Plato's Conception of Justice and the Question of Human Dignity

PHILOSOPHY AND CULTURAL STUDIES REVISITED/HISTORISCH GENETISCHE STUDIEN ZUR PHILOSOPHIE UND KULTURGESCHICHTE

Edited by/herausgegeben von
Seweryn Blandzi

VOL. 4

PETER LANG

Marek Piechowiak

Plato's Conception of Justice and the Question of Human Dignity

PETER LANG

Bibliographic Information published by the Deutsche Nationalbibliothek
The Deutsche Nationalbibliothek lists this publication in the Deutsche Nationalbibliografie; detailed bibliographic data is available on the internet at http://dnb.d-nb.de.

Library of Congress Cataloging-in-Publication Data
A CIP catalog record for this book has been applied for at the Library of Congress.

This project was financed with funds from the National Science Centre (Poland) under grant number DEC-2013/09/B/HS5/04232.

SWPS UNIVERSITY

Cover Design: © Olaf Gloeckler, Atelier Platen, Friedberg
Cover Image: © Marek Piechowiak

ISSN 2510-5353
ISBN 978-3-631-65970-0 (Print)
E-ISBN 978-3-653-05425-5 (E-PDF)
E-ISBN 978-3-631-71090-6 (EPUB)
E-ISBN 978-3-631-71091-3 (MOBI)
DOI 10.3726/978-3-653-05425-5

Peter Lang – Berlin · Bern · Bruxelles · New York · Oxford · Warszawa · Wien

This publication has been peer reviewed by Krzysztof Wroczyński and Wojciech Żełaniec.

www.peterlang.com

For Celina, Teresa, Dorota and Zofia

Contents

Preface 15

1 Introduction 17

1.1 What this book is about 17

1.2 Dignity as a fundamental value in law 17

1.3 Why Plato? 19

1.4 Objectives 22

1.5 Interpreting Plato 28

1.6 The structure of this book 31

2 The *Timaeus* on dignity: the Demiurge's speech 35

2.1 The *Timaeus* as a dialogue on justice 35

2.2 Formal aspects of the text 39

2.3 The complexity and mortality of the soul 40

2.4 Dignity as existential perfection 41

2.5 Prohibition on instrumental treatment 43

2.6 Human beings and the gods 46

2.7 The human being in relation to the whole 47

3 Justice as a virtue 53

3.1 Introductory remarks 53

3.2 Some terminological issues 54

3.3 Justice and happiness—justice as the most important of all matters 58

3.3.1 Justice as the subject of the best possible art 58

3.3.2 The greatest evil and the greatest good 59

3.3.3 Utility as the foundation of one's good 62

3.4 Traditional formulae describing just actions 64
3.5 The *Republic* as a dialogue on the individual 67
3.6 The model of the state and the teaching of virtues 69
3.6.1 Improvement of man 69
3.6.1.1 Socratic questions 69
3.6.1.2 Is the soul simple or complex? 75
3.6.1.3 How to find justice in the state 79
3.6.2 Wisdom 80
3.6.3 Courage 83
3.6.3.1 Common understanding of courage 83
3.6.3.2 The specificity of Plato's approach 84
3.6.3.3 'What things are to be feared' and human freedom 86
3.6.4 Moderation 89
3.6.5 Justice in the model of the state 91
3.6.5.1 Introduction 91
3.6.5.2 What justice in the state is 92
3.6.5.3 Weakness of the evidence 94
3.6.5.4 Beyond triviality 95
3.6.5.5 Happiness of the state or happiness of the individual? 96
3.7 What in truth is justice? 97
3.7.1 Description of justice 97
3.7.2 Justice in the model of the state as εἴδωλον—a phantom of justice 100
3.7.3 The *Phaedrus* and the model of the state in the *Republic* 104
3.7.3.1 Discourse in ink and discourse in the soul 104
3.7.3.2 The subject of inner discourse and the aim of knowledge 107
3.7.4 Justice as the internal unity and health of the soul 108
3.7.5 Versatility of the just man 110
3.7.6 Unity of virtues in just actions 116

4 The content of just actions 121
4.1 Socrates talks to himself about justice 121
4.1.1 Preliminary remarks 121
4.1.2 The form of the argument 123
4.1.3 Detailed analyses 127
4.1.4 The 'head' of Socrates' conversation about justice 131
4.1.5 A difficult step in the argument and Plato's teaching on the Good 133
4.1.5.1 From the justice in the soul to the justice of actions 133
4.1.5.2 Shadows and statues of justice 134
4.1.5.3 The Good 135
4.1.5.4 Education 138
4.1.5.5 Reconsidering the difficulties in the argumentation in the *Gorgias* 142
4.1.6 Further applications 144
4.2 Negative and positive characteristics of just actions 145
4.2.1 The harm principle 145
4.2.2 Just actions as something beneficial for others 148

5 Justice of the law and justice of the state 153
5.1 Foundations 153
5.2 The wisdom and freedom to shape one's life and Plato's alleged totalitarianism 157
5.2.1 Converging arguments against Plato's totalitarianism 157
5.2.2 Wisdom as the knowledge that oversees just actions 161
5.2.3 The failure of Isaiah Berlin's argument 162
5.2.4 Freedom to shape one's own life 167
5.2.4.1 Short-term life planning 167
5.2.4.2 Long-term life planning 168
5.2.5 Concluding remarks 173

5.3 Punitive justice 173
5.3.1 Preliminary remarks 173
5.3.2 Rhetoric as a counterfeit of punitive justice 174
5.3.3 The principal aims of punishment 177
5.3.4 The health of the soul as the foundation of justice 179
5.3.5 Equality of proportions as a basis for the determination of punishment 180
5.3.6 Injustice which punishment cannot repair 182
5.3.7 The inevitability of punishment by the gods and two aims of the law 185
5.3.8 Civil law aspects of punishment 186
5.3.9 Concluding remarks 187

6 Equality 189

6.1 Initial remarks 189

6.2 Equality in dignity 189

6.3 Proportionate equality as a basis for shaping actions 191
6.3.1 Preliminary remarks 191
6.3.2 Arithmetic equality 192
6.3.3 Geometric equality as the foundation of true justice 193
6.3.4 Aristotle's continuation of Plato's teaching on geometric proportion 197
6.3.5 Concluding remarks 200

6.4 Justice and friendship 201
6.4.1 Preliminary remarks 201
6.4.2 Friendship with oneself 201
6.4.3 Equality as the foundation of friendship 202
6.4.4 Friendship as an aim of laws 203
6.4.5 Non-violence in implementing justice 207
6.4.6 Justice in giving and receiving 208
6.4.7 Concluding remarks 211

7 **Some key issues in Plato's conception of justice** 213
7.1 What is more excellent—justice of the soul or justice of action? 213
7.2 Which activity is best and what is its best object? 219
7.2.1 Preliminary remarks 219
7.2.2 What is a proper object of love? What is a proper object of just actions? 220
7.2.2.1 Abstract form or concrete individual—challenging Gregory Vlastos 220
7.2.2.2 Engendering and birth as an aim of love 222
7.2.2.3 Loving imperfect creatures 223
7.2.2.4 Loving an individual 223
7.2.3 Just actions over contemplation 225
7.2.3.1 Back home from the top of the heavens—what are souls free of mortal deficiency doing? 225
7.2.3.2 Back to the cave from the light of the sun—what is the use of abstract forms? 228
7.2.3.3 What does the Good—the Demiurge—do? 231
7.2.4 The *Timaeus* and Plato's teaching on justice 233
7.2.5 The elderly Cephalus on justice: foreword as epilogue 238
7.2.6 Closing remarks 240
7.3 The sharing of wives: testing the interpretation on a 'hard case' 240
7.3.1 Preliminary remarks 240
7.3.2 The dolphin of Arion—an introduction by Plato's Socrates 242
7.3.3 Non-geometrical but erotic necessities 243
7.3.4 Some instructions on how to read Plato 247
7.3.5 What can be gained from the discussion about women? 248
7.3.5.1 Fundamental equality of the sexes 248
7.3.5.2 No justification for subordinating weaker minds to stronger ones 250
7.3.5.3 The highest standards of friendship 251
7.3.5.4 How to establish friendship in the soul 252
7.3.6 Closing remarks 252

8 Conclusions 255

8.1 Dignity 255

8.2 Justice of the soul 257

8.3 Justice of actions 259

8.4 Justice of laws and the state 261

Bibliography 265

I Works of Plato 265

a Collections 265

b Dialogues 265

II References 267

Indexes 279

Index Locorum 281

General Index 289

'There will always be metaphysics in the world, and what is more in everyone, especially in every thinking man.'

Immanuel Kant, *Prolegomena to any Future Metaphysics that can Present itself as a Science,* 367, trans. Peter G. Lucas.

'The whole point of our legislation was to allow the citizens to live supremely happy lives in the greatest possible mutual friendship.'

Plato, *Laws,* 743c, trans. Trevor J. Saunders.

Preface

This book is the result of many years of research. I would like to thank Jacek Sobczak, who supported me in writing an early outline of this project; Dorota Zygmuntowicz for her helpful critiques of the early draft of this book; Wojciech Żełaniec and Krzysztof Wroczyński for their helpful comments; and Jerzy Czarnowski for his suggestions and encouragement during my work on this book. Last but not least, I extend my thanks to the students who attended my seminars at Zielona Góra University and Adam Mickiewicz University for helping me to deepen my understanding of Plato.

Since I am not a native speaker of English, I needed help in the preparation of the manuscript. I wish to thank my wife Celina, Jerzy Czarnowski, and—most of all—Thomas Anessi and John Catlow, who reviewed the final version, for sharing their linguistic expertise. I am also grateful to Emilia Przylepa for her help in reviewing the Greek expressions introduced in the text. I would also like to thank Marek Moszyk for his ideas on the choice of cover photo.

I have decided to leave some references to the scholarship written in Polish, although it is not accessible to many readers of this book. I feel obliged to pay tribute at least to some of the works written in Polish which shape my thinking about Plato.

Last but not least my thanks go to the Polish National Science Centre—without its generous financial support this book could not have appeared.

Earlier versions of some sections of this book have been previously published as follows:

Parts of the Introduction and Chapter II are based on 'Plato and the Universality of Dignity' (2015), and 'Przemowa Demiurga w Platońskim „Timajosie" a współczesne pojęcie godności' [Demiurge's Speech in Plato's "Timaeus" and the Contemporary Notion of Dignity] (2013).

Parts of Chapter III, Section 7 were published as 'Platońskie widziadło sprawiedliwości' [Plato's Phantom of Justice] (2013).

Chapter IV is based on 'Sokrates sam ze sobą rozmawia o sprawiedliwości' [Socrates in a Dialogue with Himself on Justice] (2009).

The analysis of I. Berlin's argument contained in Chapter V, Section 2 was presented in 'Tomasza z Akwinu koncepcja prawa naturalnego. Czy Akwinata jest myślicielem liberalnym?' [Thomas Aquinas' Conception of Natural Law: Is Aquinas a Liberal Thinker?] (2013).

Chapter V, Section 3 was published (with minor changes) as 'Plato's Conception of Punitive Justice' (2015).

Parts of Chapter VI, Section 3 were published as 'Kallikles i geometria. Przyczynek do Platońskiej koncepcji sprawiedliwości' [Callicles and Geometry: On Plato's Conception of Justice] (2013).

1 Introduction

1.1 What this book is about

Plato's thought is a cornerstone of European philosophy and European culture. As Alfred N. Whitehead once wrote, 'The safest general characterization of the European philosophical tradition is that it consists of a series of footnotes to Plato'.[1] In philosophical reflection about law and the state it is impossible to ignore the notions and issues introduced by Plato into philosophical debate and into culture in general. As Martin Heidegger noted, one has to accept that we are talking the language of Plato even if one does not share his views.[2]

This book is chiefly about Plato's account of justice. Nevertheless, certain substantially modern questions underlie this effort—questions that are vital for understanding the foundations of modern-day legal orders. Plato is therefore read here from the perspective of the legal orders functioning today rather than from the perspective of the philosophy of law.

In the book, I focus on human dignity, which is broadly recognised as the source of all human rights, the axiological basis of law, and a criterion of justice. Did Plato have any idea about human dignity, so critical to modern legal orders? If so—and this is what I argue for in this book—then dignity should play a crucial role in Plato's understanding of justice. Since the concept of justice stands at the centre of his philosophy, it also seems to be essential to understanding the overall Platonic project. Is it the case that Plato provides the foundations for modern-day human rights protection rather than for modern-day totalitarianism?

1.2 Dignity as a fundamental value in law

Dignity is generally regarded today as a fundamental value across legal systems at both the international and national levels. It is considered inviolable,[3] and therefore

1 Whitehead, *Process and Reality* (1929), p. 39.

2 Heidegger, *The End of Philosophy*, p. 386: 'All metaphysics, including its opponent, positivism, speaks the language of Plato'.

3 *Charter of Fundamental Rights of the European Union* (2000), Article 1: 'Human dignity is inviolable. It must be respected and protected'. In relation to the international protection of human rights at UN level, point two of the *Proclamation of Teheran* (1968) recognises directly the inviolability of these rights and indirectly the inviolability of dignity as the source of these rights: 'The Universal Declaration of Human Rights states a common understanding of the peoples of the world concerning the inalienable and inviolable rights of all members of the human family and constitutes an obligation for the members of the international community'. Cf. *Basic Law for the Federal Republic of Germany* (1949), Article 1: '(1) Human dignity shall be inviolable. To respect and protect it shall be the duty of all state authority. (2) The

should never be sacrificed for the sake of other values—the possessor of dignity is an end in itself, an autotelic end, and can never be treated purely instrumentally. A very important consequence of recognition of the inviolability of dignity is its impact on how we understand the relationship between an individual, the law, and the state: the aim of laws founded upon the recognition of dignity and human rights, and the aim of a state based on such laws, is the goodness of the individual; thus, individuals are not meant to serve the state and the law, but rather, the state and the law are meant to serve the individual.

As something inherent to, and thus inseparable from, human beings, dignity is considered to be universal. As Article 1 of the *Universal Declaration of Human Rights* (1948) states: 'all human beings are born free and equal in dignity and rights', regardless of culture, regardless of time, regardless of level of development, physical or mental ability, or any other mutable human qualities. This universality of dignity provides the basis for the universality of the human rights which derive from it.[4]

The dignity which is at stake here, and which can be called the 'dignity of a person', should be distinguished from dignity as moral excellence or as an honour,[5] or dignity of other types.[6] The dignity of a person—as the source of all human rights—is a fundamental value found across legal systems. And only dignity of this kind is recognised as being equal in all human beings and an inherent quality which is present independently of any action by its holder or other persons, or of one's life circumstances.

It is something of a paradox that the recognition in law of the inherent nature of the dignity of a person and of its universality is accompanied in contemporary culture by the widespread acceptance of cultural relativism—the belief that values are a 'product' of a given culture rather than something which exists objectively, independently of human activity. If such a point of view is adopted, it ought to be acknowledged that dignity, as an axiological foundation of the legal system, is also a product of the culture of a given time and place, and thus the attribution to it of certain characteristics is not based on cognition (knowledge) of reality; dignity cannot therefore be considered as existing objectively. The assumption that dignity

---

German people therefore acknowledge inviolable and inalienable human rights as the basis of every community, of peace and of justice in the world'; *The Constitution of the Republic of Poland* (1997), Article 30: 'The inherent and inalienable dignity of the person shall constitute a source of freedoms and rights of persons and citizens. It shall be inviolable. The respect and protection thereof shall be the obligation of public authorities'.

4 *Vienna Declaration and Programme of Action* (1993), I, 1: 'The universal nature of these rights and freedoms is beyond question'. Cf. *Convention on the Rights of Persons with Disabilities* (2006), Preamble, (c).

5 On these kinds of dignity as viewed by Plato see Galewicz, 'Leontios i trupy', *passim.*

6 See Piechowiak, 'Auf der Suche', pp. 290–291, where twelve principal types of dignity are distinguished.

is conditioned by culture inevitably leads to its conceptual 'disenchantment'. As viewed from such a perspective, an inherent dignity simply does not exist. At best, the inherence and universality of dignity, its being innate (inborn) to all human beings, might be regarded as a legal fiction, a convenient tool for constructing legal systems which are expected by the legislator to produce certain outcomes. However, one consequence of this would be a repudiation of the universality of human rights, meaning that the promotion of their protection could justifiably be considered a manifestation of cultural imperialism.

If the concept of dignity as it is used in modern law expresses something inherent (innate, inborn, intrinsic) which is not created by culture, then it is to be expected that the reality encompassed within the concept of dignity should also have been considered in the past. An important argument in favour of recognising the cultural relativism and fictional nature of the legal concept of dignity is the claim that dignity was recognised only in modernity and that the concept was a product of the philosophical thought specific to this period—particularly that of Immanuel Kant, who is generally considered the father of the concept of dignity as it is used today in the language of law and jurisprudence. Yet, it is relatively common knowledge that reflections on dignity were present during the Renaissance in the treatises of such authors as Gianozzo Manetti and Giovanni Pico della Mirandola. It is less often observed that a well-developed concept of human dignity (including its recognition as the basis for personhood and for the normative status of its holder) had already been developed in the Middle Ages.[7] However, it should be noted that even a radical historicity of the notion of dignity cannot be considered sufficient reason for rejecting the existence of inherent dignity, since one could argue that the development of culture leads to the creation of better intellectual tools, like concepts or ideas, for understanding reality, and that we should not suppose that things corresponding to certain concepts did not exist in the past merely because the concepts themselves had not yet been invented.

1.3 Why Plato?

It would be momentous for establishing the universality of dignity if reflections on the concept of dignity, or—more likely—on what today is understood and expressed through this concept, could be found in ancient philosophy. Deliberations on how Plato's work provides insights into the dignity of a person, rather than providing a basis for a totalitarian framework contrasting with the dignitarian approach,

7 For a comparison of the philosophical conceptions of dignity proposed by Kant and Aquinas, see Piechowiak, 'Auf der Suche', *passim*. In the context of the problem of universality of human rights, P. Leuprecht in his book *Reason, Justice and Dignity* explores the sources of human rights, analysing the thoughts of Confucius and Mencius (pp. 7–30); Avicenna, Averroes and Ibn Khaldun (pp. 31–74); and Bartolomé de las Casas and Francisco de Vitoria (pp. 75–99).

nonetheless seem to be absent in contemporary academic discussions about the universality of human rights and their foundation in universal dignity. One of the reasons for this is that Plato is nowadays often seen—due largely to Karl Popper's book *The Open Society and Its Enemies*[8]—as someone who laid down the theoretical foundations of totalitarianism, as someone who provided justifications for the view that an individual is meant to serve the state rather than the state to serve the individual. Plato is seen as one who rejects the fundamental thesis upon which the recognition of universal human dignity is founded. In the *Republic*, in developing his model of a hypothetical state, Plato writes that

> it isn't the law's concern to make any one class in the city outstandingly happy but to contrive to spread happiness throughout the city by bringing the citizens into harmony with each other through persuasion or compulsion and by making them share with each other the benefits that each class can confer on the community. The law produces such people in the city, not in order to allow them to turn in whatever direction they want, but to make use of them to bind the city together.[9]

In accordance with the absolute subordination of the good of an individual to the good of the state, the state sets aims for particular individuals to specialise in. Every citizen

> must be brought to that which naturally suits him—one man, one job—so that each man, practicing his own, which is one, will not become many but one; and thus, you see, the whole city will naturally grow to be one and not many.[10]

The ultimate aim of the laws and organisation of a state seems to be the very existence of the state as a supreme good: 'Is there any greater evil we can mention for a city than that which tears it apart and makes it many instead of one? Or any greater good than that which binds it together and makes it one?'[11]

---

8 Popper, *The Open Society and Its Enemies*, vol. 1: *The Spell of Plato.*

9 Plato, *Republic*, 519e–520a, trans. Grube; cf. ibid., 420b–421c.

10 Plato, *Republic*, 423d, trans. Shorey. I base my analysis on the Greek texts (*Platonis Opera*, ed. Burnet. Oxford: E. Typographeo Clarendoniano, 1903 ff.; *The Perseus Project*, ed. Crane, http://www.perseus.tufts.edu). English translations have been selected on the basis of their accuracy in a given context, and thus, excerpts of the same dialogue are sometimes rendered through different translations, although the quotations are mostly after Plato, *Complete Works*, ed. Cooper (Indianapolis—Cambridge: Hackett Publishing Company, 1997). I decided not to propose my own English translations of the relevant passages. When looking for an adequate rendering of the original in different translations of the same text I realised that I can almost always find a satisfactory solution, and therefore trying to be original would be artificial and time-consuming. There were also pragmatic reasons behind leaving mostly Lamb's translations of the *Gorgias* in Section 5.3, an earlier English version of which was prepared independently of the other chapters.

11 Plato, *Republic*, 462a–b, trans. Grube.

Plato is considered by some to have created the theoretical foundations for, and to have been an adherent of, two basic types of totalitarianism.[12] The totalitarianism of the first type takes the view that the good of a member of a political community is entirely subordinated to the good of the community, and that if there is a conflict in the realisation of these goods, then the well-being and continued existence of the community prevails, and thus an individual can be rightly sacrificed for the benefit of the whole. Totalitarianism of the second type postulates that the authorities (the laws, the state) should exercise full control over all aspects of the life of all members of the political community. Neither of these two types necessarily implies the other. It is possible to propose full control over the life of citizens for their own benefit and not for the benefit of the state or community. It is also possible to recognise the well-being of the state as the highest value and nevertheless not demand full control over individuals. Whenever Plato's conception of justice is examined here, the question of totalitarianism of both types is always present somewhere in the background. Was he really blind to dignity as a reason for the non-instrumental treatment of each human being? Was he blind to the importance of individuality and autonomy for personal development? And when thinking about the place occupied by Plato's philosophy in European culture, some other intriguing general questions have to be posed. Is an essentially totalitarian philosophy the cornerstone of European culture? Was Plato's work so attractive through the centuries because he advocated a state in which every citizen was bound only to one occupation, and the life of each individual was completely subordinated to the benefit of the state as a whole? One could suggest that other issues were important for his readers. But this seems an insufficient explanation. The issue of justice, which is inevitably engaged in the problem of totalitarianism, is central to Plato's thought, which is systemic in character. Fundamental flaws in his theory of justice would be an important indication of the fundamentally defective nature of Plato's philosophy as a whole.

Plato is still held to be a totalitarian, though not an extreme one, as Karl Popper alleged, whereas his philosophy is considered to be paternalistic and, like totalitarian approaches, to take no or little account of the autonomy of an individual. As Christopher Taylor writes, his theory

> in common with other varieties of paternalism conceals a crucial evaluative gap. He needs to show that an adequate conception of a good life need not include any

---

12 A slightly different approach is that of C. C. W. Taylor, who speaks of two features that characterise totalitarianism—authoritarianism and ideology; authoritarianism is 'a system in which the ordinary citizen has no significant share (...) in the making of political decisions'; an ideology is 'a pervasive scheme of values, intentionally promulgated by some person or persons and promoted by institutional means in order to direct all or the most significant aspects of public and private life towards the attainment of the goals dictated by those values'; Taylor, 'Plato's Totalitarianism', p. 280. These two features do not have to appear together, ibid., p. 281.

> substantial measure of autonomy, but he makes no attempt to do so. Indeed he shows no sign of awareness of the problem.[13]

I wish to challenge this kind of view in a radical way, arguing that Plato was not only aware of this problem, but that his philosophy also provides strong arguments for striving for the participation of all citizens in making political decisions and, moreover, that there is room for free determination of the goals to be pursued.

The fact that Plato is suspected of helping to develop totalitarian views makes his philosophy—seemingly paradoxically—all the more attractive for research on human dignity. For the recognition of the universality of the inherent dignity, it is much more significant if reflections on such a dignity are found in a theory which argues against such recognition than in theories which are known to support it.

There is at least one more reason to include Plato in the contemporary debate on dignity. Although observable human features (like our genome) can be accepted as criteria, as 'diagnostic' traits, for identifying a holder of dignity, if dignity is universal, inherent, and equal, it nevertheless seems to be something metaphysical, independent of any observable, changeable human traits (such as thinking, choosing, acting, or behaving in a particular way). Plato is certainly someone who has something to say about such a kind of reality and about how to learn something about it.

1.4 Objectives

This study aims to give a comprehensive exposition of Plato's conception of justice as seen from the perspective of human dignity. Today, as in Plato's thought, the issue of justice is considered crucial for understanding the relationship between an individual and the state and the law, and for understanding the aims of laws and how and why to build a political community. It also turns out that reflection on human dignity in Plato's philosophy provides a perspective from which these issues can and should be viewed today.

The present study is not aimed directly at identifying flaws and weaknesses in interpretations of Plato's writings that advocate or accept the thesis that he developed a totalitarian project. Nevertheless, an approach is proposed here that very strongly opposes such interpretations. This approach rests on identifying in Plato's works reflections on that which is today called 'dignity'. Such an approach makes apparent his recognition in human beings of 'something' which is inherent, equal, and positively distinguishes them in such a way that they should be treated as aims in themselves. Moreover, these reflections play a fundamental role in the construction of Plato's overall conception of justice and, essentially, of Plato's philosophy as a whole. Plato's project turns out to be a far cry from any form of totalitarian

13 Taylor, 'Plato's Totalitarianism', p. 295.

thinking. He emerges as much less 'idealistic' and as appreciating the earthly condition of human existence much more than is usually assumed.

The problem of justice leads to the core of Plato's philosophy. It is regarded by Plato as one of the most important issues or—from some points of view—the single most important. It is argued that the first, most significant question that Plato aims to answer concerns how to be a good man, how to lead a good life. The simplest answers he supplies to these questions are that to be good means to be just; to lead a good life means to act justly. It seems that the whole of Plato's philosophy is developed with a view to giving rational consideration to these questions. Both ontological and epistemological issues are subordinated to reflection on practical ones.[14] As the ordering of questions indicates, practical philosophy is Plato's first philosophy. An illustration of this is the myth of the cave, which is a standard point of reference in epistemology and ontology, but is nevertheless placed by Plato in Book VII of the *Republic*—the dialogue about justice. Plato's philosophy is of a systemic kind—his teaching on being and cognition is essential for understanding moral issues. It is not the case that the practical philosophy is 'attached' to ontology or epistemology—rather the exact opposite. The problem of justice turns out to be central to the whole of Plato's philosophy because it leads straight to the most fundamental ontological questions concerning the foundations of existence and to epistemological issues concerning the acquisition of knowledge about what justice is and what the content of just actions is.

Although Plato does not speak a language which directly expresses existential aspects of reality by using the verb 'be' ('εἶναι') in its existential meaning,[15] nevertheless the question remains whether in using other words he is still talking about what is nowadays signified by 'existential aspect'. Does Plato consider the question of the foundations of being (existence) as an issue distinct from the problem of the 'content' of a being? I am arguing that the problem both of justice and of dignity (of what nowadays is called 'dignity'), the issue of the inner unity of the human being (soul), is crucial for Plato. A special unity turns out to underlie the immortality of the soul, and acquiring or losing justice can be understood as acquiring or losing inner unity. Unity is central to Plato's understanding of the Good as the source of existence and being.[16] Therefore, in the framework of Plato's conception of justice, when read as a contribution to contemporary debates, I consider it

14 Gajda, *Platońska droga do idei*, p. 76: 'The philosophical conception of forms (ideas) as entities which are transcendent [to the visible world] was born on the basis of reflection on values in the world where—as it seemed—all moral values failed', my translation.

15 C. Kahn argues that in Greek philosophy there is not a distinct concept of existence and existence is apprehended in predicative form: 'X is Y'; 'X exists' means for Plato 'X is something' (εἶναί τι); see Kahn, 'Why Existence Does Not Emerge', pp. 72–73; extensively on this issue, see Kahn, *The Verb 'be'*.

16 Plato, *Republic*, 509b; see Krämer, '*Epekeina tēs ousias*', *passim*.

justified to talk about the existential aspect of beings as the aspect pertaining to inner unity.

Plato's practical philosophy is often seen as being focused on legal or political issues. Some claim that the Academy was a kind of 'school of law' where legal and political issues dominated;[17] Leo Strauss advocates the view that all of Plato's dialogues deal more or less directly with political matters.[18] Nevertheless, the analyses that follow suggest that the goodness of the individual and his actions come first not only in building a theory of a good society, but also that they are unquestionable goals for the state and the law. Plato's deliberations about justice in the state are often entirely subordinated to understanding the justice of an individual and his actions. Although some teaching contained in the *Republic* applies both to an individual and to the state (the city), there are still cases where the theses are relevant to an individual and not to the state; for instance, this is evidently the case when courage is considered. The analyses show that the overall narrative introduced by Plato in the *Republic* clearly indicates that his deliberations about the state serve first of all to understand an individual's striving for fulfilment. Discrepancies in the possibilities for applying certain claims to both an individual and the community should therefore be resolved in favour of the individual. Plato provides his reader with advice on how to proceed in this way. One example, which is extensively analysed below, can be found in Book IV of the *Republic*, where Plato's Socrates not only clearly indicates that his statements are about an individual when he starts with the words 'and in truth justice is',[19] but also asks his audience to treat with caution some crucial conclusions about justice that are reached in considerations about the hypothetical state, saying explicitly that justice 'isn't concerned with someone's doing his own externally'.[20] Eric A. Havelock notices that this clear statement 'seems to imply a repudiation of a great deal of what Plato has previously said',[21] and 'previously' the model of the hypothetical state was developed. Havelock continues–'if justice does not apply to outward action, it becomes an inner and private condition, a morality of the self but not of society'.[22] The model of the hypothetical state cannot be treated as a paradigm for

---

17 Dembiński, *Późny Platon*, pp. 15, 18–19; see e.g. Plato, *Republic*, 473d.

18 Strauss, 'Plato', p. 33.

19 Plato, *Republic*, 443c–e, trans. Grube.

20 Plato, *Republic*, 443c–e, trans. Grube.

21 Havelock, *The Greek Concept of Justice*, p. 322.

22 Havelock, *The Greek Concept of Justice*, p. 322. Havelock affirms that 'Plato's moral philosophy cannot shake off paradox nor need we require that it should', ibid. Plato certainly uses paradox as a means to boost thinking on specific issues; however, I am convinced that Plato wants his reader to develop a coherent approach to the problem of justice; in this study I aim to present such an approach, consistently rejecting the view that Plato's considerations about the hypothetical state in the *Republic* are part of a political project, and consistently favouring the perspective

a political project and there is no isomorphism between justice for the city and justice for the individual.[23]

This does not mean that Plato is not interested at all in the justice of laws or of the state. Nevertheless, before these problems are considered, the issues concerning the individual have to be solved—and these solutions should be applied to questions about the justice of laws and the state. Moreover, if an individual and not the state is an aim in itself, the question of how to be a good person becomes paramount. Justice of an individual turns out to be key to understanding the aims of law and state and the justice of them.

If the dignitarian approach is the right one, then the benefits to an individual should be recognised to be the aim of laws. In Book V of the *Laws*, Plato's Athenian takes this position univocally and without reservations: 'The whole point of our legislation was to allow the citizens to live supremely happy lives in the greatest possible mutual friendship'.[24] This statement serves as a kind of a leitmotif throughout this book. In many elaborations of Plato's philosophy it is considered only in passing[25] or is interpreted as stating something about the happiness of the state rather than of individuals.[26] This is surprising because in classical philosophy, an aim which is the *causa finalis* is the most important among all causes (it is the cause of all causes—*causa causarum*) which helps us to understand the given reality (in this case, the laws and the state).

The benefit to an individual, his happiness, is not simply safety and the preservation of life, which are goods apprehended easily on the basis of sensual

---

of an individual as paramount in Plato's conception of justice. Cf. Santas, *Goodness and Justice*, pp. 150–153.

23 Cf. Santas, *Understanding Plato's Republic*, e.g. pp. 57–58, 104–105, 119; Santas does not examine at all what Plato's Socrates states about what in truth justice is, in opposition to the phantom of justice in the state which concerns external actions (Plato, *Republic*, 443c), which I find to be crucial for understanding Plato's *Republic*. Santas is not an exception; the issue seems to be usually left unconsidered; see e.g. collections: Ferrari (ed.), *The Cambridge Companion to Plato's Republic*; Kraut (ed.), *The Cambridge Companion to Plato*; McPherran (ed.), *Plato's Republic: A Critical Guide*; or monographs: Schofield, *Plato: Political Philosophy*; Bobonich, *Plato's Utopia Recast*. Cf. Vasiliou, *Aiming at Virtue in Plato*, pp. 248–249; Vasiliou examines the above-mentioned passage from the *Republic* (443c) but he concentrates on the virtue of an individual and does not consider the consequences for understanding political justice.

24 Plato, *Laws*, 743c, trans. Saunders; cf. ibid., 631b–c (Book I): 'it is no accident that the laws of the Cretans have such a high reputation in the entire Greek world. They are sound laws, and achieve the happiness of those who observe them'.

25 M. Schofield in his book *Plato: Political Philosophy* invokes this passage only in one footnote (p. 191 note 89). T. Irwin in *Plato's Ethics* mentions it only once, while considering happiness in general; Irwin (1995), p. 347 (231).

26 Bobonich, *Plato's Utopia Recast*, p. 421; cf. Plato, *Laws*, 697a–b.

experience, but also consists of being as great as possible.[27] This goes beyond that which is visible and concerns acquiring and practising virtues,[28] most of all justice. Hence, the conception of justice turns out to be crucial for understanding the aims of laws. It can be stated simply that the proper and primary aim of laws and of any state is to ensure that each member of the political community acts justly.

It should be observed that in Book III of the *Laws* one can already find a different enumeration of the aims of the state: 'One should always remember that a state ought to be free and wise and enjoy internal harmony, and that this is what the lawgiver should concentrate on in his legislation'.[29] And this is not the only place where the aims of laws (of legislation) are considered. This last enumeration is accompanied by a remark of a methodological nature:

> When we say that the legislator should keep self-control or good judgement or friendship in view, we must bear in mind that all these aims are the same, not different. Nor should we be disconcerted if we find a lot of other expressions of which the same is true.[30]

Although in Plato's writing there are a few formulas describing the aims of law, the formula from Book V of the *Laws*: 'The whole point of our legislation was to allow the citizens to live supremely happy lives in the greatest possible mutual friendship'[31] seems to be particularly convenient for deliberations on justice. On the one hand, this formula leads to deliberations about the subjective aspects of justice—justice as virtue (which presupposes good judgement, self-control, and courage), and about acting justly (which presupposes justice as virtue). Moreover, happiness will be accepted to be a common good and an unquestionable goal of laws and the state for centuries to come after Plato. On the other hand, maximising friendship turns out to be both a necessary condition for maximising justice and happiness, and—at the same time—a direct effect of practising justice.

It is surprising that although the issue of justice stands at the centre of Plato's philosophy, a comprehensive, monographic study concerned directly with Plato's conception of justice is scarcely to be found.[32] If the interpretation presented here

---

27 Plato, *Laws*, 707c: 'we differ from most people in not regarding mere safety and existence as the most precious thing men can possess, but rather the gaining of all possible goodness and the keeping of it throughout life', trans. Bury. Cf. Aristotle, *Politics*, 1252b: the city-state 'comes into existence for the sake of life, it exists for the good life', trans. Rackham.

28 Plato, *Laws*, 770c–e.

29 Plato, *Laws*, 693b, trans. Saunders.

30 Plato, *Laws*, 693c, trans. Saunders.

31 Plato, *Laws*, 743c, trans. Saunders.

32 There are, however, monographs on Plato's political and moral philosophy which do not organise their arguments around the issue of justice (e.g. Bobonich, *Plato's Utopia Recast*; Schofield, *Plato: Political Philosophy*; Rosen, *Plato's Republic*). The most comprehensive approaches to the problem of justice can be found in Vasiliou, *Aiming at Virtue in Plato*, and in Santas, *Understanding Plato's Republic*, though my

is—essentially—a correct one, then the conclusion should be drawn that without taking due account of Plato's reflections on dignity, it is hardly possible to build a comprehensive and consistent reconstruction of Plato's conception of justice.

The objectives of this study are not limited to historical issues. Indeed, historical questions are not of primary importance to the author. The book is written from the perspective of the 'user' of Plato's philosophy and not as a purely historical inquiry. Plato is treated as a partner in the contemporary debate on dignity and justice. I hope that the presented reconstruction of Plato's conception of justice will contribute not only to a better understanding of the European philosophical tradition of thought about the individual in law and state, but also to a better understanding of the human being in the contemporary world. Following Augustine of Hippo—one does not go to school merely to learn what one's teachers are thinking.

The adoption of the 'user's' standpoint was a reason for the decision to take 'state' and not 'city' as the equivalent of the Greek 'πολιτεία'. Cities corresponding to the political entities of ancient times are rarely encountered nowadays, and the issues Plato's work bears on are relevant to contemporary thinking about the state.

In the analyses proposed below, it is accepted that culture, including philosophical works, theories, ideas, and concepts, sometimes functions as a tool for cultivating or taming nature—understood as something given which exists independently of culture, although an adequate comprehension of the 'content' of such reality is impossible; it is always only partial, aspectual. There is a rational hope, and it is presupposed here, that Plato—in the framework of his own culture, using his language, his concepts, theories, and myths—was talking about something which remains the same irrespective of the epoch, audience, interpretation, approach, and so on: something that is referred to when the terms 'human being' and 'dignity' are used nowadays. Studying Plato, therefore, provides an opportunity to better understand the prerequisites for being a human and for constructing laws and a state which can be considered just. One more benefit of studying Plato today derives from the fact that the modern concepts used in ethics, legal, and political philosophy are inevitably rooted in tradition. Therefore, the better one understands the philosophical tradition, the better one understands contemporary reflection on the human being.[33]

---

interpretation not only addresses directly the issue of justice throughout the whole book but also is essentially different. Popper's *Open Society* is still counted as the most embracive elaboration of Plato's political and moral philosophy, and this might be one of the key reasons why his account remains so influential. As concerns my reading on individual justice, Irvin's *Plato's Ethics* should be mentioned, although it does not focus on the issue of justice (cf. Irvin, 'Questions about Justice'); see also Blackburn, *Plato's Republic.* In the Polish literature, the only book devoted directly to Plato's concept of the state is Jarra, *Idea państwa u Platona*, published in 1918. For a short introduction, see Dahl, 'Plato's Defence of Justice'.

33 See Gadamer, *Wahrheit und Methode*, pp. 279–281.

1.5 Interpreting Plato

When searching through Plato's writings for reflections on dignity, it is not necessary to look for particular words in Greek that seem to render the English 'dignity' or Latin 'dignitas'. There would be not much use in focusing, for example, on the word 'ἀξία'. It is much more important—and this path will be followed here—to look for something that possesses relevant characteristics, irrespective of what it is called. In the case of dignity, the search is for something inherent, inalienable, and common to all people, and which forms a foundation for one's being a goal in oneself and for the most fundamental moral principles, such as that which prohibits the purely instrumental treatment of others, as well as—to use the language of Aristotle—a foundation to wish good to someone for his own sake (to love an individual for himself) and not because a relationship with him is useful or pleasant.[34]

Since the terms, concepts, and theories used in a given time and place are considered to be intellectual tools for recognising and becoming familiar with something existing in reality, the universality of dignity and human rights would not be undermined by an acknowledgement that the use of specific terms and concepts to refer to them is relative to a particular culture or time, or to the broader theoretical contexts in which they occur. In the works of Plato, elements should be sought which are included in the concept of dignity today (such as being inborn or being an aim in itself), and the specific functions these elements fulfil should be considered—for instance, how they define the relationship between the individual and the state. Such elements can be considered an anticipation of the modern-day concept of dignity. However, a crucial question is whether reflections on what today is expressed by means of the concept of dignity can be found in the works of Plato, whether these works contain reflections on something objective (given) to which modern terms or concepts refer.

In the course of this study, it will be shown that Plato's work does contain essential components of the modern concept of dignity, and reflection on 'something' that possesses the properties ascribed to dignity nowadays. Therefore, although Plato did not have at his disposal a single term or a concept (understood as a meaning of a term) which would correspond to the modern term or concept of dignity, it is justified to use the term 'dignity' as designating something considered by Plato. It is partly the 'user's perspective' that I am adopting, the attempt to include Plato in contemporary debates, that encourages me to use the term 'dignity' to denote this 'something' that Plato sees as an equal and inherent basis for one's being an aim in oneself, although in Plato's time the concept of dignity—as an intellectual invention comprising a whole bundle of intuitions which are ascribed to dignity today—had not yet been developed.

It can be noted that Plato also discusses what dignity is, an issue that even today—despite the widespread recognition of many of dignity's features—is hard to

34 See Aristotle, *Nicomachean Ethics*, 1156a–b; cf. Price, *Love and Friendship*, pp. 104–105.

reach consensus on.[35] This issue is important for the future place of thinking about dignity and human rights in today's culture—unless we have an answer to the question of what dignity is, we are powerless against the charge that the modern legal concept of dignity is only a legal fiction, and that there is nothing in reality that is denoted by the term 'dignity'. I am arguing that Plato, while considering the basis of the special status and special treatment of human souls, reaches to ontological questions of inner unity as the foundation of immortality and of continuing existence.[36] To put it in the contemporary language of philosophy—that which is constitutive for dignity Plato sees in the existential aspect of beings and not in the qualities they are endowed with. This allows dignity to be recognised as being inherent, independent of the changeable characteristics of each human being.

Plato encourages his readers not to accept what he is saying merely because it is said by him. He encourages them to accept only that which they discern themselves. He is like a guide on an expedition—he uses this metaphor explicitly in the *Republic* when he sets the stage for drawing conclusions from his model of the hypothetical state.[37] Plato wants his reader to learn by himself; he leads to different 'places' from which it is possible to apprehend something true about reality itself and to find one's own answer to the questions 'what does it mean to be good?' and 'how to live a good life?' He also leads his readers to 'places' from which it is

---

35 M. Rosen rhetorically asks if we have at all to be able to point to an objective feature which would be the foundation of the duty to respect humanity (Rosen, *Dignity: Its History and Meaning*, p. 157). He regards respect as the basic feature specific for addressing someone who possesses dignity; and this respect has its roots in our duties, which 'are so deep a part of us that we could not be the people we are without having them. In failing to respect the humanity of others we actually undermine humanity in ourselves' (p. 157). Finally, Rosen admits that 'dignity in the sense of being treated with respect for one's humanity is not the fundamental ground of human rights that the Kantian (or Catholic) use of the term would imply' (p. 157). One should add: not only the Kantian or Catholic, but also that of anyone who takes seriously the international and—in many countries—constitutional protection of human rights. In fact, Rosen fails even to consider dignity as a source of human rights which is inherent to a human being; he suggests rather that we are unable to explore this issue. A similar direction is taken by J. Waldron in his influential book *Dignity, Rank, and Rights*, seeing dignity as a temporarily conditioned 'invention' based on the 'sortal' status which 'represents a person's permanent situation and destiny so far as the law is concerned' (p. 59); a high status of this kind (nobility) has been extended over time to become universal and equally conferred upon every human being.

36 G. Kateb pays attention to the existential component in contemporary thinking on human dignity; the existence of any human being requires no justification, no reasons: 'The question: Of what value is a human life? is indecent. The question: Why do you want to stay alive? is a tyrant's question. It should not be asked; any answer will always be off the mark'; Kateb, *Human Dignity*, p. 40.

37 Plato, *Republic*, 432b. See Section 3.6.5.

possible to apprehend something true about dignity, although he does not refer to it in the way we do today.

Moreover, Plato quite often uses different words to describe the same 'object', even when crucial issues are at stake; for example, when he refers to the parts of the hypothetical state. Plato's Socrates talks about the same part of the hypothetical state using such descriptions as 'rulers', 'the kind of judges and guardians', and 'the guardian class', and does so in passages which follow one another closely.[38] There is no doubt that he is describing the same model of the hypothetical state, using different words to refer to the same parts of the state. Similarly, it can be argued that he uses different words to refer to that which is beneficial.[39] One has to remember what the Visitor says to Young Socrates in the *Statesman*: 'if you preserve in not paying serious attention to names, you will be seen to be richer in wisdom as you advance to old age'.[40]

A similar way of guiding the reader is found when Plato recounts various stories or myths, for instance, those about the soul. Different words, different stories, and different narratives may lead to a concept (notion) which, in turn, directs towards what really counts, to something given which is independent of notions, words, or narratives and which should be discerned by the reader himself. I argue that Plato creates for the modern reader an opportunity to discern and to grasp intellectually that which is called 'dignity' today.

The way in which Plato philosophises—his clear prioritising of that which is given over linguistic expressions and their meanings—means that interpreting Plato is always difficult. Of course, every interpretation starts with language and also finds its expression in language, in certain words, stories, narratives, and in thoughts which are guided by them. Nevertheless, what is aimed for here is to reveal, together with Plato, a certain reality, something given which is of crucial importance for living 'supremely happy lives in the greatest possible mutual friendship'.[41] Therefore, the writing of this book is—ultimately—an endeavour of a systematic and not a historical kind. Nonetheless, since Plato should be the one who leads, every effort possible within the framework of this project has been made to convey what Plato, as the author of certain works, would wish us to think.

In interpreting Plato's texts, special attention has been given to the formal 'frames' he provides. These 'frames' contain Plato's suggestions on how to read particular excerpts. There are often direct statements on what a given quotation is about, and what the primary concern is of the author. There are also statements (like the phrase 'but in truth justice was'[42]) regarding to what extent the text should be read 'directly' and to what extent metaphorically. Similarly, there are signals as

38 Plato, *Republic*, 433c, 434b, 434c.
39 Plato, *Republic*, 336c–d.
40 Plato, *Statesman*, 261e, trans. Rowe.
41 Plato, *Laws*, 743c, trans. Saunders.
42 Plato, *Republic*, 443c, trans. Bloom.

to whether something is said in full seriousness or serves rather as intellectual training or even as entertainment (as when there is talk about a dolphin of Arion[43] or directly about jesting[44]). In this respect, the recommendations of the Tübingen School are followed. Due respect is also given to the unwritten teachings; nevertheless, this school of interpretation underlies the analyses below more as an inspiration than a foundation.[45]

The interpretation proposed here is a unitarian one.[46] It is accepted that there is a continuity in Plato's views on the very foundations of justice (of being or becoming good). Continuity does not mean that there is no evolution or development. At least since Plato's recognition of the complexity of the soul, there are no contradictions in the way he perceives the basic issues related to justice. The main reading of Plato in this book starts with the *Timaeus*—apparently a dialogue from the late period—in which an interpretative key for the whole of Plato's doctrine on justice is found. Since it is argued in the present book that the model of the hypothetical state constructed in the *Republic* is not a model of a perfect (ideal) political organisation, a consistent conception of the justice of the state is sought on the basis of not only the *Republic* and the *Laws*, but also in the context of the *Gorgias* and even the *Apology*.

1.6 The structure of this book

If understanding the dignity of an individual underlies the understanding of a human being, an attempt to understand Plato's doctrines of justice and the relationship of the individual to the state should not begin—as most such attempts do—with an analysis of works dealing directly with the state or the law. A better starting point, and the one that will be used in the present analysis (Chapter 2), is an early part of the speech of the Demiurge to the gods in the *Timaeus*, one of Plato's later dialogues. This text is analysed here to identify Plato's viewpoint on the question of what quality positively and radically distinguishes certain creatures from other beings, and simultaneously provides a reason for treating these creatures in a radically different way than other beings which do not possess

---

43 Plato, *Republic*, 453d.

44 Plato, *Republic*, 536c.

45 See e.g. the collection *The Other Plato*, ed. Nikulin.

46 Cf. Kahn, *Plato and the Socratic Dialogue*, pp. 38–42; see Shorey, 'The Unity of Plato's Thought'. See also J. Annas' comments on ancient, unitarian, readings of Plato, Annas, *Platonic Ethics, Old and New*, pp. 27–30. The evolutionary character of Plato's writings is argued for (using hermeneutics developed by Umberto Eco) by Olejarczyk, *Dialogi Platona*; cf. Pacewicz, 'O ewolucyjnym charakterze'. Pacewicz proposes to distinguish the evolution of Plato's philosophical views, which took place between the early and the middle period, and their development, between the middle and the late period.

this quality. An analysis of the *Timaeus* indicates that Plato recognises important aspects of the autotelic nature of certain creatures, not only of gods but also of human beings. This is reflected not only in his recognition of human beings as being the essential end (purpose, aim) of the natural world but also in his clearly expressed recognition that the purpose of the law and the state is the benefit of the individual. Moreover, one of the principal objectives of law is to lead to the equality of all members of a community. I would like to make clear, however, that I do not regard the correctness of the conclusions drawn from my analyses of the Demiurge's speech in the *Timaeus* to be a precondition for the correctness of my other findings related to Plato's conception of justice. These conclusions play rather heuristic than justificatory functions; they provide directions in the process of interpretation of Plato's works. They are consistent with other parts of my investigation, and it would be possible to present Plato's conception starting with an exploration of justice of the soul and justice of actions, and then investigating the Demiurge's speech and showing that the conclusions reached therefrom are congruent with the earlier findings.

The middle part of this book contains considerations pertaining directly to the issue of justice in Plato's works (Chapters 3–6). Here I distinguish clearly, as Plato does himself, three primary contexts in which justice is considered: justice as a virtue, which comprises the question of justice addressed by Plato in the model of the hypothetical state (Chapter 3); the justice of actions (Chapter 4); and the justice of the state and laws, which also includes punitive justice (Chapter 5). The issues of equality and friendship, which are directly involved in Plato's understanding of justice, especially in the justice of laws and the state, are considered separately (Chapter 6).

In the considerations of justice as a virtue herein (Chapter 3), two topics are clearly distinguished: justice in the model of the hypothetical state and what justice in truth is. My analyses of these topics refer mostly to the *Republic*. First, Plato's argumentation on justice in the hypothetical state is reconstructed, and this leads to the statements—widely accepted as genuine Platonic views—that justice consists in 'doing one's own work',[47] that everyone should be occupied with only one job, and that a few wise persons should organise in great detail the life of all members of the political community for the benefit of the state. What follows is a comprehensive examination of the limitations—indicated by Plato himself—on applying the conclusions drawn from the construction of the hypothetical state to the issue of justice as such. Plato's teaching about discourses designed for the acquisition of knowledge are also analysed (the crucial arguments are drawn from the *Phaedrus*).

Full credit is given to the statements in Book IV of the *Republic*, which he preceded with the words 'but in truth [τὸ δέ γε ἀληθές] justice was'.[48] It is argued

47 Plato, *Republic*, 433a, trans. Grube.
48 Plato, *Republic*, 443c–e, trans. Bloom.

that the postulate of devoting one's entire life to one occupation for the benefit of the state—which is often taken for the view of Plato himself—is held by him to be only a phantom of justice, and that the story about the model of the state is not to be read as a project for an ideal state. Constructing a model of the state is entirely subordinated to answering the question of how to be good, how to be just. If there are incongruencies between how Plato applies this model of justice in relation to the state and to an individual, they should always be resolved by giving priority to the individual. It is argued that the justice of an individual, the virtue of justice, is the existential (and therefore the highest and the most fundamental) perfection of a human being, based on an inner unity established by means of harmony and order. Someone who has mastered justice practises all the cardinal virtues. He is a comprehensively developed person, and he is not occupied with only one type of work that is typical for the members of one of the parts of the hypothetical state. To the contrary, he engages in activities typical for the members of all classes in the model of the hypothetical state. Moreover, the just person is guided by himself and not by a small group of sages.

Being just is a necessary condition for acting justly (Chapter 4). The issue of how to determine the content of just actions is examined here through an examination of the *Gorgias*, with special attention being given to Socrates' dialogue with himself, which is an exceptional formal means used by Plato to point out the most important issues. The analysis of the argumentation presented in the *Gorgias* leads my deliberations to an interpretation of the myth of the cave in the *Republic*. Plato's teaching on education, understood as a process of directing the learning power towards the right objects, and his teaching on the Good (the Form of the Good) and on the invisible realm turn out to be indispensable for understanding his argumentation concerning acting justly. Plato provides systemic reasoning for the thesis that justice is the good of others—justice never harms anybody (including one's enemies), but justice does that which benefits another. It becomes evident that in determining the content of just actions, it is the relation of an action to a specific addressee, and not to an abstract form (idea), which is of primary importance.

Plato's conception of the justice of laws and the state (Chapter 5) is secondary to his understanding of an individual as being endowed with dignity (being an aim in oneself). The good of individuals is the primary aim of laws and the state. Laws and the state serve to secure and to encourage just actions and justice as the virtue of an individual. The existence of the state is far from being the highest value—sometimes it may be better to destroy the state or to go into exile than to allow the rulers to make the lives of the ruled worse. Plato recognises the freedom to shape one's own life in both the short and long term. This recognition is deeply rooted in his conception of wisdom and courage—wisdom as a reason for a given action univocally provides only knowledge about what should be avoided, and not about what should be done here and now. Regarding Plato as an ideologist or even champion of totalitarianism turns out to be fundamentally misguided.

Plato's conception of punitive justice (Chapter 5) very clearly exposes the priority of the individual over the state and laws. A punishment is a kind of medication for the individual. Making human souls better, and not benefitting some state or any legal order, is the primary end of punitive justice.

Other inquiries directly concerning Plato's conception of justice include those related to equality and friendship (Chapter 6). Using the language of mathematics—mostly the concept of geometric proportion—Plato points to unity as a fundamental ontological issue concerning justice. In Plato's deliberations on equality, the priority of the individual (and not of abstract forms) in determining the content of just actions is also apparent. The content of just actions is based on a proportion of a certain kind which binds together an acting subject, a just action, and the addressee of the action. However, the very formal structure of this proportion rests on knowledge of something general which belongs to an invisible realm.

Since the greatest possible friendship is one of the two primary aims of laws, and since genuine friendship requires equality, equality between members of a political community therefore also becomes one of the fundamental goals to be achieved, though it is a goal which is placed in the distant future. Moreover, since acting justly is a prerequisite for happiness and friendship, and since such acting has—in principle—other people as its addressees, the principle of subsidiarity finds a grounding in Plato's approach: the state's role is not to provide goods for its citizens but to create conditions for just interactions between members of the political community who are helping each other.

Considerations pertaining directly to the conception of justice in general are followed by an examination of particular issues relating to justice (Chapter 7). This examination aims to show how the presented conception of justice 'works'. It is also meant as a form of test of the proposed interpretation. Initially, it is briefly argued that in Plato's approach not the justice of the soul, but acting justly is the highest perfection of a human being. Then more extensive consideration is given to the best activities a human being can perform and to their objects (addressees). It is argued that the best thing a human being can do is to act justly (to do what is beneficial for others) and not engage in pure contemplation. The proper objects of just deeds (of love) are other people and not abstract forms.

The final chapter is devoted to considerations concerning the sharing of wives (community of wives), as presented by Plato in the *Republic*. An interpretation of these excerpts in a non-totalitarian framework seems to be a very difficult task. Yet, it turns out that such an interpretation is possible, if due attention is given to the remarks which precede the considerations. Plato clearly indicates that these are not based on knowledge but are like the song of a poet and a kind of an instructive jest where 'erotic necessities' are at stake, rather than the geometrical necessities which are appropriate to philosophical inquiry. There are indications that the story about the sharing community of wives is meant not only as an exercise in gaining wisdom but also as a test of courage for the listener of Plato's Socrates and readers of the *Republic*.

2 The *Timaeus* on dignity: the Demiurge's speech

2.1 The *Timaeus* as a dialogue on justice

In seeking to identify an anticipation of the concept of dignity in Plato's works, it is appropriate to examine those texts devoted directly to what best distinguishes certain beings, like the gods or humans, from all other beings, and those which have important consequences in the form of postulates concerning the appropriate treatment of these beings.[49] Fundamental remarks on this question can be found in the *Timaeus*, in the speech of the Demiurge addressed to the gods whom he has created. Before making a closer examination of excerpts from that speech, a few remarks are needed with regard to the place of this text in the works ofPlato.

The *Timaeus* is a late work, and it is recognised as one of the most important and mature in Plato's oeuvre. The dialogue is considered to be a work on cosmology and on nature; it is a discourse on Plato's ontology, one that introduces what in the present day may be described as natural science. However, the present analysis shows the *Timaeus* to be in fact a dialogue—first and foremost—about moral issues concerning the individual.[50] In establishing the main questions relating to the dialogue, it is imperative to take into account both the question advanced by Plato and his aims, not simply what the respective figures in the dialogue have to say. This is of particular importance in the case of Plato, because the search for answers is

49 See Roskal, *Astronomia matematyczna*, pp. 107–121 for a discussion of the reading of the *Timaeus* in the context of cosmology and science.

50 Research on the *Timaeus* as a direct continuation of the *Republic*, and therefore as a treatise on justice (moral issues), seems unsatisfactory. Carone, *Plato's Cosmology*, offers an extensive study on the ethical dimensions of Plato's cosmology, devoting two chapters directly to an interpretation of the *Timaeus* (pp. 24–78); however, she does not challenge the paradigmatic view that, according to Plato, the best life is the life of a philosopher, and 'that the Forms are the highest goal of the philosopher' (p. 78), a view that is radically challenged by the present study (cf. Section 7.2.4). In accordance with the compatibilist reading of Plato which is favoured here, G. Carone sees a clear continuation of Plato's ethical view expressed in his early- and middle-period dialogues by pointing in his cosmology to the performative consistency in the behaviour of stars, which corresponds with 'consistency not only among one's thoughts, but also between one's thoughts and one's deeds' (p. 7). Nevertheless, she interprets the late dialogues as Plato's response to the elitism of his middle dialogues, a response which aims at some kind of reconciliation with the more egalitarian approach to happiness that is present in Plato's early-period dialogues. Cf. Paczkowski, '*Timajos* Platona', *passim*; Paczkowski points out the educational functions of the beauty of the universe revealed in the *Timaeus*.

conducted by means of stories and myths. In determining the principal questions that are the subject of the *Timaeus*, its reading requires paying special attention to the commentaries which open and close the main arguments, commentaries whose contents—at first glance—seem not to be directly related to the argument.

The introduction to this dialogue indicates that it is a continuation of the *Republic*. If this is in fact the case, there ought therefore to be a continuation of the issues previously raised, and especially of the main question as to what constitutes the justice of an individual person. Plato's Socrates points explicitly to the 'incompleteness of yesterday's discussion', that is the discussion rendered in the *Republic*:

> I'd like to go on now and tell you what I've come to feel about the political structure we've described. My feelings are like those of a man who gazes upon magnificent looking animals, whether they're animals in a painting or even actually alive but standing still, and who then finds himself longing to look at them in motion or engaged in some struggle or conflict that seems to show off their distinctive physical qualities. I felt the same thing about the city we've described.[51]

Nevertheless, it is striking that the *Timaeus* is not a dialogue about the state. The conclusion of the main argument (89d–90d) relates directly to man and his spirit. As in the *Republic*, there is an account of three types of spirit, and the discourse strives to answer a question in the realm of practical philosophy—how is one to be a good man? Shortly before concluding the dialogue (90d–e), Plato's Timaeus directly addresses the task set at the beginning—the 'initial assignment, that of tracing the history of the universe down to the emergence of humankind'. In the light of Plato's declaration that the discourse in the *Timaeus* is a continuation of the discourse contained in the *Republic*, the account of the universe and its history serves to describe man as a moral actor; just as the *Republic* is first and foremost a dialogue on the individual striving for justice as moral perfection and not about a possible state—'the city we've described' is actually 'the soul we've described', or rather 'the human we've described'.

The characterisation of the main figure, Timaeus, is also significant for identifying the main issues of the dialogue. He is portrayed positively through and through; he is not a Sophist with whom Plato's Socrates would cross swords. If the *Timaeus* were a treatise on cosmology, or on the philosophy of nature, broadly speaking, Timaeus as the main figure of the dialogue ought to be portrayed primarily as a natural historian, as someone devoted to 'science'. This, however, is not the case. Plato draws our attention to the character and education of those who in this dialogue are to continue the main deliberations contained in the *Republic*. In relation to Timaeus, Plato's Socrates first emphasises that he comes from 'an Italian city under the rule of excellent laws'[52] ('εὐνομωτάτης [...] πόλεως'—more literally translated 'of a most well-governed state'[53]) and that he is no worse than

51 Plato, *Timaeus*, 19b–c, trans. Zeyl.
52 Plato, *Timaeus*, 20a, trans. Zeyl.
53 Plato, *Timaeus*, 20a, trans. Lamb.

anyone in that city as far as his wealth or origins are concerned, that 'he has come to occupy positions of supreme authority and honor in his city'[54] and—finally—'that he has attained (...) the very summit of eminence in all branches of philosophy'.[55] The last remark concerns, in this context, philosophy in general, with no particular regard for reflections on natural history or on the cosmos as a whole. It should be noted, however, that the characterisation of Timaeus begins with a reference to the excellent laws governing his city and his personal contribution to establishing those laws, as he has held the highest offices in the state. It is worth noting, especially from the perspective of the hypothetical state depicted in the *Republic*, that his life has been comprehensively fulfilled: he is a philosopher, he—as a public official—has taken care to enact wise solutions, and he is a wealthy man. There is no indication whatsoever that he was wrong in engaging in any of these different kinds of activity.

Recognising that the *Timaeus* is mostly an anthropological dialogue where the main question remains that of justice, it is easy to understand why this very same dialogue includes Critias' commentary on the story of Solon about Atlantis.[56]

In this light, it is worth recalling as well the words of Plato's Cleinias in Book X of the dialogue *Laws*,[57] most likely written after the *Timaeus*[58]:

> It's vital that somehow or other we should make out a plausible case for supposing that gods do exist, that they are good, and that they respect justice more than men do. Such a demonstration would constitute just about the best and finest preamble our penal code could have.[59]

Plato's Athenian notices that before it is possible to make convincing arguments for the existence of gods who are good and respect justice, one has first to deal with (and refute) the doctrine—held then to be scientific (the doctrine referred to here is that of the ancient atomists)—that the cause of the cosmos coming into existence, together with all living beings, 'was neither intelligent planning, nor a deity, nor art, but (...) nature and chance'.[60] Further on, these views from the domain of cosmology and ontology are contrasted against views on the state and law, as Plato's Athenian remarks: 'that government, in particular, has very little to do with nature, and is largely a matter of art; similarly legislation is never a natural process but is based on technique, and its enactments are quite artificial'.[61]

---

54 Plato, *Timaeus*, 20a, trans. Zeyl.

55 Plato, *Timaeus*, 20a, trans. Lamb; this translation is more accurate than that of Zeyl because it points to the excellence of Timaeus in mastering philosophy.

56 Plato, *Timaeus*, 20d–26c.

57 See Paczkowski, '*Timajos* Platona', p. 227.

58 See Cornford, *Plato's Cosmology*, pp. 7–8; Owen, 'The Place of the "Timaeus"', *passim*.

59 Plato, *Laws*, 887b, trans. Saunders.

60 Plato, *Laws*, 889c, trans. Saunders.

61 Plato, *Laws*, 889d–e, trans. Saunders.

A confirmation of the method of interpretation accepted here, in which the *Timaeus* is read primarily as concerning justice or—more broadly—a life well led, is that a clear link between anthropological and cosmological issues is also made in the *Phaedo*. In this dialogue, Plato's Socrates, like his Timaeus, undertakes to resolve issues which—at first glance—belong to the realm of biology. He discusses the precise causes of how an organism works and functions, thereby relating these questions to cosmology. In commenting critically on the views of philosophers of natural history, Plato's Socrates relates:

> one man surrounds the earth with a vortex to make the heavens keep it in place, another makes the air support it like a wide lid. As for their capacity of being in the best place they could possibly be put, this they do not look for, nor do they believe it to have any divine force, but they believe that they will some time discover a stronger and more immortal Atlas to hold everything together more, and they do not believe that the truly good and 'binding' [τὸ ἀγαθὸν καὶ δέον] binds and holds them together.[62]

Cosmological issues lead Plato's Socrates to the problems of good and the principles of being, which will prove crucial for an understanding of the moral perfection of the human being.

Here one should note that Plato's Timaeus clearly speaks about the fact that his account of natural history (questions of biology and physics, from the modern perspective) does not relate to eternal truths, but to what is probable:

> And should one take a break and lay aside accounts about the things that always are, deriving instead a carefree pleasure from surveying the likely accounts about becoming, he would provide his life with a moderate and sensible diversion.[63]

In the light of the introduction to the dialogue, however, this account is not simply a lecture on natural history, for that would break the unity of the dialogue; its goal is to reach a better understanding of something that is beyond nature itself. Therefore, it can be assumed that the story told by Timaeus about the creation of the cosmos—based on such knowledge of nature as was available in the times of Plato—fulfils functions similar to those of Plato's myths.[64]

In contrast, however, to the account of justice contained in the *Republic*, where some elements of the characteristics of justice in the model of the hypothetical state were described as a phantom—εἴδωλον, something ostensible[65]—in the *Timaeus* there is no such direct questioning of the conclusions drawn from the account. Plato's Timaeus remarks that the visible cosmos is an image (εἰκών) of

---

62 Plato, *Phaedo*, 99b–c, trans. Grube.

63 Plato, *Timaeus*, 59c–d, trans. Zeyl.

64 See Paczkowski, '*Timajos* Platona', pp. 232–233; Paczkowski emphasises the role of the story told by Plato's Timaeus in revealing (as do myths) beauty, which is essential for education, and in introducing order to the individual's soul and to the state.

65 See Section 3.7.2.

something invisible which is a model (παράδειγμα) of it.[66] He warns that the accounts he gives are accounts of something that 'is itself a likeness, will be analogous thereto and possess likelihood'[67] Moreover, he adds in direct reference to the account of the universe itself that Socrates should not be surprised 'if it turns out repeatedly that we won't be able to produce accounts on a great many subjects—on the gods or the coming to be of the universe—that are completely and perfectly consistent and accurate'.[68] The visible universe and that which is invisible have to be taken into consideration if one wishes to understand human beings as subjects of moral perfection (justice).

2.2 Formal aspects of the text

The key text—split into smaller sections to make it easier to analyse—reads as follows:

> when all gods had come to be, both the ones who make their rounds conspicuously and the ones who present themselves only to the extent that they are willing, the begetter of this universe spoke to them. This is what he said:
>
> 'O gods, works divine whose maker and father I am, whatever has come to be by my hands cannot be undone but by my consent.
>
> Now while it is true that anything that is bound is liable to being undone, still, only one who is evil would consent to the undoing of what has been well fitted together and is in fine condition.
>
> This is the reason why you, as creatures that have come to be, are neither completely immortal nor exempt from being undone.
>
> Still, you will not be undone nor will death be your portion, since you have received the guarantee of my will—a greater, more sovereign bond than those with which you were bound when you came to be.'[69]

The analysed excerpt from the speech is not addressed to humans, but to more perfect beings—the gods who are to help the Demiurge in forming the world, including the formation of human beings endowed with a mortal body. The analysis here will focus on a general question that concerns more than just humanity: what, according to Plato, determines the specific, qualitatively superior position of certain beings that carries with it consequences of a normative nature, namely, the

66 Plato, *Timaeus*, 29b. It is worth noting that the hypothetical state described in the *Republic* is also called a 'model' ('παράδειγμα') of a state, and not an 'ideal' of it; Plato intends to discuss a 'modelled' state and not an ideal state; see Zygmuntowicz, *Praktyka polityczna*, p. 45.

67 Plato, *Timaeus*, 29c, trans. Lamb.

68 Plato, *Timaeus*, 29b–c, trans. Zeyl.

69 Plato, *Timaeus*, 41a–b, trans. Zeyl.

requirement of special, privileged treatment for these beings. It is also important to identify in what way this treatment should be special.

First, certain formal aspects of the speech of the Demiurge need to be specifically addressed. In reading Plato, one needs to consider the formal choices made by the author, such as who expresses particular views. In the above excerpt, it needs to be taken into account that Plato puts these words into the mouth of the creator of the world, who is certainly considered a being of special excellence. He is speaking to the gods whom he has created, and it is relevant that the addressees of his speech are conspicuous by their excellence—in intellect, as well as in other respects—because this means that it is possible to speak to them about difficult subjects in a straightforward manner.

These are clear signs on the formal level that the statements made by the Demiurge are considered by Plato to be particularly weighty. Of course, the speech is itself formulated as part of a myth. The functions performed in Plato's works by the myths he relates are a separate issue, wider discussion of which is not possible—or seemingly even necessary—here. Plato provides a succinct statement about this issue in the *Gorgias*, where his Socrates comments on the telling of a myth, saying to the Sophist Callicles:

> Maybe you think this account is told as an old wives' tale, and you feel contempt for it. And it certainly wouldn't be a surprising thing to feel contempt for it if we could look for and somehow find one better and truer than it.[70]

In some cases myths are the best thing we have to approach the truth.

2.3 The complexity and mortality of the soul

To reconstruct the reasoning used in the analysed portion of the speech, one may begin with the statement that all things which are comprised of elements ('bound') can be broken down (are 'liable to being undone'), and thus in themselves are not immortal.[71] All things that are created or born are complex; therefore, even the gods are not 'exempt from being undone' and hence are not inherently indestructible or immortal.

The statements analysed here are generally underappreciated. They appear to imply that Plato's arguments for the immortality of the soul as discussed in the literature (including textbooks), most of which are contained in the *Phaedo*,[72] are

70 Plato, *Gorgias*, 527a, trans. Zeyl.

71 A similar very general statement related to the possibility of being destroyed can be found in the *Republic*: 'everything that comes into being must decay'. Plato, *Republic*, 546a, trans. Grube.

72 Arguments based on similarities of the soul to what is eternal and unchanging, based on its internal unity; on the rule of the soul over the body; on kinship to what is divine, and opposition to what is mortal—*Phaedo*, 78b–80b; on analysis of the nature of the soul as the principle of life—*Phaedo*, 105c, *Phaedrus*, 245c; on inborn

deemed inconclusive by Plato himself. They may offer comfort to those facing death and provide guidance to those in search of answers to eschatological questions, but they are not proofs in the full sense of the word. The human soul is a created 'thing', it is 'born', it is 'complex', so in itself it is not indestructible or immortal. In terms of their complexity and the consequent lack of indissolubility that is vested in the very nature (internal structure) of being, all beings are alike—gods, human souls and the whole world of things. Moreover, if the complete unity can be found only in the Good itself—in the Form of the Good which may be equated with the form (idea) of the unity—then all other forms (ideas) are also complex. It can also be argued that forms are composed of elements as a precondition for the presence of differences between them and a precondition of the functions they fulfil in the process of cognition.[73]

2.4 Dignity as existential perfection

What is special about those to whom the speech is addressed? In terms of their genesis, they were created (formed) directly by the Demiurge. Do these beings, however, possess in themselves something that would provide a reason for referring to them or treating them in a special, privileged way? Plato explains that what is created directly by the Demiurge is 'well fitted together and is in fine condition'—'καλῶς ἁρμοσθὲν καὶ ἔχον εὖ'.[74] Instead of 'well fitted together', a more apt translation would be a word-for-word rendition of 'καλῶς ἁρμοσθέν'—'beautifully accommodated' or—using language related to music—'beautifully tuned'. The meaning of 'ἁρμόζω' often comprises a normative element—it can mean not only 'fit' but also 'fit well'. Therefore instead of 'beautifully fitted together', the translation 'beautifully well fitted together' seems to be more adequate in this context. To preserve this normative intuition I will use a calque—'beautifully harmonised'.[75]

---

knowledge and anamnesis—*Phaedo*, 95c–d; on the claim that the soul cannot be destroyed by an evil proper to it (injustice)—*Republic*, 609a–611b. An example of such a textbook is Reale, *History of Ancient Philosophy* (pp. 140–144); Reale notes the argument from the *Timaeus*, but does not pay any attention to the fact that this argument comprises presuppositions which radically challenge all other arguments (Reale call them 'proofs'). The argument in favour of the immortality of the soul based on the will of the Demiurge and Plato's own questioning of the conclusiveness of the arguments formulated in the *Phaedrus* are overlooked by L. P. Gerson in his monograph *Knowing Persons*; these problems are not mentioned either in the chapter devoted to the *Phaedo* (Gerson, *Knowing Persons*, pp. 50–98) or in his analyses of the *Timaeus* (Gerson, *Knowing Persons*, pp. 239–250).

73 See Blandzi, *Henologia*, pp. 141–142; Blandzi argues that Plato's forms are complexes of structure (φύσις) and border (πέρας), and they are constituted by relations.

74 Plato, *Timaeus*, 41b, trans. Zeyl.

75 Taking into account the importance of beauty and harmony in Plato's philosophy, a word-for-word translation seems the most accurate. This basic intuition is also lost

Several questions may be asked here: Why this particular phrase? Is the harmonising of the parts directly related to being 'in fine condition' (ἔχον εὖ)? Do these two characteristics refer to the same reality, as frequently happens in Plato's writings? Is beautiful harmonisation something more than just a question of the aesthetic values that ought to be recognised and protected?

To understand the magnitude of the matter at hand, one has to look at the overall context of Plato's system. Apprehending immortality from the point of view of inner unity establishes links between the existence of a certain being and unity. Inner unity turns out to be the foundation of being. Plato clearly recognises different kinds of inner unity, and the differences in this respect correspond to different kinds of existence—continuing and not continuing existence. There are certain 'stages' of inner unity and they are also 'stages' of perfection. What is decisive for being more or less perfect is not the 'content' of the elements which are bound together, but the inner integrity, inner unity itself. The idea that there are certain 'stages' of unity which correspond to 'stages' of being just and acting justly is also present in Plato's deliberations about justice. These considerations lead to the heart of Plato's ontology. In the *Republic*, the Good (the Form of the Good) is the highest idea,[76] something qualitatively more perfect than anything else: 'although the good is not being, but superior to it in rank and power'.[77] The symbol of the Good is the sun:

> the sun not only provides what is seen with the power of being seen, but also with generation, growth, and nourishment although it itself isn't generation. (...) Therefore, (...) not only being known is present in the things known as a consequence of the good, but also existence and being [τὸ εἶναί τε καὶ τὴν οὐσίαν] are in them besides as a result of it.[78]

The issue of the Good is crucial for understanding justice, and it is an issue I will return to more than once. It is essential to take into consideration that—especially with the aid of Plato's so-called unwritten teachings—it is possible to reasonably identify the Good (the Form of the Good) with the One (the Form of the Unity)[79]

---

in the Lamb translation: 'fairly joined together'. See Wesoły, 'Platońska koncepcja harmonii', p. 111.

76 For an extensive analysis see Ferber, *Platos Idee des Guten*; in his monograph Ferber analyses only Plato's 'written' teaching contained in the *Republic*; for a general introduction, see e.g. Santas, 'The Form of the Good in Plato's Republic', *passim*.

77 'οὐκ οὐσίας ὄντος τοῦ ἀγαθοῦ, ἀλλ' ἔτι ἐπέκεινα τῆς οὐσίας πρεσβείᾳ καὶ δυνάμει ὑπερέχοντος', Plato, *Republic*, 509b, trans. Grube; Shorey translates: 'the good itself is not essence but still transcends essence in dignity and surpassing power'. See Krämer, '*Epekeina tēs ousias*', *passim*; Krämer translates: 'the good itself is no substance [οὐσία], but rather beyond being [οὐσία], exceeding it in rank and power'; ibid., p. 39.

78 Plato, *Republic*, 509b, trans. Bloom.

79 E.g. Aristoxenus, *Elementa Harmonica*, II, 39.8–40.4; Aristotle, *Nicomachean Ethics*, 1095a–b; *Metaphysics*, 987b–988a, 1091b; *Eudemian Ethics*, 1218a; for the sources

and, more generally, good with unity. Granting existence can be understood as granting unity, according to the basic intuition that unity is the basis of existence, of being something distinct from everything else. What has no unity does not exist, it breaks down and ceases to exist. Giving unity is first of all a matter of existence, of giving or strengthening existence.[80] 'Beautiful harmonisation' is the basis of the inner unity, and thus of perfection in the order of existence—the more something is internally harmonised, the more it is internally united; the more it is united, the more it exists. One more correlation should be mentioned here that is of fundamental importance for an understanding of justice and just action: the more something exists, the more it resembles the Good itself.

Thus, if dignity becomes associated with unity based on internal harmony ('beautiful harmonising'), then dignity proves to be a special 'property' belonging to the order of existence. Attributing dignity to a thing first and foremost expresses something about how that thing exists and not about what it is like. The existence and the manner of existence encompass the existing thing as a whole, and thus encompass all the traits of a given individual.[81] If dignity is thus understood and ascribed to human beings, then the special quality related to dignity is acquired by everything that is within a human being: both the biological and the psychological or spiritual. Such an approach shapes a general ontological framework which seems to be promising in the search for an explanation of why human rights protect not only that which is specific to human beings, such as being free and rational, but also potentially to all aspects of being a human. Nevertheless, the issue needs closer examination, since it has to be considered to what extent the statements of the Demiurge about gods apply also to human beings.

2.5 Prohibition on instrumental treatment

A particular form of internal perfection based on internal unity and the manner of existence that accompanies it are reasons for the special treatment of those who possess it, as Plato writes: 'only one who is evil would consent to the undoing of

---

see Gaiser, *Platons ungeschriebene Lehre*; Reale, *Autotestimonianze e rimandi dei dialoghi di Platone*; see Pacewicz, *Między dobrem a jednością*, pp. 82–92, 145–147; Reale, *History of Ancient Philosophy*, pp. 77–83; see also Gaiser, *Testimonia Platonica*; Szlezák, *Reading Plato*; Ferber, *Warum hat Plato*; on Plato's unwritten doctrines in the context of the problem of understanding law and justice, see Incampo, *Sul fondamento*, pp. 91–139. Against equating the Good with the One, see Pacewicz, *Między dobrem a jednością*, esp. p. 173.

80 See Krämer, '*Epekeina tēs ousias*', *passim*; Szlezák, 'The Idea of the Good', *passim*; Incampo, *Sul fondamento*, pp. 93, 110; Blandzi, *Platoński projekt*, pp. 200–201.

81 To put it as Thomas Aquinas did—'being as we understand it here is the actuality of all acts, and therefore the perfection of all perfections' ('quod dico esse est actualitas omnium actuum, et perfectio omnium perfectionum'), Thomas Aquinas, *De potentia*, q. 7, a. 2, ad 9, trans. English Dominican Fathers.

what has been well fitted together [beautifully harmonised] and is in fine condition'.[82] The Demiurge himself is good, the best of causes, and the 'most excellent of all that is intelligible and eternal'.[83] For this reason, it is impossible for him ever to want to destroy someone who has been beautifully harmonised and is in fine condition.

Moreover, the Demiurge emphasises that the addressees of his speech will never be destroyed: 'you will not be undone nor will death be your portion'. Thus, the reason for special treatment is always present—in the language of today, it is innate or inherent. This reason can be described as a particular unity of being, a particularly perfect way of existence, a beautiful internal harmony, or simply as dignity itself.

One can also argue that since dignity is understood as existential perfection, this perfection is radically inherent (inseparable) and is independent of any particular quality or qualities and of the manner in which an individual acts. It is, therefore, impossible to lose dignity without losing one's very existence. The wish—the very will (βούλησις) of the Demiurge—for these particular beings to survive is not a one-off act, for the guarantees of survival exist at present and will do so in the future; the Demiurge will therefore never wish to destroy them.

The Demiurge's argumentation for the continuing existence of gods is in complete accord with the aforementioned systemic context that demands dignity be treated as perfection in the existential aspect of a being. Here, dignity is in a radical way inseparable from and independent of particular traits. Thus the Demiurge speaking to the gods foresees no situation where the direct fruits of his labours lose their fundamental perfection based on an act of direct creation by him (that they are 'beautifully harmonised' and 'in fine condition'), perfections which are the reasons for the continuing will of the Demiurge for their existence.

The Demiurge's will with respect to ensuring existence rests in something that is found in the subject itself and is not dependent on what choices the subject makes. It should be noted, however, that in the Platonic world the gods always act in a just way. Nevertheless, it is not any particular choice of action that is the reason for the Demiurge's will to secure their continuing existence.

It should be emphasised that the prohibition on destroying a possessor of dignity is absolute in the sense that it was not formulated with a view to achieving goals that go beyond the good of the possessors of dignity themselves, such as the good of the state or the universe as a whole, but with a view to their inner

82 Plato, *Timaeus*, 41a–b, trans. Zeyl.

83 Plato, *Timaeus*, 29a, 37a, trans. Zeyl; see Reale, *History of Ancient Philosophy*, pp. 113–114. There is no need to resolve here the question of whether the Demiurge is to be identified with the Good symbolised by the sun in the myth of the cave. I am accepting the view that the story in the *Timaeus* about the Demiurge concerns the same reality as the stories about the Good in the *Republic* or the story about the Supervisor of the Universe in the *Laws*.

perfection which is called here 'dignity'—their being beautifully harmonised and in good condition, which is a basis for their inner unity and therefore existence. The possessors of dignity are ends in themselves, although this does not exclude the possibility that such entities are essential for the whole of the universe to be perfect and that, in this sense, they benefit the whole.[84]

Here it is important that the will for their continuing existence—a specific way of treating others—rests on the specific characteristics of the subject. Such a characteristic is possessed by everything that is directly created by the Demiurge,[85] and therefore everything that is directly created by him is also willed by him, due to the fact that this particular being possesses a certain special inner harmony and beauty (unity), and not because of its belonging to a certain kind or species of beings. That which is particular, not that which is general, is what matters here. Neither is the usefulness (for example, for the preservation of a species) of the particular being the reason for the Demiurge's will for its continuing existence. In other words, such a being is willed for its own sake. It is therefore an end in itself—or following Aristotle, who identifies an end with a good, it is the good in itself and not an instrumental good; it is a *bonum honestum*, which in the later tradition is recognised to be dignity.[86] On account of the fact that the Demiurge's will is the foundation of the very existence of things which are wished by him, the way of existence also accords with the way a being is willed by the Demiurge. It is therefore also possible to state that such a being exists for its own sake and not on account of something else. Consequently, postulates may be formulated that describe the proper treatment of the possessors of dignity.

The statement that destroying a possessor of dignity (of unity based on a beautiful internal harmony) would be the act of a bad entity is true not only for the Demiurge, but is universal—no being, in so far as it is good, would want to threaten the existence of a possessor of dignity. From a systemic point of view, according to Plato, striving to be good is an innate tendency ('desire') of all that exists—striving for existence is striving for an internal unity that is equal to goodness. This needs closer consideration. Nevertheless, without going into details, the analyses justify a general prohibition on destroying beings endowed with dignity. In other words, whenever such an entity is the addressee of an action, one has to bear in mind that—regardless of its individual characteristics—as a result of dignity itself (internal structure) it has a right to its own existence, which should always be respected in all actions addressed towards it. This idea is in line with the personalistic norm as it is formulated today, regarded as a simple consequence of recognising dignity.[87]

---

84 See e.g., Plato, *Timaeus*, 41b–c; idem, *Laws*, 903b–e.

85 Plato, *Timaeus*, 41c.

86 'Dignitas significat bonitatem alicujus propter seipsum', Thomas Aquinas, *Scriptum super Sententiis*, lib. 3, d. 35, q. 1, a. 4, qc. 1, co.

87 As Immanuel Kant writes: 'man and generally any rational being exists as an end in himself, not merely as a means to be arbitrarily used by this or that will, but in all

2.6 Human beings and the gods

The Demiurge's speech is addressed to the gods. How far do the findings about their excellence also apply to human beings? In the *Timaeus*, Plato writes that in creating the universe, the Demiurge himself creates particles that the gods will use to create human beings. These particles are immortal because they are created directly by the Demiurge, and thus possess the same excellence that is the reason for the immortality of the gods themselves. Plato's Demiurge says to the gods in the closing passage of his speech:

> And to the extent that it is fitting for them to possess something that shares our name of 'immortal', something described as divine and ruling within those of them who always consent to follow after justice and after you, I shall begin by sowing that seed, and then hand it over to you. The rest of the task is yours. Weave what is mortal to what is immortal, fashion and beget living things. Give them food, cause them to grow, and when they perish, receive them back again.[88]

Later in the dialogue, Plato writes about this immortal part of human beings:

> Now we ought to think of the most sovereign part of our soul as god's gift to us, given to be our guiding spirit. This, of course, is the type of soul that, as we maintain, resides in the top part of our bodies. It raises us up away from the earth and toward what is akin to us in heaven, as though we are plants grown not from the earth but from heaven. In saying this, we speak absolutely correctly.[89]

There may be doubts as to whether this divine part in man is but one of the three parts of the soul that Plato distinguishes—namely reason—or whether it is the whole soul, which is composed of three elements. There would seem to be good arguments for the latter.

Human souls as created directly by the Demiurge are certainly also composed of some elements, since everything created or generated is complex. In respect to the gods, Plato's Timaeus talks about their being 'well fitted together [beautifully harmonised] and (...) in fine condition'.[90] There is no reason not to apply this description to a human soul as well. In considering what elements comprise the soul that has been formed directly by the Demiurge, it is natural to refer to the dialogue *Phaedrus*, where the entire soul—symbolised by 'the natural union of

his actions, whether they concern himself or other rational beings, must be always regarded at the same time as an end'; Kant, *Fundamental Principles of the Metaphysic of Morals*, 64–65 (428), and in consequence—'So act as to treat humanity, whether in thine own person or in that of any other, in every case as an end withal, never as means only', ibid., 66–67 (429).

88 Plato, *Timaeus*, 41c–d, trans. Zeyl.

89 Plato, *Timaeus*, 90a, trans. Zeyl.

90 Plato, *Timaeus*, 41b, trans. Zeyl.

a team of winged horses and their charioteer'[91]—is composed of three elements. According to the account given there, the soul as a tripartite whole is immortal—it can be incarnated, but it can also exist without a body.[92] The elements are analogous to those of which the gods (created directly by the Demiurge) are composed—'the gods have horses and charioteers that are themselves all good and come from good stock'.[93]

Coming back to the *Timaeus*, an act of direct creation concerns the particle that rules, the one that governs (ἡγεμονοῦν) those who wish to act justly. Does this, however, necessarily mean that only a rational part of the soul would be created directly by the Demiurge? Making human beings act justly is thus the first task assigned to human souls. When one refers to the dialogue *Phaedrus*, following in the footsteps of the gods can be regarded as a metaphor for acting justly. Thus in describing the procession of the gods journeying through the universe—to which whoever wishes may join—Plato avers that every one of these gods acts as befits him, does his own work[94]—meaning, in accordance with Plato's basic formula describing justice: each acts justly. In the *Republic*, when Plato writes on the specific functions of the soul that cannot be ascribed to anything else (no doubt referring to the soul as a tripartite whole), he expounds: 'taking care of things, ruling, deliberating, and the like'[95] and to give life is the work of the soul (ψυχῆς ἔργον).[96] To follow justice and the gods can, therefore, be considered in principle as the work of the entire soul, not only of reason as a part of it. What is clear is that this particular element in us, created directly by the Demiurge, gives character to the whole human being—'raises us up away from the earth'.[97]

2.7 The human being in relation to the whole

In terms of the universe, man is an essential element of the perfection of the whole. In speaking to the gods and setting them the task of creating man, the Demiurge avers:

> There remain still three kinds of mortal beings that have not yet been begotten; and as long as they have not come to be, the universe will be incomplete, for it will still lack within it all the kinds of living things it must have if it is to be sufficiently complete.[98]

91 Plato, *Phaedrus*, 246a, trans. Nehamas, Woodruff.
92 Plato, *Phaedrus*, 246d–248e.
93 Plato, *Phaedrus*, 246a–d, trans. Nehamas, Woodruff.
94 'πράττων ἕκαστος αὐτῶν τὸ αὑτοῦ', Plato, *Phaedrus*, 247a.
95 'τὸ ἐπιμελεῖσθαι [to be someone's mentor] καὶ ἄρχειν καὶ βουλεύεσθαι', Plato, *Republic*, 353d, trans. Grube.
96 Plato, *Republic*, 353d.
97 Plato, *Timaeus*, 90a, trans. Zeyl.
98 Plato, *Timaeus*, 41b–c, trans. Zeyl; see Plato, *Laws*, 903b–e.

Nonetheless, as in the case of the gods, in accepting the thesis that the aim of creating human beings is the perfection of the whole, it is not an obstacle to accept the thesis that their existence remains an end in itself, and this is due to their particular perfection. It should also be noted that the relation of a human being to the whole of the universe is an entirely different issue to that of the relation of a human being to the state and law.

It is very important to notice that a human soul, having been created directly by the Demiurge and being 'beautifully harmonised and in fine condition'—in short, 'possessing' dignity—came to be destined to exist in the body, in contrast to the gods, as creatures which—composed of soul and body—is mortal. The existence of such creatures is necessary for the universe to be perfect.[99] Human souls as an element of bodily creatures are willed by the Demiurge, but it is also true that the mortal creatures composed of an immortal soul and mortal body are wanted by the Demiurge, although they were not created directly by him. Therefore, it can be concluded that existence in the body is compatible with the very nature of the human soul. It can also exist in the form of an animal. Plato's Timaeus speaks not simply about souls changing their bodies, but also says that 'all the animals exchange their forms, one for the other, and in the process lose or gain intelligence or folly',[100] as if being 'mixed' creatures were their primary form of being. By 'primary' I mean here—normal, in accordance with the order of the universe and in accordance with the will of the Demiurge. The description in the *Timaeus* of the formation of a mortal soul in specific parts of the body by the gods[101] can be read as not implying that only the rational part of the soul was created directly by the Demiurge and the appetitive and spirited are mortal were created by the gods. Rather, this description concerns that which is specific to a given mortal creature. When Plato's Timaeus concludes this description referring to 'the most sovereign part of our soul as god's gift to us',[102] this part can be identified not with the rational part but with a guiding spirit—a daimon—which, in accordance with the myth of Er in the *Republic*, is not a part of the soul as such but is appointed to the fate chosen by the soul.[103] It represents the knowledge needed to live a good life in the way that the individual has chosen.

According to such a reading, death is not conceived as liberation from earthly conditions, which is a precondition for leading a true life. Here one should not be misled when Plato's Timaeus says that in dying the soul 'finds it pleasant to take its flight'.[104] This claim concerns the way of dying—a death may be pleasant 'when

99 Plato, *Timaeus*, 41b–c.
100 Plato, *Timaeus*, 92c, trans. Zeyl.
101 Plato, *Timaeus*, 69a–81e.
102 Plato, *Timaeus*, 90a, trans. Zeyl.
103 Plato, *Republic*, 617d–e. See Section 5.2.4.2.
104 Plato, *Timaeus*, 81d–e, trans. Zeyl.

the aging process has run its course',[105] but 'a death that is due to disease or injury is painful and forced'.[106] I shall consider this issue further, particularly in Chapter 7.

If it is natural for the human soul to form a composition together with the body, then questions about justice, about how to be good, and how to live a good life, are questions about the here and now. Knowledge concerning an invisible realm is needed to live a good life as a creature composed of a soul and a body, and as creatures which strive for (and as far as possible find) accomplishment and happiness in the here and now. Only in this way can the will of the Demiurge be fulfilled and the universe gain its perfection. At the same time, an individual has to find his own fulfilment in this world as an aim in himself, because the soul, which is the source of existence and of all activities of the human being, exists as an aim in itself.

Plato, evidently, sees a qualitative difference between human beings and other entities in the visible world. Other living things (such as plants[107]) were created by the gods for the benefit of human beings, and benefiting human beings can therefore be regarded as the plants' aim. At the end of the story about the creation of human beings, Plato writes in the *Timaeus*:

> Of necessity, however, it came about that he lived his life surrounded by fire and air, which caused him to waste away and be depleted, and so to perish. The gods, therefore, devised something to protect him. They made another mixture and caused another nature to grow, one congenial to our human nature though endowed with other features and other sensations, so as to be a different living thing. These are now cultivated trees, plants and seeds, taught by the art of agriculture to be domesticated for our use. (...) All these varieties were planted by our masters, to whom we are subject, to nourish us.[108]

In this context it is apt to note that the special character of the human soul—which is also the reason that the Demiurge will not cease to want its continuing existence, regardless of all changeable, specific traits—is also independent of the moral quality of the soul. This is stated categorically when Plato raises the issue of punishment (as will be discussed further in Section 5.3), the aim of which, in principle, is the good (benefit) of those punished. Admittedly, Plato accepts the possibility of moral decline to the extent that no punishment can heal the soul; in this instance, an appropriate punishment is one that lasts forever and serves to deter others.[109] The most important point, however, is that even extreme moral decline will not lead the Demiurge to cease to wish for the existence of the soul. The reason for

105 Plato, *Timaeus*, 81e, trans. Zeyl.
106 Plato, *Timaeus*, 81e, trans. Zeyl.
107 In his story, Plato speaks only of the creation of plants by the gods—animals are generated from people; see Plato, *Timaeus*, 90d–92c.
108 Plato, *Timaeus*, 77a, 77c, trans. Zeyl.
109 Plato, *Gorgias*, 525b; *Republic*, 615e.

such an act of will still holds—in spite of its moral decline, the soul remains 'beautifully harmonised' and 'in fine condition'. The recognition of dignity in spite of any negative moral qualities is a typical feature in the understanding of personal dignity in modern legal systems.

One may object to this line of argumentation by invoking the *Phaedrus*, where Plato's Socrates, in his account of what the human soul is like, looks for reasons why immortal souls incarnate.[110] According to the story comparing a soul to a chariot, the soul seems to be at home when travelling through 'heaven', and incarnation is due to a certain structural imperfection in the human soul—the lowest part of the soul sometimes hinders it in acting in accordance with the judgment of reason.[111] Properly educated human souls, it seems, never incarnate. The account in the *Timaeus* is different. Incarnation is necessary for the perfection of the universe, and it is good gods who supply the bodily elements of human beings. There is no mention of the imperfection of souls being a necessary condition for incarnation. The human soul is also understood as being 'beautifully harmonised' and 'in fine condition'. The main reason for incarnation is of a positive nature—it contributes to the perfection of the universe. I shall return later to the interpretation of the *Phaedrus*; nevertheless, it may be noted here that there is no need to posit an incongruence between the accounts from the *Phaedrus* and the *Timaeus* as long as the myth about the chariot, according to the suggestions contained in the myth of the cave from the *Republic*, is read as a story about education performed in this life in order to lead it justly.

The question of the relationship between human beings and the universe as a whole is also present in a well-known and beautiful excerpt from the dialogue *Laws*, where the Athenian states:

> What we say to the young man should serve to convince him of this thesis: 'The supervisor of the universe has arranged everything with an eye to its preservation and excellence, and its individual parts play appropriate active or passive roles according to their various capacities. These parts, down to the smallest details of their active and passive functions, have each been put under the control of ruling powers that have perfected the minutest constituents of the universe. Now then, you perverse fellow, one such part – a mere speck that nevertheless constantly contributes to the good of the whole – is you, you who have forgotten that nothing is created except to provide the entire universe with a life of prosperity. You forget that creation is not for your benefit; you exist for the sake of the universe. (...) But you're grumbling because you don't appreciate that your position is best not only for the universe but for you too, thanks to your common origin.'[112]

110 Plato, *Phaedrus*, 246a–257b.
111 Plato, *Phaedrus*, 246d–248e.
112 Plato, *Laws*, 903b–c, trans. Saunders.

This quotation would seem, at first glance, to justify recognising Plato as one who ascribes to totalitarianism. It should be noted, however, that first, in the context of the cited excerpt, the good of the individual is not sacrificed for the good of the whole, though it is a part of it: 'your position is best not only for the universe but for you too'; and second, the above quotation does not relate to the ties between the individual and state, and for this reason its content cannot be advanced as an argument for Plato's totalitarian convictions.

In relation to the universe, human beings are an essential element for the perfection of the whole, and, in this sense, are for the good of the whole. However, as in the case of the gods, acceptance of the thesis that the purpose of the creation of human beings is the perfection of the whole does not preclude the thesis that their existence is an aim in itself, a result of their particular perfection. It should also be noted that the relationship of humans to the whole of the universe is essentially a different question from that of their relationship to the law and the state.

3 Justice as a virtue

3.1 Introductory remarks

A correct interpretation of Plato's work requires one first establish which problems he considers to be the most important. This is an essential step in formulating the principal questions to which he wishes to provide answers and in reconstructing the principal pillars of his arguments.

In this context, it is necessary to differentiate between various forms of justice, such as the justice of actions, justice of the soul, justice of the hypothetical state as a reflection of the justice of the soul, punitive justice, and justice of the law and state. Reconstructing the argumentative architecture of Plato's teaching on justice, it can be observed that he starts with the question of why it is better to act justly rather than unjustly. This is a very intriguing question because, according to the basic intuitions in Greek culture related to justice, acting justly means acting for the benefit of another and not for the benefit of oneself. But why should a reasonable person do something for others, possibly losing some of his own possessions or sacrificing benefits as a consequence? This problem leads to the question of the justice of the soul as something that conditions just actions and is a result of such actions. The question of why one should act justly thus leads to the question of why one should be just, why one should acquire the virtue of justice. In order to provide an answer to questions about justice as a virtue, Plato constructs a model of the state that is in fact a model of the soul. Once we are equipped with answers to questions concerning the justice of the individual—of his soul and his actions—it is possible to address the issue of justice of the law and state *per se*. The issue of punitive justice as one that restores lost justice is, on the one hand, linked to questions pertaining to the justice of the individual. On the other hand, punitive justice presupposes the functioning of a legal system, and considerations on punitive justice reveal important features of the relations between an individual and the state (laws). Therefore, the topic of punitive justice is preceded here by reflections on the justice of the state and laws.

Before delving into the analysis proposed by Plato, it is worth pointing out several elements of the cultural context, noting first and foremost, the basic intuitions in the Greek language and culture relating to justice and the law. Plato explores these intuitions and refers to them in his argumentation; however, on vital points he goes further. The interpretations of Plato's teachings on justice which place great emphasis on directing every person 'to do his own work'—the one thing that a person is best at—in fact, go only halfway. Admittedly, arguments for doing one's own work are indeed presented in Plato's writings, and the interlocutors of Plato's Socrates generally agree with these arguments, sometimes eagerly, and therefore a reader may form the impression that these arguments, which coincide with some basic intuitions contained in the Greek language and culture, encapsulate the very nature of Plato's teachings. I argue, however, that as far as justice is concerned, establishing the essence of Plato's teachings demands going far beyond these intuitions, which prove to be more of a starting point than an end point in his elaboration of a theory of justice.

3.2 Some terminological issues

Plato's teachings on justice—indeed, like all of his philosophy—arise naturally from Greek culture. This also applies to its immersion in language. I would like to cast light on those elements that lead to certain arguments which are considered Plato's 'standard-bearers', arguments integral and specific to his philosophy.

It is appropriate to start with Plato's epistemology. His doctrine of recollection—*anamnesis* (ἀνάμνησις) as providing the foundations for understanding the way human knowledge is acquired, correlates with the Greek etymology of the word 'truth'—'ἀλήθεια'. Truth is a denial of forgetfulness as personified by Lethe (Λήθη), who guards the sources of the waters from which those entering Hades (or returning from it) drink. The word 'μνήμη'—'memory'—is the source from which derives the name of Mnemosyne (Μνημοσύνη), the daughter of Uranus and Gaia. She is the personification of memory and, as the mother of the nine Muses, the mother of all teaching and the arts. Defining true cognition as *anamnesis* suggests the restoration of memory (and thus the act of reminding) to be the essence of the process of cognition.

A similar reference to Greek culture, one based on intuitions rooted in etymology, can be found in Plato's teachings on justice. In his times, the word 'θέμις', which can also be rendered as 'justice', had already lost its significance for teaching on justice. The goddess Themis (Θέμις) personified divine laws and divine justice. She was also responsible for divining the will of the gods—she taught Apollo the art of divination, and the cult of Themis was present in Delphi before that of Apollo. She was also connected with oracles, who revealed the will of gods. The word 'θέμις' as used in the *Iliad* signifies mainly the ordinances of the king which are sanctioned by the gods, and the unwritten rules of human behaviour.[113] Since the authority of θέμις rested mostly on the authority of the gods, its moral significance was not obvious.

The moral dimension of justice came to be closely associated with the term 'δίκη', and from the time of Hesiod this was probably the most important category in moral reflection.[114] Dike, the personification of human justice, was a daughter of Themis and Zeus. Originally, the word 'δίκη', from which 'δικαιοσύνη' ('justice') and 'δίκαιος' ('just', 'righteous') are derived, meant 'a normal course of events, a standard way of behaviour', being a condition or action signifying what is to be expected, the normal course of things.[115] In this context, William Guthrie noted

113 Janik, *Terms of the Semantic Sphere of* δίκη *and* θέμις, p. 115.
114 Janik, *Terms of the Semantic Sphere of* δίκη *and* θέμις, p. 116.
115 Guthrie, *The Greek Philosophers*, p. 6.

that the earliest meaning of 'δίκη' 'in Greek literature is certainly no more than the way in which a certain class of people usually behave, or the normal course of nature. There is no implication that it is the right way, nor does the word contain any suggestion of obligation'.[116]

Such a non-moral meaning is to be found in Homer, who certainly shaped the minds of the Greeks in the times of Plato. In the *Odyssey*, Penelope uses the expression 'as is the *dike* of lords' to describe 'the way they are wont to behave;'[117] akin to doing or saying something cruel or overweening or having favourites, which is not in her view something that should serve as an example and is certainly something the 'good master Odysseus'[118] never did. A similar usage of *dike* can be found in Hippocrates: 'Death does not follow these symptoms in the course of *dike*', which means simply 'does not normally follow'.[119] The normative meaning of 'δίκη' is already fully formed, and possesses its own personification in the form of the goddess Δίκη, a century before Plato, in the poetry of Aeschylus.[120]

Guthrie argues that the definition of justice (δικαιοσύνη) elaborated in the long discussion in the *Republic* and which is based on a rejection of the meaning of the word 'δίκη' current in Plato's own day, represents a return to its original meaning and, according to Guthrie, should be regarded as Plato's final definition, his ultimate conclusion:

> justice, *dikaiosyne*, the state of the man who follows *dike*, is no more than 'minding your own business', doing the thing, or following the way, which is properly your own, and not mixing yourself up in the ways of other people and trying to do their jobs for them.[121]

---

116 Guthrie, *The Greek Philosophers*, p. 6.

117 Guthrie, *The Greek Philosophers*, p. 6.

118 Guthrie, *The Greek Philosophers*, p. 6; see Homer, *Odyssey*, IV, 689 f.; see ibid., XIV, 58 f., where Eumaeus mentions 'the *dike* of serfs like myself, who go ever in fear', quoted after Guthrie, *The Greek Philosophers*, p. 6.

119 Guthrie, *The Greek Philosophers*, p. 6; see Hippocrates, *De capitis vulneribus*, 3; quoted after Guthrie, *The Greek Philosophers*.

120 Guthrie, *The Greek Philosophers*, p. 7. In Hesiod one encounters the moral dimension of justice which is crafted in opposition to either ὕβρις (pride) or βία (act of violence); however, as Havelock argues, Hesiod's considerations of justice still belong—in their core—to the oral culture 'which was incapable of conceptualizing justice apart from its pragmatic application in day-to-day procedure. In oral thought it remains a method, not a principle'. Havelock, *The Greek Concept of Justice*, pp. 216–217.

121 Guthrie, *The Greek Philosophers*, p. 7. W. K. C. Guthrie observes that this original meaning of 'δίκη' 'was rooted in the class-distinctions of the old Homeric aristocracy, where the appropriate action was summed up in a man's knowing his proper place and sticking to it and to Plato, who was founding a new aristocracy, class-distinctions—based this time on a clearly thought-out division of functions determined by psychological considerations, but class-distinctions nevertheless—were the mainstay of the state'; ibid.

In the course of this study, I shall argue that a return to the original meaning of 'δίκη' goes only halfway to revealing the specific Platonic conception of justice, one focusing on the justice of the individual, in which 'minding your own business' no longer adequately characterises just actions. Furthermore, class distinctions in the state will be rejected as a paradigm for the organisation of the state itself.

Nevertheless, the proposed interpretation is also immersed in the primary meanings of 'δίκη', though somewhat differently than suggested by Guthrie. The etymology of 'δίκη' leads to the root 'δεiκ', which occurs in 'δείκνυμι'—'to show', 'indicate'.[122] This suggests a shift from the descriptive aspect: 'how things are', 'how things are wont to be', to that of the prescriptive: 'what should be the case'. Notwithstanding, there is yet another more important matter to consider. According to its primary meaning, δίκη is the 'dividing line between two properties'.[123] Due to the fact that a path or road often ran along these lines, it came to mean 'a way' or 'path',[124] and further, 'a normal course of events'. These roads or paths mark out the way of those travelling in a particular direction, indicating the destination for which they have set out. In respect to ontology, however, much more significant is the fact that these lines establishing borders also provide order and form, and that these borders establish a field, something distinct, as an entity. This intuition is highly important in philosophy, and constitutes one of the central elements of Greek philosophy, including pre-Socratic ontology.[125] In Greek philosophy, the fundamental ontological principle is that 'to be' means 'to be defined'.[126] This in turn takes the form: 'to be' means 'to be bound', to have boundaries which provide shapes. Therefore, boundaries (also: limits, ends) are understood as something defining quantity and/or quality.[127] Therefore, the better (more strongly) something is defined, the more it in fact exists. Justice is originally thus related to the very constitution of something, and therefore, to its very existence. It will be argued that in Plato's philosophy relating justice to the 'strength' of existence is foundational to thinking on justice as the most fundamental virtue of man. The more one is just, the more one in fact exists, even though one may have less.

The intuitions that are fundamental for Plato's concept of justice, especially the justice of actions, can also be found in the etymology of the word 'νόμος', which in Greek is a basic word used to denote law. In identifying the content or shape of just action, Plato focuses on what is 'commensurable' with an addressee of action in the sense that it is profitable, beneficial or, at least, not harmful to him. 'Νόμος' was used primarily to designate laws whose authority rested on the authority of a human community to establish laws for itself, but it could also

122 *Etymologisches Wörterbuch der Griechischen Sprache*, pp. 116–117.
123 Kubok, *Prawda i mniemanie*, p. 99.
124 Guthrie, *The Greek Philosophers*, p. 6.
125 This issue is discussed in a monograph by Kubok, *Problem apeiron*.
126 Kahn, 'Being in Parmenides and Plato', p. 173 [244].
127 Kubok, *Problem apeiron*, p. 47.

denote a customary law or a custom—that which is generally accepted.[128] The noun 'νόμος' is derived from the verb 'νέμω'—'I allocate, pasture, feed or apportion food' (the noun 'νομεύς' means 'herdsman').[129] These fundamental intuitions indicated by etymology also lead to the act of caring for others[130] and to equality based on a certain measure, a certain fit, and a position between extremes. When feeding it is necessary to distribute food which is appropriate both in quality and in quantity—not too much and not too little. Such a way of thinking on equality, usually associated with Aristotelian teachings on virtue, also lies—as it transpires—at the fundaments of Plato's understanding of just actions and descriptions of the form of such actions (see Section 6.3).

From the verb 'νέμω' also derives the name of the goddess Nemesis, who was the daughter of Nyx (the Night) and sister of Moirai, the goddesses of destiny. Nemesis personifies the just revenge of the gods, since 'νέμεσις' also signifies justified indignation, just anger, or morally motivated fear.[131] Sometimes, like Erinyes, she was seen as a power which punishes crimes, but first of all she was recognised as a power against a lack of restraint, for instance, against the arrogant pride of rulers or against the excessive prosperity of mortals. Hence, she distributes good fortune (happiness) and misfortune, keeping watch so as to ensure that no one's success exceeds the boundaries marked out for them.[132]

Such allocation or distribution is also reflected in the general Greek designation of a deity, god, goddess, or spiritual semi-divine being inferior to the gods—daimon (δαίμων). The expression 'δαίμων' was often used to denote the divine power itself. This word is derived from 'δαίεσθαι', the middle voice of 'δαίω'—'I distribute'.[133] A deity, therefore, is someone who 'becomes apportioned'. Here, there is a correlation with Plato's teachings on the Good as the highest form (idea), which by nature tends to spread (in Latin: *bonum est diffusivum sui*) and to share its goodness, which means providing existence and order. Because the good comprises justice, the understanding of the Good also defines the Platonic paradigm of understanding justice.

---

128 Later on, νόμος was used also in reference to the Law of Moses as divine law. Nevertheless, the laws—νόμοι—based on the authority of the community itself were sometimes in opposition to the laws—θέμιστες—based on divine authority. Cf. Gagarin, *Writing Greek Law*, pp. 33–36.

129 Cf. e.g. Plato, *Statesman*, 267e, where the statesmen are called 'the herdsmen of humanity', trans. Rowe.

130 See Plato, *Statesman*, 275e, 276d.

131 Grimal, *Concise Dictionary*, pp. 289–290.

132 Kubiak, *Mitologia Greków*, p. 39.

133 Liddell, Scott, Jones, *A Greek–English Lexicon*, p. 366.

3.3 Justice and happiness—justice as the most important of all matters

3.3.1 Justice as the subject of the best possible art

The *Gorgias* is devoted to rhetoric as the best of the arts; at the same time, next to the *Republic*, it is the most important dialogue devoted to justice. Turning to Callicles, Plato's Socrates avers:

> I'd like to find out from the man [Gorgias] what his craft can accomplish and what it is that he both makes claims about and teaches. As for the other thing, the presentation, let him put that on another time, as you suggest.[134]

In a later comment by Polos there is a reference to an art (τέχνη) which is the most beautiful and the best, to which only the best of individuals could devote themselves.[135] Socrates' question directs our attention towards the subject of the most beautiful and best of the arts, what this art 'makes claims about and teaches'. The fundamental problem perceived by Plato's Socrates concerns not what the rhetoric of Gorgias states and teaches, but rather, what is taught by rhetoric itself, the most beautiful and best of the arts, and therefore one that relates to the most important of matters.[136] In the course of the dialogue, it becomes clear that the proper subject of the most beautiful and best of the arts is justice—that is, the justice of man (the soul) and his actions. Each of the arts has as its aim the good, that is, the perfection of that which is the object of actions performed during the exercising of a given art.[137]

In the case of the most beautiful and best of the arts, this object is man (the soul), and the aim is to make him good and beautiful. Justice can therefore be understood to be the appropriate good for man. True art entails understanding the nature of the things it relates to and a familiarity with causes, which means that actions undertaken that shape a given thing are thought through and have an aim (the goodness of its object), which imbues these actions with a particular order.[138]

It is worth noting that in the *Gorgias* Plato is not concerned with justice in general—an abstract form (idea) of justice—but with the justice of a specific, existing individual (soul). What is particularly important, therefore, in the context

---

134 Plato, *Gorgias*, 447c, trans. Zeyl; 'craft' here is the translation for 'τέχνη', often rendered also as 'art'.
135 Plato, *Gorgias*, 448c.
136 See Stauffer, *The Unity of Plato's* Gorgias; I agree with one of the main theses of D. Stauffer's book, that in the *Gorgias* only a kind of rhetoric is criticised and not rhetoric as such.
137 See Jaeger, *Paideia*, vol. 2, p. 131.
138 Plato, *Gorgias*, 465a, trans. Zeyl.

of the issue under consideration, is that the subject of the best of the arts is not justice of the state.

The formulation of a definition of the subject of rhetoric helps Plato's Socrates to analyse the Sophists' claim that the rhetoric practised by them is the best of the arts, and, moreover, to draw conclusions about justice. Responding to Socrates' question, Gorgias answers:

> The persuasion I mean, Socrates, is the kind that takes place in law courts and in those other large gatherings (...). And it's concerned with those matters that are just and unjust.[139]

Socrates emphasises the weight of the issue by saying: 'I don't suppose there's anything quite so bad for a person as having false belief [δόξα] about the things we're discussing right now'.[140] It is thus justice and injustice that come to the fore. Socrates sums up one of the comments by Gorgias:

> Hold it there. You're right to say so. If you make someone an orator, it's necessary for him to know what's just and what's unjust, either beforehand, or by learning it from you afterwards.[141]

In the course of discussion, justice turns out to be the subject matter of the best possible art.

3.3.2 The greatest evil and the greatest good

Similar conclusions concerning the importance of justice are reached when Plato's Socrates asks directly the question of what is the greatest evil and the greatest good. Adeimantus, in clarifying the principal question in the *Republic*, says: 'No one, whether in poetry or in private conversations, has adequately argued that injustice is the worst thing a soul can have in it and that justice is the greatest good'.[142] Plato's Socrates accepts the view that justice represents the greatest good and injustice the greatest evil, and takes up the challenge to argue adequately for this claim.

The relationship between justice and happiness is directly addressed in Book IX of the *Republic*, where different types of characters (related to types of constitutions) are considered. When Plato's Socrates has to answer the question who 'is first in happiness, who second, and so on in order'[143], he holds it to be an easy task, and orders them according to virtue and vice, justice and injustice: 'the

139 'περὶ τούτων ἅ ἐστι δίκαιά τε καὶ ἄδικα', Plato, *Gorgias*, 454b, trans. Zeyl.
140 Plato, *Gorgias*, 458a–b, trans. Zeyl.
141 Plato, *Gorgias*, 460a, trans. Zeyl.
142 Plato, *Republic*, 366e, trans. Grube.
143 Plato, *Republic*, 580b, trans. Grube.

best, the most just, and the most happy is the most kingly (...) and the worst, the most unjust, and the most wretched is the most tyrannical'.[144]

In the *Gorgias* injustice and causing injustice are considered the greatest evils. In summing up the discussion with Polos on the subject of punishment and its avoidance, Socrates asks rhetorically: 'Does it follow that injustice, and doing what is unjust, is the worst thing there is?'[145] Somewhat further, this question is re-addressed with regard to the general issue of punishment—the unjust usually has the opportunity to 'return to health' thanks to an appropriate punishment, and therefore: 'So, doing what's unjust is the second worst thing. Not paying what's due when one has done what's unjust is by its nature the first worst thing, the very worst of all'.[146]

Here it can already be noticed that the accent should be on the action, on the commission of injustice—'the greatest evil is to commit injustice'[147]—rather than on the state of the soul itself. An analogous thesis—that the greatest evil is to commit injustice and not to bear any punishment for it—appears at the beginning of the dialogue with Callicles as something that philosophy says, always speaking the same thing.[148]

Consequently, committing injustice also transpires to be a greater evil than being subjected to it. Plato's Socrates, in the discussion with Polus, remarks that he who unjustly sentences to death is more deserving of pity than he who has been sentenced to death.[149] The general question of happiness is strongly linked with the thesis 'that doing what's unjust is worse than suffering it'[150]; this thought is continued in further parts of the dialogue: 'one who does what's unjust is always more miserable than the one who suffers it, and the one who avoids paying what's due always more miserable than the one who does pay it'.[151]

Plato's Socrates therefore points to justice and injustice as the basic criteria for one's actions:

> Do we agree that sometimes it's better to do those things we were just now talking about, putting people to death and punishing them and confiscating their property, and at other times it isn't? (...) I say that when one does these things justly, it's better, but when one does them unjustly, it's worse.[152]

---

144 Plato, *Republic*, 580b–c, trans. Grube.
145 'ἆρ' οὖν συμβαίνει μέγιστον κακὸν ἡ ἀδικία καὶ τὸ ἀδικεῖν', Plato, *Gorgias*, 479c–d, trans. Zeyl.
146 Plato, *Gorgias*, 480d, trans. Zeyl.
147 Plato, *Gorgias*, 469b, trans. Zeyl.
148 Plato, *Gorgias*, 482a–b.
149 Plato, *Gorgias*, 469b.
150 Plato, *Gorgias*, 473a, trans. Zeyl; cf. ibid., 469b.
151 Plato, *Gorgias*, 479e, trans. Zeyl; cf. ibid., 473a, 474b.
152 Plato, *Gorgias*, 470b–c, trans. Zeyl.

This statement is made by Plato's Socrates in the judicial context of sentencing, nevertheless, he generalises the context and recognises justice to be moral perfection as such. The argumentation in favour of accepting justice and moral excellence to be basic criteria for action involves linking the justice or injustice of the subject of these actions with happiness:

> the matters in dispute between us are not at all insignificant ones, but pretty nearly those it's most admirable to have knowledge about, and most shameful not to. For the heart of the matter is that of recognizing or failing to recognize who is happy and who is not.[153]

It should be noted here that it is not the happiness of the state or society that is of primary concern, but that of particular individuals. Happiness, in the view of both Socrates and his opponents, is the most certain of goods,[154] one that is not subject to doubt. The controversy mentioned concerns what happiness consists of or what makes people happy. Plato's Socrates argues that this is justice. The degree to which one is just is directly related to the degree of one's happiness:

> The happiest man, then, is the one who doesn't have any badness in his soul, now that this has been shown to be the most serious kind of badness. (...)
>
> And second, I suppose, is the man who gets rid of it. (...) This is the man who gets lectured and lashed, the one who pays what is due. (...)
>
> The man who keeps it, then, and who doesn't get rid of it, is the one whose life is the worst.[155]

One of the theses put forward after Socrates' dialogue with himself in the *Gorgias* is that the possession of justice and self-control makes 'happy people happy', and the possession of badness makes 'miserable people miserable'.[156] Being just, as being in opposition to being unjust and wicked, decides on the beauty and the good of man: 'the admirable and the good [καλὸν καὶ ἀγαθόν—beautiful and good] person, man or woman, is happy, but that the one who's unjust and wicked is miserable'.[157] After Socrates' dialogue with himself, which can be held to be the culmination of the *Gorgias*, happiness is also associated with being a good man, as well as being good and beautiful—and therefore also just—in one's actions: 'the good man does well and admirably [εὖ τε καὶ καλῶς] whatever he does, and (...) the man who does well is blessed and happy [μακάριόν τε καὶ εὐδαίμονα]'.[158] In these statements the

153 Plato, *Gorgias*, 472c, trans. Zeyl.
154 Cf. Xenophon, *Memorabilia*, IV, 2, 33.
155 Plato, *Gorgias*, 478d–e, trans. Zeyl; cf. ibid., 472e.
156 Plato, *Gorgias*, 508b, trans. Zeyl.
157 'τὸν μὲν γὰρ καλὸν καὶ ἀγαθὸν ἄνδρα καὶ γυναῖκα εὐδαίμονα εἶναί φημι, τὸν δὲ ἄδικον καὶ πονηρὸν ἄθλιον', Plato, *Gorgias*, 470e, trans. Zeyl.
158 Plato, *Gorgias*, 507c, trans. Zeyl.

term 'justice', sometimes together with other descriptions of positive moral qualities, is used to indicate the goodness of a person or of his actions.

Linking justice with happiness is of primary importance for defending the view that justice is desirable as such, regardless of the gains or losses in someone's possessions. This is the focus of the above arguments. Questions of whether happiness consists of being just—having justice in the soul—or of acting justly, or perhaps is something caused by justice, are not central here. Nevertheless, it is references to acting justly that dominate. The view that justice in the soul underlies (causes) happiness is compatible with the claim that happiness consists of acting justly, since justice in the soul causes such actions. The question of whether justice in the soul or acting justly is more perfect will be considered separately in Section 7.1.

3.3.3 Utility as the foundation of one's good

In Ancient Greece and its culture, as in Plato, good is strictly linked with beauty. Plato's Socrates starts his argument by characterising beauty with the aid of two categories. One the elements of this pair is pleasure (ἡδονή), while the other is use, benefit, expediency (χρεία,[159] ὠφελία[160]). In the course of his argument, the latter element is recognised as the foundation of good.[161] Illustrations from medicine make it obvious that what is pleasurable and what is useful are two very different things; someone's good is associated here with the useful,[162] and with the pleasurable—in as much as it serves the good.

Analogously, that which is ugly, repulsive (αἰσχρόν) is characterised through suffering (λύπη) and evil (κακόν),[163] with the last being linked with harm (βλάβη).[164]

159 'Take admirable bodies first. Don't you call them admirable [beautiful] either in virtue of their usefulness, relative to whatever it is that each is useful for, or else in virtue of some pleasure, if it makes the people who look at them get enjoyment from looking at them?' ('οἷον πρῶτον τὰ σώματα τὰ καλὰ οὐχὶ ἤτοι κατὰ τὴν χρείαν λέγεις καλὰ εἶναι, πρὸς ὃ ἂν ἕκαστον χρήσιμον ᾖ, πρὸς τοῦτο, ἢ κατὰ ἡδονήν τινα, ἐὰν ἐν τῷ θεωρεῖσθαι χαίρειν ποιῇ τοὺς θεωροῦντας'), Plato, *Gorgias*, 474d, trans. Zeyl.

160 'Don't you call shapes and colours admirable [beautiful] on account of either some pleasure or benefit or both?' ('ἢ διὰ ἡδονήν τινα ἢ διὰ ὠφελίαν ἢ δι' ἀμφότερα καλὰ προσαγορεύεις'), Plato, *Gorgias*, 474e, trans. Zeyl.

161 Socrates does not protest when Polos says to him: 'your present definition of the admirable in terms of pleasure and Good is an admirable one' ('ἡδονῇ τε καὶ ἀγαθῷ ὁριζόμενος τὸ καλόν'), Plato, *Gorgias*, 475a, trans. Zeyl. For the principal argument on this subject, see ibid., 476e–477a.

162 Plato, *Gorgias*, 478c.

163 'And so is my definition of the shameful in terms of the opposite, pain and bad, isn't it?' ('οὐκοῦν τὸ αἰσχρὸν τῷ ἐναντίῳ, λύπῃ τε καὶ κακῷ'), Plato, *Gorgias*, 475a, trans. Zeyl.

164 Plato, *Gorgias*, 475a–b, 477c.

Injustice becomes associated with the ugly and evil (harm). The most repulsive is that which is the worst.[165] The greatest evil, therefore, is that which causes the greatest harm:

> But what is surpassing in greatest harm would, I take it, certainly be the worst thing there is. (…) Injustice, then, lack of discipline and all other forms of corruption of soul are the worst thing there is.[166]

Already at this point it can clearly be seen—and further analysis confirms this—that at the heart of Plato's concept of justice lies what is useful,[167] and not the obligation or duty encapsulated in the norms of actions.[168]

The answer to the question of why it is better to act justly rather than unjustly demands an examination of how just or unjust actions are related to the inner state of the soul—which constitutes the justice of the soul. Why is it better to have a just soul than an unjust one? An answer to this question necessarily involves pointing to some kind of benefits gained by an acting subject. Plato is testing the traditional formulae of justice, analysing whether they are apt for comprehending what is useful for a soul. Looking at justice from the perspective of usefulness would seem—at first glance—to be a standpoint typical of the Sophists. There is, however, a basic conceptual difference, arising from a difference in the criteria defining that which is useful. For the Sophists—on account of their acceptance of sensualism—the criteria lay in that which can be perceived by the senses, in 'those which one feels',[169] and can be understood in terms of possessing something—health, wealth, political power, etc.

---

165 'εἰ δὴ αἰσχίστη, καὶ κακίστη', Plato, *Gorgias*, 477c.

166 'ἀλλὰ μὴν που τό γε μεγίστῃ βλάβῃ ὑπερβάλλον μέγιστον ἂν κακὸν εἴη τῶν ὄντων. (…) ἡ ἀδικία ἄρα καὶ ἡ ἀκολασία καὶ ἡ ἄλλη ψυχῆς πονηρία μέγιστον τῶν ὄντων κακόν ἐστιν', Plato, *Gorgias*, 477d–e, trans. Zeyl.

167 Cf. e.g. Plato, *Republic*, 344e, where in the discussion with Thrasymachus the issue of justice is characterised as a matter 'to determine which whole way of life would make living most worthwhile for each of us', trans. Grube; and the issue of justice comprises an examination of 'whether just people also live better and are happier than unjust ones', ibid., 352d.

168 It is difficult to agree with Stauffer who, in reference to the descriptions of justice which are analysed by Plato (*Republic*, 331e ff.), states that duty provides the very basis for justice. In Stauffer's approach the concept of good would be secondary to the concept of duty; though this is typical for ethics after Hume and Kant, it seems not to accord with Plato's position; Stauffer, *Plato's Introduction to the Question of Justice*, pp. 11–14.

169 Most likely Protagoras is the most succinct in characterising the Sophist's epistemology in Plato's *Theaetetus*—'it is impossible to think that which is not or to think any other things than those which one feels; and these are always true', Plato, *Theaetetus*, 167a–b; trans. Fowler.

Plato's criterion is found in what is beyond the sensual. The key is determining the specificity of the benefits brought by just actions to their subject. This problem can be formulated–following Adeimantus–as follows: why should injustice be blamed and justice praised not 'by mentioning the reputations, honours, and rewards that are their consequences'.[170] I am arguing that the criterion is–ultimately–the perfection of the subject in respect to existence and being. Just actions–actions for the benefit of another person–may cause various losses to the acting subject, but generally speaking, these are losses in the domain of belongings, possessions. That which is truly useful is that which contributes to the strengthening of one's existence, or that which mitigates its degeneration. In this way, usefulness is placed on the level of being, beyond losing or acquiring something one 'has'. The attainment of virtues is a means for acting justly, which contributes to the unity and therefore to the existence of their subject. The very existence of human actions has its foundation in the goodness of the acting subject.

3.4 Traditional formulae describing just actions

In the *Republic*, reflection on the formulae defining justice begins even in the short, introductory conversation of Socrates with Cephalus–justice 'is speaking the truth and paying whatever debts one has incurred'.[171] This definition will soon be rejected as being incongruent with our thinking about justice in a situation when someone who is of sound mind entrusts us with a weapon and then demands it be returned when he loses his mind.[172]

Then there is a consideration of the definition of justice proposed by Simonides of Ceos, a poet of the sixth and fifth centuries BC, whom Plato's Socrates describes as 'a wise and godlike man'.[173] According to the text of the *Republic*,[174] Simonides claimed that 'it is just to give to each what is owed to him' ('τὸ τά ὀφειλόμενα ἑκάστῳ ἀποδιδόναι δίκαιόν ἐστι').[175] The context indicates that this was a definition

170 Plato, *Republic*, 366e, trans. Grube. S. Blackburn formulates the main problem of the *Republic*, describing this very issue as Glaucon's challenge: 'show that morality, in and of itself and regardless of its consequences, benefits the possessor, and that immorality similarly harms him'. Blackburn, *Plato's Republic*, p. 44. This seems imprecise, however–benefiting the possessor is a consequence of justice (morality). Then the core of the issue is the specificity of this benefit.

171 'τὴν ἀλήθειαν αὐτὸ φήσομεν εἶναι ἁπλῶς οὕτως καὶ τὸ ἀποδιδόναι ἄν τίς τι παράτου λάβῃ', Plato, *Republic*, 331c, trans. Grube.

172 Plato, *Republic*, 331c.

173 Plato, *Republic*, 331e, trans. Grube.

174 In the preserved texts of Simonides of Ceos himself the passage containing the analysed description of justice has not been preserved; see R. G. Bury, footnote to the *Republic*, 331e, in Plato, *Republic*, trans. Bury.

175 Plato, *Republic*, 331e, trans. Grube.

commonly known and accepted.[176] Plato's Socrates does not reject it, but he warns against such an interpretation of this formula, according to which justice would be considered in categories of returning debts taken. The above-mentioned argument about returning a weapon to someone who is not of sound mind, advocates against this interpretation, for it would imply that it would be just to return something even in a case when the thing being returned might cause harm to him. This argument is supplemented by the observation that in this situation one would have to deem it just to return the thing even in the case when the lending party is a friend, which could lead to a conflict with the obvious intuition that it is just that one always acts to assure the good of one's friends.[177] It is better, therefore, instead of speaking of returning a debt to someone, to say that 'it is just to give to each what is appropriate to him' ('τὸ προσῆκον ἑκάστῳ ἀποδιδόναι').[178]

Neither does Plato's Socrates consider the above formula entirely satisfactory.[179] This is because it could be understood to mean that it is just to return good for good and evil for evil. Plato's argumentation aims to demonstrate that justice—in its fundamental understanding—must not be conceived purely in categories of returning debts taken, nor should one conceive of it in categories of exchange. Plato's Socrates, therefore, challenges the view that justice is based on harming foes and extending services to friends: 'it is never just to harm anyone'.[180] Justice cannot be properly apprehended in thinking that is typical in war; it presupposes a kind of friendship (or at least striving for friendship) and hence excludes treating someone as a foe.[181] Plato's thinking about justice not only goes beyond categorising others as a foe, but also beyond treating others as competitors in acquiring something which can be possessed by defeating someone.[182]

---

176 Plato, in his analyses of justice elsewhere, also refers to Simonides; see Plato, *Republic*, 334b, 334e.

177 Plato, *Republic*, 332a–b, trans. Grube.

178 Plato, *Republic*, 332c, trans. Grube.

179 In the later Byzantine legal tradition, the analysed formula 'what is due' ('τὸ προσῆκον') was given in Greek using the word ἴδιος—'appropriate, personal, specific to the individual (such as a name), private'. See 'τὸ δὲ δίκαιον ἑκάστῳ νέμει τὸ ἴδιος'—'Iustum autem suum cuique tribuit', *Basilicorum* lib. II, tit. I, I, quoted following *Basilicorum libri LX* 1933; the definition of justice by Ulpian from the *Digest* 'iustitia est constans et perpetua voluntas ius suum cuique tribuendi' (*Dig.* 1, 1, 10 pr.), is translated as: 'Δικαιοσύνη ἐστὶ σταθηρὰ βούλησις καὶ διηνεκὴς ἑκάστῳ τὸ ἴδιον ἀπονέμουσα δίκαιον', *Basilicorum* lib. II, tit. I, X. Plato and Aristotle use the word ἴδιος, though not in the contexts of describing justice which are analogous to the quoted descriptions; see ἴδιος in Liddell, Scott, Jones, *A Greek–English Lexicon*, p. 818.

180 'οὐδαμοῦ γὰρ δίκαιον οὐδένα ἡμῖν ἐφάνη ὂν βλάπτειν', Plato, *Republic*, 335e, trans. Grube.

181 Cf. Legutko, *Sokrates*, pp. 412–413; see Section 6.4.

182 Cf. the opening passages of the *Laws*; Plato, *Laws*, 626b–628e.

It should be noted that in principle Plato is not against characterising justice as returning to each what is owed to them; but he is decidedly against particular interpretations of Simonides' formula. Plato's Socrates remarks that neither Simonides—described earlier as 'wise and godly'—nor Bias of Prien and Pittakos of Mytilene[183]—who were ranked among the Seven Sages of Greece—postulated the harming of foes and doing of favours to friends. He suggests that harming foes and favouring friends is a way of thinking that 'belongs to Periander, or Perdiccas, or Xerxes, or Ismenias of Corinth, or some other wealthy man who believed himself to have great power'.[184] Here, Plato lists examples of rulers who in his times, in terms of political power and possession, were considered to 'have great power'. Plato writes that they believed themselves to have great power, or—as Paul Shorey translates it—that in their conceit they had great power, hinting that the true greatness of acts cannot be measured by what people usually consider as a measure of success in life, or by what is modelled on what someone who has unlimited power (who is an absolute ruler) can do. The fields of activity indicated by Plato where 'achievements' only appear to constitute success in life remain unchanged despite the passing of the ages. The appearances or phantoms of successful life in these fields in actuality define injustice. When in Book II of the *Republic* Plato describes a perfectly unjust man and the plans made by such a man, he writes:

> He rules his city because of his reputation for justice; he marries into any family he wishes; he gives his children in marriage to anyone he wishes; he has contracts and partnerships with anyone he wants; and besides benefiting himself in all these ways, he profits because he has no scruples about doing injustice.[185]

The 'achievements' listed above reflect what is known in the Christian tradition as conceit, lust and greed,[186] fields that can, in brief, be couched in terms of power, sex, and money.

Returning to the analysed formulae describing justice, it should be noted that in the *Gorgias* Plato himself uses a formula—'if he did what's appropriate with respect to human beings, he would be doing what's just'[187]—which is very similar to the

---

183 Plato, *Republic*, 335e, trans. Grube.

184 Plato, *Republic*, 336a. Despite the services of Periander to Corinth (tradition speaks of forty years of rule) and many dicta preserved in the annals, he remained a controversial figure, known to be hot-tempered, and a figure subject to misfortune as a result; see Diogenes Laertius, *Lives of Eminent Philosophers*, 1, 94–100. Cf. Kubiak, *Literatura Greków*, pp. 112–117.

185 Plato, *Republic*, 362b, trans. Grube.

186 *The First Epistle General of John*, 2, 16: 'For all that is in the world, the lust of the flesh, and the lust of the eyes, and the pride of life, is not of the Father, but is of the world', *Holy Bible*, King James Version, 1991.

187 'περὶ μὲν ἀνθρώπους τὰ προσήκοντα πράττων δίκαι' ἂν πράττοι', Plato, *Gorgias*, 507b, trans. Zeyl; Lamb translates: 'when he does what is fitting as regards men, his actions will be just'.

one considered in Book I of the *Republic* in the polemic with Thrasymachus.[188] Both formulae refer to the adequacy of something to someone—the fittingness of something (of an action) with respect to someone—as the essence of just actions. This question is discussed in a further section of this book concerned specifically with the justice of actions (Chapter 4).

Plato's Socrates demonstrates that just actions are aimed at the good of the addressee of the actions, and at another's good, including when the addressee is someone weak and underprivileged;[189] slaves are also included.[190] Since to be just is to care not about oneself but about someone else, justice leads to the loss of one's own belongings, and thus—as Thrasymachus concludes—it is best to be unjust as much as possible and demand justice from others who thus do what benefits us; then personal gain will be the greatest, though only the strong are able to do this:

> justice is really the good of another, the advantage of the stronger and the ruler, and harmful to the one who obeys and serves. Injustice is the opposite, it rules the truly simple and just, and those it rules do what is to the advantage of the other and stronger, and they make the one they serve happy, but themselves not at all.[191]

It can be observed, therefore, that the considerations on justice in the *Republic* begin with reflections on the justice of one's actions—and that the road to this leads through an examination of what is the justice of the soul. There is a similar structure in the *Gorgias*—reflection on the justice of the soul leads to questions concerning the justice of actions. A question that becomes central is why it is better to act justly than unjustly, since justice in actions results in another's good, not one's own.

3.5 The *Republic* as a dialogue on the individual

In accordance with the aim described at the beginning of the *Republic*, the fundamental question addressed relates to the justice of the individual and not the state. An analysis of the state can be said to be a heuristic operation. The state, as an instrument of enquiry, is a model of man (the soul). As Plato's Socrates comments:

> The investigation we're undertaking is not an easy one but requires keen eyesight. Therefore, since we aren't clever people, we should adopt the method of investigation that we'd use if, lacking keen eyesight, we were told to read small letters from a distance and then noticed that the same letters existed elsewhere in a larger size and on a larger surface. We'd consider it a godsend, I think, to be allowed to read the

188 'it is just to give to each what is appropriate to him [τὸ προσῆκον ἑκάστῳ ἀποδιδόναι]', Plato, *Republic*, 332c, trans. Grube.

189 Plato, *Republic*, 339b–342e.

190 Plato, *Laws*, 777d–e.

191 Plato, *Republic*, 343c–d, trans. Grube.

> larger ones first and then to examine the smaller ones, to see whether they really are the same.[192]

Since justice exists both in man and in the state, and because the state is larger, it will be easier to see justice in it. It is evident, however, that the enquiry aims at understanding the justice of an individual. In describing his methodology Plato's Socrates also indicates that he will not be examining a real state or a 'ready-made' ideal state, but that the subject of examination is a mental representation of a state 'under construction'.[193] The mental building of a state by Plato is a methodological operation of a heuristic nature that can be compared to similar operations proposed by other thinkers, such as the construct of the hypothetical original position—for instance, John Rawls' use of the hypothesis of the veil of ignorance—so as to identify the fundamental principles ordering social life.

The particular framework for examining justice is defined at the beginning of the dialogue and will be confirmed at the point where Plato's Socrates answers the question of what justice is, which takes place in Book IV (443c–444a). This passage closes the analysis which was begun by the declaration that what constitutes the justice of the soul will be searched for by means of a construct of the state as a model of the soul (368b). Plato, therefore, writing on the justice of the individual, speaks of what 'in truth justice is' and describes justice through a mental reconstruction of a hypothetical state as an apparition or phantom (εἴδωλον) of true justice (443c).

This is confirmed by a subsequent closure relating to the construct of the state, one attesting to the fact that this model is one for the formation of the soul and not—at least, not without essential adjustments—for the formation of the state. This can be found at the conclusion to Book IX, which closes the enquiry on the hypothetical state. In the matter of a just person's participation in politics, Glaucon remarks: 'You mean that he'll be willing to take part in the politics of the city we were founding and describing, the one that exists in theory, for I don't think it exists anywhere on earth'.[194] Socrates in turn replies:

> But perhaps, I said, there is a model of it in heaven, for anyone who wants to look at it and to make himself its citizen on the strength of what he sees. It makes no difference whether it is or ever will be somewhere, for he would take part in the practical affairs of that city and no other.[195]

---

192 Plato, *Republic*, 368c–d, trans. Grube.

193 'If we could watch a city coming to be in theory, wouldn't we also see its justice coming to be, and its injustice as well? (...) And when that process is completed, we can hope to find what we are looking for more easily?' Plato, *Republic*, 369a–b, trans. Grube.

194 Plato, *Republic*, 592a, trans. Grube.

195 Plato, *Republic*, 592b, trans. Grube.

The end, therefore, is not the formation of a real state shaped according to the invented model—'it makes no difference whether it is or ever will be somewhere'. The emphasis instead is placed on the individual, who wishes to exemplify the model of the state and to make *himself* its citizen (ἑαυτὸν κατοικίζειν).[196] Thus what matters is the formation of the self in relation to the conclusions arising from the construction of the model of the state.

Before issues relating directly to justice are discussed in detail, the teachings of Plato will be analysed in respect to the cardinal virtues developed for understanding justice itself.

3.6 The model of the state and the teaching of virtues

3.6.1 Improvement of man

3.6.1.1 Socratic questions

Analyses of Plato's model of the state must take into account the context established in the discussion between the Sophists and Socrates. This discussion aims to answer questions about individual justice, which are understood as issues about the improvement of a man, about becoming good. A question comes to the fore: 'what does it mean to be a good man?' Answering it is indispensable for addressing problems concerning individual improvement, such as 'how to become good?' and 'how to help others in becoming good?'

A good starting point for further considerations is a question posed by Socrates, who follows a postulate contained in the 'Delphic inscription' that commands: know yourself.[197] It is impossible to take proper care of oneself or others without an understanding of man. Plato explains this in a simple way in a dialogue between Socrates and Alcibiades:

> *Socrates*: Now if we didn't know what a shoe was, would we have known what skill makes a shoe better?

---

196 Cf. Voegelin, *Plato and Aristotle*, p. 146, commenting on the *Republic*, 592b: 'Sliding through the metaphor to reality, participation in politics now means concern with the transpolitical politeia that is set up in heaven and will be realized in the soul of the beholder. The soul is a one-man polis and man is the "statesman" who watches over its constitution. The dissolution through the ultimate shift to the soul and its transcendent order, however, does not cancel the validity of the whole preceding inquiry into the paradigm of the good polis'. However, it is argued below that such a cancellation (regarding central elements of the paradigm of the good *polis*) takes place explicitly when Plato's Socrates, while drawing conclusions from the construction of the hypothetical state as the model of the soul, says what justice in truth is and what is only a phantom of it (Plato, *Republic*, 443c–444a). See Section 3.7.

197 See Plato, *Phaedrus*, 229a–230b.

Alcibiades: No, we couldn't have.
Socrates: Nor would we have known what skill makes a ring better if we didn't know what a ring was.
Alcibiades: True.
Socrates: Well then, could we ever know what skill makes us better if we didn't know what *we* were?
Alcibiades: We couldn't.

(...)

Socrates: (...) this is the situation we're in: if we know ourselves, then we might be able to know how to cultivate ourselves, but if we don't know ourselves, we'll never know how.[198]

Plato and his Socrates are evidently inspired here by their own Greek tradition. Plato was certainly familiar with the ode 'For Hieron of Syracuse' by one of the most prominent poets, Pindar, who wrote it about a century before Plato. Pindar goes to the point in an unsurpassably concise way: 'γένοι' οἷος ἐσσὶ μαθών'—'Learn and become who you are'[199] or 'Become what you are, having learned it'.[200] To realise this postulate requires maturity; in the next verse, Pindar warns: 'To children, you know, an ape is pretty, always pretty'.[201] To know who you are is not a simple thing, but it is indispensable for the development of a man. Pindar introduces a seeming paradox—how can I become who I am? I am who I am. Everyone is who they are. Nevertheless, Pindar's expression involves thinking which is characteristic of philosophy, especially practical philosophy. The question of who I am is a question about the invisible essence, the nature, of man. It is a question about something which establishes the aim of development, a model of being good, something normative telling me what I should be like and how I should act. At the same time, it is something which constitutes one's being in the here and now.[202]

---

198 Plato, *Alcibiades*, 128e–129a, trans. Hutchinson.

199 Pindar, *Pythian 2, For Hieron of Syracuse Chariot Race*, 70, trans. Svarlien.

200 Quoted after Patrick Kurp (http://evidenceanecdotal.blogspot.com/2011/02/become-what-you-are-having-learned-it.html) who attributes this translation to Elroy L. Bundy, supposedly in *Studia Pindarica* (1962), however this translation is hardly to be found in Bundy's book.

201 Pindar, *Pythian 2, For Hieron of Syracuse Chariot Race*, 71. The ape as a symbol of a spoiled spirited part of the soul is used by Plato in the *Republic*, 590b: 'And aren't flattery and slavishness condemned because they subject the spirited part to the moblike beast, accustoming it from youth on to being insulted for the sake of the money needed to satisfy the beast's insatiable appetites, so that it becomes an ape instead of a lion?', trans. Grube.

202 In Aristotelian philosophy the form of a substance has two aspects: ἐντελέχεια—a pattern of fulfilment, of development, which, as an aim, provides direction for development, and ἐνέργεια—a source of actions performed here and now; cf. e.g. Aristotle,

The main alternative for understanding who a man is was metaphorically depicted by Plato in the introductory part of the dialogue *Phaedrus*. After focusing attention on the problem of knowing oneself and discarding questions relevant to enquiry into the world of nature, Plato's Socrates outlines his own project: 'I look (...) into my own self: Am I a beast more complicated and savage than Typhon, or am I a tamer, simpler animal with a share in a divine and gentle nature?'[203]

The first Greek word used to describe Typhon—πολύπλοκον, rendered here by 'complicated'—means tangled (like a labyrinth), confusing, without order; the second—ἐπιτεθυμμένον—means savage and also furious. Typhon was one of the least sympathetic (and the deadliest) creatures in Greek mythology. According to Hesiod's *Theogony*, Typhon was 'terrible, outrageous and lawless'.[204]

Plato uses the figure of Typhon as an image of man seen from the philosophical perspective of the Sophists. Of particular interest here is their position, introduced here by Plato more as a model for the purpose of philosophical discussion than as faithful presentation of a philosophical position.[205] Plato's challenge to the Sophists' view in the domain of ethics concerns not only those views belonging to philosophical anthropology, but reaches into the foundations of both ethics and anthropology, drawing on the fields of epistemology and ontology. The basic declaration on the sources of trustworthy cognition accepted by the Sophists is placed by Plato in the mouth of Protagoras (who historically laid down the foundations for Sophist philosophy) in the dialogue *Theaetetus*: 'it is impossible to judge what

---

Metaphysics, 1022a, 1032b. In the case of man, this form can be called humanity—'something' everyone has in common and which is an ontological foundation of belonging to the human species.

203 Plato, *Phaedrus*, 230a, trans. Nehamas, Woodruff.

204 Hesiod, *Theogony*, 306–307, trans. Evelyn-White.

205 Cf. Corey, *The Sophists in Plato's Dialogues*. I agree with Corey that the Sophists in Plato's dialogues are not portrayed as 'deliberate deceivers or evildoers' (p. 211); I also agree that Plato seems neither to offer nor to intend a general criticism of the Sophists (p. 228). From the point of view of justice as a central subject of Plato's philosophy I do not find Corey's distinction between the Sophists (who claim that they are teaching virtue) and rhetoricians (who do not claim this, p. 12) to be of great importance. The opponents of Plato's 'positive characters', like Socrates, Parmenides, the Eleatic Stranger and the Athenian Stranger, serve to illuminate Plato's position by placing it in contrast to certain standpoints. In the course of this book I will call these opponents 'the Sophists' since they share certain fundamental epistemological views clearly exposed by Plato's Protagoras (a protoplast of the Sophists) which close the way out of the cave and therefore the way to learn truths which are indispensable for the formulation of the proper conception of justice. Cf. Tell, *Plato's Counterfeit Sophists*; and a collection of essays: O'Grady (ed.), *The Sophists*.

is not, or to judge anything other than what one is immediately experiencing; and what is immediately being experienced is always true'.[206]

Taking into account the range of meanings of the Greek πάσχω, instead of 'what one is immediately experiencing', it may be translated as 'what one feels'.[207] It should be noted, however, that 'what one feels' is not limited by the Sophists to what is given in sensual experience, understood as being provided by the senses. We should remember that the concept of the five basic senses was developed later by mediaeval Arabic thinkers. 'What one feels' also comprises what is experienced emotionally—for instance, what is feared or desired. If human knowledge is limited to such sources, then it is obvious that the whole universe, which is recognised as real and which should be taken into account in rational considerations on man and his conduct, is essentially of a sensual nature. Man is also a part of this universe. If one asks about guidelines in our life, such as how to find aims whose realisation would fulfil a human life, then it is clear that a rational being will follow what is recognised as real and what can be apprehended. From the perspective of the Sophists' philosophy this 'real' and 'cognisable' is limited to that which one feels.

The practical consequences of this standpoint are presented in a speech by Plato's Callicles:

> this is what's admirable and just by nature—and I'll say it to you now with all frankness—that the man who'll live correctly ought to allow his own appetites to get as large as possible and not restrain them. And when they are as large as possible, he ought to be competent to devote himself to them by virtue of his bravery and intelligence, and to fill them with whatever he may have an appetite for at the time. But this isn't possible for the many; I believe.[208]

Where appetites reign there is no order. For the ancient Greeks (perhaps the atomist doctrine is an exception) any order is based on reason. If appetites reign 'the man who'll live correctly' becomes more tangled and furious than Typhon. The fundamental virtues of bravery—courage (ἀνδρεία) and intelligence or prudence (φρόνησις)—are only the means (like oars) for the accomplishment of aims established by human appetites.

If what one feels, what is immediately experienced, is the only credible source of knowledge, then there is only the here and now. There is no place for an invisible 'who I am' which provides hints about who I should become. Actual desires determine the aims of actions, and there are no criteria allowing one to say that

206 'οὔτε γὰρ τὰ μὴ ὄντα δυνατὸν δοξάσαι, οὔτε ἄλλα παρ' ἃ ἂν πάσχῃ, ταῦτα' δὲ ἀεὶ ἀληθῆ', Plato, *Theaetetus*, 167a–b, trans. Levett.

207 Plato, *Theaetetus*, 167a–b, trans. Fowler: 'it is impossible to think that which is not or to think any other things than those which one feels; and these are always true'. Levett's translation 'to judge' seems to be better than 'to think' as suggested by F. N. Fowler.

208 Plato, *Gorgias*, 491e–492a, trans. Zeyl.

certain aims should be desired and others not. People are fundamentally unequal if only that which is observable is taken into account. Nature itself shows that only a very few are able to fulfil their desires. The actual ability to act and to subdue others discloses the law of nature—'nature itself reveals that it's a just thing for the better man and the more capable man to have a greater share than the worse man and the less capable man'.[209] There is the justice of nature which shows 'that the superior rule the inferior and have a greater share than they'.[210] Human laws—established by the majority of those who are weak and unable to secure for themselves the fulfilment of their desires—are against the laws of nature. The many who are weak become detractors of the few who are strong

> because of the shame they feel, while they conceal their own impotence. Further, they say that a lack of discipline is shameful (...) and so they enslave men who are better by nature and while they themselves lack the ability to provide for themselves fulfillment for their pleasures, their own lack of courage leads them to praise self-control and justice.[211]

The weak use education and the law to control those who are better by nature. Plato's Callicles, without any hesitation, and with powerful words, presents views which are not only of interest to scholars but which were openly promulgated in connection with the ideology promoted by the Nazi regime in the 20th century, claiming that some people are by nature superior to others and by nature should rule over those who are by nature worse:

> We mould the best and the most powerful among us, taking them while they're still young, like lion cubs, and with charms and incantations we subdue them into slavery, telling them that one is supposed to get no more than his fair share, and that that's what's admirable and just. But surely, if a man whose nature is equal to it arises, he will shake off, tear apart, and escape all this, he will trample underfoot our documents, our tricks and charms, and all our laws that violate nature. He, the slave, will rise up and be revealed as our master, and here the justice of nature will shine forth.[212]

---

209 Plato, *Gorgias*, 483d, trans. Zeyl.

210 Plato, *Gorgias*, 483d, trans. Zeyl.

211 Plato, *Gorgias*, 492a–b, trans. Zeyl. Callicles continues: 'As for all those who were either sons of kings to begin with or else naturally competent to secure some position of rule for themselves as tyrants or potentates, what in truth could be more shameful and worse than self-control and justice for these people who, although they are free to enjoy good things without any interference, should bring as master upon themselves the law of the many, their talk, and their criticism?', ibid., 492b–c, trans. Zeyl.

212 Plato, *Gorgias*, 483e–484b, trans. Zeyl.

Plato perfectly realises that such doctrines have an impact that goes beyond relations between individuals; his Callicles claims: 'Nature shows that this is so in many places; both among the other animals and in whole cities and races of men'.[213]

Callicles sums up his powerful exposition by referring directly to Socrates:

> the truth of it, Socrates—the thing you claim to pursue—is like this: wantonness, lack of discipline, and freedom, if available in good supply, are excellence and happiness; as for these other things, these fancy phrases, these contracts of men that go against nature, they're worthless nonsense![214]

The speech delivered by Plato's Callicles in the *Gorgias* is a kind of manifesto describing the point of reference of Plato's critics. Plato's response to the Sophists' view is complex and comprises all of the principal elements articulated above, situated in different philosophical disciplines. He realises that a proper response must rebuild the Sophists' doctrine at all levels of philosophical thinking. Therefore, on the level of epistemology, not the senses, but reason is the foundation of knowledge. On the level of ontology—real being, the real world, which is of the highest importance in terms of the question of how to live, is that which is an object of reason and of knowledge acquired by reason alone. The human soul belongs to this real world. To questions of what to do, what are the aims proper for man, it is reason—not 'what one feels'—that provides the answers. Appetites and desires are merely means, while bravery and prudence are the aims that should be pursued. Education and human laws, as far as they are shaped by reason, are essential in becoming just and acting justly. All human souls share the same fundamental excellence—being created directly by the Demiurge. On the basic level of human relations, this excellence 'requires' one to pay equal attention to the continuing existence of every human being, and this can be realised by caring for their well-being. Moreover, Plato's project aims at a society of individuals who are equal in a more general sense, because one of the primary aims of law is 'to allow the citizens to live (...) in the greatest possible mutual friendship'[215] and true friendship presupposes equality.

The guidelines for an understanding of man are laid down in the description of a creature that Plato's Socrates contrasts with the Typhon—'a tamer, simpler animal with a share in a divine and gentle nature'.[216] The creature is not savage and furious, but tamed and 'cultivated' (ἡμερώτερον), not complicated and confusing, but simple and comprehensible (ἁπλούστερον), possessing something divine and modest, without arrogance or pride.[217]

---

213 Plato, *Gorgias*, 483d, trans. Zeyl.

214 Plato, *Gorgias*, 492c, trans. Zeyl.

215 Plato, *Laws*, 743c, trans. Saunders.

216 'ἡμερώτερόν τε καὶ ἁπλούστερον ζῷον, θείας τινὸς καὶ ἀτύφου μοίρας φύσει μετέχον', Plato, *Phaedrus*, 230a, trans. Nehamas, Woodruff.

217 Greek 'ἄτυφος' has the same root (but with the negating *a*-) as 'Τυφῶν'; in the Stoic philosophy 'ἄτυφος' (free of arrogance, not puffed up) becomes one of the

3.6.1.2 *Is the soul simple or complex?*

To answer the question of what it means to be good, the question must be resolved of whether the soul, as a 'centre' of being and acting, is simple and consists of only one element, or if it is composed of parts which nonetheless form a special unity. If there is only one element in the soul, then the answer will also be simple–to be good means to develop potentialities innate to this element, to acquire perfection which is proper for it. If, however, the soul is composed of several elements, the answer cannot be simple–to be good presupposes at least that every part of the soul has its own specific perfection.

Plato's Socrates as presented in the early dialogues claims that a human soul as the constitutive element of being human, the principle of human life, is simple. There is only one element–the one responsible for being rational. If the soul were simple in the ontological sense as not being composed of any other elements, there would be no problem in justifying its immortality; what is simple in this sense cannot disintegrate. Plato does not seem to accept this kind of simplicity of the soul. In the *Phaedo*, where the tripartite conception of the soul is not referred to, although the problem of immortality of the soul is extensively considered, an argument based on ontological simplicity is hardly to be seen. Moreover, in the speech of the Demiurge in the *Timaeus*, it is clear that Plato does not accept the ontological simplicity of created souls. Even the gods are not simple, because they were created by the Demiurge by binding certain elements together. The problem of the simplicity of the soul can, however, also be considered as a problem of the simplicity of its nature, of its 'content'–its characteristics as the principle of actions which are proper for the soul.

On the level of practical philosophy, while considering question of moral perfection, the simplicity of the soul as simplicity of its nature provides the basis for a quite simple answer to the question of what it means to be good. If only rationality characterises the soul and constitutes the very nature of man, then becoming good consists in perfecting what constitutes the nature of man. Therefore, there is only one virtue–wisdom, which is excellence in relation to that which is rational. All other virtues, including justice, are forms of wisdom. It is very plausible that the real Socrates adhered to this view. Plato's presentation of Socrates' views in the early dialogues coincides with other sources. As Xenophon relates:

> He said that Justice and every other form of Virtue is Wisdom. 'For just actions and all forms of virtuous activity are beautiful and good. He who knows the beautiful and good will never choose anything else, he who is ignorant of them cannot do them, and even if he tries, will fail. Hence the wise do what is beautiful and good, the unwise cannot and fail if they try. Therefore since just actions and all other forms of beautiful

---

fundamental descriptions of a true philosopher; *Cleanthes Stoicus*, 1.127, Liddell, Scott, Jones, *A Greek–English Lexicon*, p. 274.

> and good activity are virtuous actions, it is clear that Justice and every other form of Virtue is Wisdom.'[218]

Wisdom is not only a necessary but also a sufficient condition for good conduct. A man who is wise never does anything wrong. Xenophon writes:

> When asked further whether he thought that those who know what they ought to do and yet do the opposite are at once wise and vicious, he answered: 'No; not so much that, as both unwise and vicious. For I think that all men have a choice between various courses, and choose and follow the one which they think conduces most to their advantage. Therefore I hold that those who follow the wrong course are neither wise nor prudent.'[219]

No wise (prudent) man ever does anything that would be harmful to what is the most important for him; and wrongdoing is harmful to his soul. These Socratic views are also presented by Plato's Socrates in the *Euthydemus*:

> it seems likely that with respect to all the things we called good in the beginning [e.g. being rich, healthy, and handsome, noble birth, power, and honor], the correct account is not that in themselves they are good by nature, but rather as follows: if ignorance controls them, they are greater evils than their opposites, to the extent that they are more capable of complying with a bad master; but if good sense and wisdom are in control, they are greater goods. In themselves, however, neither sort is of any value. (...) Then what is the result of our conversation? Isn't it that, of the other things, no one of them is either good or bad, but of these two, wisdom is good and ignorance bad?[220]

In other dialogues different views on this subject are presented by Plato's Socrates. These views rely on the human experience expressed by Phaedra in Euripides' *Hippolytus*–'we know and understand what is noble but do not bring it to completion'.[221] Plato develops a tripartite theory of the soul[222] which allows for an explanation of this phenomenon. Every human soul is composed of three parts: rational, spirited and appetitive. An answer to the question of what it means to be good

---

218 Xenophon, *Memorabilia*, III, 9, 5, trans. Marchant.

219 Xenophon, *Memorabilia*, III, 9, 4, trans. Marchant; cf. ibid., IV, 2, 33.

220 Plato, *Euthydemus*, 281d–e, trans. Sprague.

221 Euripides, *Hippolytus*, 380–381, trans. Kovacs; Phaedra explains also the reason for this: 'we know and understand what is noble but do not bring it to completion. Some fail from laziness, others because they give precedence to some other pleasure than being honorable', ibid., pp. 380–382. The best known expression of this universal experience was given a few centuries later by Ovidius' Medea: 'I see a better course and I approve, but follow its defeat', Ovidius, *Metamorphoses*, 7.20–21, trans. More.

222 For a collection of essays see Barney, Brennan and Britain (eds.), *Plato and the Divided Self*.

will therefore be much more complicated than the Socratic one. At first glance, the goodness of something that is composed of parts presupposes the goodness of each part; each part should possess a perfection specific to it. In addition, though, a fourth excellence is needed—the one responsible for the perfection of the whole; and this is justice. As will be seen, Plato does not follow this path very strictly—one part of the soul does not have a perfection of its own. Nevertheless, he accepts that there are four fundamental perfections of the soul and of man—four fundamental virtues, known later as cardinal virtues, which provide 'hinges' for a moral life (the Latin '*cardo*' means 'hinge'[223]): wisdom, courage, temperance and justice.

The main arguments for the recognition of the three parts of the soul are provided by Plato shortly before he concludes what justice truly is,[224] and after constructing his model of the state and explaining the cardinal virtues using the example of the parts of the state. Closing the argumentation, Plato's Socrates suggests that the model of the state was constructed 'by itself', outside of considerations about the soul, as it was developed independently of reflection upon the soul, and was only later applied to issues related to the soul:

> Well, then, we've now made our difficult way through a sea of argument. We are pretty much agreed that the same number and the same kinds of classes as are in the city are also in the soul of each individual.[225]

Nevertheless, taking a closer look at Plato's remarks on virtues in the state, they become fully understandable only from an anthropological, individual perspective—some of these remarks, such as those on courage, go against intuitions related to the state but are very intuitive in relation to an individual. Understanding the *Republic* becomes much more intuitive if the dialogue is read with a realisation that the model of the state is actually built for the purpose of understanding the individual and not the state. The argument for the presence of three elements in the soul is much more precise than that concerning the three parts of the state, which is based mostly on reflection upon what we need in a state—'it's our needs, it seems, that will create it'.[226] Many elements are necessary in the state because there are many different needs. Why are there exactly three basic parts? The recognition of the three parts of the state seems to originate in Plato's analyses of the inner experience of the self, which provide an argument for the presence of three elements in the soul.

Plato develops the tripartite theory of the soul referring to a common inner experience: people responding differently to the same thing at the same time. Taking as an example someone who is thirsty, Plato's Socrates observes that 'the

---

223 Later (not before Augustus) *cardo* means also 'that on which everything else turns or depends, the chief point or circumstance'; Lewis, Short, *A Latin Dictionary*, p. 291.

224 Plato, *Republic*, 437a–441c, trans. Grube.

225 Plato, *Republic*, 441c, trans. Grube.

226 Plato, *Republic*, 369c, trans. Grube.

soul of the thirsty person, insofar as he's thirsty, doesn't wish anything else but to drink, and it wants it and is impelled towards it'.[227] But 'sometimes there are thirsty people who don't wish to drink',[228] for example, if they think it can be harmful to their health; this is a result of rational calculation. Plato argues that 'It can't be (...) that the same thing, with the same part of itself, in relations to the same, at the same time, does opposite things'.[229] He concludes that

> it isn't unreasonable for us to claim that there are two [parts], each different from another. We'll call the part of the soul with which it calculates the rational part and the part with which it lusts, hungers, thirsts, and gets excited by other appetites the irrational appetitive part, companion of certain indulgences and pleasures.[230]

In the soul there is, therefore, a rational part (λογιστικόν) and an appetitive part (ἐπιθυμητικόν).

Plato points out one more kind of inner experience. Sometimes anger is directed against what is desired—'anger sometimes makes war against the appetites, as one thing against another'.[231] Plato's Socrates tells a story which was probably well-known to his audience:

> Leontius, the son of Aglaion, was going up from the Piraeus along the outside of the North Wall when he saw some corpses lying at the executioner's feet. He had an appetite to look at them but at the same time he was disgusted and turned away. For a time he struggled with himself and covered his face, but, finally, overpowered by the appetite, he pushed his eyes wide open and rushed towards the corpses, saying, 'Look for yourselves, you evil wretches, take your fill of the beautiful sight!'[232]

Anger is motivated by rational calculation, and Plato uses military terminology to describe this:

> when appetite forces someone contrary to rational calculation, he reproaches himself and gets angry with that in him that's doing the forcing, so that of the two factions that are fighting a civil war, so to speak, spirit allies itself with reason.[233]

There should be, then, a third element—a spirited part of the soul (θυμοειδές), different from the rational and appetitive parts. The inner experience proves also that the spirit never allies itself with appetite, but always with intellect, preventing one from doing 'what reason has decided must not be done'.[234] The spirit is a helper of

227 Plato, *Republic*, 439a–b, trans. Grube.
228 Plato, *Republic*, 439c, trans. Grube.
229 Plato, *Republic*, 439b, trans. Grube.
230 Plato, *Republic*, 439d, trans. Grube.
231 Plato, *Republic*, 440a, trans. Grube.
232 Plato, *Republic*, 439e–440a, trans. Grube. The story was originally narrated by the comic dramatist Theopompus; Nails, *The People of Plato*, p. 186.
233 Plato, *Republic*, 440a–b, trans. Grube.
234 Plato, *Republic*, 440b, trans. Grube.

the rational part. It is clearly different from the rational part because the strength of the spirit is often different from the strength of the intellect, as can be clearly seen in the case of children, who are full of spirit right from their birth, but in whose case rational calculation comes much later.[235]

Experience also shows that the result of the fight between reason and appetite is not preordained. We sometimes act in accordance with rational calculation and against appetite, sometimes in accordance with appetite and against rational calculation. This depends on the condition of the spirited part, how far reason can rely on the spirit, and on whether this third part is well-trained or spoilt and corrupted. Reason itself does not fight with appetite and does not get angry; this is the work of the spirited part, which may also be called the militant or angering part. The spirit, which is a helper of reason, is like a dog serving a shepherd.[236] As the perfection of reason, wisdom does not suffice to be good and to act rightly. We also need other virtues that cannot be equated with wisdom.

The Platonic state, which is a model of the soul, is composed of three classes (γένη)—the class of guardians (φυλακικόν), of auxiliaries (ἐπικουρικόν) and of money-makers (χρηματιστικόν).[237] These classes represent the three parts of the soul—rational, spiritual and appetitive. As is typical for Plato, who focuses on notions and not words themselves, he refers to the classes using a number of different terms. For example, he talks about the counsellors and guardians (βουλευτικοὶ καὶ φυλακοί), warriors (πολεμικοί) and craftsmen (δημιουργοί);[238] the rulers (ἄρχοντες), soldiers (στρατιῶται) and the ruled (ἀρχόμενοι);[239] and he does not stick to the same sets of descriptions, for instance, one can find reference to the deliberative class (τὸ βουλευτικὸν γένος), the auxiliary (τὸ ἐπικουρητικὸν γένος), and the money-makers (τὸ χρηματιστικὸν γένος).[240]

3.6.1.3 How to find justice in the state

Looking for an answer to the question of what justice in the state is, Plato assumes that there are four basic—cardinal—virtues in the state. This assumption originates in the old Hellenic ethics of the city-state. Aeschylus, before Plato, writes in the *Seven Against Thebes* about four fundamental virtues, but the list is slightly different and includes piety.[241] This issue will be taken up later.

In the *Republic*, Plato takes for granted as an assumption that there are four virtues—justice, wisdom, courage, and moderation. Because the modelled state

---

235 Plato, *Republic*, 441a–b.
236 Plato, *Republic*, 440d.
237 Plato, *Republic*, 434c.
238 Plato, *Republic*, 434a–b.
239 Plato, *Republic*, 433c–d.
240 Plato, *Republic*, 441a.
241 See Jaeger, *Paideia*, vol. 1, p. 106; Jaeger refers to Aeschylus, *Seven Against Thebes*, 610; see Section 3.6.5.4.

is perfect, all four virtues should be present in it. Plato's Socrates first discovers wisdom in the state, as it is the easiest to find. Next come courage and moderation. Justice is the most difficult to see. Plato assumes that justice is equal to that excellence of the state which remains after the other three virtues are found and which can be equated to none of them.[242] This methodology of finding what justice is seems quite poor from a logical point of view. It can be argued that it is not justified: why is it that exactly four virtues are fundamental; why is this particular collection of virtues and not a completely or slightly different set assumed; why is wisdom among these virtues and not, as in earlier city-ethics, godliness; why should exactly four basic perfections be present in the model of the state? The logical obscurity that is quite apparent here speaks in favour of treating the account of the hypothetical state as being subsidiary in character, like the myths recounted by Plato, and not as a philosophical argument. A philosophical character can be assigned, however, to the above-mentioned argument for the partition of the soul into three main elements.

3.6.2 Wisdom

Wisdom can be easily perceived in the model of the state. It is a perfection of the rulers, who are called the complete guardians. Wisdom is

> a kind of knowledge belonging to some of the citizens that counsels not about the affairs connected with particular matters in the city, but about how the city as a whole would best deal with itself and the other cities.[243]

Not the will of the guardians, but their knowledge is the basis for shaping actions. A normative order has objective foundations that are knowledgeable. According to this description of wisdom, it is not limited to the knowledge of general rules. It is practical knowledge—the city is wise because 'it's of good counsel'.[244] It should be pointed out that this is not pure theoretical knowledge based on contemplation of eternal truths for their own sake. Wisdom as knowledge is an instrumental value—it is acquired to attain other goals, to enable the city to 'best deal with itself and the other cities'. Wisdom is clearly distinguished from knowledge about particular things, like the knowledge of carpenters or farmers; it concerns the city as a whole.

---

242 Plato, *Republic*, 427e–428a, 433c.

243 'ἔστι τις ἐπιστήμη ἐν τῇ ἄρτι ὑφ' ἡμῶν οἰκισθείσῃ παρά τισι τῶν πολιτῶν, ᾗ οὐχ ὑπὲρ τῶν ἐν τῇ πόλει τινὸς βουλεύεται, ἀλλ' ὑπὲρ αὑτῆς ὅλης, ὅντινα τρόπον αὐτή τε πρὸς αὑτὴν καὶ πρὸς τὰς ἄλλας πόλεις ἄριστα ὁμιλοῖ', Plato, *Republic*, 428c–d, trans. Bloom. Grube's translation suggests an interpretation that goes too far; he writes that this knowledge is about 'the maintenance of good relations, both internally and with other cities', but the text refers to the city's relations with itself rather than internal relations.

244 Plato, *Republic*, 428b, trans. Bloom; εὔβουλος—prudent, well-advised; Grube translates here: 'because it has good judgment'.

Plato does not explain and does not provide any example of what it means for the city as a whole to 'best deal with itself and the other cities'. At first glance, it seems that this represents knowledge about what is beneficial for the state as a whole—for its existence and power. However, how can one understand that it deals as a whole with itself? How can a state act as a whole towards itself? It is not impossible, but certainly a wide range of presumptions would have to be considered. This problem disappears when we adopt an anthropological interpretation. In this case, the description of wisdom reads as follows:

> Wisdom is a kind of knowledge belonging to a part of the soul that counsels not about the affairs connected with some particular thing in a man (soul), but about how a man as a whole would best deal with himself and other people.

Wisdom is moral knowledge about acting. The action, which is considered from a moral point of view, is always the action of a man as a whole. It is the intellect being able to care for the whole soul[245] and, moreover, for the body, as well.[246]

Moral knowledge which governs actions related to the individual and towards other people is very different from knowledge about particular elements of man, such as knowledge about biology, psychology, or medicine. Like moral knowledge, expertise in medicine is of a practical nature; nevertheless, medicine provides answers about what we should do to be or to become healthy, but not about what we simply should do. Moral knowledge—wisdom—cannot be found in the sciences. It is clear that if one acts in accordance with his moral knowledge, some 'parts' of the individual can be disturbed or even damaged as a consequence. The existence of the whole is what matters. Every part has to be unconditionally subordinated to the benefit of the whole.

When this view is expressed through the metaphor of the state, then on the level of the hypothetical state it has to be recognised that every part (every citizen) of the state should exist for the benefit of the state as a whole and could be sacrificed for it. Is this Plato's view, however, on the organisation of a real state? If the *Republic* is read as a treatise on the soul, then additional arguments would be needed to ascribe totalitarian views to Plato. While reading about wisdom, it has to be remembered that Plato warns explicitly against the direct application of his analyses of justice in the model of the state to the real state, when he speaks about a phantom of justice (see below). An argument of a general nature based on Plato's dignitarian approach in the *Timaeus* has to be kept in mind—it is individuals and not a state or any community who are wished by the Demiurge for themselves, and this dignitarian approach, moreover, is entirely congruent with Plato's univocal

---

245 Plato, *Republic*, 441e.

246 Plato, *Republic*, 442b: 'these two parts also do the finest job of guarding the whole soul and body against external enemies—reason by planning, spirit by fighting, following its leader, and carrying out the leader's decisions through its courage', trans. Grube; see Galewicz, 'Leontios i trupy', p. 53.

statements about the aims of laws, which appear in the *Laws*: 'The whole point of our legislation was to allow the citizens to live supremely happy lives in the greatest possible mutual friendship'.[247]

Reading Plato's exposition on wisdom from this perspective, something comes to the fore which proves crucial to an understanding of his account of freedom—a fundamental issue where totalitarianism is concerned. Plato's Socrates applies his description of wisdom in the state to an individual following explanations about courage, and in this context he states that we call someone wise 'because of that small part of himself that rules in him and makes those declarations and has within it the knowledge of what is advantageous for each part and for the whole soul, which is the community of all three parts'.[248] What are 'those declarations' made by 'that small part of himself'? According to the precedential statement of Plato's Socrates, these are 'the declarations of reason about what is to be feared and what isn't'.[249] According to this statement, the moral knowledge contained in wisdom indicates univocally what should be avoided, and not what should be done. This has important consequences for the very possibility of finding out—cognitively—what precisely an individual should do in a given situation to fulfil himself. If only the boundaries of acting justly can be cognitively specified, it is possible that there is usually more than one good way of acting which can be justly chosen. To determine how to act justly here and now thus requires not only knowledge, but also a decision on the form of action.

To provide a comprehensive picture of Plato's account of wisdom, it is necessary to mention here (and these issues are developed below) that the knowledge that constitutes wisdom is acquired by a given individual. It is not something learnt from someone else. Considering the myth of the cave, it has to be remembered that education does not consist in 'putting' knowledge into one's mind, but in enabling the soul to learn what is important. Plato's Socrates explicitly states that 'education isn't what some people declare it to be, namely, putting knowledge into souls that lack it, like putting sight into blind eyes'.[250] Positively speaking—education is a craft concerned with effectively turning around the intellectual part ('the instrument with which each learns'[251]) and this is possible only by turning around the whole soul.[252]

On the level of the model of the state, Plato's Socrates—in respect to the guardians—mentions that

> Those orders we give them (...) are neither as numerous nor as important as one might think. Indeed, they are all insignificant, provided, as the saying goes, that they guard

247 Plato, *Laws*, 743c, trans. Saunders.
248 Plato, *Republic*, 442c, trans. Grube.
249 Plato, *Republic*, 442c, trans. Grube.
250 Plato, *Republic*, 518b–c, trans. Grube.
251 Plato, *Republic*, 518c, trans. Grube.
252 Plato, *Republic*, 518c–d.

> the one great thing, though I'd rather call it sufficient than great. (...) Their education and upbringing, for if by being well educated they become reasonable men, they will easily see these things for themselves, as well as all the other things we are omitting.[253]

As the guardians represent the intellectual part of the soul, and therefore also the learning power, then the entire content of wisdom is in fact personalised, is acquired autonomously. On this point, it seems to be very difficult (if not impossible) to interpret the texts about wisdom and education as statements about both the individual soul and the state. If wisdom is knowledge which is individually acquired, then it cannot be understood as the content of legislation produced by rulers.

3.6.3 Courage

3.6.3.1 Common understanding of courage

The second virtue which Plato discovers in the model of the state is courage. It is relatively easy to see because—like wisdom—it is a perfection of one given part of the state (this will not be the case with moderation). Nevertheless, there are difficulties in apprehending its essence. Plato wants to convince the reader to adopt an understanding of courage which runs counter to the common intuition of this virtue as a perfection important for the social life of the state. According to its common understanding in Greek culture, courage is, first of all, a virtue possessed by a warrior on the battlefield—a courageous warrior keeps the line in the face of fear of death. Such intuitions about courage can be found in the *Nicomachean Ethics*, where Aristotle describes bravery as 'a mean about feelings of fear and confidence',[254] as something between fear and confidence. As regards the relationship to fear, 'death is the most frightening of all'.[255]

> Nevertheless, not even death in all conditions, e.g. on the sea or in sickness, seems to be the brave person's concern. In what conditions, then, is death his concern? Surely in the finest conditions. And these are deaths in war, since they occur in the greatest and finest danger; and this judgment is endorsed by the honours given in cities and by monarchs.[256]

Of course, on the battlefield, fear is not the only dominant emotion which jeopardises the ability to maintain the line and obedience to orders. The desire for glory or the desire to be first to grab precious loot may also play a significant role. However, it is counterintuitive to claim that it is courage that restrains them.

253 Plato, *Republic*, 423d–e, trans. Grube.
254 Aristotle, *Nicomachean Ethics*, 1115a, trans. Irwin.
255 Aristotle, *Nicomachean Ethics*, 1115a, trans. Irwin.
256 Aristotle, *Nicomachean Ethics*, 1115a, trans. Irwin.

Plato in his approach moves, however, in that direction and credits courage for restraining all kinds of emotions which can endanger that which is rational.

3.6.3.2 *The specificity of Plato's approach*

Plato knows that he has to redirect the thoughts of his reader. This is why his Glaucon states twice that he has difficulties in understanding Socrates' views on courage. This is quite unusual in Plato's dialogues:

> *Socrates*: The city is courageous, then, because of a part of itself that has the power to preserve through everything its belief about what things are to be feared, namely, that they are the things and kinds of things that the lawgiver declared to be such in the course of educating it. Or don't you call that courage?
> *Glaucon*: I don't completely understand what you mean. Please, say it again.
> *Socrates*: I mean that courage is a kind of preservation.
> *Glaucon*: What sort of preservation?
> *Socrates*: That preservation of the belief that has been inculcated by the law through education about what things and sorts of things are to be feared. And by preserving this belief 'through everything', I mean preserving it and not abandoning it because of pains, pleasures, desires, or fears.[257]

By means of Glaucon's interventions and Socrates' repeating the same view twice in slightly different words, Plato draws the reader's attention to the novelty of his proposal, and warns the reader not to follow common intuitions about courage. To be courageous is to be someone who preserves rational convictions despite pain, pleasures, desires, or fears. The emotions that pose a threat to courage are not limited to fear or confidence.[258] Plato refers to all four of the most fundamental feelings (passions): pain—reaction to actual evil; pleasure—reaction to actual good; desire—reaction to expected good; and fear—reaction to expected evil. Plato writes about a common psychological mechanism known as rationalisation, which consists of a modification of rational convictions because of feelings experienced. The problem of courage as formulated by Plato goes beyond the problem of the relationship between λόγος (reason, word, speech) and ἔργον (action, deed), which was clearly

---

257 Plato, *Republic*, 429b–d, trans. Grube; courage is later presented within the framework of the model of the state as 'the preservation among the soldier of the law-inspired belief about what is to be feared and what isn't', ibid., 433c; cf. ibid., 442b–c. Cf. Plato, *Laws*, 630c, where Plato's Athenian recalls Theognis' formula 'loyalty in a crisis'.

258 Similarly, Plato, *Laws*, 633c–d; cf. remarks in the *Laws* that even the best legislators fail to care about exercising courage in the face of pleasures and desires, ibid., 634a–c.

formulated in the fifth-century Athenian culture.[259] In the foreground is not the requirement that actions remain in concord with convictions, but something more fundamental: the preservation of the beliefs that are the reasons for actions.

Plato's account of courage provides a good argument for the thesis that his model of the state is constructed from an anthropological perspective and serves primarily as a tool for understanding the individual. His description of courage becomes clear and intuitive if it is interpreted from an individual point of view. The lawgiver stands for the rational part of the soul which provides moral knowledge—wisdom. The class of auxiliaries who are the bearers of courage symbolises the spiritual part of the soul, which takes part in an inner struggle between the rational and appetitive part of the soul. Courage is therefore understood as *the power to preserve one's beliefs about what things are to be feared, namely, that they are things and kinds of things that the intellect has declared to be such in the course of education.*

This conclusion is clearly accepted by Plato's Socrates when he speaks about a courageous individual: 'we call a single individual courageous, namely, when it preserves through pains and pleasures the declarations of reason about what is to be feared and what isn't'.[260] Similarly to the understanding of wisdom, the account of education in the myth of the cave confirms this interpretation as the overriding one, and calls into question the possibility of applying Plato's teaching about courage to the organisation of a state according to his model. In the very process (course) of education in the proper sense, there is no place for anyone to declare that something is such and such (for example, 'what things are to be feared'). The process of learning is a personal process.

The artificiality of the model of the state in relationship to a real state is clearly visible when the subject of feelings is considered. According to the model, these are the members of the auxiliary class. They have to struggle against passions and desires. In fact, this should be the problem of the money-making class. This picture of the state, in which neither the perfect (complete) guardians nor the craftsmen are considered to be subjects of courage in the sense designated by Plato, presupposes that their maintaining self-control over their feelings is not important. How could this be explained in the framework of the model of the state? And according to the description of courage in the model of the state, this struggle takes place primarily in the souls of members of the auxiliary class. At the same time the members of the militant class are to control the behaviour of the craftsmen (the members of the money-making class). It is presupposed that the craftsmen are not to deal with their own passions, this being the job of the soldiers. This is certainly not what is expected in the perfect real state.

---

259 Balot, *Courage in the Democratic Polis*, p. 129. This common understanding of courage in terms of a relationship between reason and action is referred to by Plato's Socrates in the *Laches*, 193e.

260 Plato, *Republic*, 442b–c, trans. Grube.

At first glance, Plato's approach to courage is consistent with the common one in that fear is an element of the description of courage. On closer examination, however, it is found that fear serves two functions. Plato first uses fear to define what should be avoided, to define duties. This fear is not to be overcome; it plays a positive role. The second function of fear is similar to the function it plays in the common account of courage—it is a feeling that drags us from our duties and one that ought to be overcome (like fear in the face of death on the battlefield). In contrast to the common view, however, for Plato such fear is only one (and not necessarily the first) of four basic passions which should be overcome. Courage consists in this case in overcoming that fear which helps not to fear something else. For example, if stealing is to be feared (according to the wisdom acquired by the perfect guardians or simply by reason), and that means one should not steal, then one is courageous in overcoming the fear of poverty, but also in overcoming the desire to become wealthier, which pulls man away from this obligations. The overcoming of fear ceases to characterise all kinds of courage.

3.6.3.3 'What things are to be feared' and human freedom

In reading what Plato writes about courage it is easy to recognise another element which is far from intuitive in relation to the state. Plato repeats twice, in complex and—taking into account Glaucon's interventions—very carefully elaborated statements, that what is at stake is beliefs about 'what things are to be feared', and not simply beliefs about what should be done. According to this account, Plato's lawgiver, or the laws established by him and addressed to the members of the auxiliary class, deal only with that which is to be feared,[261] and are therefore limited to what should be avoided, usually expressed through prohibitions. Moreover, Plato's account of courage suggests that the lawgiver concentrates on what is to be feared and the borders between what is to be feared and what is not—'we call a single individual courageous, namely, when it preserves through pains and pleasures the declarations of reason about what is to be feared and what isn't'.[262]

In the *Laches* Plato's Socrates pays attention to the knowledge of fearful and hopeful things, where hopeful things are 'those that do not produce fear'.[263] This description of hopeful things ('θαρραλέα'—'that may be ventured on') is counterintuitive because obviously not everything which does not produce fear gives hope. Such a counterintuitive description confirms the interpretation proposed here, which states that practical knowledge about concrete action is limited to knowing what is forbidden, and that this knowledge does not indicate directly what should be done in the here and now.

261 Plato, *Republic*, 429b–d, 430a–b, 433c.
262 Plato, *Republic*, 442b–c, trans. Grube.
263 Plato, *Laches*, 198b, trans. Sprague.

Moreover, the common experience of every state, and also Plato's further description of his state, prove that every law (even one addressed only to the auxiliary class, which is endangered by passions) comprises both prohibitions and orders. Such a significant departure from quite obvious truths about the state and the law is very puzzling. It suggests that what is at stake are matters of the highest importance, but—again—for an understanding of the individual and not the state.

Plato's statements about courage in the *Republic* are a reminder of the well-known passage of the *Apology* in which Plato's Socrates explains his presence before the court:

> I have a divine or spiritual sign (...). This began when I was a child. It is a voice, and whenever it speaks it turns me away from something I am about to do, but it never encourages me to do anything [προτρέπει δὲ οὔποτε].[264]

'A divine or spiritual sign', or rather 'a divine and spiritual voice' ('θεῖόν τι καὶ δαιμόνιον φωνή'), Socrates' daimon can be understood as a voice of conscience which is also a voice of reason, or at least a voice saying something that is in accordance with wisdom. It can be learned from the myth of Er that this voice of practical reason, represented by the daimon for this particular person and his fate, takes into account the specificities of the person's way of life, of the fate chosen.[265] There is no doubt that Plato appoints this voice only to pronounce judgments of a negative nature. It says what is not to be done—what is to be feared. If it remains silent, it provides information that an intended action is not something which is to be feared, and is therefore something which is not forbidden. Plato's Socrates clearly refers to this information. After his conviction, when he explains to the jury the meaning of what has occurred, the silence of his inner voice was for him a sign that what had happened to him (his being sentenced to death) was harmful neither for him nor for anybody else, and therefore that he was acting justly. Socrates points out: 'My divine sign has not opposed me, either when I left home at dawn, or when I came into court, or at any time that I was about to say something during my speech'.[266]

Importantly, the inner voice did not advise him to go to the court. To do so was a decision taken by Socrates and judged by his daimon. It is not to be excluded that in Socrates' situation his inner voice would not have been opposed to a different action than going to the court or—at least—giving a different speech before the court.

So Plato precisely distinguishes knowledge about what is to be feared and what is not, from knowledge about what should be done. Wisdom, or at least that part of it which directly and univocally shapes actions, is limited to the first kind of knowledge. One knows what should not be done, but not what one should do,

264 Plato, *Apology*, 31c–d, trans. Grube.
265 Plato, *Republic*, 617d–e; see Section 3.10.3.2.
266 Plato, *Apology*, 40b–c, trans. Grube.

perhaps with the exception of cases when only one way of acting is permissible and all others are wrong (are to be feared); however, even here knowledge about what should be done is secondary to knowledge about what should be avoided.

Recognising the objective foundations of moral judgment as pertaining to what should be avoided has important consequences for the understanding of human freedom. Usually, one does not choose between what should not be done and what should be done. If one chooses between doing A or B, the basic normal situation of choice is the choice between two permissible ways of acting; neither A nor B is to be feared—the inner voice remains silent.

The fact that wisdom, and especially that part of wisdom which determines what concerns the spirited part, is limited to knowledge of 'what things are to be feared' (and not what should be done here and now), has very far-reaching consequences for the interpretation of Plato's dialogues. Plato's intention is to help us to find knowledge on how the state should not be organised or what one should not do, and—secondarily—what is permissible. There will, however, be no knowledge about the one, sole right way of organising the state or the one, single right way for an individual to act.

There are also significant implications for the question of Plato's alleged totalitarian views. If the *Republic* were to be interpreted as a dialogue about the organisation of a state, then one would have to consider not only that reason is able to determine explicitly only what should not be done and what is permissible, but also that Plato ascribes to the auxiliary the duty of 'executing' this knowledge. If rulers were to choose an option from among those that are not to be feared, that would not be of concern for the auxiliary, and this means that it is not for the state to carry out the decisions of rulers. This is very counterintuitive, and therefore provides another argument that the *Republic* should not be read as a treatise about the organisation of the state. It is also a very strong argument against assigning to Plato the totalitarian view that the state should control every aspect of the life of the ruled. On the contrary, Plato's views resemble here a basic conviction underlying modern human rights protection: that the general conditions of organising a just society are objectively founded, and there is space for a free determination of concrete social orders and for a free determination of individual lifestyles.

Moreover, Plato leaves no doubt that the wisdom which would be necessary to design a happy life for the ruled cannot be acquired by man. To call someone wise is proper only for a god; a man can only be a lover of wisdom—a philosopher.[267] These matters will be referred to later on in the section devoted to Plato's account of freedom (Chapter 5).

267 See Plato, *Phaedrus*, 278d.

3.6.4 Moderation

The third virtue found in the model of the state is moderation (σωφροσύνη). In the *Republic* the short introductory dialogue between Socrates and Glaucon suggests that after considering wisdom and courage it would be possible to look for justice itself, but it is advisable to consider moderation first. Some issues that are essential to the concept of moderation also play a vital role in understanding justice. At the very beginning of his analyses, Plato's Socrates observes that moderation is a kind of consonance and harmony ('συμφωνίᾳ τινὶ καὶ ἁρμονίᾳ');[268] consonance and harmony are crucial for in Plato's concept of justice, as they are fundamental for the unity of the soul and its strength of existence. They are clearly related to order, and therefore—according to a view commonly accepted in Greek culture—to the activity of reason.

To understand Plato's account of moderation, some attention should be given to the translation of the word 'σωφροσύνη'. The first intuitions link it with reason, with sound reason. However, in accordance with long-standing tradition σωφροσύνη is understood as moderation or temperance. Aristotle linked σωφροσύνη with pleasures and pains,[269] which are among the four basic passions clearly related to appetites (desires). This would suggest that it was an excellence of only one part, the appetitive part, of the soul or of the craftsman class in the state, which is evidently not the position of Plato. In Latin, 'σωφροσύνη' is translated as '*prudentia*' ('prudence') or '*temperantia*' ('moderation'). 'Prudence' is understood mainly as 'the ability to govern and discipline oneself by the use of reason'.[270] This meaning is, however, very close to the meaning of 'wisdom' as understood by Plato, and in the context of his philosophy, translating 'σωφροσύνη' as 'prudence' would lead to confusion. The meaning of '*temperantia*', like English 'moderation' or 'temperance', remains strongly connected with mastering passions or desires, with self-control, and its relation to reason and reasonable order is lost. When reading translations of Plato's writings about moderation, the connection between the latter and reason should be kept in mind. The Greek 'σώφρων' originates from 'σῶς' ('safe and sound', also 'alive and well') and φρήν ('mind', also 'heart', as seat of the passions). From this point of view, 'moderate' ('σώφρων') means 'of sound mind'.[271]

According to the *Republic*, moderation is more difficult to see than wisdom or courage, because it is not related to one particular part of the state: 'unlike courage and wisdom, each of which resides in one part, making the city brave and wise respectively, moderation spreads throughout the whole'.[272] It is a mistake, then,

268 Plato, *Republic*, 430e; cf. ibid., 431e.
269 Aristotle, *Nicomachean Ethics*, 1107b.
270 *The Merriam-Webster Dictionary*, /www.merriam-webster.com/dictionary/prudence/.
271 In the Polish translation by Witwicki 'σωφροσύνη' is rendered by '*rozwaga*', which is close to '*roztropność*'—'prudence' and '*rozum*'—'reason'; the verb '*rozważać*' means 'to weigh up different—and possibly opposing—reasons for action'. Cf. Section 4.1, an analysis of the *Gorgias*, 506c–507c.
272 Plato, *Republic*, 431e–432a, trans. Grube.

to treat moderation as a perfection of only the craftsman class or of the appetitive part of the soul. Plato's Socrates starts with the common intuitions which link moderation with self-control. He immediately objects, however, to this understanding of moderation because such control is impossible in one and the same subject (element, part)—the same would at the same time rule and be ruled.[273]

In the model of the state, moderation takes place when 'the desires of the inferior many are controlled by the wisdom and desires of the superior few',[274] 'if indeed the ruler and the ruled in any city share the same belief about who should rule'.[275] Moderation comprises not only the perfect guardians and the money-makers but also the auxiliaries. Plato's Socrates proposes the following description:

> Moderation (...) actually stretches throughout the whole, from top to bottom of the entire scale, making the weaker, the stronger and those in the middle—whether you wish to view them as such in terms of prudence, or, if you wish, in terms of strength, or multitude, money or anything else whatsoever of the sort—sing the same chant together. So we would quite rightly claim that this unanimity is moderation, an accord of worse and better, according to nature, as to which must rule in the city and in each one.[276]

Plato's account of moderation in the state stresses not the pure control of rulers over the ruled but a rational order based on unanimity (ὁμόνοια—oneness of mind, concord) and accord (συμφωνία—harmony, harmonious union). This presupposes that the ruled rationally recognise their inferiority in the state, which requires that they have sound judgment in matters of the state, which is the property of the rulers. This makes the account of the state slightly inconsistent, for if the ruled had sound judgment, considerable humility would also be required from them, which Plato does not mention at all. There is of course another option, namely that the ruled are manipulated, that they do not have any sound judgment about their position in the state, but only share a belief about this.[277] Then, however, would a true unanimity or true agreement be possible? That Plato does not consider these problems is again an argument that in writing the *Republic* he was actually concerned with the understanding of the individual and not the state.

An anthropological interpretation is much more intuitive. In a moderate soul the relations between its parts are well ordered and based on the nature of each of its parts or on the nature of the whole soul as composed of three elements. The expression 'according to nature' ('κατὰ φύσιν') used by Plato's Socrates in his description of moderation can be understood as referring to 'worse' and 'better'—as G. M. A. Grube does, who has 'this agreement between the naturally worse

273 Plato, *Republic*, 430e–431a.
274 Plato, *Republic*, 431c–d, trans. Grube.
275 Plato, *Republic*, 431d–e, trans. Grube.
276 Plato, *Republic*, 432a, trans. Bloom.
277 In the *Republic*, 431d–e; Plato writes about δόξα—belief—and not about knowledge.

and the naturally better'[278]—or as referring to 'agreement'—then moderation is characterised as 'natural agreement'.[279] The latter conforms to a description of a moderate man found in the *Phaedrus*—a man is moderate if his internal elements accord to each other as in 'the natural union of a team of winged horses and their charioteer'.[280]

The question arises of whether moderation—as it 'spreads throughout the whole'[281]—is the perfection of the state and of the soul as a whole. The answer is that it is not. It concerns the relations between the parts. The perfection of the whole as the whole is justice based on a unity which concerns the very existence of an individual and of all he consists of, including his perfections—virtues.

3.6.5 Justice in the model of the state

3.6.5.1 Introduction

After discovering three cardinal virtues in the model of the state, Plato's Socrates looks for the fourth fundamental perfection that is different from the three already disclosed, which should be justice.[282] The analysis of this perfection is preceded with introductory remarks which serve to stress the importance of the problem and the difficulties in comprehending it. Those who are trying to learn what justice is, Socrates compares to hunters—'we must station ourselves like hunters surrounding a wood and focus our understanding, so that justice doesn't escape us and vanish into obscurity, for obviously it's around here somewhere'[283]—and he talks about the need to pray before continuing the quest for justice.[284] He also says that 'the place seems to be impenetrable and full of shadows. It is certainly dark and hard to search through. But all the same, we must go on'.[285]

The dialogue between Socrates and Glaucon[286] directs attention to the problems of talking about justice. Using the metaphor of hunting, it can be said that in this hunt, justice cannot be bagged—it cannot be adequately described, but it can be

278 'This unanimity, this agreement between the naturally worse and the naturally better as to which of the two is to rule both in the city and in each one, is rightly called moderation' ('ὥστε ὀρθότατ' ἂν φαῖμεν ταύτην τὴν ὁμόνοιαν σωφροσύνην εἶναι, χείρονός τε καὶ ἀμείνονος κατὰ φύσιν συμφωνίαν ὁπότερον δεῖ ἄρχειν καὶ ἐν πόλει καὶ ἐν ἑνὶ ἑκάστῳ'), Plato, *Republic*, 432a, trans. Grube. Bloom's translation, which is preferred here, does not forejudge whether 'natural' applies to being 'better' or 'worse' or else 'natural agreement' is meant.
279 This reading is suggested in the Polish translation by Witwicki.
280 Plato, *Phaedrus*, 246a, trans. Nehamas, Woodruff.
281 Plato, *Republic*, 431e–432a, trans. Grube.
282 Plato, *Republic*, 432b, 433c.
283 Plato, *Republic*, 432b, trans. Grube.
284 Plato, *Republic*, 432c.
285 Plato, *Republic*, 432c, trans. Grube.
286 Plato, *Republic*, 432b–d.

'seen'. The quest for justice is bloodless hunting—Socrates encourages Glaucon to follow him: 'look and try eagerly to catch sight of it, and if you happen to see it before I do, you can tell me about it';[287] but Glaucon responds—'you'll make better use of me if you take me to be a follower who can see things when you point them out to him'.[288] This is a warning not to take literally what will shortly be said about justice in the state. What will be said only points out justice, which a follower of Plato's Socrates must perceive on his own.

3.6.5.2 What justice in the state is

In looking for justice, Plato's Socrates searches for a principle that underlies the construction of the whole model of the state. This principle is 'that everyone must practice one of the occupations in the city for which he is naturally best suited'.[289] Here is the broader context:

> *Socrates*: Then listen and see whether there's anything in what I say. Justice, I think, is exactly what we said must be established throughout the city when we were founding it—either that or some form of it. We stated, and often repeated, if you remember, that everyone must practice one of the occupations in the city for which he is naturally best suited.
>
> *Glaucon*: Yes, we did keep saying that.
>
> *Socrates*: Moreover, we've heard many people say and have often said ourselves that justice is doing one's own work and not meddling with what isn't one's own [τὸ τὰ αὑτοῦ πράττειν καὶ μὴ πολυπραγμονεῖν δικαιοσύνη ἐστί].
>
> *Glaucon*: Yes, we have.
>
> *Socrates*: Then, it turns out that this *doing one's own work* [τὸ τὰ αὑτοῦ πράττειν]—provided that it comes to be in a certain way—is justice.[290]

To sum up, justice in the model of the state consists in 'doing one's own work'[291]. Plato's Socrates also remarks that justice is 'having and doing of one's own'[292], and the sole aim in the delivery of judgment by the perfect guardians is 'that no citizen should have what belongs to another or be deprived of what is his own'.[293]

Plato's Socrates characterises justice also by means of an opposition to injustice. He notices that the most dangerous for the state would be the exchange of

---

287 Plato, *Republic*, 432c, trans. Grube.
288 Plato, *Republic*, 432c, trans. Grube.
289 Plato, *Republic*, 433a, trans. Grube.
290 Plato, *Republic*, 433a–b, trans. Grube, emphasis added.
291 Plato, *Republic*, 433a, trans. Grube; see Plato, *Republic*, 433b, 433d; see Plato, *Charmides*, 161b.
292 'τε καὶ ἑαυτοῦ ἕξις τε καὶ πρᾶξις', Plato, *Republic*, 433e–434a, trans. Grube.
293 'ὅπως ἂν ἕκαστοι μήτ' ἔχωσι τἀλλότρια μήτε τῶν αὑτῶν στέρωνται', Plato, *Republic*, 433e, trans. Grube.

roles between classes: 'meddling and exchange between these three classes, then, is the greatest harm that can happen to the city and would rightly be called the worst thing someone could do to it'.[294] This is injustice. Finally, justice in the state is characterised as something contrary to injustice: 'for the money-making, auxiliary, and guardian classes each to do its own work in the city, is the opposite. That's justice, isn't it, and makes the city just?'[295] Glaucon answers: 'I agree. Justice is that and nothing else'.[296] This is the final statement of the considerations aimed at establishing what is justice in the model of the hypothetical state.

The answer seems to be quite unattractive and trivial—the mountain gave birth to a mouse. The introductory remarks about difficulties and the need for prayer now seem to have been out of proportion. These observations are quite obvious to a careful reader, and Plato is certainly aware of this; he therefore allows his Socrates to prepare the audience for a disappointment. Before announcing the 'revelations', he relieves the tension built up around the problem of what justice in the state is, downplaying the difficulties:

> what we are looking for seems to have been rolling around at our feet from the very beginning, and we didn't see it, which was ridiculous of us. Just as people sometimes search for the very thing they are holding in their hands, so we didn't look in the right direction but gazed off into the distance, and that's probably why we didn't notice it.[297]

At this stage of the considerations, there is actually no novelty in the understanding of justice. Plato's Socrates merely restores the original meaning of 'justice'—well-known from Homer. Was it necessary to go to such lengths? What is new in comparison with the results established by the consideration of the three virtues seems very trivial—to exercise a certain perfection requires the proper action of the subject of that perfection and of all its parts. This is of course true, and it is also a very basic truth, but in no way specific to considerations about the state or the soul. Why should it be called 'justice'? The distribution of tasks is already accomplished by exercising wisdom and moderation, and courage takes care of the proper execution of obligations. Moreover, the excellence of 'doing one's own work' is a very basic perfection, which provides no adequate reasons for being praised as an especially admirable virtue specific to the state or the soul. It is difficult at this point to pass judgment upon the special perfection of justice as virtue, since the criteria have not been disclosed. All of the first three virtues seem to be more complex. Moderation is a much better candidate for a virtue of particular excellence, as it is based on harmony; wisdom seems to be more excellent, as it links the human soul with the 'higher world'; courage, in turn, introduces wisdom into practice.

---

294 Plato, *Republic*, 435b–c, trans. Grube.
295 Plato, *Republic*, 435c, trans. Grube.
296 Plato, *Republic*, 435d, trans. Grube.
297 Plato, *Republic*, 432d–e, trans. Grube.

3.6.5.3 Weakness of the evidence

The evidence used by Plato's Socrates for his characterisation of justice in the state is strikingly weak. First of all, he points out that justice as the perfection of the state 'is what was left over when moderation, courage, and wisdom have been found'.[298] This argument has a presupposition that is far from being obvious or proven. A necessary condition for the soundness of this argument is that in the state there are exactly four virtues—exactly those listed. Then, after discovering three of them, one could argue that the one which is left is justice. Plato's Socrates, however, neither provides any reason that there are exactly four virtues in the state and exactly those listed, nor does he indicate that this was ever demonstrated. For contemporaries of Plato, it was well-known that in talking about the four basic virtues, he was referring to the old Hellenic ethics of the state. As mentioned earlier, in the *Seven against Thebes* by Aeschylus, we read about 'a moderate, just, noble, reverent man'.[299] In Greek we have 'σώφρων δίκαιος ἀγαθὸς εὐσεβὴς ἀνήρ'.[300] Greek 'ἀγαθὸς' means, first of all, 'good', but in the Greek culture of those times to be a good man was actually the same as to be a good male (ἀνήρ, gen. ἀνδρός), whose first obligation towards his community was to defend it, and therefore his first virtue was courage (ἀνδρεία). There are, therefore, the virtues of moderation, justice, courage and piety. The place of Plato's wisdom was occupied by piety. Plato, of course, is fully aware of this tradition. For example, in the *Gorgias*, right in the centre of the considerations about justice (justice accompanied by piety), Plato's Socrates says about a good man that, 'if he did what's appropriate with respect to man, he would be doing what's just, and with respect to the gods he would be doing what's pious'.[301] Moreover, in the *Protagoras*, Plato lists five fundamental virtues: knowledge, justice, courage, temperance, and piety (ἐπιστήμη, δικαιοσύνη, ἀνδρεία, σωφροσύνη, ὁσιότης).[302] In the *Republic* itself, by the end of Book IX only three fundamental virtues are mentioned: moderation, justice, and reason (σωφροσύνη, δικαιοσύνη, φρόνησις).[303]

It is also striking that Plato's Socrates tries to convince his audience by pointing out that the proposed solution that 'justice is doing one's own work and not meddling with what isn't one's own'[304] is something that 'we've heard many people say and have often said ourselves'.[305] Talking about what many people say suggests that something is broadly recognised, and Homer comes naturally to the fore. Referring to what people are wont to say may be persuasive, but it is a very

---

298 Plato, *Republic*, 433b–c, trans. Grube.
299 Aeschylus, *Seven Against Thebes*, 610, trans. Smyth.
300 Aeschylus, *Seven Against Thebes*, 610, trans. Smyth.
301 Plato, *Gorgias*, 507b, trans. Zeyl. See Vlastos, 'Socratic Piety', *passim*.
302 Plato, *Protagoras*, 330b, trans. Lomardo, Bell.
303 Plato, *Republic*, 591b, trans. Grube.
304 Plato, *Republic*, 433a–b, trans. Grube.
305 Plato, *Republic*, 433a, trans. Grube.

weak argument, especially for Plato, for whom Homer—being a poet—is hardly an authority in philosophical matters.[306] Nevertheless, common opinion is for Plato usually a preliminary for serious considerations. The narrative which accompanies his final statements about justice in the state suggests, therefore, that it is only a starting point, a point of reference for a philosophical quest.

3.6.5.4 Beyond triviality

How can we move beyond the triviality and—let it be said—logical obscurity of this argument? First, it should be recalled that when Plato's Socrates takes us on a bloodless hunting expedition, giving answers about what justice is, he is not 'bagging his prey' but only pointing to something that his follower should spot for himself. It could be said that, with regard to 'doing one's own work', one should look at the modelled state as an existing whole, and then try to discern the excellence of it as a whole, and not only the excellence of its parts or the excellence of the relations between them.

Second, knowing this, it is possible to focus on something that is said—seemingly as an incidental remark—when justice in the state is characterised as 'doing one's own work'. Plato's Socrates notices that from the perspective of moderation, courage and wisdom, this doing one's own work 'provided the power by which all these others came into being; and, once having come into being, it provides them with preservation as long as it's in the city'.[307] This view Plato repeats in a slightly different manner, stating that justice is 'the power that consists in everyone's doing his own work'.[308] What is at stake is actually the power (δύναμις). Further, this is power of a very special kind, since it gives and sustains one's very being, and such a power can be taken as a manifestation of something divine, especially when we consider the myth of the cave in the *Republic* and the characteristics of the Good symbolised by the sun. What justice does in the soul is analogous to the work of the Good in the universe.

Third, an important hint can be found in the above-quoted passage from the *Republic*, which concerns the principle of the construction of the hypothetical state:

306 E.g. Plato, *Republic*, 600e.

307 'τὸ ὑπόλοιπον ἐν τῇ πόλει ὧν ἐσκέμμεθα, σωφροσύνης καὶ ἀνδρείας καὶ φρονήσεως, τοῦτο εἶναι, ὃ πᾶσιν ἐκείνοις τὴν δύναμιν παρέσχεν ὥστε ἐγγενέσθαι, καὶ ἐγγενομένοις γε σωτηρίαν παρέχειν, ἕωσπερ ἂν ἐνῇ', Plato, *Republic*, 433b–c, trans. Bloom; the Bloom translation is more accurate here. Grube translates: 'the power that makes it possible for them to grow in the city and that preserves them when they've grown for as long as it remains there itself'. He translates 'ἐγγίγνομαι' as 'make possible', which seems to be correct but too weak, especially if it concerns δύναμις.

308 'ἡ τοῦ ἕκαστον ἐν αὐτῇ τὰ αὑτοῦ πράττειν δύναμις', Plato, *Republic*, 433d, trans. Grube.

> This was meant to make clear that each of the other citizens is to be directed to what he is naturally suited for, so that, doing the one work that is his own, he will become not many but one, and the whole city will itself be naturally one not many.[309]

A reason is given why everyone should do his own work—'he will become one and also the whole city will itself be naturally one'. This reason can be held to be that at which Plato's Socrates is pointing during the bloodless hunt. Taking into account Plato's ontology and his views on the Good and the One (and also on the good and the one as an inner unity in general) as a foundation of being, one can see what is actually of highest importance in justice. An inner unity is the basis of existence, it is the power (δύναμις) that gives and sustains the very being of the virtues and of their subject. It comprises a soul (a man) as a whole. This kind of perfection of a being is qualitatively higher than any perfection of the elements or of relations between the elements of that being. The foundation of existence is a necessary condition for the reality of any perfection.

3.6.5.5 Happiness of the state or happiness of the individual?

In the model of the hypothetical state, the well-being of the state is given clear priority over the interests (happiness) of an individual or—rather, importantly—of the classes of the state and of individuals only as their members:

> we should consider whether in setting up our guardians we are aiming to give them the greatest happiness, or whether—since our aim is to see that the city as a whole has the greatest happiness—we must compel and persuade the auxiliaries and guardians to follow our other policy and be the best possible craftsmen at their own work, and the same with all the others. In this way, with the whole city developing and being governed well, we must leave it to nature to provide each group with its share of happiness.[310]

Consequently, the well-being and happiness of the state as a whole is recognised—in this model—as an aim of laws:

> that it's not the concern of law that any one class in the city fare exceptionally well, but it contrives to bring this about in the city as a whole, harmonizing the citizens by persuasion and compulsion, making them share with one another the benefit that each is able to bring to the commonwealth. And it produces such men [the people who are able to see the good] in the city not in order to let them turn whichever way each wants, but in order that it may use them in binding the city together.[311]

---

309 Plato, *Republic*, 423d, trans. Grube.

310 Plato, *Republic*, 421b–c, trans. Grube.

311 Plato, *Republic*, 519e–520a, trans. Bloom. This translation points out that well-being ('εὖ πράξει'; some translations e.g. Grube, have 'happiness') should be contrived 'in the city as a whole'.

It is important to remember that this is a model that serves to understand the goodness (justice) of an individual soul. It is in fact a model of the real soul and not a model of a real state. Therefore, conclusions should first be drawn concerning the individual, and only then about the state, and only in as much as they do not contradict the conclusions pertaining to the individual.

If the view that everything in the soul—the well-being of every part—serves to benefit the whole soul is to be expressed on the level of the state as a model of the soul, then the simplest way is to recognise the subordination of every class of the state to the benefit of the whole. Every part also has to perform its function—it has to do its own work. The subordination of each class of the state to the benefit of the whole is a statement which is accepted as a metaphorical expression of Plato's answer to the central question he is considering: what does it mean to be good and what are the conditions of being good? Of course, if the goodness of the soul as a whole (justice) is at stake, then the perfection of its parts is a condition for the goodness of the whole only as long as they contribute to the perfection of the whole.

Let us quote the *Laws* again: 'The whole point of our legislation was to allow the citizens to live supremely happy lives in the greatest possible mutual friendship'.[312] Plato does not change his mind. He takes the same direction in the *Gorgias*, the *Phaedrus* and the *Theaetetus*; moreover, a careful reading of the *Republic* itself leaves no doubt that the theses about the complete subordination of the citizen to the state and about sticking to one occupation proper to a particular class are accepted by Plato only in the framework of the hypothetical state constructed to understand justice in an individual soul. An indication that only the model is meant here is also given in both of the last quotations. Plato does not talk about the happiness of citizens in contrast to the happiness of the state, but about the happiness of groups (ἔθνος) or the well-being of a class (γένος), which clearly symbolises a part of the soul.

3.7 What in truth is justice?

3.7.1 Description of justice

Plato's Socrates applies his analysis of the model of the state to the problem of the justice of the individual—the justice of the soul. He poses a seemingly rhetorical question: 'Well, then, is the justice in us at all indistinct? Does it seem to be something different from what we found in the city?'[313] Pointing to obvious cases of injustice, such as temple robberies, thefts, betrayals of friends, not keeping an oath or other agreement, adultery, disrespect for one's parents, and neglecting the gods,

312 Plato, *Laws*, 743c, trans. Saunders.

313 Plato, *Republic*, 442d, trans. Grube.

Plato's Socrates draws the conclusion that a just man, who is in opposition to one who commits injustice, is one who is internally ordered like a just state, which was described earlier: 'every part within him does its own work, whether it's ruling or being ruled'.[314] Justice is nothing less 'than this power, the one that produces men and cities of the sort we've described'.[315]

Plato does not stop at these conclusions. The most important things remain to be said. As was mentioned before, the view that the core of justice is acting in accordance with what is proper for one's social status or social role is an old Hellenic idea, present in Homer and in the basic intuitions the Greek language connects with justice. In saying that 'doing one's own work' is the core of justice, Plato rejects the meaning of the word 'justice' that was current in his own day, which linked justice with the fulfilment of duties formulated in laws, and goes back to its original meaning.[316] However, it needs to be stressed here that Plato does not finish his enquiry at this point, as many interpreters claim or suggest.[317] It is true that Plato points out the importance of the results already achieved when talking about the fulfilment of a dream and about divine aid:

> Then that dream of ours has reached its perfect fulfilment. I mean our saying that we suspected that straight from the beginning of the city's founding, through some god, we probably hit upon an origin and model for justice.[318]

Yet this is actually only the beginning—the scene being set. His first step in the direction of something that is difficult to comprehend has already been taken—justice does not rest simply in acting in a certain way, but is the power that produces men and cities that act justly.

Before exploring further what justice really is, Plato explicitly and clearly distances himself (or—rather—distances the truth about justice) from the view that doing one's own work is justice itself. In the previous quotation, Plato's Socrates is already talking about hitting upon 'an origin and model for justice'. In the original text, the terms 'ἀρχή' and 'τύπος' are used. The first of these, read in the context of the second, should not be understood as a technical philosophical term describing the essence of something; the translations 'origin' or 'beginning'—as used by Grube—are adequate. The term 'τύπος' signals that only a model of justice has been found, only an impression, like the impression from a seal or carved

314 Plato, *Republic*, 443b, trans. Grube.
315 Plato, *Republic*, 443b, trans. Grube.
316 Guthrie, *The Greek Philosophers*, p. 7.
317 For the most prominent and most influential, see Popper, *The Open Society and Its Enemies*, vol. 1: *The Spell of Plato*; see Guthrie, *The Greek Philosophers*, p. 7.
318 Plato, *Republic*, 443b–c, trans. Bloom. Bloom's translation of 'εἴδωλον' as 'phantom' is more adequate to the proposed interpretation; on the meanings of 'εἴδωλον' see the next paragraph.

figure, or an outline of it. The distance from the already discovered principle of justice is widened in the next statement made by Plato's Socrates:

> And this, Glaucon, turns out to be after all a kind of phantom [εἴδωλον] of justice—that's also why it's helpful—the fact that the shoemaker by nature rightly practices shoemaking and does nothing else, and the carpenter practices carpentry, and so on for the rest.[319]

The performance by each individual of only one single action is merely a phantom (εἴδωλον) of justice. The word 'εἴδωλον' requires special attention, and its meaning will be a subject of attention in the paragraphs that follow. It clearly serves here to signal a distance to the truth about justice and what is expressed by the words of Plato's Socrates, who continues:

> But in truth justice was [τὸ δέ γε ἀληθές], as it seems, something of this sort; however, not with respect to a man's minding his external business, but with respect to what is within, with respect to what truly concerns him and his own. He doesn't let each part in him mind other people's business or the three classes in the soul meddle with each other, but really sets his own house in good order and rules himself; he arranges himself, becomes his own friend, and harmonizes the three parts, exactly like three notes in a harmonic scale, lowest, highest and middle. And if there are some other parts in between, he binds them together and becomes entirely one from many, moderate and harmonized. Then, and only then, he acts, if he does act in some way—either concerning the acquisition of money, or the care of the body, or something political, or concerning private contracts.[320]

It should be emphasised that the cited passage begins with 'but in truth' ('τὸ δέ γε ἀληθές'). Moreover, Glaucon, Socrates' partner in the dialogue, responds to his exposition by saying: 'Socrates, (...) what you say is entirely true' ('παντάπασιν, ἦ δ' ὅς, ὦ Σώκρατες, ἀληθῆ λέγεις').[321] This is a frame used by Plato to stress the most important part of the recapitulation of his examination of justice based on the analysis of the model of the hypothetical state constructed by him in the *Republic*.

The following paragraphs deal first with the meaning of 'εἴδωλον', rendered here as 'phantom'. This analysis is crucial to a proper understanding of the methodological status of the justice discovered in Plato's hypothetical state and for interpreting the principle of 'doing one's own work'. It is also crucial because it makes clear why some common interpretations of Plato's teaching on justice are in error. Next, the core of Plato's understanding of justice in the soul is elaborated upon, and this leads to the principle of unity and to the metaphor of the health of the soul. Finally, the versatility of just men and the unity of virtues are discussed. Since in the passage under discussion a clear distinction is drawn between justice

319 Plato, *Republic*, 443c, trans. Bloom.
320 Plato, *Republic*, 443c–e, trans. Bloom.
321 Plato, *Republic*, 444a, trans. Bloom.

of the soul (man) and justice of actions, the latter of these will be carefully analysed as the next, essential step in elaborating Plato's understanding of justice.

3.7.2 Justice in the model of the state as εἴδωλον—a phantom of justice

Considered from the perspective of attaining knowledge about justice, Plato's describing something as 'εἴδωλον', a phantom of justice, carries a certain duality. On the one hand, εἴδωλον can be useful and helpful; on the other, it is something misleading and confusing, distracting one from the truth.[322] Most translations of the passage under analysis (443c) point to the positive aspect of εἴδωλα, but the negative side should also be borne in mind;[323] indeed, it should be recognised in this context as paramount.

The positive function played by εἴδωλα in the acquisition of knowledge is mentioned by Plato in the *Seventh Letter*:

---

322 It is worth noting that Francis Bacon understood εἴδωλα—in Latin '*idola*', in English 'idols'—in a purely negative way, as being only a constraint on the developing sciences; see Bacon, *Novum organum*, chapters 38–62 (pp. 19–35); in chapter 38 (p. 19) Bacon writes: 'The idols and false notions which have already preoccupied the human understanding, and are deeply rooted in it, not only so beset men's minds that they become difficult of access, but even when access is obtained will again meet and trouble us in the instauration of the sciences, unless mankind when forewarned guard themselves with all possible care against them'.

323 Clearly visible in the Polish translation by Witwicki: 'A to było, Glaukonie, pewne widziadło sprawiedliwości, ale bardzo się nam przydało' (*Republic*, 443c)—word for word: 'But that was, Glaucon, only a phantasm of justice but it was very helpful'. Witwicki suggests here an opposition: 'although it was a phantasm, nevertheless it was useful'. Grube translates 'εἴδωλόν τι' as 'a sort of image' but this translation loses the dual character of the original expression and may suggest that an image in the proper sense (εἴκων) is meant. In the Parmenides (132c) there is a warning not to mix εἴδωλα with images (εἴκονες). The dual character is also not present in Shorey's translation 'a sort of adumbration', and he comments in a footnote that 'The contemplation of the εἴδωλον, image or symbol, leads us to the reality. The reality is always the Platonic Idea. (...) In the case of spiritual things and moral ideas, there is no visible image or symbol (Politicus [*Statesman*], 286a), but imperfect analogies, popular definitions, suggestive phrases, as τὰ ἑαυτοῦ πράττειν, well-meant laws and institutions serve as the εἴδωλα in which the philosophic dialectician may find a reflection of the true idea'. But Shorey's comment clearly does not fit the usage of 'εἴδωλόν' in the analysed passage; first, the expression 'But in truth justice was', which follows the description of εἴδωλόν (of justice), does not refer to the Platonic idea, but to an individual existing in the here and now; second, the state in which there is a strict division of labour cannot be taken as a 'well-meant' (just) institution because of the versatility of the just man (who possesses all cardinal virtues; see Section 3.7.6) which is included in the understanding of what justice in truth is.

> For every real being, there are three things that are necessary if knowledge of it is to be acquired: first, the name; second, the definition; third, the image; knowledge comes fourth [ἓν μὲν ὄνομα, δεύτερον δὲ λόγος, τὸ δὲ τρίτον εἴδωλον, τέταρτον δὲ ἐπιστήμη], and in the fifth place we must put the object itself, the knowable and truly real being.[324]

Each of the four instruments—name, definition, image, and knowledge—needed to grasp the 'truly real being' is by nature defective.[325] Later on, when the three elements necessary for acquiring knowledge are considered, instead of the word 'εἴδωλον', Plato uses 'ὄψις' in connection with 'αἰσθήσις'—'visions and sense-perception':

> it is by means of the examination of each of these objects, comparing one with another—names and definitions, visions and sense-perceptions [ὀνόματα καὶ λόγοι ὄψεις τε καὶ αἰσθήσεις], proving them by kindly proofs and employing questionings and answerings that are void of envy—it is by such means, and hardly so, that there bursts out the light of intelligence and reason regarding each object in the mind of him who uses every effort of which mankind is capable.[326]

It can be assumed that 'visions and sense-perceptions' is here an equivalent of 'image'—'εἴδωλον'. Therefore, the justice in the model of the state, described in the *Republic* as 'εἴδωλον'—'image, phantom', is the third of the elements, next to the name and definition, which serves in the acquisition of the knowledge about justice expressed after the phrase 'But in truth' (443c–e).

In the myth of the cave, εἴδωλα are the reflections of men and other objects in the water which are seen by someone who has been liberated from the cave. Beholding the reflections in the water is a step towards seeing the sun, which follows from watching the shadows in the world outside the cave, but is prior to watching the night sky with its stars and the moon.[327] Although it is placed in the real world—in the world of forms (ideas), of 'intellectual' entities—εἴδωλον is something remote from that which is real. The model of the hypothetical state can

---

324 Plato, *Letter VII*, 342a, trans. Morrow. *Letter VII* is treated here as having been written by Plato himself; its authenticity has recently been challenged in Burnyeat, Frede, *The Pseudo-Platonic Seventh Letter*, although their argumentation has been questioned by Kahn, 'Review'.

325 Plato, *Letter VII*, 343d.

326 Plato, *Letter VII*, 344b, trans. Bury; in Morrow's translation 'ὀνόματα καὶ λόγοι ὄψεις τε καὶ αἰσθήσεις' is rendered—less adequately—as 'names, definitions, and visual and other perceptions'. Plato is referring not to the act of perception but to what is perceived, and in this direction should go the understanding of 'αἰσθήσεις' here; analogous to the rendering of 'αἰσθήσεις θεῶν' by 'visible appearances of the gods'; see Liddell, Scott, Jones, *A Greek–English Lexicon*, p. 42.

327 Plato, *Republic*, 516a; cf. Plato, *Statesman*, 286a, where εἴδωλον is a material (apprehended by sensual experience) image of something.

be regarded as such a kind of intellectual entity. It should be stressed, however, that it is not a 'shadow' of the form (idea) of the state, but it does provide a 'shadow' of justice—that is to say, justice in the model of the hypothetical state is a 'shadow' of what justice in truth is.

Of key importance to the proposed interpretation is what Plato's Critias says in the *Timaeus* about the model of the state developed in the *Republic*: the citizens and the state are portrayed 'in mythical fashion' ('ὡς ἐν μύθῳ').[328] Neither Socrates nor anybody else from the audience objects to this statement.

Also in the *Timaeus*, Plato's Socrates points out limitations in the explanatory power of the story told in the *Republic*:

> I'd like to go on now and tell you what I've come to feel about the political structure we've described. My feelings are like those of a man who gazes upon magnificent looking animals, whether they're animals in a painting or even actually alive but standing still, and who then finds himself longing to look at them in motion or engaged in some struggle or conflict that seems to show off their distinctive physical qualities. I felt the same thing about the city we've described.[329]

In these contexts, εἴδωλα play a positive role, though there are clear limitations in 'reading' them. They certainly cannot be taken directly as normative paradigms of entities which are used to point at a certain reality lying beyond that which is observable. I would venture to claim that the model of the hypothetical state described in the *Republic* must not be treated as a paradigm of a state in the visible realm, just as the chariot described in the *Phaedrus*[330] must not be treated as a paradigm for the construction of chariots. Both the state and the chariot are εἴδωλα which serve to help in understanding the soul and its moral perfection (justice).

When interpreting Plato's account of justice presented in the *Republic* it should also be kept in mind that when the term 'εἴδωλον' is used there is also a warning present: we are dealing with something two-faced. The pejorative meaning of 'εἴδωλον' is used by Plato's Socrates when he describes the abilities of those who return to the cave from the outside world: 'you'll know what each of the phantoms is, and of what it is a phantom, because you have seen the truth about fair [beautiful], just, and good things'.[331]

Similarly, the pejorative meaning is present in his consideration of artistic activities—'Shouldn't we set down all those skilled in making, beginning with Homer, as imitators of phantoms of virtue and of the other subjects of their making? They don't lay hold of the truth'.[332] Plato's Socrates observes that 'The

328 Plato, *Timaeus*, 26c, trans. Zeyl.
329 Plato, *Timaeus*, 19b, trans. Zeyl.
330 E.g. Plato, *Phaedrus*, 246d–248e.
331 Plato, *Republic*, 520c, trans. Bloom.
332 Plato, *Republic*, 600e, trans. Bloom.

maker of the phantom, the imitator, we say, understands nothing of what *is* but rather of what looks like it *is*'.[333]

The purely pejorative sense of 'εἴδωλον' can be found in the *Gorgias*, where the rhetoric developed by the Sophists is described as a phantom (εἴδωλον) of one part of the art of politics: punitive justice.[334] It only imitates punitive justice and is thus actually harmful because its aim is liberation from punishment, the latter being beneficial as it restores health to a sick soul. Rhetoric is a form of flattery that contains no knowledge, but is only 'a knack and a routine'.[335] Similarly, one element of flattery is sophistry, which imitates the art of legislation (beneficial for healthy souls), and—in relation to caring for the body—a second part of flattery is cosmetics (beauty-culture), which imitates the art of gymnastics (beneficial for healthy bodies), and pastry baking (cookery), which imitates medicine (beneficial for sick bodies).[336] Plato is not sparing in his negative descriptions of rhetoric as flattery, calling it an 'εἴδωλον' of one part of politics, as well as 'shameful' ('αἰσχρός') and 'bad' ('κακός'):[337] 'it guesses at what's pleasant with no consideration for what's best',[338] 'it has no account of the nature of whatever things it applies by which it applies them, so that it's unable to state the cause of each thing'.[339]

In the *Theaetetus* εἴδωλον stands in direct opposition to reality and truth. It is very difficult to distinguish one from the other because εἴδωλα pretend to be true. Plato's Socrates compares his art to the art of midwifery, stressing not only the difficulty of his art but also its importance, which rests in the ability to distinguish phantoms—εἴδωλα—from that which is real:

> the work of the midwives is a highly important one; but it is not so important as my own performance. And for this reason, that there is not in midwifery the further complication, that the patients are sometimes delivered of phantoms [εἴδωλα] and sometimes of realities [ὅτε ἀληθινά], and that the two are hard to distinguish. If there were, then the midwife's greatest and noblest function would be to distinguish the true from the false offspring (…).

333 Plato, *Republic*, 601b–c, trans. Bloom, emphasis in the text.
334 Plato, *Gorgias*, 463c–d; the translation of Zeyl—'oratory is an image of a part of politics'—does not reflect the pejorative connotation of 'εἴδωλον' in this context. Lamb and Hamilton, Emlyn-Jones render 'εἴδωλον' here as 'a semblance'. The Polish translation by Witwicki leaves no doubt about the negativity in describing rhetoric as 'εἴδωλον': rhetoric is 'cząstki politycznej upiorem'—'a wraith of a part of politics'.
335 Plato, *Gorgias*, 463b, trans. Zeyl.
336 Plato, *Gorgias*, 465b–c.
337 Plato, *Gorgias*, 463d.
338 Plato, *Gorgias*, 465a, trans. Zeyl.
339 Plato, *Gorgias*, 465a, trans. Zeyl.

> And the most important thing about my art [of midwifery] is the ability to apply all possible tests to the offspring, to determine whether the young mind is being delivered of a phantom, that is, an error [εἴδωλον καὶ ψεῦδος], or a fertile truth.[340]

This survey of the different meanings of 'εἴδωλον' and the different functions played by εἴδωλα in pursuing knowledge leads to the conclusion that this notion retains a twofold character. Because justice in the hypothetical state, namely doing one's own work, is an εἴδωλον of justice, it is useful for understanding justice, but on the other hand, it can also be misleading. It would pose a fundamental danger to learn what in truth justice is if justice in the hypothetical state were confused with justice itself. In the *Phaedrus*, Plato's Socrates warns with strong words: 'to be unaware of the difference between a dream-image and the reality of what is just and unjust, good and bad, must truly be grounds for reproach even if the crowd praises it with one voice'.[341]

3.7.3 The *Phaedrus* and the model of the state in the *Republic*

3.7.3.1 Discourse in ink and discourse in the soul

In the *Republic* Plato constructs a model of the state for heuristic and didactic purposes—he uses it to explain to the reader the justice of the soul. The *Republic* is a type of discourse which Plato himself would classify as a discourse written down in ink[342] or—at best—the spoken discourse of a dialectician.[343] In the *Phaedrus* he distinguishes different discourses, and his Socrates warns that

340 See Plato, *Theaetetus*, 150a–c, trans. Levett; cf. ibid., 150e. Cf. Plato, *Sophist*, 234c–e; Plato's Stranger is talking about εἴδωλα λεγόμενα—spoken copies which can be used to trick young people and 'to make them believe that words are true and that the person who's speaking to them is the wisest person there is', ibid., 234c, trans. White. In the *Timaeus*, εἴδωλα are mentioned in quite a different sense, as performing non-cognitive functions. They control the appetitive part of the soul which 'was not going to understand the deliverances of reason and that even if it were in one way or another to have some awareness of them, it would not have an innate regard for any of them, but would be much more enticed by images and phantoms night and day', Plato, *Timaeus*, 71a, trans. Zeyl; cf. Gerson, *Knowing persons*, pp. 241–243.

341 'τὸ γὰρ ἀγνοεῖν ὕπαρ τε καὶ ὄναρ δικαίων καὶ ἀδίκων πέρι καὶ κακῶν καὶ ἀγαθῶν οὐκ ἐκφεύγει τῇ ἀληθείᾳ μὴ οὐκ ἐπονείδιστον εἶναι, οὐδὲ ἂν ὁ πᾶς ὄχλος αὐτὸ ἐπαινέσῃ', Plato, *Phaedrus*, 277d–e, trans. Nehamas, Woodruff; 'ὕπαρ τε καὶ ὄναρ' is rendered as 'a dream-image and the reality' but it could be also understood as 'day and night', 'always', 'under all circumstances', and this is the direction chosen by Fowler: 'For whether one be awake or asleep, ignorance of right and wrong and good and bad is in truth inevitably a disgrace, even if the whole mob applaud it'.

342 See Plato, *Phaedrus*, 276c.

343 Plato, *Phaedrus*, 276e.

> those who think they can leave written instructions for an art, as well as those who accept them, thinking that writing can yield results that are clear or certain, must be quite naïve (...) how could they possibly think that words that have been written down can do more than remind those who already know what the writing is about.[344]

In the conclusion to the *Phaedrus*, Plato's Socrates observes that 'no discourse worth serious attention has ever been written in verse or prose'.[345]

In opposition to this kind of discourse stands 'a discourse [λόγος] that is written down, with knowledge, in the soul of the listener; it can defend itself, and it knows for whom it should speak and for whom it should remain silent'.[346] The discourse written in the soul—as Plato's Phaedrus states—'can be fairly called an image [εἴδωλον]' of 'the living, breathing discourse of the man who knows'.[347]

Someone who is very wise, someone 'who knows what is just, noble, and good',[348] uses the art of dialectic:

> The dialectician chooses a proper soul and plants and sows within it discourse accompanied by knowledge—discourse capable of helping itself as well as the man who planted it, which is not barren but produces a seed from which more discourse grows in the character of others. Such discourse makes the seed forever immortal and renders the man who has it as happy as any human being can be.[349]

Plato's Socrates observes that in the case of perfect discourses (speeches), not only the listener learns something, but so does the one who speaks:

> only what is said for the sake of understanding and learning, what is truly written in the soul concerning what is just, noble, and good can be clear, perfect, and worth serious attention: Such discourses should be called his own legitimate children, first the discourse he may have discovered already within himself and then its sons and brothers who may have grown naturally in other souls insofar as these are worthy; to the rest, he turns his back. Such a man, Phaedrus, would be just what you and I both would pray to become.[350]

The one who speaks discovers something 'within himself', but he also sees what has grown naturally in other souls, and can learn from this (having a midwife's ability to distinguish mere phantoms from true thoughts[351]). The listener has to read what is written in his own soul. In other words, he has to see himself being led to a place where he can spot the desired subject. This resembles clearly the description

344 Plato, *Phaedrus*, 275c–d, trans. Nehamas, Woodruff.
345 Plato, *Phaedrus*, 277e, trans. Nehamas, Woodruff.
346 Plato, *Phaedrus*, 276a, trans. Nehamas, Woodruff.
347 Plato, *Phaedrus*, 276a, trans. Nehamas, Woodruff.
348 Plato, *Phaedrus*, 276a, trans. Nehamas, Woodruff.
349 Plato, *Phaedrus*, 276e–277a, trans. Nehamas, Woodruff.
350 Plato, *Phaedrus*, 278a–b, trans. Nehamas, Woodruff.
351 See Plato, *Theaetetus*, 150c–d, where Socrates is talking about his ignorance.

of hunting for justice in the *Republic* (432b), which proceeded directly from the formulation of conclusions about what justice in the model of the state is.[352]

It is therefore perfectly normal that genuine knowledge about something, which is to be discovered in one's own soul, always has a different content than that of a discourse written in ink or spoken. A discourse which is spoken or written in ink is only a means to write genuine knowledge into the soul of a reader or listener. From this point of view—even without a clear declaration that an essential part of it is only a phantom of justice—it is quite obvious that the description of the 'ideal' state contained in the *Republic* should not be taken for something directly expressing genuine knowledge about justice, all the less so about the state. This description is—at best—part of the art of dialectic. What counts is what emerges in the mind of the reader, and this must not be simply a mental reflection of a discourse written in ink. The reader must not only possess certain intellectual abilities to understand what is spoken, but also needs to look for the knowledge himself. The story leads to 'places' where it is easier to spot what is most important. The forest (or deserted, dark places) one has to go through while hunting is not only something which hides secrets and makes cognition difficult, but it symbolises the knowledge needed to spot justice; there is no other way than the difficult one. The forest where justice is hidden, that is the context of interpretation, is very broad and comprises not only what is expressed in other parts of the *Republic*, but also what is said in other works of Plato; the *Phaedrus* seems to be of particular importance since it deals directly with the issue of acquiring knowledge.

The *Republic* evidently cannot be treated as a source of knowledge on how to organise the state. If the model of the hypothetical state in the *Republic* were taken directly as an instruction on how to create a perfect state, then a paradox would emerge: the *Republic* itself could not serve as a textbook on any of the stages in the education of perfect rulers because it does not fit the criteria provided for such textbooks, especially because of its extensive use of images of visible reality.[353] This paradox vanishes if—as is argued throughout this book—the *Republic* is about an individual soul, and the state that is actually at stake is within the subject. What Plato suggests is that the real education that takes place within a soul is not possible solely by means of images imitating what is visible. Talking about education in the model of the state, Plato means that an inner discourse about justice, beauty and good goes beyond everything that can be apprehended by sensual experience. The model of the hypothetical state is a means to reach the invisible realm, not a model serving to create—even if that were possible—a state in the visible realm. Proposing a factual realisation of this model goes in the opposite direction to that which Plato's methodology suggests. To use the language of the *Phaedrus*: the model of the state is a means of writing in the soul of a reader 'the living and

352 See Section 3.6.5.

353 See Smith, 'Images, Education and Paradox', *passim*.

breathing discourse'[354] on the justice of an individual; it is not a project for a state in the visible realm.

3.7.3.2 *The subject of inner discourse and the aim of knowledge*

Inner discourse concerns that which is the main subject of the knowledge of the person who writes the discourse, 'who knows what is just, noble [καλῶν—beautiful], and good'.[355] That justice is placed first in this enumeration in the *Phaedrus* is no accident. As will be argued, justice is founded on inner order and harmony, and therefore on beauty; at the same time, this is the foundation of the unity that contributes to the goodness of the soul. Therefore, it is also understandable that the final prayer in the *Phaedrus* is a prayer, first and foremost, for inner beauty:

> O dear Pan and all the other gods of this place, grant that I may be beautiful inside. Let all my external possessions be in friendly harmony with what is within. May I consider the wise man rich. As for gold, let me have as much as a moderate man could bear and carry with him. Do we need anything else, Phaedrus? I believe my prayer is enough for me.[356]

Answering Socrates' prayer, Phaedrus says: 'Make it a prayer for me as well. Friends have everything in common'.[357] If inner beauty is an aim of learning, then knowledge about justice, beauty, and good (the Good) or contemplation of the forms (ideas) of justice, beauty, and good has a practical purpose, which is acquiring a certain moral quality and acting according to it. The knowledge which is pursued is about how a man as a whole would best deal with himself and other people; it is wisdom as described earlier in the *Republic*.[358] This knowledge is never complete—wisdom belongs to the gods; therefore, the philosopher as a lover of wisdom looks to his partners in his discussions as true friends who allow him to develop a living discourse that teaches both the speaker and the listener.

The prayer to become a wise man is not a prayer to be someone whose aim in life consists simply in contemplating truth, in a kind of theoretical activity, but one who seeks to become just and act in a just way, and to interact with others, to become their friend and to help them become just and act in a just way. It is understandable then that there is a direct link between the living discourse in the soul and happiness—this discourse 'renders the man who has it as happy as any human being can be'.[359]

---

354 Plato, *Phaedrus*, 276a, trans. Nehamas, Woodruff.
355 Plato, *Phaedrus*, 276c, trans. Nehamas, Woodruff.
356 Plato, *Phaedrus*, 279b–c, trans. Nehamas, Woodruff.
357 Plato, *Phaedrus*, 279c, trans. Nehamas, Woodruff.
358 Plato, *Republic*, 428c–d, 443e, see Section 3.6.2.
359 Plato, *Phaedrus*, 276e–277a, trans. Nehamas, Woodruff.

Reading the final prayer, one can also observe that the desired ideal of life is not the life of a perfect guardian, a philosopher as described in the *Republic*. It is someone who also establishes an external harmony, which also comprises a means for decent living—'As for gold, let me have as much as a moderate man could bear and carry with him'.[360] This issue will be addressed below (Section 3.7.5) when the versatility of a just man is considered.

3.7.4 Justice as the internal unity and health of the soul

In the search for reasons why justice is the greatest excellence, the 'first' virtue, one finds a clear indication in Plato's fundamental description of what justice really is ('but in truth justice is...') in Book IV of the *Republic* (443c–e). Explaining why doing its own work by each part of the soul is so important, Plato's Socrates states that thanks to inner harmony (or in the words of the *Phaedrus*—inner beauty) someone who is just 'becomes entirely one from many [παντάπασιν ἕνα γενόμενον ἐκ πολλῶν]'.[361] The reason is given why justice is so important. The unity is an ontological perfection, the perfection of a being, and—moreover—an existential perfection: the more something (someone) is internally united (not divided, in-dividual), the more—the more strongly—it (he) exists. From this point of view, it is clear that justice of the soul is a quite different perfection from moderation, which also stretches into the whole soul. The latter deals with relations between the parts, while the first is a perfection of the whole *par excellence*. It comprises all elements and—by providing existence—also provides the specificity of a given way of existence.

It also becomes clear why in Plato's state, which is a model of the soul, every element has to be subordinated to the benefit of the state. This reflects the simple thought that everything in the soul has to contribute to its existence.

Commenting on the statement about what justice in truth is, Plato's Socrates compares justice to health.

> To produce health is to establish the parts of the body in a relation of mastering, and being mastered by, one another that is according to nature, while to produce sickness is to establish a relation of ruling, and being ruled by, one another that is contrary to nature.
>
> ...

360 Plato, *Phaedrus*, 279b–c, trans. Nehamas, Woodruff; cf. idem, *Laws*, 728e–729a: 'Both [money and goods], in excess, produce enmity and feuds in private and public life, while a deficiency almost invariably leads to slavery. No one should be keen on making money for the sake of leaving his children as rich as possible, because it will not do them any good, or the state either. A child's fortune will be most in harmony with his circumstances, and superior to all other fortunes, if it is modest enough not to attract flatterers, but sufficient to supply all his needs', trans. Saunders.

361 Plato, *Republic*, 443c–e, trans. Bloom.

> Then, in its turn, (...) isn't to produce justice to establish the parts of the soul in a relation of mastering, and being mastered by, one another that is according to nature, while to produce injustice is to establish a relation of ruling, and being ruled by, one another that is contrary to nature?[362]

Health and justice are, respectively, states of the body and of the soul which are 'according to nature' ('κατὰ φύσιν'), while sickness and injustice are states of the body and of the soul which are 'contrary to nature' ('παρὰ φύσιν'). Nature as a criterion of justice, of moral correctness, is not the same nature to which the Sophists referred, which can be apprehended on the basis of sensual experience, but instead belongs to the invisible realm.[363]

Recognition that justice is the health or well-being of the soul leads to a solution to the problem introduced by Thrasymachus at the beginning of the *Republic*—does it better pay to act justly and to be just or to act unjustly and to be unjust?[364] The conclusion is drawn—as being obvious—not by Plato's Socrates this time but by Glaucon, who represents someone who is very eager to expand his own knowledge but is not exceptionally brilliant (although he is not stupid either):

> If life doesn't seem livable with the body's nature corrupted, not even with every sort of food and drink and every sort of wealth and every sort of rule, will it then be livable when the nature of that very thing by which we live is confused and corrupted, even if a man does whatever else he might want except that which will rid him of vice and injustice and will enable him to acquire justice and virtue?[365]

Also in the *Gorgias* Plato describes justice as the health of the soul by analogy to the health of the body—'there's a state of fitness for each of these [body and soul]'.[366] Plato uses terminology taken from medicine: 'εὐεξία', translated here as 'fitness', means also 'good habit of body', 'good health', 'vigour', or 'good condition'.[367] A healthy soul is described also as 'χρηστή'—good in the sense of being able to fulfil tasks which are proper to it, strong, serviceable; like a ship which passes safely through a storm to reach the harbour of its destination. In the *Gorgias* Callicles, expressing the thoughts of Plato's Socrates, refers to health and strength with the word 'ἰσχύς'—'strength', 'might', 'power'. The use of several different terms to describe one reality, a certain state of the soul, is an example of a procedure typical of Plato, whereby he tries to explain something which is beyond sensual experience. Health, fitness, being 'serviceable' and power rest on regularity and order ('ἤ [τυχοῦσα] τάξεώς τε καὶ κόσμου τινός').[368]

---

362 Plato, *Republic*, 444d, trans. Bloom.
363 Cf. Jaeger, *Paideia*, vol. 2, p. 134.
364 Plato, *Republic*, 343d–344c.
365 Plato, *Republic*, 445a–b, trans. Bloom.
366 Plato, *Gorgias*, 464a, trans. Zeyl.
367 Cf. Jaeger, *Paideia*, vol. 2, p. 389, note 30.
368 Plato, *Gorgias*, 504b.

All the aforementioned categories concern the soul as a whole; they describe a virtue of the soul as such, a virtue that allows one to perform actions that are specific to the soul, like managing, ruling, deliberating or living.[369] And the soul's own specific virtue which conditions the soul's specific functions is justice.[370]

The health of the body, although it requires the proper functioning of its internal elements, is something qualitatively different from the characteristics of particular elements, and also different from the characteristics of the relations between them. Regularity and order are the foundations of health and justice (and this applies analogously to any object produced by craftsmen, such as shipwrights or house builders);[371] nevertheless health and justice are something different than regularity and order. Health and justice allow one to act according to nature. The acting of the body or of the soul as a whole cannot be explained adequately in terms of the functioning of the internal elements, although their proper functioning is a prerequisite of the proper functioning of the whole.

The description of justice using the terms 'health', 'fitness', 'power', or 'strength' converges with the ontological understanding of justice proposed here: justice is first of all a strength of existence based on an internal unity of the soul—the more a soul is just, the more it exists. This finds its consequences in identifying just actions as those which are godlike, which are specific for the Good.[372]

3.7.5 Versatility of the just man

The analyses of the passage concerning what in truth justice is (*Republic*, 443b–444a) leads to important conclusions about the occupation or—rather—occupations of a just man and about the whole project of building a state strictly divided into social classes. If 'the fact that the shoemaker by nature rightly practices shoemaking and does nothing else, and the carpenter practices carpentry, and so on for the rest'[373] is only a kind of phantom—εἴδωλον—of justice, then the whole project of a state divided into three classes in which an individual, devoted to only one occupation (one kind of basic activity) and existing entirely for the sake of the state, is questioned as a project for a real state. And it is questioned by Plato himself. Taking into account where the expression 'but in truth' (443c) is placed, justice concerns what is within an individual. It is clear that knowledge about forms (ideas) is subordinated to knowledge on how to be a good man in the here and now, how to be a just man. But decisive for the proposed interpretation is

369 Plato, *Republic*, 353d.
370 Plato, *Republic*, 353e.
371 Plato, *Gorgias*, 503e–504a.
372 Cf. Weiss, *Philosophers in the Republic*, pp. 164–207; Weiss points to the specificity of actions which are acts of justice and not of moderation—these are actions which protect the interests of others, which are beneficial for them. See Chapter 4, esp. Section 4.2.2.
373 Plato, *Republic*, 443c, trans. Bloom.

the statement that 'in truth justice was (...) something of this sort [of being occupied only with one occupation]; however, *not with respect to a man's minding his external business*'.[374] Therefore it is not the case that individual justice is an addition to the justice realised externally in a state or externally at all. Plato's Socrates unambiguously states that justice does not concern man's minding his external business, while the entire model of the hypothetical state is based on strict specialisation in the citizens' actions, which means doing something externally. Even if it involves learning or exercising virtues, this concerns how an individual acts as a whole. While explaining what justice in truth is, then, what is meant is action by specific parts of the soul.

In the light of the analysed passage, which explains what justice is in truth, someone who is just deals with different tasks and occupations. His actions concern the acquisition of money or private contracts (as is typical of the ruled in the model state), he cares for the body (as is important for warriors) and undertakes 'something political'—'πολιτικόν τι' (which is the domain of the rulers). There are therefore actions which in the model were strictly separated, and Plato's Socrates explicitly warns not to mix them.[375] Here a realisation of these different tasks is understood as the 'external business' of someone who is just and who is able to perform proper actions in each of these domains. The model of the hypothetical state as a paradigm for a state in the visible realm falls apart completely.

A similar description of the comprehensive activities of a perfect man—a person of understanding—is provided at the end of Book IX of the *Republic*. From the systematic viewpoint, taking into account the place this description occupies in the dialogue as a whole, it should be regarded as being of highest importance for understanding the aims Plato wished to accomplish, and therefore of highest importance for the interpretation of other parts of the *Republic*. This is the place where Plato's Socrates—after considering different types of constitutions (governments) related to types of character—actually draws final conclusions related to the main question of the *Republic*—what does it mean to be a just man, what does it mean to a be good man? All the efforts of such a man have the aim 'that his entire soul settles into its best nature, acquires moderation, justice, and reason [σωφροσύνην τε καὶ δικαιοσύνην μετὰ φρονήσεως]'.[376] Such a man undertakes activities typical of the members of all classes present in the model of the state. First, he will value studies that produce this state of his soul,[377] which is typical of the philosophers—the rulers of the state (perfect guardians). Second, he will cultivate the harmony of his body.[378] He does this for the sake of the consonance of his soul, and he strives to be strong,

374 Plato, *Republic*, 443c, trans. Bloom, emphasis added; Grube translates here 'It [justice] isn't concerned with someone's doing his own externally'.
375 Plato, *Republic*, 433e–434c.
376 Plato, *Republic*, 591b, trans. Grube.
377 Plato, *Republic*, 591c.
378 Plato, *Republic*, 591c.

healthy and beautiful, 'unless he happens to acquire moderation as a result';[379] nevertheless, he undertakes activities typical of soldiers, who are auxiliaries in the model of the state. Plato's Socrates mentions also that such a man will 'keep order and consonance in his acquisition of money'.[380] There is no doubt that Plato's Socrates is considering one and the same man engaged in different activities.

Evidently Plato in his writings does not stick to the presumably strict rule that everyone should be appointed to only one occupation, even when he characterises his model of the state. Talking about education in Book VII, he states clearly and without any hesitation that 'our guardian must be both a warrior and a philosopher'.[381]

One may object that the engagement of a perfect man (or an almost perfect man) in different activities is a burden which has to be accepted because the state he lives in is not a perfect one. But this objection is very difficult to defend if Plato's remark about the division of labour as a phantom of justice is taken seriously. He clearly states that justice understood as performing only one's own occupation does not characterise 'someone's doing his own externally',[382] and justice in the state evidently concerns one's external business—external acting. Plato bases the opposition between a phantom of justice and what justice is in truth on an opposition between external and internal doing, and not on oppositions between classes as is the case in his model of the state, where he remarks that meddling and exchange between three classes 'is the greatest harm that can happen to the city',[383] and in the perspective of the model of the state, Plato's Socrates observes that 'when the same person tries to do all these things at once (...) [it will] bring the city to ruin'.[384]

A strong argument that versatility is an essential characteristic of someone who is just can be drawn from the *Timaeus*, where there is talk about diseases and their curing. Plato's Timaeus starts with a general observation that 'all that is good is beautiful, and what is beautiful is not ill-proportioned. Hence we must take it that if a living thing is to be in good condition, it will be well-proportioned'.[385] Certainly, this remark also concerns someone who is just. The parts of the soul have to be well-proportioned, and this proportion is seen by Plato's Timaeus in strict connection to the body and actions which are indispensable for its health. He is surprisingly radical about the importance of the harmony between soul and body, and not only for the health of both of them: 'In determining health and

379 Plato, *Republic*, 591c, trans. Grube.
380 Plato, *Republic*, 591d, trans. Grube.
381 Plato, *Republic*, 525b, trans. Grube.
382 'οὐ περὶ τὴν ἔξω πρᾶξιν τῶν αὑτοῦ', Plato, *Republic*, 443c, trans. Grube; Bloom translates: 'not with respect to a man's minding his external business'.
383 Plato, *Republic*, 434b, trans. Grube.
384 Plato, *Republic*, 434b, trans. Grube.
385 Plato, *Timaeus*, 87c, trans. Zeyl.

disease or virtue and vice no proportion or lack of it is more important than that between soul and body'.[386] To preserve the health of the body and of the soul one should care about each part of the body and of the soul as well:

> The mathematician, then, or the ardent devotee of any other intellectual discipline should also provide exercise for his body by taking part in gymnastics, while one who takes care to develop his body should in his turn practice the exercises of the soul by applying himself to the arts and to every pursuit of wisdom, if he is to truly deserve the joint epithets of 'fine and good.' And the various bodily parts should also be looked after in this same way, in imitation of the structure of the universe.[387]

The presented paradigm of someone who is beautiful and thus also just presupposes the exercising of not only all cardinal virtues but also different types of 'external' doing, although these external doings do not constitute justice themselves.

There are also other arguments that doing one thing as one's own work does not characterise justice in a perfect state, but only in a model of a state constructed to understand the justice in the soul.

One crucial argument rests on the recognition of happiness and friendship between citizens as two principal aims of law.[388] The happiness of citizens and friendship are therefore fundamental characteristics of the perfect state. True friendship is possible only between equals, first of all, between those who are equal in virtues. Plato clearly links happiness with being just, which itself presupposes the possession of wisdom, courage and moderation. Therefore, the citizens in a perfect state cannot be only perfect guardians. Someone possessing all four cardinal virtues is able to perform occupations which in the model of the hypothetical state were specific to a particular class. It should also be noted that it is a just man, and thus someone possessing all four basic virtues, who acts 'either concerning the acquisition of money, or the care of the body, or something political, or concerning private contracts'.[389]

The interpretation proposed here allows one to avoid the well-known problem of whether the citizens of the perfect state could be happy.[390] Plato clearly accepts that in the model of the hypothetical state the vast majority could not be happy and could not have a relationship of friendship. These are the third class, the people whose whole life is devoted to increasing material wealth. A statement on this can be found at the very beginning of the *Republic*, in Socrates' dialogue with Cephalus, who had inherited a substantial fortune and multiplied it a little. What is important for Plato's Socrates is that Cephalus has not devoted his entire life to

386 Plato, *Timaeus*, 87d, trans. Zeyl.
387 Plato, *Timaeus*, 88c–d, trans. Zeyl.
388 Plato, *Laws*, 743c.
389 Plato, *Republic*, 443e, trans. Bloom.
390 See Section 6.4.6.

increasing his wealth, and that he cares about money because it is useful and not for its own sake:

> you don't seem to love money too much. And those who haven't made their own money are usually like you. But those who have made it for themselves are twice as fond of it as those who haven't. Just as poets love their poems and fathers love their children, so those who have made their own money don't just care about it because it's useful, as other people do, but because it's something they've made themselves.[391]

If people care about money for its own sake, it 'makes them poor company, for they haven't a good word to say about anything except money'.[392] Being poor company, they are not able to develop true friendship. They cannot be happy because they have not attained a high level of morality.

If happiness and friendship are the principal aims of law and of the state based on that law, then the hypothetical state modelled by Plato's Socrates, in which a large group of people devote their lives to increasing their wealth, cannot be recognised as a paradigm for creating a state in the visible realm. When one rejects the view that the principle requiring devotion to only one occupation applies to the perfect state, one no longer faces the aforementioned problem of the exclusion of significant groups of citizens from being happy and living in true friendship.

One can argue that a strict division of occupations between classes could be justified by natural differences in individual abilities only in an imperfect state which is on its way to becoming a perfect state. Then, however, the model of the hypothetical state from the *Republic* would be a paradigm for an imperfect state but not for a perfect one. This would be contrary to the basic assumption that we are dealing with a model of a perfect state. This is another argument for regarding the model state only as a means for understanding justice in the soul.

This analysis confirms that to reach a proper understanding of the justice in the state, the aims of laws—happiness and friendship[393]—and therefore a recognition of the ancillary, instrumental value of the state and law have to be taken into account.

In the model of the hypothetical state, narrow specialisation—appointing each individual to only one occupation which he can perform best, according to his nature—was justified by the good of the state as a supreme good. If the good of the state is only an instrumental value, then a different argument is needed to justify a strict division of the main types of occupations. The instrumental character of the law and state is certainly and directly recognised in the *Laws*—they are tools for reaching happiness (virtues) and friendship.[394]

One could argue that both the *Laws* and the *Timaeus* are late dialogues, and that Plato changed his view on the instrumental character of the law and the state.

---

391 Plato, *Republic*, 330b–c, trans. Grube.
392 Plato, *Republic*, 330c, trans. Grube.
393 Plato, *Laws*, 743c.
394 Plato, *Laws*, 743c.

Plato himself never mentions such a change of mind on that fundamental issue. But more importantly, there are clear remarks on the instrumental character of the state in the introductory part of the *Republic* itself. The city (the state) arose because people are not self-sufficient: 'because people need many things, and because one person calls on a second out of one need and on a third out of a different need, many people gather in a single place to live together as partners and helpers. And such a settlement is called a city'.[395]

The versatility of the just man coincides with the Greek paradigm of being a good man. The central virtue of the good one was magnanimity, greatness of soul—*μεγαλοψυχία*,[396] which was accomplished when greatness in the moral respect was accompanied by other goods, including material assets. In this perspective it fits very well that at the end of the *Phaedrus* Plato's Socrates concludes his final prayer with remarks relating to material wealth: 'As for gold, let me have as much as a moderate man could bear and carry with him'.[397]

One must also bear in mind that Socrates, who is the best possible instance of being a philosopher, also holds offices as required of a citizen and takes part in military campaigns, presenting outstanding courage.[398] It can also be assumed that Plato's own expeditions to Asia Minor and Crete were mercantile expeditions. Taking into account Plato's depiction of Socrates, one has to exclude such an interpretation of the *Republic* that a strict division of occupations between the members of three classes would be proper for perfect citizens in the perfect state. Differences between people which make them suited to perform different jobs[399] do not exclude the possibility that the same citizen may accomplish activities typical of all classes of the model state.

Another important argument in favour of the versatility of a just person is provided by the *Timaeus*, when the participants in the discussion are introduced. Both Timaeus and Critias, who are the main speakers, are portrayed as thoroughly positive figures. In this dialogue, their expositions seem to be closer to Plato's views than those of Socrates. Both Timaeus and Critias are depicted as being very versatile, as possessing the virtue of magnanimity. About Timaeus himself Plato's Socrates states that

> He's from Locri, an Italian city under the rule of excellent laws. None of his compatriots outrank him in property or birth, and he has come to occupy positions of supreme authority and honor in his city. Moreover, he has, in my judgment, mastered the entire

395 Plato, *Republic*, 369b–c, trans. Grube.

396 See Aristotle, *Nicomachean Ethics*, 1123a–1125a; see Paczkowski, 'Klasyczna filozofia grecka', p. 82.

397 Plato, *Phaedrus*, 279b–c, trans. Nehamas, Woodruff.

398 Plato, *Symposium*, 219d–221c.

399 Cf. Plato, *Republic*, 370a, trans. Bloom: 'each of us is naturally not quite like anyone else, but rather differs in his nature; different men are apt for the accomplishment of different jobs'.

> field of philosophy. As for Critias, I'm sure that all of us here in Athens know that he's no mere layman in any of the areas we're talking about.[400]

The examples of Timaeus (and also of Socrates to some extent) suggest one more quite strong argument against accepting in a perfect state a strict division of occupations between people belonging to different classes as indicated in the model of the hypothetical state.

An argument against the strict division of occupations can also be made based on the overall aims of Plato's philosophy. If one asks what is the paramount concern of Plato as a philosopher (or at least one of his principal aims), it is quite clear that it is to acquire virtue as such—the attainment of moral perfection by each person. It is also obvious that acquiring moral perfection consists in acquiring justice, which itself also presupposes mastering wisdom, courage and moderation, and this is clearly a process. Mastering these virtues requires engaging in activities in which they can be exercised, and these activities are proper for the members of different classes of the hypothetical state. This leads to the conclusion that someone striving for justice should in fact engage in activities typical of different classes, and likewise, that someone who has already mastered justice is apt to exercise well (justly, good, beautifully) different activities typical of the members of different classes in the hypothetical state. This includes engaging in politics (as is typical of the perfect guardians—the philosopher-rulers), caring about his body and physical strength (as is typical of soldiers), and increasing his wealth (as is typical of money-makers). Taking this into account, it is clear that the passage 443c–e of the *Republic* concerning what in truth justice is describes different activities of a simply just man and not of different people belonging to different classes.

3.7.6 Unity of virtues in just actions

Acquiring the virtue of justice presupposes mastering wisdom, courage and moderation. It should be stressed, however, that the virtue of justice is not simply a sum of other virtues. From an ontological point of view it is very different, since it is 'located' on the level of existence, while the other virtues are perfections in the essential aspect (of the 'content' of being human). This is an important distinction in Aristotle's approach to general justice, a notion that corresponds to Plato's notion of justice as virtue. In the Aristotelian conception, however, justice has its own specificity, as it is 'the only virtue that seems to be another person's good'.[401] The difference between justice and other virtues lies in the means of exercising it, and in the addressee of the deeds based on it—'justice is complete virtue to the highest degree because it is the complete exercise of complete virtue. And it is the complete exercise because the person who has justice is able to exercise virtue in

---

400 Plato, *Timaeus*, 20a, trans. Zeyl.

401 Aristotle, *Nicomachean Ethics*, 1130a, trans. Irwin.

relation to another, not only in what concerns himself'.[402] Therefore, justice can be aptly characterised by the proverb quoted by Aristotle himself: 'And in justice all virtue is summed up'.[403] In Plato's approach, justice can also be characterised as being 'another person's good', though in being situated on an existential level and as providing power to exercise all other virtues it differs profoundly from them and cannot be understood simply in terms of being a sum and in terms of the specificity of its addressees. Moreover, Plato's considerations on wisdom and courage clearly refer to the exercising of these virtues in relation to others, and therefore justice is not the only one virtue which is another person's good.

It should be noticed that in the description of what in truth justice is (*Republic*, 443c–e), the justice of the soul is seen from the perspective of just actions: 'Then, and only then, he acts, if he does act in some way—either concerning the acquisition of money, or the care of the body, or something political, or concerning private contracts'.[404] An action engages the whole subject, all parts of its soul—all the 'three classes' are acting together. There are no people representing any social class in it. For a just action, wisdom, courage and moderation are needed in the same subject. In a real state all these virtues are required from every citizen, and all of them should act justly. This is also seen clearly when Plato's description of virtues is considered. For example, the core of courage consists in following reason especially in the face of emotions which drive someone to act in a way contrary to what reason advises him to do. It is a virtue required from everyone and is far from being specific to soldiers. Of course, the whole of Plato's account of cardinal virtues, as interpreted here, does not exclude the possibility that some individuals possess special abilities to be soldiers and to fight in defence of the state.

It is clear that the conceptualisation of the justice of an individual as presented here is incompatible with the justice in the model of the hypothetical state constructed in the *Republic*. According to this model, the citizens belonging to particular classes do not actually need to develop all four virtues to the greatest possible extent. Moreover, the justice of individual citizens is not the proper subject of consideration. While the model is being constructed, justice is searched for and found in the state as a whole and not in particular citizens occupied with their own specific jobs. Plato's Socrates does not pay particular attention even to the justice of the perfect guardians (the philosopher-rulers). Implementation of the strict division of classes made on the grounds of essential differences in the virtues of the members of these classes would result in the 'dissociation' of the constitutive parts of individual souls; it would lead to precisely opposite effects in the individuals to those required by the justice of the soul. The rulers would guide the members of the other classes 'externally' with the help of laws and the members of the auxiliary class. The producers would simply be compelled to do

402 Aristotle, *Nicomachean Ethics*, 1129b, trans. Irwin.
403 Aristotle, *Nicomachean Ethics*, 1129b, trans. Irwin.
404 Plato, *Republic*, 443e, trans. Bloom.

what is required by law, neither understanding the reasons for introducing specific laws nor even internalising the values promoted by the laws (as is the case with members of the auxiliary class) would be needed. If the internal integration of the three parts of the soul is a foundation for justice and for happiness, then not the perfect guardians (philosopher-rulers) but the members of the auxiliary class seem to be closest to realising internal unity, since they internalise the law as congruent with their education and are trained in acting in accordance with the law and with their own convictions. If one accepts that Plato is not an ethical intellectualist, as the real Socrates was, and that knowledge is not a sufficient condition for acting rightly, then in the hypothetical state even some philosophers must be compelled by auxiliaries to act in accordance with laws. Finally, let us return to a statement which is fundamental for the conception of the justice in the model of the hypothetical state:

> This was meant to make clear that each of the other citizens is to be directed to what he is naturally suited for, so that, doing the one work that is his own, he will become not many but one, and the whole city will itself be naturally one not many.[405]

Though it could be plausible that 'one man—one work' helps in creating the unity of the state, it is very difficult to understand how doing one job for one's whole life could possibly contribute to the internal unity of the intellectual, spirited and appetitive parts of the soul of a particular citizen. It might contribute to the unity between innate abilities and actions, but it has nothing to do with the justice (understood as the unity of the three parts of the soul) and moral perfection of an individual.

In a perfect state all citizens aim to acquire justice and need all of the cardinal virtues. The perfect guardians (the philosopher-rulers) evidently need courage—understood as the application of wisdom to their actions; they also need inner harmony, comprising their emotions. Soldiers need wisdom in their souls even if it is not 'produced' by them, and clearly need temperance. Similarly, managing an enterprise and even being a simple craftsman requires not only temperance. Courage is also indispensable, and in running a larger enterprise, knowledge of the reasons for actions, and therefore, wisdom, is also certainly indispensable. Courage in particular is understood by Plato in such a way that it is necessary for every citizen. This clearly indicates that the model of the hypothetical state is completely subordinated to the understanding of individual justice.

Recognition of the versatility of the just man and the unity of virtues aimed towards the acquisition of justice by every citizen does not exclude the formulation of proposals concerning the division of occupations between citizens. Individual abilities are, of course, important in citizens' decisions about what they should choose in their lives. Nevertheless, the abilities related to the particular classes in the model of the hypothetical state are not decisive for choosing a particular way

---

405 Plato, *Republic*, 423d, trans. Grube.

of life—everyone needs them to live a good, just life. Very telling is the choice—depicted in the myth of Er—made by Odysseus, who personifies cleverness and the best abilities needed for being a warrior. He chooses 'the life of a private individual who did his own work'.[406] Plato suggests that it was the right choice. The issue of choosing a way of life will be considered in detail below (Section 5.2.4).

406 Plato, *Republic*, 620c, trans. Grube.

4 The content of just actions

4.1 Socrates talks to himself about justice

4.1.1 Preliminary remarks

Up to this point, the inquiry has been focused on the justice of the soul. This analysis was indispensable for understanding the justice of actions. A link between these two kinds of justice has already been found in the passage from Book IV of the *Republic* analysed above, which starts with words: 'And in truth justice is'.[407] In this passage, Plato makes a crucial point about the connection between justice in the soul and the justice of actions:

> One who is just (...) puts himself in order, is his own friend, and harmonizes the three parts of himself like three limiting notes in a musical scale—high, low, and middle. He binds together those parts and any others there may be in between, and from having been many things he becomes entirely one, moderate and harmonious.
>
> Only then does he act. And when he does anything, whether acquiring wealth, taking care of his body, engaging in politics, or in private contracts—in all of these, he believes that *the action is just and fine that preserves this inner harmony and helps achieve it, and calls it so*, and regards as wisdom the knowledge that oversees such actions. And he believes that *the action that destroys this harmony is unjust, and calls it so*, and regards the belief that oversees it as ignorance.[408]

A person acts justly because he is just, while just actions preserve justice in the soul and help to achieve it. Wisdom is the knowledge which oversees such actions. The question arises, however, where the one who is just should look to obtain wisdom viewed as knowledge about how man as a whole should deal with himself and other people in the best possible way.[409] The answer is complex. One part of it has already been elaborated upon—one should learn about the justice of the soul and about the other cardinal virtues. These are, nonetheless, principles of action which can be called formal. They pertain to the 'inner' side of an action, that is, they are concerned with what is on the inside of an acting subject. But what determines the external shape of an action? The answer to this question combines two major elements. First, the power of cognition should be turned towards the intelligible realm, and one has to learn about the Good itself. One learns how to act by seeing how the Good acts. A crucial text concerning a genuine education in general and learning about the Good in particular is the well-known myth

---

407 Plato, *Republic*, 443c, trans. Grube.
408 Plato, *Republic*, 443d–e, trans. Grube, emphasis added.
409 Cf. Plato, *Republic*, 428c–d, see Section 3.6.2.

of the cave in Book VII of the *Republic.* The first principle of external action is also of a formal nature—just action benefits others. The myth of the cave will be examined, however, from a broader perspective established through an analysis of a key passage from the *Gorgias* that reveals the second major element of what determines the shape of just actions: knowing the intelligible realm is not enough to obtain wisdom understood as knowledge which shapes external action. If one recognises that just action benefits others, it is necessary to know the addressees of the action. This point is not trivial, because there are two very different possible approaches to the origin of norms or values understood as reasons for just actions. The first approach recognises a strict division between 'be' and 'ought'—actions are shaped by norms whose content is determined independently of learning about the addressees of an action (there is no source of normativity in the addressee); this determination of the content of norms can be done by a lawgiver, for example, or by an objective intelligible realm (by norms 'existing' in the intelligible realm, in the world of forms). The second approach recognises that the reason for a given shape of an action is to be found first of all in its addressee—the action should be fitting and beneficial for the latter. General, abstract norms can and should be formulated, but they are secondary to the relation of congruity between an action (or its effect) and its addressee.

How important the difference is between these two approaches is clearly visible if one asks the question 'why should I do it?' In the first approach, the answer is 'Because it is required by law', and this means I act for the sake of the law. In the second approach the answer is 'Because it is beneficial for the addressee'—something should be done for the sake of a fellow man. The crucial difference between these two approaches remains regardless of whether the law in the first approach is only an arbitrary creation of men or objectively given in an intelligible realm (such as natural law, the law of reason, *logos,* etc.). In this first approach the principal aim of just actions is situated *prima facie* 'outside' an individual. An analogous structure can be found in conceptions that advocate prioritising the state over the individual—the reason for action rests, ultimately, in that which is beneficial for the state and is created by the state as its laws. The second approach favours the individual, and it will be argued here that Plato's conception of just action represents this second approach. It is also appropriate to the contemporary conception of human rights—human dignity, as their source, is inherent, innate to a human being; they are not a creation of any state or international community, nor are they discovered in the normative sphere, separate from concrete individuals.

Plato's approach to these issues is analysed here mostly on the basis of a passage from the *Gorgias* which directly addresses the problem of the justice of actions. This problem also appears in the *Republic*; nevertheless, it is worthwhile to pay attention to Socrates' dialogue with himself in the *Gorgias*[410] because of the exceptional form in which Plato expresses there his views on justice.

---

410 Plato, *Gorgias,* 506c–507c.

4.1.2 The form of the argument

At one point of the discourse presented in the *Gorgias*, at the 'top' of the dialogue, or in the 'head' of the discussion, as it is called in the text itself,[411] Plato lets his Socrates conduct a discussion with Socrates himself. This formal technique is exceptional in Plato's writings,[412] and it would be difficult to overestimate its importance. Even if Plato's Socrates' declaration that 'the things I say I certainly don't say with any knowledge at all; no, I'm searching together with you',[413] it remains true that the wisest man is discussing justice with the wisest man.[414] And even if he does not have knowledge at the start of the discussion, he is certainly someone who is able to deliver good thoughts.[415] Plato's Socrates is playing simultaneously the roles of a midwife and of someone who is pregnant with the truth.[416]

The dialogue of Socrates with himself follows directly his discussion with Callicles, who has defended rhetoric as a craft which helps to free one from punishment. As often happens in discussions with Socrates, Callicles reaches such a point that if the discussion continued he would have to admit the truth of a statement contradicting his own originally expressed position. When Socrates draws the conclusion that 'So to be disciplined is better for the soul than lack of discipline, which is what you yourself were thinking just now',[417] which clearly contradicts Callicles'

411 Plato, *Gorgias*, 505c–d.

412 Olson, 'Socrates Talks to Himself in Plato's Hippias Major', refers to a kind of dialogue conducted by Socrates with himself in the *Hippias Major* (*Greater Hippias*), 286c ff. But this dialogue of Socrates with himself appears not in such a pure form as in the *Gorgias*, and therefore its importance for interpretation is rather limited. Leaving aside the problem of Plato's authorship of the *Hippias Major*, it has to be observed that in this dialogue—unlike in the *Gorgias*—Plato's Socrates does not directly disclose his identity as his own partner in the discussion; the 'second Socrates' remains unidentified as Socrates. Also unlike in the *Gorgias*, in the *Hippias Major* there is someone who actively participates in the discussion of the 'apparent' Socrates with the 'hidden' Socrates—Hippias evokes questions posed by the 'hidden' Socrates. Moreover, the 'apparent' Socrates aims to elaborate his standpoint as congruent with Hippias' views and presents it as their joint stance. Last but not least, the discussion does not lead to clear conclusions directly related to the subject of the conversation.

413 Plato, *Gorgias*, 506a, trans. Zeyl. Cf. Plato, *Apology*, 23a–b, trans. Grube: 'What is probable, gentlemen, is that in fact the god is wise and that his oracular response meant that human wisdom is worth little or nothing, and that when he says this man, Socrates, he is using my name as an example, as if he said: "This man among you, mortals, is wisest who, like Socrates, understands that his wisdom is worthless"'.

414 Cf. Plato, *Apology*, 21a.

415 Cf. Plato, *Phaedrus*, 235c–d: 'I know my own ignorance. The only other possibility, I think, is that I was filled, like an empty jar, by the words of other people streaming in through my ears', trans. Nehamas, Woodruff.

416 Cf. Plato, *Theaetetus*, 148e–151d.

417 Plato, *Gorgias*, 505b, trans. Zeyl.

initial views, the latter does not want to confirm this statement. Therefore, he simply breaks the process of argumentation, saying: 'I don't know what in the world you mean, Socrates. Ask somebody else (...) And I couldn't care less about anything you say, either. I gave you these answers just for Gorgias' sake'.[418] Gorgias and Polus had withdrawn from the discussion earlier. No one volunteers to continue the discussion with Socrates. So Callicles suggests that Socrates could continue himself: 'Couldn't you go through the discussion by yourself, either by speaking in your own person or by answering your own questions?'[419] Socrates agrees and chooses to continue in the form of such a dialogue. The advantages and disadvantages of this form are considered in the *Gorgias* itself. These remarks significantly contribute to understanding what will be said in this exceptional dialogue.

At the very beginning of the *Gorgias*, before Plato's Socrates begins arguing with Gorgias, the advantages of dialogue and the concision of expositions are extensively discussed, and Socrates explicitly requires such forms from his counterpart:

> Well now, Gorgias, would you be willing to complete the discussion in the way we're having it right now, that of alternately asking questions and answering them, and to put aside for another time this long style of speechmaking like the one Polus began with? Please don't go back on your promise, but be willing to give a brief answer to what you're asked.[420]

Similarly, before arguing with Polus, Socrates insists that Polus answer and ask questions and curb his long style of speech, the style he tried to use at first.[421] Advocating these requirements, Socrates reasons:

> If you spoke at length and were unwilling to answer what you're asked, wouldn't I be in a terrible way if I'm not to have the freedom to stop listening to you and leave? But if you care at all about the discussion we've had and want to straighten it up, please retract whatever you think best, as I was saying just now. Take your turn in asking and being asked questions (...), and subject me and yourself to refutation.[422]

Plato's Socrates sometimes violates these conditions himself, but in doing so he provides reasons for it. After a longer speech he has just delivered there is an explanation:

> Perhaps I've done an absurd thing: I wouldn't let you make long speeches, and here I've just composed a lengthy one myself. I deserve to be forgiven, though, for when

418 Plato, *Gorgias*, 505c, trans. Zeyl.
419 Plato, *Gorgias*, 505d, trans. Zeyl.
420 Plato, *Gorgias*, 449b, trans. Zeyl. Cf. e.g. a remark in the *Republic* about Thrasymachus emptying 'this great flood of words into our ears all at once like a bath attendant', Plato, *Republic*, 344d, trans. Grube.
421 Plato, *Gorgias*, 461d.
422 Plato, *Gorgias*, 461e–462a, trans. Zeyl.

> I made my statements short you didn't understand and didn't know how to deal with the answers I gave you, but you needed a narration. So if I don't know how to deal with your answers either, you must spin out a speech too. But if I do, just let me deal with them. That's only fair [just—δίκαιον].[423]

Concise forms of speaking are proper for profound and smart people. It is a more perfect means of consideration than a lecture or a speech, if the counterparts are smart and profound thinkers. The expression 'That's only fair'—'that will only be just [δίκαιον γάρ]'[424] which closes the quotation should not be underestimated. What is just is something that is proper for someone in the sense that it fits, is adjusted to him, in this case—specifically—to his intellectual abilities. If someone is smart, the short form suffices; if someone does not understand concise language, a longer argument is needed.

Concise talking presupposes certain knowledge which has not been directly disclosed. Therefore, in interpreting Socrates' dialogue with himself, it has to be acknowledged that some important knowledge needed to understand the issues discussed by Socrates is not provided in the text of the dialogue itself. One also has to be open to thinking about Plato's so-called unwritten teachings.

In spite of Plato's Socrates' own declarations that his knowledge is limited, simply by choosing the form of a dialogue, and by being concise in asking and answering, he is apparently saying: 'I have knowledge about that which I am discussing. I have mastered my subject'. This choice also indicates that the one who speaks is smart and skilful.

The choice of a short form and the assumption of the expertise of both partners in the discussion do not preclude the possibility that questions will be asked about simple matters. While talking with Gorgias about the subject of the best art, Plato's Socrates warns him:

> But so you won't be surprised if in a moment I ask you again another question like this, about what seems to be clear, and yet I go on with my questioning—as I say, I'm asking questions so that we can conduct an orderly discussion. It's not you I'm after; it's to prevent our getting in the habit of second-guessing and snatching each other's statements away ahead of time. It's to allow you to work out your assumption in any way you want to.[425]

When the most important matters are at stake, they only appear to be clear. Being clear, in turn, is related not only to intellectual abilities, to the power of learning itself; it is also important in which direction that power is turned.[426] Gorgias is a paradigm of a man with exceptional knowledge and intellectual skill. Plato's

423 Plato, *Gorgias*, 465d–466a, trans. Zeyl.
424 Plato, *Gorgias*, 466a, trans. Zeyl.
425 Plato, *Gorgias*, 454b–c, trans. Zeyl.
426 Cf. Plato, *Republic*, 518b–c; see Section 4.1.5.4.

Socrates remarks that questions about clear, or rather seemingly clear, matters are needed 'so that we can conduct an orderly discussion'. Asking simple questions should 'prevent our getting in the habit of second-guessing and snatching each other's statements away ahead of time' and help work out assumptions or—more accurately—complete an argument in accordance with assumptions.

Before starting the discussion with himself, Plato's Socrates gives clear signs that matters of primary importance have not yet been considered: 'What'll we do now? Are we breaking off in the midst of the discussion?'[427] In fact, the 'head' of the whole story about justice is still lacking—Plato's Socrates remarks: 'They say that it isn't permitted to give up in the middle of telling stories, either. A head must be put on it, so that it won't go about headless'.[428]

Also important are Socrates' considerations about the disadvantages of dialoguing with himself. He remarks that this situation will fit the words of the comic poet Epicharmus: 'One man doing the work of two'.[429] Here, it is difficult not to take into account what Plato's Socrates says in the *Republic* about justice in the model of the hypothetical state—everyone should do, according to 'what he is naturally suited for, (...) the one work that is his own'[430] and 'justice is doing one's own work and not meddling with what isn't one's own'.[431] Asking and answering questions are essentially different 'works', like delivering a child (the work of a midwife) and giving birth (the work of a mother). Nevertheless, Plato's Socrates does not follow the principle of doing only one work, arguing that 'it looks as though I have no choice at all'.[432] This confirms the thesis that the principle of 'doing one's own work' applied to individuals in the state is only a phantom (εἴδωλον) of true justice.[433] Moreover, Socrates' consenting to do 'the work of two', accompanied by his mentioning the problems of doing so, indicates that something very important is at stake.

Recognition that Socrates' dialogue with himself concerns the most important matters is also of great importance for further interpretation of the previously analysed passage from the *Republic* that states what in truth justice is.[434] In the *Gorgias*, considerations about the justice of the soul are summarised in an exceptional form—Socrates' dialogue with himself—and the argument will culminate in deliberations on acting justly and on what is decisive for shaping such acting, or, in other words, what determines wisdom as the knowledge which oversees just

427 Plato, *Gorgias*, 505d, trans. Zeyl.
428 Plato, *Gorgias*, 505c–d, trans. Zeyl.
429 Plato, *Gorgias*, 505e, trans. Hamilton, Emlyn-Jones; Zeyl translates 'one man, for what two men were saying before'.
430 Plato, *Republic*, 423d, trans. Grube.
431 Plato, *Republic*, 433a–b, trans. Grube.
432 Plato, *Gorgias*, 505e, trans. Zeyl.
433 Plato, *Republic*, 443c.
434 Plato, *Republic*, 443c–444a; see Section 3.7.

actions. This dialogue of Socrates with himself also reveals the most important subject of the *Gorgias*; this is neither rhetoric nor punitive justice, but justice as such.

4.1.3 Detailed analyses

To facilitate analysis, the text is rewritten in such a way that the structure of the dialogue of Socrates with himself is clearer (questions are marked as [*Socrates 1*] and answers as [*Socrates 2*]). It is also made visible which utterances Plato's Socrates addresses to himself and which are addressed to the audience (to Callicles). The successive pronouncements in the dialogue are also numbered; these numbers will be referenced in the subsequent analysis.

1 [*Socrates*] [506c] Listen, then, as I pick up the discussion from the beginning.

2 [*Socrates 1*] Is the pleasant the same as the good?

3 [*Socrates 2*] It isn't, as Callicles and I have agreed.

4 [*Socrates 1*] Is the pleasant to be done for the sake of the good, or the good for the sake of the pleasant?

5 [*Socrates 2*] The pleasant for the sake of the good.

6 [*Socrates 1*] [506d] And pleasant is that by which, when it's come to be present in us, we feel pleasure, and good that by which, when it's present in us, we are good?

7 [*Socrates 2*] That's right.

8 [*Socrates 1*] But surely we are good, both we and everything else that's good, when some excellence has come to be present in us?

9 [*Socrates 2 / Socrates*] Yes, I do think that that's necessarily so, Callicles.

10 [*Socrates 1*] But the best way in which the excellence of each thing comes to be present in it, whether it's that of an artifact or of a body or a soul as well, or of any animal, is not just any old way, but is due to whatever organization, correctness, and craftsmanship [τάξει καὶ ὀρθότητι καὶ τέχνῃ] is bestowed on each of them. Is that right?

11 [*Socrates 2*] Yes, I agree.

12 [*Socrates 1*] [506e] So it's due to organization that the excellence of each thing is something which is organized and has order? [τάξει ἄρα τεταγμένον καὶ κεκοσμημένον ἐστὶν ἡ ἀρετὴ ἑκάστου;]

13 [*Socrates 2*] Yes, I'd say so.

14 [*Socrates 1*] So it's when a certain order, the proper one for each thing, comes to be present in it that it makes each of the things there are, good? [κόσμος τις ἄρα ἐγγενόμενος ἐν ἑκάστῳ ὁ ἑκάστου οἰκεῖος ἀγαθὸν παρέχει ἕκαστον τῶν ὄντων;]

15 [*Socrates 2*] Yes, I think so.

16 [*Socrates 1*] So also a soul which has its own order is better than a disordered one? [καὶ ψυχὴ ἄρα κόσμον ἔχουσα τὸν ἑαυτῆς ἀμείνων τῆς ἀκοσμήτου;]

17 [*Socrates 2*] Necessarily so.

18 [*Socrates 1*] But surely one that has order is an orderly one? [ἀλλὰ μὴν ἥ γε κόσμον ἔχουσα κοσμία;]

19 [*Socrates 2*] Of course it is.

20 [*Socrates 1*] [507a] And an orderly soul is a self-controlled [σώφρων] one?

21 [*Socrates 2*] Absolutely.

22 [*Socrates 1*] So a self-controlled soul is a good one. [ἡ ἄρα σώφρων ψυχὴ ἀγαθή.]

23 [*Socrates*] I for one can't say anything else beyond that, Callicles my friend; if you can, please teach me.
[*Callicles*] Say on, my good man.

24 [*Socrates 1*] I say that if the self-controlled [σώφρων] soul is a good one, then a soul that's been affected the opposite way of the self-controlled [σώφρων] one is a bad [κακή] one. And this, it's turned out, is the foolish and undisciplined [ἄφρων τε καὶ ἀκόλαστος] one.

25 [*Socrates 2*] That's right.

26 [*Socrates 1*] And surely a self-controlled person would do what's appropriate with respect to both gods and human beings. For if he does what's inappropriate, he wouldn't be self-controlled. [καὶ μὴν ὅ γε σώφρων τὰ προσήκοντα πράττοι ἂν καὶ περὶ θεοὺς καὶ περὶ ἀνθρώπους: οὐ γὰρ ἂν σωφρονοῖ τὰ μὴ προσήκοντα πράττων;]

27 [*Socrates 2*] That's necessarily how it is.

28 [*Socrates 1*] And of course [507b] *if he did what's appropriate* with respect to human beings, he would be doing what's just, and with respect to gods he would be doing what's pious, and one who does what's just and pious must necessarily be just and pious. [καὶ μὴν περὶ μὲν ἀνθρώπους *τὰ προσήκοντα πράττων* δίκαι' ἂν πράττοι, περὶ δὲ θεοὺς ὅσια: τὸν δὲ τὰ δίκαια καὶ ὅσια πράττοντα ἀνάγκη δίκαιον καὶ ὅσιον εἶναι.]

29 [*Socrates 2*] That's so.

30 [*Socrates 2*] [507c] Yes, and he would also necessarily be brave, for it's not like a self-controlled man to either pursue or avoid what isn't appropriate, but to avoid and pursue what he should, whether these are things to do, or people, or pleasures and pains, and to stand fast and endure them where he should. So, it's necessarily very much the case, Callicles, that the self-controlled man, because he's just and brave and pious, as we've recounted, is a completely good man, that the good man does well and admirably whatever he does, and that the man who does well is blessed and happy [τὸν σώφρονα, ὥσπερ διήλθομεν, δίκαιον ὄντα καὶ ἀνδρεῖον καὶ ὅσιον ἀγαθὸν ἄνδρα εἶναι τελέως, τὸν δὲ ἀγαθὸν εὖ τε καὶ καλῶς πράττειν ἃ ἂν πράττῃ, τὸν δ' εὖ πράττοντα μακάριόν τε καὶ εὐδαίμονα εἶναι],

while the corrupt man, the one who does badly, is miserable. And this would be the one who's in the condition opposite to that of the self-controlled one, the undisciplined one whom you were praising.

31 [*Socrates*] So this is how I set down the matter, and *I say that this is true.*[435]

In the *Gorgias*, the problem of rhetoric seems to be the main subject of the dialogue as a whole. Nevertheless, rhetoric provides an opportunity to talk about justice and being good. Plato's Socrates initially recalls the distinction between the good and the pleasant and their relationship to one another: the pleasant is done for the sake of the good, and not the good for the sake of the pleasant (1–5).

The next sequence of questions and answers aims to determine what constitutes the excellence of each thing (6–15). An 'inner', 'proper' excellence of a given thing—its virtue (ἀρετή)—is considered. The good which makes us good is a certain virtue. Because the justice of the soul is a virtue, understanding justice requires understanding what a virtue is. Plato's Socrates remarks that virtue is a result of 'organization, correctness, and craftsmanship'—'τάξει καὶ ὀρθότητι καὶ τέχνῃ' (10). These three elements have to be 'fitted' to a given thing;[436] this thing may also be a soul or a part of it. A given thing requires a certain 'organization, correctness, and craftsmanship' that are proper for it.

Virtue itself is a kind of order (κόσμος). In this context, Plato's Socrates also describes it as a certain order which is proper (οἰκεῖος) for each thing (14); it is not any order in an abstract sense. In the text which follows, the word 'order'—'κόσμος'—becomes a basic description of excellence—a virtue of the soul (14, 16, 18, 20). This order—and this is what is of primary importance—makes its subject good (14).

Plato's Socrates notes also that the ordered (κοσμία) soul is moderate (σώφρων), prudent, and reasonably controls itself. At first glance, the inference from being ordered to being moderate seems not to be clear. It becomes understandable if the description of moderation (σωφροσύνη) as one of the cardinal virtues in the *Republic* is considered. Plato writes that it 'resembles a kind of harmony [ἁρμονία]';[437] it is a kind of unanimity (ὁμόνοια—oneness of mind), an accord (συμφωνία—harmonious union).[438]

In considering the connection between order (harmony) and reason in Plato's Socrates' argumentation, one has to remember the view which was commonly

435 Plato, *Gorgias*, 506c–507c, trans. Zeyl, emphasis added.

436 Plato uses 'ἀποδίδωμι'—'give back', 'restore', 'return', 'render what is due'; the same verb is to be found in the Simonides' classic description of justice invoked and analysed by Plato in the *Republic*, 331e: 'it is just to give to each what is owed to him' ('τὸ τὰ ὀφειλόμενα ἑκάστῳ ἀποδιδόναι δίκαιόν ἐστι'), trans. Grube.

437 Plato, *Republic*, 431e, trans. Grube.

438 Plato, *Republic*, 432a.

accepted by the ancient Greek philosophers,[439] that order is impossible without reason as its cause. Therefore there is no order which would not be reasonable. When the question of the inner order of the soul is considered from this point of view, then moderation is to be understood as prudence, as something reasonable. As was mentioned above, the very etymology of the Greek 'σωφροσύνη' (moderation) points to, above all, reason and not moderation understood as temperance. Order and harmony are constitutive of beauty, which is clearly attributed to the Good.[440]

Moderation as prudence is a foundation of justice in the soul as it concerns the relations between the three parts, and therefore the soul as a whole. From this perspective, it seems not to be accurate to reduce moral perfection to wisdom and to treat the analysed excerpts as an expression of ethical intellectualism, which is held to be a characteristic Socratic (and/or early-Platonic) view. In the *Republic*, moderation (σωφροσύνη) is clearly differentiated from wisdom (σοφία). The former is a certain order and harmony, while the latter is a kind of knowledge about the actions of the subject.[441] Moderation and wisdom are two essentially distinct virtues. In the analysed passage of the *Gorgias*, order is referred to as a foundation of the former.[442]

From the issue of being moderate—self-controlled—Plato's Socrates comes back to the issue of being good: 'So a self-controlled soul is a good one' ('ἡ σώφρων ψυχὴ ἀγαθή')(22). At this point, considerations summarising the teaching about justice in the soul end. In this recapitulation there are no new elements beyond those which were talked about before the Socrates' dialogue with himself began. Socrates felt compelled to speak with himself and to do 'the work of

439 Perhaps the views of the ancient atomists were an exception.

440 See e.g. Plato, *Republic*, 509a.

441 Plato, *Republic*, 428c–d.

442 Arguments in favour of ethical intellectualism that refer to the *Gorgias* (460b) are not convincing. The text reads as follows: 'Isn't a man who has learned a particular subject the sort of man his knowledge makes him?' ('ὁ μεμαθηκὼς ἕκαστα τοιοῦτός ἐστιν οἷον ἡ ἐπιστήμη ἕκαστον ἀπεργάζεται'), and: 'isn't a man who has learned what's just a just man too?' ('ὁ τὰ δίκαια μεμαθηκὼς δίκαιος'), trans. Zeyl. This passage refers first to skilfulness in a certain occupation, such as shoemaking or carpentry. In Greek, 'ἐπιστήμη' means not only 'knowledge' but also 'professional skills'; both meanings are related to 'acquaintance' with a matter. The Greek 'μανθάνω' means 'learning', not only by study, but also by practice; it means also 'acquire a habit of'. It can be argued not only from a linguistic but also from a systemic point of view that in the context analysed here 'ἐπιστήμη' means skilfulness rather than knowledge, and 'μανθάνω' means 'learning by practice' rather than 'learning by study'. In the *Republic*, Plato's Socrates, after explaining that—in truth—justice is an inner harmony in the soul, points out just actions and not learning as something 'that preserves this inner harmony and helps achieve it'; wisdom is 'the knowledge that oversees such action' (*Republic*, 443e). Cf. Legutko, *Sokrates*, p. 446; Koszkało, 'Rozwój pojęcia woli', pp. 160–161.

two'[443] and to provide the 'head' for the discussion, because the most important things had not yet been disclosed. Therefore, it should be assumed that the part following after this recapitulation is the 'head' of the discussion, where Plato's Socrates has placed the new element that is of primary importance for understanding justice. This element is composed of two statements of Socrates—numbered here as 26 and 28. What is said in 507c (statement 31) can be seen as a closing remark—as something like 'breathing out', drawing additional conclusions.

4.1.4 The 'head' of Socrates' conversation about justice

The first statement of this part of Socrates' dialogue with himself (from statement 26) links the virtue of moderation as prudence with action:

> And surely a self-controlled person would do what's appropriate with respect to both gods and human beings. For if he does what's inappropriate, he wouldn't be self-controlled.
>
> καὶ μὴν ὅ γε σώφρων τὰ προσήκοντα πράττοι ἂν καὶ περὶ θεοὺς καὶ περὶ ἀνθρώπους: οὐ γὰρ ἂν σωφρονοῖ τὰ μὴ προσήκοντα πράττων;[444]

The crucial words: 'τὰ προσήκοντα πράττοι' are translated by Donald Zeyl as 'do what's appropriate', and by Walter Lamb as 'do what is fitting' ('as regards both gods and men'). The expression 'τὰ προσήκοντα' in Hellenistic philosophy usually means 'duty', 'obligation (*officium*)', and 'τὰ προσήκοντα πράττειν' can be rendered here as 'to do one's duty', 'to fulfil an obligation'. However, the analysed expression used by Plato draws attention to the 'fit' between an action (something done) and a person.[445] This is also clearly the case when equality as a foundation of

---

443 Plato, *Gorgias*, 505d, trans. Zeyl.

444 Plato, *Gorgias*, 507a, trans. Zeyl.

445 Cf. Stauffer, *Plato's Introduction to the Question of Justice*, pp. 11–15. I agree with Stauffer that Plato begins with an exploration of ordinary opinions on justice and that these opinions are expressed in the language of duty or of obligation; I also coincide with his view that 'Plato ultimately defends a position that is in opposition to Kant's' (p. 15). However, I disagree with his claim that Plato 'begins from the same concerns and starting point as Kant' (p. 15). The methodological status of moral duties is very different for Plato than for Kant. Kant takes moral obligations as something unquestionable, a moral law which he not only regards with awe and admiration (see conclusion of Kant, *Critique of Practical Reason*, 161), but which is the data underlying his practical philosophy—the fundamental question he poses concerns the transcendental conditions of the very possibility of unconditional moral obligations. For Plato, the obligations he considers play mostly heuristic functions, they direct the focus to the good of an addressee of an action (as in the considerations of the returning of a borrowed weapon to a friend who has become mentally ill; see Plato, *Republic*, 331c) and the fundamental questions are: how one becomes a good man and what it means to be a good man. For suggestions for further reading on Plato's duty-based approach, see Stauffer, *Plato's Introduction*, p. 11 note 23.

justice is considered—this issue will be addressed below in Chapter 6. Very similar intuitions are connected with Aristotle's epikeia (τό ἐπιεκής), which is a correction of that which is based simply on being in accordance with generally formulated norms (legal justice).[446] This correction is founded on a relation of something being proper or fitting for someone, as a mean between excess and deficiency.[447]

The importance of that which is expressed by 'τὰ προσήκοντα πράττειν'—'do what's appropriate', 'do what is fitting'—is suggested by a repetition of the same view by means of its negative—'For if he does what's inappropriate, he wouldn't be self-controlled'.[448]

The next step leads to the 'peak' of Socrates' dialogue with himself(28):

> And of course if he did what's appropriate with respect to human beings, he would be doing what's just, and with respect to gods he would be doing what's pious, and one who does what's just and pious must necessarily be just andpious.
>
> καὶ μὴν περὶ μὲν ἀνθρώπους τὰ προσήκοντα πράττων δίκαι' ἂν πράττοι, περὶ δὲ θεοὺς ὅσια: τὸν δὲ τὰ δίκαια καὶ ὅσια πράττοντα ἀνάγκη δίκαιον καὶ ὅσιον εἶναι.[449]

There are several reasons to attribute a key importance to this expression. First, it appears when Socrates is in dialogue with himself and contains an answer to the most important questions posed earlier—it directly says what the justice of an action is, indicating a necessary connection between just actions and the justice of the soul.[450] Moreover, it is the last statement in the dialogue of Socrates with himself. It is also the last short one (excluding short confirmations) enunciated before the longer exposition of the conclusions (30) and the closing statement (31): 'So this is how I set down the matter, and I say that this is true'.[451] The statement 'I say that this is true' should also be taken into account in considering the importance of the analysed passage. As was demonstrated above, according to Plato's Socrates the briefness of the expression indicates both the proficiency of the speaker and addressee and the importance of what is said. The longer utterance (30) beginning

446 Aristotle, *Nicomachean Ethics*, 1137b.

447 Aristotle, *Nicomachean Ethics*, 1106a–b.

448 Plato, *Gorgias*, 507a, trans. Zeyl; Lamb translates: 'for he could not be sensible if he did what was unfitting'.

449 Plato, *Gorgias*, 507a–b, trans. Zeyl.

450 Cf. *Republic*, 443c–e; this passage, commented on extensively above (Section 3.7), in which Plato's Socrates explains what in truth justice is, ends also with a statement about the necessary connection between being just (justice in the soul) and acting in a just way: 'And if there are some other parts in between, he binds them together and becomes entirely one from many, moderate and harmonized. *Then, and only then*, he acts, if he does act in some way—either concerning the acquisition of money, or the care of the body, or something political, or concerning private contracts', trans. Bloom, emphasis added.

451 Plato, *Gorgias*, 507c, trans. Zeyl.

'Yes, and he would also necessarily be brave'[452] is addressed directly to Callicles and not to the 'second' Socrates. It is much longer than any of the previous utterances. It certainly contains important statements, but these concern not justice itself but applications and consequences of views about the justice of the soul and the justice of an action (most of all, its relations to courage and happiness are considered).

What is very interesting here is that in explaining what is crucial for shaping just action Plato's Socrates refers neither to general knowledge drawn from the world of forms (ideas) nor to generally formulated norms. The relation between an action and its addressee is in the foreground. Someone who is just acts with regard to individuals, and his actions should be 'adjusted', 'fitting', 'appropriate' to their addressee. Consequently, wisdom which is knowledge about just action must contain knowledge about individuals. It is clear that an action is formed 'in favour' of its addressee—a man or a god. It is not shaped to comply with generally formulated law, understood as a system of norms; in other words, compliance with the law is not the ultimate aim of an action in respect to its moral quality, but rather 'compliance' with the addressee of an action.

It will be argued below that this standpoint is in full accordance with Plato's teaching about the Good. This crucial issue in the conception of justice can be better understood by looking carefully at the myth of the cave from Book VII of the *Republic*, which—within the framework of a quest for understanding justice—concerns 'the effect of education and of the lack of it on our nature'.[453]

4.1.5 A difficult step in the argument and Plato's teaching on the Good

4.1.5.1 From the justice in the soul to the justice of actions

It is argued here that the goodness of an individual (his justice and his acting in a just way) and not knowledge itself (the contemplation of truth) is the primary concern of an acting individual. In the text of the *Gorgias*, there are indications that in developing the argumentation contained in Socrates' dialogue with himself Plato assumes—on the part of the listeners—some knowledge about the highest (pure) good—the Good and its relations to other beings. Before this dialogue starts, Plato makes it clear that short statements are enough only for the most profound thinkers. Socrates' dialogue with himself presented in the *Gorgias* is the finest example of concise argumentation—no wonder, as it is a conversation between the two wisest Athenians. To fully understand this argumentation it is indispensable to be aware of the knowledge which is presupposed.

What is the most difficult part of Socrates' argument? The careful reader sees a kind of gap in the transition from the summary of the teaching about the justice of

452 Plato, *Gorgias*, 507c, trans. Zeyl.
453 Plato, *Republic*, 514a, trans. Grube.

the soul (2–25) to statement about justice of acting contained in the 'head' of the discussion (26, 28). If this gap remains unfilled, then the most important assertions seem to lack a proper foundation. This argumentative step leads from the affirmation that the self-controlled (prudent) soul (σώφρων ψυχή) 'is a good one' (24)[454] to the claim that 'a self-controlled person would do what's appropriate with respect to both gods and human beings' (26).[455] The phrase 'do what's appropriate with respect to both gods and human beings' explains what 'is a good one' means. Why should this be accepted? The key word is 'good'. Knowledge about good is necessary to fill in the (alleged) argumentative gap. In the explanation of justice, the core of Plato's ontology is at stake. This is the reason why the myth of the cave—placed at the beginning of Book VII—is fundamental for understanding the justice of an individual and justice in general.

4.1.5.2 Shadows and statues of justice

The myth of the cave is about our nature in respect to education and its lack. It is introduced by Plato's Socrates saying: 'Next, I said, compare the effect of education and of the lack of it on our nature to an experience like this'.[456] It should be read, of course, also as a myth that tells us something about justice, and therefore about education and the lack thereof in the understanding or realisation of justice. There are clear signs in the myth itself indicating that questions about justice form the primary perspective for the reflection on education contained in it. When Plato's Socrates talks about returning to the cave, he points out the first disputes concerning justice. The one who returns to the cave

> behaves awkwardly and appears completely ridiculous if he's compelled, either in the courts or elsewhere, to contend about the shadows of justice or the statues of which they are the shadows and to dispute about the way these things are understood by people who have never seen justice itself.[457]

Interestingly, in these considerations of justice, it is neither abstract forms (ideas) nor general principles, but concrete actions which are considered in the courts, and that are of primary importance. The prisoners in the cave share some convictions about justice which are drawn from the observation of the shadows. These convictions are commonly accepted by the 'prisoners'. They can be identified by taking into account the conception of justice which initiated the discussion. According to this conception, as Glaucon presented it (though not being its adherent), it can be concluded that the people who have never been outside the cave

---

454 Plato, *Gorgias*, 507a, trans. Zeyl.
455 Plato, *Gorgias*, 507a, trans. Zeyl.
456 Plato, *Republic*, 514a, trans. Grube.
457 Plato, *Republic*, 517d, trans. Grube.

> say that to do injustice is naturally good and to suffer injustice bad, but that the badness of suffering it so far exceeds the goodness of doing it that those who have done and suffered injustice and tasted both, but who lack the power to do it and avoid suffering it, decide that it is profitable to come to an agreement with each other neither to do injustice nor to suffer it. As a result, they begin to make laws and covenants, and what the law commands they call lawful and just. This, they say, is the origin and essence of justice. It is intermediate between the best and the worst. The best is to do injustice without paying the penalty; the worst is to suffer it without being able to take revenge. Justice is a mean between these two extremes. People value it not as a good but because they are too weak to do injustice with impunity. Someone who has the power to do this, however, and is a true man wouldn't make an agreement with anyone not to do injustice in order not to suffer it. For him that would be madness. This is the nature of justice, according to the argument, Socrates, and these are its natural origins.[458]

These views are congruent with the Sophists' scientific approach based on sensual experience and applied to research on law and justice. One can say that according to nature 'The advantage of the stronger (...) is just',[459] as Thrasymachus claimed. Or—in the words of Callicles from the *Gorgias*—'nature itself reveals that it's a just thing for the better man and the capable man to have a greater share than the worse man and the less capable man'.[460] This Sophists' manifesto on justice as presented by Plato's Callicles[461] is a very powerful statement of a view which is consistently built on the foundations laid down by Protagoras: it is impossible to judge anything other than what one feels (one's immediate experiences).[462]

The laws and covenants made as a result of an agreement which aims to minimise the suffering of injustice by those who are unable to exercise injustice towards others are like statues which cast shadows. These agreements are concluded with a presupposition that everybody innately strives for domination, for having more than others, and that agreements limit that which is natural. People treat each other as competitors, rivals, opponents who strive for victory by conquering others, and agreements are concluded as a protection against being defeated or conquered. These views are challenged by the myth of cave.

4.1.5.3 The Good

What is the most important knowledge regarding justice obtained outside the cave? It concerns the Good. Knowledge gained 'outside the cave' concerns 'that

458 Plato, *Republic*, 358e–359b, trans. Grube.
459 Plato, *Republic*, 338c, trans. Grube.
460 Plato, *Gorgias*, 483d, trans. Zeyl.
461 Plato, *Gorgias*, 491e–492c.
462 Plato, *Theaetetus*, 167a–b.

which is and the brightest thing that is, namely the one we call the good'.[463] In the intelligible (knowable) realm, 'the form of the good is the last thing to be seen, and it is reached only with difficulty'.[464]

Already in Book VI—before the myth of the cave is set out—there is a clear statement: 'you've often heard it said that the form of the good is the most important thing to learn about and that it's by their relation to it that just things and the others become useful and beneficial [χρήσιμα καὶ ὠφέλιμα]'.[465] In Book VI the Good is also compared to the sun. Its warmth and light was commonly recognised in Greek culture to be the source of life—'the sun not only provides visible things with the power to be seen but also with coming to be, growth, and nourishment although it is not itself coming to be'.[466] If the Form of the Good in the intelligible realm is like the sun in the visible realm, then 'not only being known is present in the things known as a consequence of the good, but also existence and being [καὶ τὸ εἶναί τε καὶ τὴν οὐσίαν] are in them besides as a result of it, although the good isn't being but is still beyond being, exceeding it in dignity and power'.[467] The Form of the Good—the Good is the source of existence of everything that exists.[468]

What are the main thoughts about the Good presented in the myth of the cave in Book VII? Plato's Socrates observes that one coming out of the cave towards the sun 'is turned towards things that are more [μᾶλλον ὄντα]'.[469] According to the myth of the cave, someone who is able to look at the sun 'would infer and conclude that the sun provides the seasons and the years, governs everything in the visible world, and is in some way the cause of all the things that he uses to see'.[470]

These thoughts are repeated and developed further:

> Once one has seen it, however, one must conclude that it is the cause of all that is correct and beautiful [ὀρθῶν τε καὶ καλῶν] in anything, that it produces both light and its source in the visible realm, and that in the intelligible realm it controls and

463 Plato, *Republic*, 518c–d, trans. Grube; see Szlezák, 'The Idea of the Good', *passim*, esp. pp. 121–123.

464 Plato, *Republic*, 517c, trans. Grube; cf. idem, *Phaedrus*, 247c–d: 'without color and without shape and without solidity, a being that really is what it is, the subject of all true knowledge, visible only to intelligence', trans. Nehamas, Woodruff.

465 Plato, *Republic*, 504e–505a, trans. Grube.

466 Plato, *Republic*, 509b, trans. Grube.

467 Plato, *Republic*, 509b, trans. Bloom; Grube translates 'but their being is also due to it' and evidently misses one crucial element of the sentence, rendering 'καὶ τὸ εἶναί τε καὶ τὴν οὐσίαν' by 'their being'.

468 Cf. Plato, *Timaeus*, 68e: 'τὸ δὲ εὖ τεκταινόμενος ἐν πᾶσιν τοῖς γιγνομένοις αὐτός'—'but Himself designed the Good in all that was generated', trans. Burnet; cf. idem, *Phaedo*, 99c.

469 Plato, *Republic*, 515d, trans. Grube.

470 Plato, *Republic*, 516b–c, trans. Grube.

> provides truth and understanding [ἀλήθειαν καὶ νοῦν], so that anyone who is to act sensibly [ἐμφρόνως πράξειν] in private or public must see it.[471]

The sun, in providing the seasons and years, symbolises the provision of order and harmony by the Good, which are the foundations of being correct (just, right) and beautiful (ὀρθῶν τε καὶ καλῶν). Order and harmony are also the foundations of an inner unity and therefore of existence.

The Good controls and provides truth and understanding (ἀλήθειαν καὶ νοῦν), therefore seeing the Good is indispensable for being able to act sensibly (ἐμφρόνως—prudently, wisely) in private and in public. It is striking that no distinctions between the social classes described in the model of the hypothetical state are mentioned. One might expect that seeing the Good would be indispensable for the perfect guardians who establish laws. But this is not the case; here—seeing the Good is necessary for sensible action in private. This favours the interpretation which advocates for the versatility of a just man and for dismissing the model of the hypothetical state as a paradigm for creating a state.

The statements about the Good made in the myth of the cave point at the activity of the Good. Since having justice in the soul is being good, obtaining similarity to the Good leads to conclusions about actions which are proper for someone who is just. These are actions which are proper for someone who is good, which reveal the very nature of the Good, which is giving and caring about the existence of everything that exists.

Referring to the so-called unwritten teachings, one can find arguments in favour of identifying the Good with the One. The Good—being at the same time the One—gives existence by providing unity (order, harmony, proportion). One may observe that to obtain the theses about justice which are advocated here, there is not in fact any need to refer directly to the unwritten teachings; it suffices to read the teaching on the Good in the *Republic* together with the stories in the *Timaeus* about the Demiurge's creation of the universe. Justice in the soul, which is its goodness, is clearly linked with its inner unity, which is based on harmony and order (proportion). The unity of elements based on harmony and proportion is the foundation of the existence of every being and of the special way of existence of that which is created directly by the Demiurge.[472]

The rule applies here that the more unity something possesses the more it exists; the more order and harmony, the more unity; the more order and harmony, the more justice. The more justice, the more goodness and participation in the nature of the Good. Therefore, the more justice, the more there is action for the benefit of others.

---

471 Plato, *Republic*, 517b–c, trans. Grube.

472 See e.g. Plato, *Timaeus*, 68e; idem, *Republic*, 509b.

4.1.5.4 Education

The above analyses of the myth of the cave is focused on the 'content' of education—the most important kind of knowledge. Nevertheless, the myth of the cave also concerns the process of education itself, what education is. It turns out that the myth reveals something not about different people (souls) living in the visible realm, but about some of them coming out to the world of forms (ideas) and then returning in another incarnation into the visible world. The myth is about the elements of an individual soul, just like the story about the hypothetical state is about an individual soul and its parts, not about different people living in a state.

Of the highest importance for any interpretation of not only the myth of the cave but also the story about the hypothetical state is the statement that '*Education isn't* what some people declare it to be, namely, *putting knowledge into souls that lack it*, like putting sight into blind eyes'.[473] This negative characterisation, of what education is not, is followed by a positive description:

> But our present discussion, on the other hand, shows that the power to learn is present in everyone's soul and that the instrument with which each learns is like an eye that cannot be turned around from darkness to light without turning the whole body. This instrument cannot be turned around from that which is coming into being without *turning the whole soul* until it is able to study that which is and the brightest thing that is, namely, the one we call the good. (...) Then *education is the craft concerned with doing this very thing, this turning around, and with how the soul can most easily and effectively be made to do it*.[474]

Education (παιδεία) in its essence consists of turning around the power to learn which is present in everyone's soul (the instrument with which each learns)[475]—and this emerges when Plato's Socrates draws conclusions from the whole story about the cave. To be educated is like coming out of the cave; it is like turning around the power to learn 'from that which is coming into being'[476]—from the world of shadows experienced by our senses (what one feels), 'to study that which is and the brightest thing that is, namely, the one we call the good'.[477] The last quotation is a statement determining what the most important knowledge is about—the most important overall, which also means the most important in respect of justice—and this is the knowledge about the Good. Nevertheless, it is paramount to realise that education is not based on an individual's leaving this world—it is a process which can take place in the here and now. Coming out of the cave consists in turning the

---

473 Plato, *Republic*, 518b–c, trans. Grube, emphasis added.

474 Plato, *Republic*, 518c–d, trans. Grube, emphasis added.

475 Plato, *Republic*, 518c: 'the virtue of reason seems to belong above all to something more divine, which never loses its power', trans. Grube.

476 Plato, *Republic*, 518c, trans. Grube.

477 Plato, *Republic*, 518c–d, trans. Grube.

power to learn towards the invisible realm. Returning to the cave requires turning the power to learn towards the visible realm, but while doing it the new knowledge about that which is invisible should be preserved. Obtaining knowledge about the invisible realm is not an aim in itself. Someone who has mastered this knowledge is still far from being perfect and far from achieving happiness. This knowledge is the foundation of being just and acting justly in this life. Being just is a matter of relations between elements of the soul, and therefore it cannot be obtained only by the rational part of the soul or by learning itself. The acquired knowledge needs to be applied. Therefore, the way back to the cave is the way to the true integrity of an individual, to becoming just, and thus the way to being more; in short, the way back to the cave is the way to happiness.

Education as a means of turning the power to learn in the right direction presupposes turning the whole soul. Therefore, education engages all parts of the soul, their cooperation and unity.[478] Thus, an initial justice or dignity in the soul is presupposed as a precondition for cooperation between the different parts of the soul. There is a striking analogy here to the story about the winged chariot in the *Phaedrus*–to obtain knowledge about the invisible realm the whole soul has to travel to the top of heaven.[479]

The two aforementioned descriptions of education contained in the myth of the cave, the negative and the positive, are decisive for the rejection of interpretations according to which someone comes the 'upper world', and gives instructions and provides knowledge to uneducated people who live in the visible realm, understood as our visible world. What is more, they also give a clear indication (if not a decisive one) that the story about the hypothetical state should not be read as a story about a real state divided into three classes, where everyone has only one occupation related most of all to his ability to learn, and where the philosopher-rulers possess knowledge which is transferred to the members of an auxiliary class. In characterising courage, Plato writes about the passing on (declaring) of a 'belief about what things are to be feared' by lawgivers to the auxiliary class in the course of their education.[480] Although in the myth of the cave Plato's Socrates talks about 'putting knowledge [ἐπιστήμη] into souls that lack it'[481] and–in the description of courage–about a belief (δόξα); nevertheless, in both cases he speaks about

478 Cf. Plato, *Laws*, 689d: 'You see, my friends, without concord, how could you ever get even a glimmer of sound judgment? It's out of the question', trans. Saunders.

479 Plato, *Phaedrus*, 246d–248e.

480 'The city is courageous, then, because of a part of itself that has the power to preserve through everything its belief about what things are to be feared, namely, that they are the things and kinds of things that the lawgiver declared to be such in the course of educating it [ὁ νομοθέτης παρήγγελλεν ἐν τῇ παιδείᾳ]', Plato, *Republic*, 429b–c, trans. Grube.

481 Plato, *Republic*, 518c, trans. Grube.

education (παιδεία), and according to the myth of the cave, education should not be understood as the transfer by anyone of any 'content' to another's soul.

Therefore, coming out of the cave should be interpreted as a process which takes place inside the soul. It is also described as 'the upward journey of the soul to the intelligible realm'.[482] Such an interpretation is also favoured by an exchange of remarks between Glaucon and Socrates at the beginning of the story. After the first description of the cave and of the prisoners, Glaucon—without being asked—observes: 'It's a strange image you're describing, and strange prisoners'.[483] And Plato's Socrates responds: 'They're like us'.[484] He intends to tell a story first of all about himself and about his listeners. He searches for answers to the question of how to be good, here and in this life. There is a temptation to identify Plato's Socrates with someone who comes from an upper reality, someone who is—in the end—killed by prisoners,[485] but on the other hand, there is an explicit statement here that Socrates counts himself as one who is bound to the rocks—he is a prisoner of the cave. Plato's Socrates is—at the same time—the one who undertakes the upward journey and the one who comes back to the cave.

Support for the presented interpretation can be found in considerations about the different stages in the process of education. Only the rational part of the soul is clearly indicated as the one which undertakes the journey out of the cave when Plato's Socrates discusses the crafts involved in the first part of the process of education (arithmetic, geometry, astronomy, and music),[486] and discusses dialectic as the art of wise conversation, which is the final stage of education. Precisely, the journey out of the cave is referred to as 'dialectic'.[487] The crafts mastered during education have the power to awaken and lead upward the best part of the soul:

> Then the release from bonds and the turning around from shadows to statues and the light of the fire and, then, the way up out of the cave to the sunlight and, there, the continuing inability to look at the animals, the plants, and the light of the sun, but the newly acquired ability to look at divine images in water and shadows of the things that are, rather than, as before, merely at shadows of statues thrown by another source of light that is itself a shadow in relation to the sun—*all this business of the*

---

482 Plato, *Republic*, 517b, trans. Grube.

483 Plato, *Republic*, 515a, trans. Grube.

484 Plato, *Republic*, 515a, trans. Grube.

485 Plato, *Republic*, 517a: 'And, as for anyone who tried to free them [prisoners] and lead them upward, if they could somehow get their hands on him, wouldn't they kill him?', trans. Grube.

486 To be precise—Plato's Socrates distinguishes five crafts, counting separately the geometry which deals with two-dimensional objects and that which deals with three-dimensional objects; Plato, *Republic*, 528a–d. In the Middle Ages, arithmetic, geometry, astronomy, and music would be called the *quadrivium*, forming—after the *trivium*—the second component of the liberal arts.

487 Plato, *Republic*, 532b.

> *crafts we've mentioned has the power to awaken the best part of the soul and lead it upward to the study of the best among the things that are,* just as, before, the clearest thing in the body was led to the brightest thing in the bodily and visible realm.[488]

The principal aim of education is strictly related to the justice of the soul and to just actions—it sees the Good, while intellect (the power to learn) should be compelled to learn about the Good: 'It is our task as founders, then, to compel the best natures to reach the study we said before is the most important, namely, to make the ascent and see the good'.[489]

Consequently, coming back to the cave to help the prisoners should also be understood as a process that takes place inside the soul. Returning to the cave comprises turning the upper part of the soul—the intellect—to matters of the spirited and appetitive parts. This is the way to become internally integrated, to obtain justice in the soul and—finally—to act in a truly just way, and it means never harming anybody and acting in a way that is beneficial for the addressee of an action. The latter is recognised not to be a rival who has to be conquered, but as a friend. The true nature of justice, which can be recognised only beyond sensual experience, is linked not with competition but with cooperation.

This way down is, for the intellect, something incongruent with its nature. When Plato's Socrates remarks that the ones who get to the contemplation of the Good 'are unwilling to occupy themselves with human affairs and that their souls are always pressing upwards, eager to spend their time above',[490] he means that the intellectual part is by its own nature directed to purely theoretical studies concerning that which is 'divine study',[491] and that the intellectual part is reluctant to occupy itself with affairs which are the proper subjects of the lower parts of the soul, especially of the appetitive one. The question why caring about justice is more perfect than contemplating truth will be considered in a more detailed way in Section 7.2;[492] nevertheless, the direction of argumentation is already visible—justice is a perfection in the existential aspect of the soul; it is the perfection of all perfections, since it provides existence for all the other perfections (virtues).

One more thing should be noted here. This turning of the intellect towards the intelligible realm in order to shape one's own actions is not a once-in-a-lifetime undertaking. It should be repeated over and over again. Describing the outlining of the constitution by philosophers in the hypothetical state, Plato's Socrates says:

> After that, I suppose that in filling out their work they would look away frequently in both directions, toward the just, fair, and moderate by nature and everything of the

488 Plato, *Republic*, 532b–d, trans. Grube, emphasis added.
489 Plato, *Republic*, 519c, trans. Grube.
490 Plato, *Republic*, 517c, trans. Grube.
491 Plato, *Republic*, 517d, trans. Grube.
492 For more standard interpretations of coming back to the cave, see e.g. Smith, 'Return to the cave', *passim*.

> sort, and, again, toward what is in human beings; and thus, mixing and blending the practices as ingredients, they would produce the image of man.[493]

This understanding of the place of looking at the intelligible in the process of shaping one's actions is quite strong evidence that the myth of the cave should be read primarily, if not exclusively, as pertaining to processes which can take place in the here and now, the processes of education, of obtaining the knowledge which is necessary for being just and acting justly.

4.1.5.5 Reconsidering the difficulties in the argumentation in the Gorgias

From the point of view of the conception of justice, the lesson learned from the myth of the cave is at least twofold. First, it concerns the way out of and back to the cave—the indispensability of turning the intellect from that which is based on what one feels to the truths which go beyond what is sensual, and the indispensability of turning the intellect with its knowledge back to matters which are proper for the lower parts of the soul. Second, the lesson concerns the most important content of knowledge about *what is*, especially in reference to the Good. This knowledge is crucial for understanding justice, because justice essentially contributes to the goodness of an individual and his actions.

If the dialogue of Socrates with himself is interpreted in the light of the teaching contained in the myth of the cave, the gap in the argumentation, the transition from statements about justice of the soul to conclusions about justice of action, has now been filled in. By providing order and harmony, the Good gives beauty and unity, and therefore existence. The better someone is, the more he is just, then the more inner unity he has, and therefore the more he exists. The more someone exists, the more he lives. Life is the foremost function of the soul—'the work of the soul [ψυχῆς ἔργον]'.[494] The better the soul is (meaning the more just it is), the better the soul accomplishes the functions which are proper to it—this was clearly stated in the *Republic* when preparations were being made for the discussions of justice—'taking care of things, ruling, deliberating, and the like'.[495] Finally, one can observe that the better someone is, the more he resembles the Good itself. Consequently, his actions resemble actions which are proper to the Good. Therefore, from a systemic point of view, someone who has justice in his soul tends—by the very nature of being just—to seek the benefit of others, to provide—as far as is possible—order, beauty, life and existence. In other words: he does what fits the addressee of his action, what is appropriate. On the one hand, 'it is never just to harm anyone';[496] on the other, justice makes good not only someone

493 Plato, *Republic*, 501b, trans. Bloom.
494 Plato, *Republic*, 353d, trans. Grube.
495 Plato, *Republic*, 353d, trans. Grube.
496 Plato, *Republic*, 335e, trans. Grube.

who is just, but also the addressee of just actions.[497] Since justice is an existential excellence based on an internal unity, then the internal unity, this 'being more', of the addressee of an action is a criterion for the quality of the action—it is just if it fits this internal unity (does not diminish it or contribute to it).

This is the first and most important challenge for the shadows and statues of justice in the cave; this challenges the presuppositions which underlie—like in Plato's Callicles' approach—the conception of justice developed by the intellect (the power to learn) on the basis of sensual experiences. Callicles has a brilliant mind, but his power to learn has not been turned in the right direction. From the perspective of the knowledge obtained in the invisible realm, it is not naturally just that everyone seeks his own profits and subdues others, or that laws and contracts serve to restrict the most powerful individuals, thus defending the majority, who are weaker. Quite the opposite is true. But to discover this, it is necessary to go beyond sensual experience—to turn around the intellect to that which is invisible and to apply knowledge to human actions.

The moral perfection of an individual, which is an excellence *per se* and not in some aspect of life, is placed by Plato on the level of existence (to be) and not on the level of possessions (to have). This explains how it is possible to lose possessions, time, health, and even one's own life (this happens when someone tries to avoid harming others and do what is profitable for them) and—at the same time—still benefit. Put simply: 'you have less but you are more'.

The last pronouncement of Plato's Socrates which treats the subject under discussion (30) directly is considerably longer, and therefore, does not fit the postulate of concise speaking, which was followed in the core of the discussion of Socrates with himself. It is addressed directly to Callicles and not to the 'second Socrates'. It repeats the main steps of the argumentation. First, justice and moderation as prudence are linked with courage. Someone who acts justly

> would also necessarily be brave, for it's not like a self-controlled man to either pursue or avoid what isn't appropriate, but to avoid and pursue what he should, whether these are things to do, or people, or pleasures and pains, and to stand fast and endure them where he should.[498]

Then, a very short summary of the next major steps in the argument is provided:

(a) because he is just and brave and pious, he is a completely good man;
(b) because he is a completely good man, he does well and admirably whatever he does;
(c) because he does well, he is blessed and happy (μακάριόν τε καὶ εὐδαίμονα).[499]

497 Plato, *Republic*, 335a–e.
498 Plato, *Gorgias*, 507c, trans. Zeyl.
499 Cf. Plato, *Gorgias*, 507c.

The argument is brought to a close with a contrasting comparison between a just man and an undisciplined man who (a') is corrupt, (b') does badly, and (c') is miserable.[500]

This résumé confirms that such a conception of good is crucial for understanding justice and for establishing a link between being just and acting in a just way. It should also be stressed that not being just, not the 'possession' of justice, but acting justly is the direct foundation of being blessed and happy. This issue will be addressed further below.

The very last sentence (31) is already on the level of meta-language. Plato's Socrates talks about that which has been said: 'this is how I set down the matter, and I say that this is true'.[501] It should be noted that it is quite exceptional in Plato's writing that his Socrates makes direct statements qualifying certain pronouncements as true.

4.1.6 Further applications

In the text which follows the dialogue of Socrates with himself, conclusions are drawn related to the aims which should be pursued. Firstly, 'a person who wants to be happy must evidently pursue and practice self-control [moderation as prudence]'.[502] The justice and moderation of an individual become the primary ends of personal and public life:

> This is the target which I think one should look to in living, and in his actions he should direct all of his own affairs and those of his city to the end that justice and self-control will be present in one who is to be blessed.[503]

Directly afterwards he presents an undisciplined person as a marauder who 'could not be dear to another man or to a god, for he cannot be a partner, and where there's no partnership there's no friendship'.[504] It is very interesting that already in the formulation of the major conclusions in the *Gorgias*, while talking about the ends of personal as well as of public life, Plato links happiness (being blessed) with friendship, as he does in our leitmotif from the *Laws*: 'The whole point of our legislation was to allow the citizens to live supremely happy lives in the greatest possible mutual friendship'.[505]

The conclusions reached in the dialogue of Socrates with himself are also applied directly to the other issues pursued earlier in the *Gorgias*. Thus, someone who has done something unjust to free himself from his misery should be his own

---

500 Cf. Plato, *Gorgias*, 507c.
501 Plato, *Gorgias*, 507c, trans. Zeyl.
502 Plato, *Gorgias*, 507c–d, trans. Zeyl.
503 Plato, *Gorgias*, 507d–e, trans. Zeyl.
504 Plato, *Gorgias*, 507e, trans. Zeyl.
505 Plato, *Laws*, 743c, trans. Saunders.

accuser and should use the art of oratory for this very purpose:[506] 'doing what's unjust is as much worse than suffering it as it is more shameful, and (...) a person who is to be an orator the right way should be just and be knowledgeable in what is just'.[507]

Further on, the objections formulated earlier by Callicles are analysed,[508] and the *Gorgias* as a whole is concluded with a myth about judgment and life after earthly death. A similar conclusion is to be found in the *Republic*, which ends with the myth of Er.

4.2 Negative and positive characteristics of just actions

4.2.1 The harm principle

The characteristics of just actions follow from the considerations about the Good. These characteristics can be described in a negative or a positive way. Firstly, a 'harm principle' is formulated. This principle applies independently of the wrongs caused by someone. In the *Crito* Plato's Socrates states: 'One should never do wrong in return, nor do any man harm, no matter what he may have done to you'.[509] This is clearly connected with justice. In the *Republic*, not harming anyone is indicated as the proper action of someone who is just—'it isn't the function of a just person to harm a friend or anyone else, rather it is the function of his opposite, an unjust person',[510] and it is linked with justice in general—'it is never just to harm anyone'.[511]

The principle of not harming anyone is a universal principle and—it needs to be stressed—all are equal in respect to its application. The contexts of the above quotations, both in the *Crito* and in the *Republic*, clearly indicate that this harm principle includes even actions addressed towards enemies. This teaching goes clearly against views which were dominant in Plato's times, and certainly not only then. As Kenneth J. Dover writes, 'It was not the Athenian custom to disguise hatred, (...) successful retaliation was a joy, and failure a horror; a man might be respected for attempting revenge and denigrated for making no attempt'.[512]

---

506 Plato, *Gorgias*, 508b.

507 Plato, *Gorgias*, 508c, trans. Zeyl.

508 The structure is similar to that of an article (*articulus*) which was used by scholars in mediaeval times: it started with doubts (*dubitatio*) and objections, with the statement of the author's position (*corpus*), and closed with responses to the objections.

509 Plato, *Crito*, 49c, trans. Grube.

510 Plato, *Republic*, 335d, trans. Grube.

511 'οὐδαμοῦ γὰρ δίκαιον οὐδένα ἡμῖν ἐφάνη ὂν βλάπτειν', Plato, *Republic*, 335e, trans. Grube.

512 Dover, *Greek Popular Morality*, p. 182.

Not harming others who are weaker becomes, for Plato, a test of being genuinely just. In the *Laws*, slaves too are explicitly mentioned:

> The best way to train slaves is to refrain from arrogantly ill-treating them, and *to harm them even less* (assuming that's possible) than you would your equals. You see, when a man can hurt someone as often as he likes, he'll soon show whether or not his respect for justice is natural and unfeigned and springs from a genuine hatred of injustice. If his attitude to his slaves and his conduct towards them are free of any taint of impiety and injustice, he'll be splendidly *effective at sowing the seeds of virtue*. Just the same can be said of the way in which any master or dictator or person in any position of authority deals with someone weaker than himself.[513]

This quotation confirms the conclusions reached in the analysis of the Demiurge's speech in the *Timaeus*. All human beings, including slaves, should be treated as aims in themselves. The postulate of not harming is justified by the individual development of a slave, and this is development of that which is most important—of moral qualities: a master who does not harm his slaves 'will be splendidly effective at sowing the seeds of virtue'.[514]

One may say that there is already present here a preferential attitude towards the poor and vulnerable. It is visible in the above statements on how to treat slaves. This preference is clearly visible in the *Laws* where the treatment of orphans is concerned. For example, a regulation is advocated that 'if a man (...) harms a child deprived of its father or mother, he must pay double the damages that he would have to pay for a crime committed against a child with both parents living'.[515]

The issue of not harming is addressed in the introductory part of the *Republic*, in the short exchange of words between Socrates and the elderly Cephalus, who in his old age is more devoted to religious matters than to philosophical disputes. Talking about the greatest benefits which can be drawn from having money, he explains what most worries a man who approaches the end of his life:

> If he finds many injustices in his life, he awakes from sleep in terror, as children do, and lives in anticipation of bad things to come. But someone who knows that he hasn't been unjust has sweet good hope as his constant companion—a nurse to his old age.[516]

According to Cephalus, wealth is beneficial to sensible and decent people:

> Wealth can do a lot to save us from having to cheat or deceive someone against our will and from having to depart for that other place in fear because we owe sacrifice

513 Plato, *Laws*, 777d–e, trans. Saunders, emphasis added. Cf. idem, *Republic*, 590c–d: 'It isn't to harm the slave that we say he must be ruled', trans. Grube.

514 Plato, *Laws*, 777e, trans. Saunders.

515 Plato, *Laws*, 927d, trans. Saunders; cf. ibid., 926c–928d.

516 Plato, *Republic*, 330e–331a, trans. Grube.

> to a god or money to a person. It has many other uses, but, benefit for benefit, I'd say that this is how it is most useful to a man of any understanding.[517]

It is worth noting that Cephalus does not worry about the laws he has broken, the obligations he has failed to fulfil or having acted against justice in general. He is concerned about harm inflicted on an individual man or about not giving something which was owed to a god. Typically, harming others hits at something that one justly possesses in a broad sense of the word. A catalogue of severely unjust acts which cause harm to others is to be found in the *Apology*, for example, in Plato's Socrates' speech defending himself before the court. The acts referred to include killing, banishing or disfranchising an innocent man.[518]

Inflicting harm on others is something opposed to what is proper for the action of the Good (the Form of the Good). The badness, the ugliness of injustice is most obvious in relation not to the addressee of an action but—far more—to the subject of an unjust action. Doing wrong should be shunned more than suffering from it—this is one of the major conclusions of the *Gorgias*: 'among so many arguments this one alone survives refutation and remains steady: that doing what's unjust is more to be guarded against than suffering it'.[519] To harm someone is much worse than to be harmed: 'to commit any unjust act at all against me and my possessions is both worse and more shameful for the one who does these unjust acts than it is for me, the one who suffers them'.[520] By harming someone the violator at the same time hurts himself—he is injured in his very existence, which is his first and most fundamental excellence. Harming others concerns one's possessions, something that one has, harming oneself by unjust action results in injustice of the soul; it undermines inner unity and therefore concerns the being itself, the excellence of existence.

The harming of oneself by causing injustice in one's own soul is something that can be done only by the subject of an action. If someone has mastered justice, nobody is able to make him unjust—as Plato's Socrates states in his apology: 'I do not think it is permitted that a better man be harmed by a worse'.[521] Nevertheless, Plato does not exclude in principle the possibility that someone may dispose or even impel someone else to unjust actions or make someone else worse in a moral sense. Since the inner unity of the parts of the soul is immune to direct interference from the 'outside', negative influence has to be understood as being indirect, although very dangerous. In the *Republic* there is an indication that this may be done by a tyrant or—more generally—a man with a tyrannical character: 'he is extremely unfortunate and goes on to make those near him like himself'.[522]

517 Plato, *Republic*, 331b, trans. Grube.
518 Plato, *Apology*, 30d, trans. Grube.
519 Plato, *Gorgias*, 527b, trans. Zeyl; see Pawłowski, 'Zasada "niekrzywdzenia" ', *passim*.
520 Plato, *Gorgias*, 508e, trans. Zeyl.
521 Plato, *Apology*, 30d, trans. Grube; Fowler translates: 'I believe it is not God's will that a better man be injured by a worse'.
522 Plato, *Republic*, 580a, trans. Grube.

The Athenian in the *Laws*, summarising the standpoint developed in the discussion, talks about the possibility that the whole political system corrupts those who are ruled.[523] In such situations Plato's Athenian admits extremely radical remedies:

> Rather than have the state tolerate the yoke of slavery and be ruled by unworthy hands, it may by absolutely necessary to allow it to be destroyed, or abandon it by going into exile. All that sort of hardship we simply have to endure rather than permit a change to the sort of political system which will make men worse.[524]

It is evident that the harm principle formulated by Plato pertains to individuals and not the state.

4.2.2 Just actions as something beneficial for others

The negative characterisation of just actions as actions which do not inflict harm certainly takes priority over a positive characterisation. Nevertheless, taking into account Plato's Socrates' description of just actions and their systemic context, which includes Plato's teaching about the Good, the positive characteristics of just actions should not be overlooked.

The discussion of Plato's Socrates with himself in the *Gorgias* led to the conclusion that doing what is appropriate with respect to human beings is doing what is just, doing what is appropriate with respect to the gods is doing what is pious,[525] and doing what is appropriate means doing that which 'fits', that which is 'in accordance' with an addressee. It is worth noting that—in agreement with the analysis of the Demiurge's speech in the *Timaeus*—men and gods are also considered in the *Gorgias* as special addresses of actions. They should be treated as aims in themselves. The description of just action in the *Gorgias* confirms their special status.

Everyone who acts towards men and gods, as far as he is good, resembles in his action the Good—the Demiurge himself. Therefore, one cannot act to destroy them or even wish them destroyed, and this is expressed in the principle which forbids harming anyone.

Not harming does not fully exhaust 'what fits'. Thus, moreover, like the Good itself, which gives life and existence, a just man in his action seeks the benefit of the addressee of this action. Already in Book I of the *Republic*, Plato's Socrates addresses the question of what it means to rule and to be a genuine ruler, arguing against Thrasymachus' view that justice is the advantage of the stronger.[526] A genuine ruler is a just ruler. In the first recapitulation of the argument, Plato's Socrates states:

523 Plato, *Laws*, 770e, trans. Saunders.
524 Plato, *Laws*, 770e, trans. Saunders.
525 Plato, *Gorgias*, 507b.
526 Plato, *Republic*, 339b–347e.

> no one in any position of rule, insofar as he is a ruler, seeks or orders what is advantageous to himself, but what is advantageous to his subject, that on which he practices his craft. It is to his subject and what is advantageous and proper to it that he looks, and everything he says and does he says and does for it.[527]

Plato here describes the ruler's action as doing 'what is advantageous and proper [συμφέρον καὶ πρέπον]'. The meaning of the Greek words 'συμφέρον' and 'πρέπον' is similar to the meaning of the expression 'τὰ προσήκοντα' used in the Gorgias and translated as 'what is appropriate', the meaning of which also includes 'being fitted' to the addressee of an action. The word 'συμφέρον', rendered in the quotation as 'advantageous', means also 'useful', 'expedient', 'fitting'. Similar intuitions are expressed by 'πρέπον'—'proper'—which can be understood as 'conspicuously fitting', 'seemly', or 'suitable'.[528]

In the *Republic* there is a number of descriptions which Thrasymachus forbids Socrates from using as descriptions of what is just. Socrates protests against this prohibition,[529] and therefore, one can conclude that precisely those descriptions are regarded by Plato as proper for a characterisation of just actions. Besides the aforementioned 'συμφέρον', these include: 'δέον'—'needful', 'which ought to be', 'binding'; 'ὠφέλιμον'—'beneficial', 'useful', 'helping', 'serviceable'; 'λυσιτελοῦν'—'profitable'; and 'κερδαλέον'—'gainful'.[530] This is another example of Plato's using several different words to explain a given notion or reality.[531] Nevertheless, it is certain that the leading intuition links justice, first and foremost, with the beneficial, with the useful. A duty is secondary to being beneficial, the beneficial is not established as secondary to the content of a duty expressed in a norm; a norm only expresses what is beneficial.

It is in the mouth of Thrasymachus, who—seemingly ironically—refers to a commonly accepted opinion about justice, that Plato places the description of justice and of the just which he actually shares himself[532] and which will be

527 Plato, *Republic*, 342e, trans. Grube.

528 Shorey renders 'πρέπον' as 'suitable'.

529 Plato, *Republic*, 337d.

530 Plato, *Republic*, 336c–d: 'καὶ ὅπως μοι μὴ ἐρεῖς ὅτι τὸν δέον ἐστὶν μηδ' ὅτι τὸ ὠφέλιμον μηδ' ὅτι τὸ λυσιτελοῦν μηδ' ὅτι τὸ κερδαλέον μηδ' ὅτι τὸ συμφέρον'—'And don't tell me that it's the right, the beneficial, the profitable, the gainful, or the advantageous', trans. Grube.

531 Language is only a means to discuss reality; cf. Plato, *Republic*, 533d–e, trans. Grube: 'we won't dispute about a name when we have so many more important matters to investigate'.

532 Thrasymachus is an excellent debater. He uses an elenctic argument himself—which is considered a typical Socratic argument: first he accepts the description of justice accepted by Socrates, and then he aims at conclusions which expose the (alleged) limitations of such a description.

paradigmatic for centuries to come: 'justice [and the just] is really the good of another'.[533] And this time the word 'ἀγαθόν'—'the good' is applied as a description of what is beneficial or useful.

Developing his argumentation, Plato's Socrates compares a genuine ruler with a shepherd and ruling as shepherding. He observes that 'Shepherding is concerned only to provide what is best for that which it is set over, and it is itself adequately provided with all it needs to be at its best when it doesn't fall short in any way of being the craft of shepherding'.[534] In the case of rulers, 'their ruling will benefit not themselves but their subjects'.[535] And where ruling is concerned 'no craft or rule provides for its own advantage, but (...) it provides and orders for its subject and aims at its advantage, that of the weaker, not of the stronger'.[536] Here, in the positive aspect of acting justly, the preferential treatment of the weaker comes to the fore.

Plato's conception of justice makes it possible to explain something which—at first glance—seems paradoxical. Since justice is the good of another, then someone acting justly has to lose something good, which becomes the good of another. How is it possible that the doer of just actions becomes good himself? The answer proposed by Plato leads to a fundamental philosophical distinction between being and having. A just man—although doing what is beneficial for another—loses to some extent what he has, his possessions, his time, his health or even his life, but he benefits himself in his first and most excellent perfection, in his existence—he exists more strongly. Just actions contribute to the justice which is in the soul and which—as an inner harmony—establishes an inner unity of the soul that is the foundation of existence. A just man exists more, even though he has less if he lost his possessions while acting for others.

There is also a systemic philosophical explanation as to why just actions are essentially those which are beneficial for others. It is provided by the teaching about the Good, which—by its nature—gives existence and all excellences to everything that exists—*bonum est diffusivum sui* ('the good is diffusive of itself', 'the good tends to spread'.) Giving existence is giving unity, and the Good is the only 'thing' which is absolutely simple and one in itself. By being just, a person converges towards the Good, and by the nature of being good, he acts to the benefit of others.

---

533 'ἡ μὲν δικαιοσύνη καὶ τὸ δίκαιον ἀλλότριον ἀγαθὸν τῷ ὄντι', Plato, *Republic*, 343c, trans. Grube. Cf. Aristotle, *Nicomachean Ethics*, 1130a, trans. Rackham: 'Justice alone of the virtues is "the good of others", because it does what is for the advantage of another' ('ἀλλότριον ἀγαθὸν δοκεῖ εἶναι ἡ δικαιοσύνη μόνη τῶν ἀρετῶν, ὅτι πρὸς ἕτερόν ἐστιν· ἄλλῳ γὰρ τὰ συμφέροντα πράττει'); cf. ibid., 1134b.

534 Plato, *Republic*, 345c–d, trans. Grube.

535 Plato, *Republic*, 345e, trans. Grube.

536 Plato, *Republic*, 346e, trans. Grube.

This is also confirmed by Plato's approach to piety and being pious. Accepting that doing 'what's appropriate (...) with respect to gods' is 'doing what's pious',[537] it should be noted that in the case of a god to harm him or to do something beneficial for him is practically impossible. As Vlastos writes in the conclusion of his analyses of piety in the *Euthyphro*, a god,

> being already perfect, does not require from us any contribution to his own well-being but only asks each of us to do for the other persons what he would be doing for them himself if he were to change places with us.[538]

And if he were to change places with us, he would do what is advantageous for others. Plato's Socrates practises piety by 'doing god's work on god's behalf to benefit his fellow townsmen'.[539] In human acting, if the shape of actions is considered, practising piety based on respect towards god (gods) turns out to be undistinguishable from practising justice.

Summing up, just actions are understood as being opposite to those which are harmful. The first characterisation of just actions focuses on not inflicting harm, but—especially when the systemic context established by the teaching about the good is taken into account—just actions are also those which are beneficial to others in the sense that they contribute to strengthening the existence, the inner unity, of their addressees.[540]

537 Plato, *Gorgias*, 507b (28), trans. Zeyl.

538 Vlastos, 'Socratic Piety', p. 76.

539 Vlastos, 'Socratic Piety', p. 76; Weiss, *Philosophers in the Republic*, pp. 129–163.

540 Plato, *Republic*, 457b: 'it is and always will be the finest saying that the beneficial is beautiful, while the harmful is ugly', trans. Grube. Cf. Weiss, *Philosophers in the Republic*, p. 10: 'it is up to us, Plato's readers, to recognize that it is justice's unselfishness, the fact that it is concerned for others, that makes it the primary virtue, the "power" that anchors all the others, both producing and preserving them (4.433b–c). It may be salutary for Glaucon and Adeimantus to confuse justice with moderation, but it is not good for us. We must see that there is beauty—nobility—in being concerned for others'.

5 Justice of the law and justice of the state

5.1 Foundations

Both the state and the law as its foundation are good if they realise the aims which are proper for them. Plato's writings indicate the priority of the individual over the state; in his late dialogue the *Laws*, he makes explicit pronouncements regarding the aims of legislation: 'The whole point of our legislation was to allow the citizens to live supremely happy lives in the greatest possible mutual friendship'.[541]

There are two principal aims of law—the happiness of the citizens and friendship between them. Friendship is strictly connected with equality, and these issues will be considered in Chapter 6. Consequently, friendship and equality are also aims of the state which creates and implements the laws.

If one takes into account that—according to the Demiurge's speech in the *Timaeus*—being someone whose existence is continuously willed, being an object of continuous care, has an inherent basis, a special unity established by an inner beautiful harmony and being in fine condition, and that this is due to its having been created directly by the Demiurge himself, it is striking that Plato nowhere in his writings mentions that the state as such or some essential element of it was created directly by the Demiurge. Neither does he speak of an inherent, ontic excellence of the state comparable to the excellence possessed by beings created directly by the Demiurge. A state as such is not desired by the Demiurge for its own sake. One can say that a state, in comparison to a human being (soul), is only a phantom (εἴδωλον) of being.[542] One of the consequences of being created directly by the Demiurge or of possessing the special innate excellence typical of gods and human souls (or their elements) is their continuing existence. Plato does not ascribe continuing existence to any state. On the contrary, the state's existence is clearly subordinated to the realisation of certain aims, which justifies the existence of the state. If these aims are not realised, the reason for the state's existence disappears. The state, like the law, serves the individual in achieving fulfilment. In a speech addressed to law-'givers' and law-'guardians', Plato's Athenian (together with Megillus and Clinias) states:

> Colleagues and protectors of our laws, we shall—inevitably—leave a great many gasps in every section of our code. However, we shall certainly take care to outline a sort of sketch of the complete system with its main points, and it will be your job to take this sketch and fill in the details. You ought to hear what your aims should be when you do this. (…) The central point to which we agree amounted to this.

541 Plato, *Laws*, 743c, trans. Saunders.

542 Speaking in the language of Aristotle—the state is not a substance but an accidence; it has only relational being and does not exist in itself.

> 'Our aim in life should be goodness and the spiritual virtue appropriate to mankind. (...) Whatever the mean, it's this aim we've described that we must all strain every muscle to achieve throughout our lives. No man, whoever he is, should ever be found valuing anything else, if it impedes his progress—not even, in the last resort, the state. *Rather than have the state tolerate the yoke of slavery and be ruled by unworthy hands, it may be absolutely necessary to allow it to be destroyed, or abandon it by going into exile. All that sort of hardship we simply have to endure* rather than permit a change to the sort of political system which make men worse.'[543]

The weight of these assessments should be appreciated bearing in mind the significance of the city-state in Greek culture for constituting the personal identity of its citizens. Here Plato's Athenian states directly that there are situations in which it is better for a state to be destroyed or it is better to go into exile.[544]

Continuing his speech, Plato's Athenian highlights the criteria for judging laws as good or bad. They are formulated as a consequence of accepting happiness, which consists of the inner, moral development of an individual, as the first aim of laws:

> This, then, is the agreed statement; now it's up to you to consider this double aim of ours and censure the laws that can do nothing to help us; but you must commend and welcome the effective ones with enthusiasm, and cheerfully live as they dictate. You must have no truck with other pursuits which aim at different 'good' (as people call them).[545]

---

543 Plato, *Laws*, 770c–e, trans. Saunders; the quotation marks are in the translation, emphasis added. It should be mentioned that the wording of the source in Greek is obscure and incomplete enough to be differently amended and translated (see Plato, *The Laws of Plato*, ed. England, vol. 1, pp. 601–602). Bury translates 'ἀνάστατον' as 'allow it to be revolutionized'. It is hard to accept as accurate the Renaissance translation by Marsilio Ficino, which fits well to a totalitarian interpretation of Plato's writings: 'Pro patria praeterea, si necesse sit, mori paratus sit antequam velit aut eversam videre civitatem iugoque servitutis subiectam a peioribus gubernari, aut fuga ipsam deserere' (*The Laws of Plato*, ed. England, vol. 1, p. 602). Ficino's text is followed by the 19th-century translation of Burges: 'he will at length even die for a state, rather than be willing to support the yoke of slavery, should there appear a necessity for it to be overthrown, and to be under the rule of worse men, or to quit it a not-state by flight', Plato, *The Laws*, in: *The Works of Plato: A New and Literal Version*, ed. Burges, London (1852), vol. V, p. 222; Ficino uses a Greek manuscript which has not been preserved to modern times; see Zygmuntowicz, *Praktyka polityczna*, p. 19. The dignitarian interpretation of Plato entirely accords with Saunders' translation (there is no talk about dying for the country).

544 Looking back on the Nazi state and the Holocaust, this statement seems strikingly current.

545 Plato, *Laws*, 770e–771a, trans. Saunders

In these fundamental issues related to the principal aims of laws, there is no significant change in Plato's views in comparison with his earlier works.[546] Similar views can easily be found in other dialogues if they are read without the prejudice that Plato develops a totalitarian project. When the phantoms of justice are put in their proper place, evidence of the recognition of the individual as the aim of the law and state stands out. For example, acknowledgment of the subordination of the state to the good of the individual is visible in the description of politics in the *Gorgias*, which certainly does not belong to the late dialogues. Politics is 'for the soul'.[547] It is a craft which aims not at the good of the state, but at the good of an individual soul—its fitness and health. One part of politics, namely legislation, is for healthy souls and makes them fit; the other part—penal justice—is a kind of medicine for souls. These two elements of politics 'always provide care (...) for the soul, with a view to what's best'.[548]

To the above quoted excerpt about the aims of laws, there is a corresponding passage in the *Gorgias* where Plato's Socrates addresses Callicles:

> But it's not for love of winning that I'm asking you. It's rather because I really do want to know the way, whatever it is, in which you suppose the city's business ought to be conducted among us. Now that you've advanced to the business of the city, are we to conclude that you're devoted to some objective other than *that we, the citizens, should be as good as possible*? Haven't we agreed many times already that this is what a man active in politics should be doing? Have we or haven't we? Please answer me. Yes we have. (I'll answer for you.)[549]

There is a certain forcefulness in Plato's Socrates' voice. As in his dialogue with himself, though on a smaller scale, he answers his own question. The insistent 'Please answer me' is the translation of ἀποκρίνου—it could also be translated simply as 'answer!' The same word was used in courts, meaning 'answer charges', 'defend oneself'.

Slightly earlier, Plato's Socrates remarks:

> Shouldn't we then attempt to care for the city and its citizens with the aim of making the citizens themselves as good as possible? For without this, as we discovered earlier, it does no good to provide any other service if the intentions of those who are likely to make a great deal of money or take a position of rule over people or some other position of power aren't admirable and good.[550]

Being as good as possible means being just. It is worth noting that the justice of an individual is mentioned here in relation to other activities performed by an

546 Cf. Sieroń, *Status jednostki i państwa w greckiej* πόλις, p. 119.
547 Plato, *Gorgias*, 464b, trans. Zeyl.
548 Plato, *Gorgias*, 464c, trans. Zeyl.
549 Plato, *Gorgias*, 515b–c, trans. Zeyl, emphasis added.
550 Plato, *Gorgias*, 513e–514a, trans. Zeyl.

individual, like making money and taking a position of rule over people, and not in relation to the state.

All affairs, both of private life and—clearly—of the state as well, should serve the acquisition of justice by an individual:

> This is the target which I think one should look to in living, and in his actions he should direct all of his own affairs and those of his city to the end that justice and self-control will be present in one who is to be blessed.[551]

The *Gorgias* finishes with an encouragement:

> So let's use the account that has now been disclosed to us as our guide, one that indicates to us that this way of life is the best, to practice justice and the rest of excellence both in life and in death. Let us follow it, then, and call on others to do so, too (...).[552]

Justice as the excellence of an individual, and not of a state, is what is meant here. There is no mention of any state at all. Of course, sacrificing one's own life for a state can be a deed of justice, and usually is, but its worth is rooted in its benefiting not the state itself, but its citizens.

In the *Republic*, if one approaches the problem from a systematic perspective, the primacy of the individual becomes clear. Plato does not question the statements which open his story about the hypothetical state and which clearly indicate the instrumental value of the state, which is created for the sake of men. Plato's Socrates begins building his model of a hypothetical state with the remark that 'a city comes to be because none of us is self-sufficient, but we all need many things', and he asks rhetorically: 'Do you think that a city is founded on any other principle?'[553] To the quoted description of the aims of laws from the *Laws*, which are happiness and friendship,[554] corresponds the description of what the state is, which precedes the consideration of the hypothetical state in the *Republic*:

> And because people need many things, and because one person calls on a second out of one need and on a third out of a different need, many people gather in a single place to live together as partners and helpers. And such a settlement is called a city.[555]

People help each other in their needs, and the aim is not to create the state as an entity possessing an aim independent of the aims (benefits) of its citizens. Moreover, it is not the state which is meant to fulfil the needs of its citizens, but the citizens themselves.

---

551 Plato, *Gorgias*, 507d, trans. Zeyl.
552 Plato, *Gorgias*, 527e, trans. Zeyl.
553 Plato, *Republic*, 369b, trans. Grube.
554 Plato, *Laws*, 743c.
555 Plato, *Republic*, 369b–c, trans. Grube.

Visible here is an anticipation of the principle of subsidiarity.[556] It guards the autonomy of individuals, families, and smaller communities against interference from higher organisations.[557] The effectiveness of the social structures formed in accordance with this principle is certainly an important argument for its implementation. Plato also provides a moral justification based on his conception of justice.[558] It is the individual who should resemble the Good and act to benefit others. The state ought to help in maximising the realisation of this aim in a given society, and thus the state must not obstruct an individual in acting to benefit others. If it unnecessarily takes the place of the individual in acting for the benefit of others, it deprives him of the opportunity to contribute to his own moral development (to act justly and to become more just).

5.2 The wisdom and freedom to shape one's life and Plato's alleged totalitarianism

5.2.1 Converging arguments against Plato's totalitarianism

The Spell of Plato, the first volume of Popper's *The Open Society and Its Enemies*, is probably the most prominent and certainly the most influential elaboration of Plato's work that directly accuses Plato of laying down the foundations of totalitarian ideology. The debate over this interpretation has a long history, and there

556 This principle, nowadays broadly accepted (for example, it is one of the fundamental principles of the European Union), requires 'that a central authority should have a subsidiary function, performing only those tasks which cannot be performed effectively at a more local level', Brown (ed.), *The New Shorter Oxford English Dictionary*, p. 3123.

557 The preamble of the Constitution of the Republic of Poland (1997) asserts that the Constitution, as the basic law for the State, is based on, among other principles, 'the principle of subsidiarity in the strengthening the powers of citizens and their communities'.

558 A moral justification of the principle of subsidiarity is also present in Roman Catholic social thought, in which this principle has its origins; its classic formulation is to be found in an encyclical of Pius XI, *Quadragesimo anno*, No. 79: 'Just as it is gravely wrong to take from individuals what they can accomplish by their own initiative and industry and give it to the community, so also it is an injustice and at the same time a grave evil and disturbance of right order to assign to a greater and higher association what lesser and subordinate organizations can do. For every social activity ought of its very nature to furnish help to the members of the body social, and never destroy and absorb them'. Cf. Leo XIII, *Rerum novarum* (1891), No. 32: 'the State must not absorb the individual or the family; both should be allowed free and untrammelled action so far as is consistent with the common good and the interest of others'.

is no need to make a detailed analysis of it here.[559] In this chapter, attention is focused on Plato's understanding of wisdom and freedom as theoretical reasons for rejecting totalitarianism as a conception proper for modelling a just society. Before exploring this, it is useful to place these arguments against Plato's alleged totalitarianism into a broader perspective, and to point out the converging argumentative *topoi.*

Certain arguments refer to the 'external' purposes which motivated Plato to present his model of the state, such as the use of the *Republic* and other dialogues as manuals in Plato's Academy. His exposition of the conception of a totalitarian state would thus function as a kind of intellectual provocation, a challenge for students meet in discussing the organisation of a state, requiring them to find counterarguments, to reflect upon the argumentation itself, and to train their skills in discerning what is realistic.[560] On crucial points, Plato does not leave his readers on their own, but provides them with indications about the direction in which they should proceed; an example of this is the story about the sharing of wives, analysed later here in Chapter 7. Plato expects his readers to learn to discern what is real and what is not, what is true and what is not. These are basic skills not only for being a good statesman but also and foremost for living a good life.

Another group of arguments refers to the 'internal' purposes of Plato's model of the hypothetical state, purposes he clearly sets himself. As was demonstrated above, his model has methodological functions; in depicting the soul, it helps one to understand justice in the soul and the justice of the actions of an individual. 'The fact that the shoemaker by nature rightly practices shoemaking and does nothing else, and the carpenter practices carpentry, and so on for the rest',[561] which is sometimes recognised to be the central point of Plato's conception of justice, is by Plato himself univocally described as εἴδωλον—a phantom of justice. Plato, wishing to be absolutely clear, precedes the final conclusions drawn from the mental experiment of building a state with the exceptionally strong expression 'but in truth justice is'; following this individual justice, and not the justice of the state, is considered.[562]

---

559 Popper's book was widely criticised. Among the most important of the critical monographs published shortly after Popper's book are G. J. de Vries, *Antisthenes Redivivus. Popper's Attack on Plato* (Amsterdam: North-Holland Publishing Company, 1952); J. Wild, *Plato's Modern Enemies and The Theory of Natural Law* (Chicago: University of Chicago Press, 1953); and R. B. Levinson, *In Defense of Plato* (Cambridge: Harvard University Press, 1953). Popper's response to his critics can be found in the 5th edition of *The Open Society* (1966). Later, a non-totalitarian interpretation was widely developed; see Zygmuntowicz, *Praktyka polityczna*, pp. 27–28; cf. Mróz, 'Rola dialogu Gorgias w Karla R. Poppera', *passim.*

560 Dembiński, *Późny Platon*, p. 19.

561 Plato, *Republic*, 443c, trans. Bloom.

562 Plato, *Republic*, 443c–e; see Section 3.7.

The justice of an individual and of his actions is the topic of the 'head' of Plato's Socrates' dialogue with himself in the *Gorgias*.[563]

One should also remember Plato's teaching about 'the living and breathing discourse'[564] which is to be written by a listener (reader) himself, and his teaching about education presented in the myth of the cave—education consists in turning the power of learning in the right direction, and not in putting knowledge in somebody else's mind.[565]

All discrepancies between Plato's comprehension of the justice of an individual and an individual's actions and his exposition of the justice in the state speak for reading the analysis of the state as merely representing a mental experiment which serves to better understand the individual.

There is also a group of arguments, presented above, against Plato's alleged totalitarianism which concern not the purposes or methods, but the 'content' of Plato's philosophy. Here belongs his apprehension of the crucial element of dignity—of one's being an aim in oneself—which clearly does not apply to the state.

To the same group belongs an argument which rests on Plato's characterisations of wisdom and courage and on recognising knowledge about 'what things are to be feared'[566] as the only knowledge directly applicable to a concrete action—the knowledge provided by reason says univocally only what should be avoided in a given situation. In the language of the model of the state—the auxiliaries, while acting courageously, deal only with knowledge about what should not be done, and therefore they can only prevent other citizens from doing wrong; they cannot direct every choice made by others, because they simply do not have knowledge about it. Since knowledge does not determine which one of the possible goods should become the aim of an action of a given subject—wisdom only presides over (oversees) good (just) actions. This applies to both short-term and long-term life planning. The metaphor of choosing one's own life with one's own daimon (δαίμων) indicates that according to Plato everyone is directed in his actions by knowledge which is strictly related to the way of life he has chosen, and at the same time, is strictly 'personal', acquired as a consequence of his own choices.

Recognition that choices are accompanied by knowledge about what should be avoided explains the priority of the harm principle in determining the shape of just actions. Certainly, this principle requires not only abstaining from active wrongdoing, but also acting when inactivity is harmful, such as when someone's life is endangered. On the other hand, there is no knowledge which would indicate specific actions that directly make their addressee happy. What leads to happiness—to the fulfilment of another—is not determined exclusively by objective factors. There are usually many possible ways of living decently. Knowledge only

563 Plato, *Gorgias*, 506c–507c; see Chapter 4.

564 Plato, *Phaedrus*, 276a, trans. Nehamas, Woodruff.

565 Plato, *Republic*, 518b–c; see Section 4.1.5.4.

566 Plato, *Republic*, 429b, trans. Grube.

oversees action; it does not determine its content univocally. Consequently, the way of living decently is not determined univocally by knowledge. Plato's thinking is very close to the modern conception of human rights as basic conditions for individual development. He provides a space for rational freedom—the free shaping of one's own life, accompanied by the recognition of the objective and cognisable foundations of right and wrong.

Wisdom as knowledge about how a man as a whole can best deal with himself and other people requires knowledge about both the invisible and visible realms, and taking into account the legitimate choices which shape one's life, which is highly individualised knowledge. The only path to wisdom leads through an encounter and dialogue with others.[567] The difficulties posed are therefore enormous. A man can only be a lover of wisdom, a philosopher, while calling someone 'wise' is 'proper only for a god'.[568]

Plato's dialogues, including, of course, the *Republic*, should not be read as providing concrete solutions; they lead the reader to places where he can see what is important for becoming good and acting in a good way, and enable him to write within himself 'the living and breathing discourse'.[569]

On the way to wisdom one realises that the visible realm is not the only one important for this discourse, and that the learning power (the intellect) should be directed to the invisible realm. Plato expects his reader to acquire there knowledge about principles of a formal nature. The most important knowledge which can be acquired in the invisible realm concerns the Good itself, and tells us that justice lies, above all, in doing that which is beneficial for others; that one can lose one's possessions and nevertheless be more. One learns about integrity, internal unity, and cardinal virtues, revealing the principles which rule what is truly one's own—what is inside one.

When it comes to determining the shape of a concrete action, one has to discern 'what things are to be feared'[570] and to come to know the border between things which are to be feared and, to use also an expression from the *Laches*, 'those that do not produce fear'[571]—hopeful things. It is necessary to come back to the visible realm and to find out what fits another—what is harmful and what is not. This provides knowledge about what makes people unhappy, but does not say what makes particular individuals happy. If happiness is the aim of laws, it is necessary to enter into dialogue and come to know the choices made by others.

567 Plato, *Theaetetus*, 150c–d.
568 Plato, *Phaedrus*, 278d, trans. Nehamas, Woodruff.
569 Plato, *Phaedrus*, 276a, trans. Nehamas, Woodruff.
570 Plato, *Republic*, 429b, trans. Grube.
571 Plato, *Laches*, 198b, trans. Sprague.

5.2.2 Wisdom as the knowledge that oversees just actions

The passage in Book IV of the *Republic* analysed extensively above, about what 'in truth justice is',[572] links justice in the soul with just actions (acting justly). Just deeds are the deeds of a just man. Wisdom is needed to properly shape them—a just man 'regards as wisdom the knowledge that oversees such actions'.[573] To describe the role of wisdom, Plato uses the term 'ἐπιστατοῦσαν', a participle of the verb 'ἐπιστατέω'—to preside over, to be in charge of, to have the care of. This wording is certainly not used by chance. In Athens and other cities, a formula used to be placed at the head of decrees: 'ἔδοξεν τῷ δήμῳ·... Νικιάδης ἐπεστάτει'—'decreed by the people: ... under the presidency of N'.[574] Plato's Socrates does not say that wisdom as a certain kind of knowledge determines what to do; it only oversees actions, or in the words of Shorey's translation, it 'presides over such conduct'.

Wisdom is characterised as a kind of knowledge about how a man as a whole should best handle himself and treat other people.[575] When it comes to action, however, a decisive role is played by the spirited part of the soul, which should be perfected by courage. As was demonstrated above,[576] the essence of courage lies in preserving certain rational convictions when actions are chosen. These convictions concern not what should be done here and now, but what should be avoided—they are 'about what things and sorts of things are to be feared'.[577] One can learn exactly what one should not do, but wisdom does not provide—at least from the perspective of the perfect performance of the spirited part—one and only one answer to the question of what should be done. Nevertheless, wisdom is, generally speaking, 'good judgment [εὐβουλία]'[578]—good judgment about how a man as a whole would best handle himself and treat other people. Looking comprehensively at Plato's considerations about acquiring wisdom, it can be accepted that wisdom as the perfection of the intellectual part of the soul comprises knowledge about the overall aim of human life, which consists in acquiring virtues and—most of all—justice, as well as living happily through just deeds.

It has to be stressed that knowledge about the cardinal virtues themselves does not provide knowledge about what is to be done. It is a kind of a 'formal' knowledge about how to act—this knowledge concerns how to 'construct' a just action, it says where and how to search for guidelines which determine the shape of

---

572 Plato, *Republic*, 443c–444a.

573 'σοφίαν δὲ τὴν ἐπιστατοῦσαν ταύτῃ τῇ πράξει ἐπιστήμην', Plato, *Republic*, 443e, trans. Grube; Shorey translates 'wisdom the science that presides over such conduct'.

574 Cf. Liddell, Scott, Jones, *A Greek–English Lexicon*, p. 659.

575 Plato, *Republic*, 428c–d, trans. Bloom; see Section 3.6.2. and comments about Bloom's and Grube's translations.

576 See Section 3.6.3.

577 Plato, *Republic*, 429c, trans. Grube.

578 Plato, *Republic*, 429c, trans. Grube.

action, but it tells neither what should be done nor what should be avoided. Thus, if acquiring cardinal virtues is established as an aim of laws and of the state, it is still far from determining the shape of the life of the citizens and of the organisation of the state itself.

5.2.3 The failure of Isaiah Berlin's argument

Plato's account of knowledge about 'what things are to be feared' leaves space for freedom while preserving the objective foundations of morality. Isaiah Berlin's argumentation that the recognition of the objective foundations of good (of right and wrong, good, and evil) logically results in accepting totalitarianism, fails because he misses Plato's point that it is possible to have objective foundations for morality that do not determine univocally which acts lead to one's happiness.[579] In his famous essay *Two Concepts of Liberty*,[580] Berlin argues that if human beings became happy by acting in a right way, by acting justly, and if what is just were determined objectively and were cognisable, then the best political order would be a totalitarian one in which a minority of wise men ruled the majority, and determined their ways of living. Berlin ascribes such a way of thinking to Plato. He aims to reject the recognition of the objective foundations for good when a social order is designed. The general scheme of his argumentation is as follows:

> if there is a necessary, logical linkage between a recognition of the objective foundations of good and a recognition of the totalitarian order as the best one,
>
> and if totalitarianism is rejected, for example on the basis of experience or common knowledge,
>
> then—using the scheme of logical indirect proof—Berlin rejects the objective foundations of good as a basis for the social order.

His challenge is very serious and deserves close attention. It is directed not only against Plato's conception of justice, but also against the whole tradition in which the objective foundations of justice are recognised.

Berlin's reconstruction of the position regarding the objective foundations of law (of the social order), which he ascribes to Plato and criticises, can be presented as follows:

> [1] According to the objectivistic position that which is just (proper, fair) is independent of subjective beliefs or individual choices, and moral and political problems are real problems; these problems refer to how things are, that is, moral evaluations say something about reality and may be true or false.

579 See also Piechowiak, 'Negative Freedom or Objective Good', *passim*.
580 Berlin, 'Two Concepts of Liberty', written in 1958.

[2] On the basis of these premises the conclusion can be drawn that: 'if moral and political problems are genuine ... they must in principle be soluble; that is to say, there must exist one and only one true solution to any problem.'[581]
[3] Therefore, to know what makes someone happy there is no need to ask him about the choices he has made or wants to make; it suffices to learn the objective foundations of moral evaluations.

To counter the adherents of such a position, Berlin actually uses Socratic argumentation: he provisionally accepts his opponents' theses ('good is cognisable and objectively founded') and draws conclusions from them until a contradiction emerges between one of the conclusions ('totalitarianism is the best social order') and other theses which are obvious and universally accepted and—importantly—accepted by the opponents of Berlin's liberal position, proponents of the objective foundations of good (of right and wrong, good, and evil). They reject the thesis that 'totalitarianism is the best social order'. Removal of the contradiction requires the negation of one of the premises on which the indirect reasoning is based, assuming at the same time that the other premises are true and also acceptable on the grounds of the given position.

The following reconstruction of Berlin's argumentation can be proposed. He accepts the following premises which are also accepted by supporters of the traditional conceptions which recognise the objective foundations of good (of right and wrong, good and evil):

1. 'The members of a society pursue happiness'.
2. 'Happiness is achieved through doing that what is good for someone'.
3. 'Some members of a society have more cognitive powers than others'. This is a very reasonable premise: if human beings vary in their cognitive abilities in many domains of cognition, it is reasonable to accept that this is the case also in the domain of justice.

These are premises which Berlin does not intend to question, and he implicitly considers them accurate, although the chosen terminology is that of the traditional conceptions of morality, which he is going to challenge, and not of modern liberalism. He himself assumes that everyone strives towards a life that will fulfil him—in the traditional approach that Berlin criticises, the road to such fulfilment leads through the realisation of positive freedom, whereas in the liberal approach the path is the realisation of negative freedom. None of these premises would have been questioned by Plato.[582]

581 Berlin, 'Two Concepts of Liberty', p. 145.
582 The first two of these premises are clearly accepted in the Aristotelian tradition to which Aquinas adheres, see e.g, Thomas Aquinas, *Summa theologiae*, II-II, q. 47, a. 15, co.: 'Wherefore since the inclination of nature is ever to something fixed, the knowledge of those means cannot be in man naturally, although, by reason of his natural disposition, one man has a greater aptitude than another in discerning them, just as it happens with regard to the conclusions of speculative sciences' ('quia

Besides this, Berlin adopts a premise containing a statement which he considers to be an element of the objectivistic position, marked above as [2]:

4. 'When forming a political order it has to be accepted that good is unambiguously objectively founded ('there must exist one and only one true solution to any problem') and that good may be a subject of cognition'.

   This is the premise of indirect reasoning that he intends to negate. If in the further steps of reasoning he is able to arrive at a contradiction, a thesis which is the negation of this premise will be proven, that is: 'It is not true that when forming a political order it has to be assumed that good is unambiguously objectively founded and may be a subject of cognition'.

The further steps of reasoning are as follows:

5. 'To be happy, one has to come to know good'—a conclusion arrived at on the basis of 1, 2, and 4.
6. 'Some members of society are better at recognising what is good'—a conclusion arrived at on the basis of 3 and 4.
7. 'The political system which is the best at leading the members of society is one in which individuals who are the best at recognising good entirely direct the lives of others without accounting for their individual choices (what is good is determined by the state of things and the way it is recognised and not the decisions of individuals); therefore, a totalitarian system is the best'—a conclusion arrived at on the basis of 1, 2, 6 and the definition of the totalitarian system.
8. 'It is not true that the political system which proves to be the best in leading the members of society is a totalitarian system'—a premise which is based on universal knowledge supported by experience; it is assumed—indeed, it is difficult to prove otherwise—that this premise is also accepted by Berlin's opponents, namely proponents of the objective foundations of good (of right and wrong, good, and evil).

There is a contradiction between premises 7 and 8. Therefore, the negation of one of the premises in the reasoning should be accepted, and Berlin suggests that premise 4 should be negated:

> 'It is not true that when forming a political order it has to be accepted that good is unambiguously objectively founded and that it may be a subject of cognition.'

This conclusion is negative—it indicates what should be rejected, and not which view should be accepted. Berlin proposes that in a well ordered society

---

inclinatio naturae semper est ad aliquid determinatum, talis cognitio non potest homini inesse naturaliter, licet ex naturali dispositione unus sit aptior ad huiusmodi discernenda quam alius; sicut etiam accidit circa conclusiones speculativarum scientiarum').

> the frontiers between individuals or groups of men [are] to be drawn solely with a view to preventing collisions between human purposes, all of which must be considered to be equally ultimate, uncriticisable ends in themselves.[583]

Human aims are understood here as aims which, in the light of the ordering of social life, do not have objective foundations—if they had, the argument presented would apply. However, Berlin is not against accepting the objective foundations of good in general, and he points at the difference between the social and individual perspectives. From the social perspective, it is not important why somebody considers something to be his good. It is possible that the only reason for being good is being wanted by a given subject; such a solution would probably be closest to Berlin's views. However, his argumentation against recognising, on the social level, the objective foundations of good does not require taking such a position on the private level. Private opinions on the topic of the good may have their basis in the vein of emotivism—something is good because of the positive emotional reaction to a given situation, real or imagined (the feeling of approval)—or in the vein of cultural relativism—something is good because of convictions based in culture and transmitted through upbringing and participation in culture. What is more, Berlin will not refuse an individual the right to recognise the objective foundations of good as long as these convictions affect private matters only and do not shape the way the political community is organised. In his view, although such opinions are false, people have the right to false opinions; however, it is inadmissible for such opinions to be accepted in the public sphere when the social order is formed, since that—according to the presented argument—would lead indirectly to the acceptance of totalitarianism as the best political system or social order in general.

Berlin's argument poses a serious challenge to conceptions which recognise the objective foundations of good. A common strategy for their defence, presented in the classical tradition, is based on the assertion that a given individual himself is able to recognise best what in a given specific situation is good, while at the same time, free choice does not co-constitute the content of good.[584] In such approaches the perfecting function of the will and free choice is exhausted in the pursuit of that which is recognised as good or in perfecting the recognition of good.[585] However, the fundamental problems posed by Berlin and the liberal tradition remain. This tradition aims to appreciate freedom in determining the shape of the fulfilment of one's life. This is an appreciation of individual life projects; appreciation of the

583 Berlin, 'Two Concepts of Liberty', p. 153, note 47.

584 Thomistic literature usually invokes Aquinas' analyses of multiplicitous relationships and the cooperation of reason (intellect) and will in human actions; see Walgrave, *Reason and Will*, pp. 78–80; Pinckaers, *The Sources*, pp. 381–386; the role of free choice in the determination of natural law is overlooked, and cognitive elements are pointed out.

585 Walgrave, *Reason and Will*, p. 81.

individuality of every person based on a variety of ways of life, and variety justified not simply by the differences in individual abilities and circumstances of life, but in variety founded on free choices made by individuals concerning their way of life. These choices should not only be tolerated by others but considered to be an important dimension of the fulfilment of a person, and therefore protected as broadly as possible by positive law. Importance is attached to the protection of the autonomy of human beings. This autonomy would be compromised by a total subjection to those who know best.

There is another problem with autonomy—if the fulfilment of man consisted in following the way which is unambiguously determined by another, even if that other was God, life would consist in the realisation of aims determined by others, and man would simply be a tool in the realisation of such aims. If one were to assume that these aims were unambiguously determined by the existing state of things or existing law (including natural law), then in fact, the human being would be for the law and not law for the human being. The perfectly lived life could then be compared to a well-done job by a driver who receives not only instructions on how to handle the car, but also a map with a precise route—the best driver is the one who is best at handling the car and best at following the route.

Can the values claimed by the liberal tradition be saved when the objective foundations of good and axiological cognitivism are recognised? Can Berlin's argument be refuted without abandoning the essential elements of the conceptions that accept the objective foundations of good?

Berlin's argument is conclusive in the matter of rejecting the objective foundations of good on the condition that the objectivistic position was adequately characterised in the premises which he assumed. One can see that Berlin assumed a premise which—in his opinion—follows from the acceptance of the objective grounding of good, but one which, on closer inspection, is not only not obvious, but proves to be wrong in the light of Plato's conception of justice. Namely, it is not obvious that since good is objectively grounded, there must be one and only one proper solution to every real moral and political problem, independently of the choices made by individuals. Plato provides an adequate counter-argument. He would agree that 'there must exist one and only one true solution to any problem',[586] but—in principle—only where problems about what should be avoided are concerned. The moral knowledge pronounced by the conscience says what should not be done—'it never encourages me to do anything'[587]—the intellect presents only one true solution to the problem 'what things are to be feared'.[588] When one excludes all things which 'are to be feared', one is usually not left with only one possible way of acting, or even way of life, being in accordance with the knowledge provided by the intellect.

586 Berlin, 'Two Concepts of Liberty', p. 145.
587 Plato, *Apology*, 31c–d, trans. Grube.
588 Plato, *Republic*, 429b–c, trans. Grube; cf. ibid., 442b–c.

5.2.4 Freedom to shape one's own life

5.2.4.1 Short-term life planning

In Book VI of the *Republic*, Plato's Socrates, while developing his story about the hypothetical state, describes how philosophers as rulers would sketch the outline of a constitution.[589] He indicates a principal reason why philosophers should do this—'they are painters who use the divine model'.[590] Translating this into teaching about individual justice, it means that the 'constitution' of an individual should be outlined by reason, which also has knowledge about something invisible and abstract—the good, justice, courage, moderation, and the like. Plato's Socrates is far from thinking that there is a general model which could be implemented and should shape human life simply according to a pattern which is already given. The process is much more complicated, and involves knowledge about concrete reality in this visible word:

> they'd look often in each direction, towards the natures of justice, beauty, moderation, and the like, on the one hand, and towards those they're trying to put into human beings, on the other. And in this way they'd mix and blend the various ways of life in the city until they produced a human image based on what Homer too called 'the divine form and image' when it occurred among human beings.
>
> (...) They'd erase one thing, I suppose, and draw in another until they'd made characters for human beings that the gods would love as much as possible.[591]

Both directions—towards the invisible (intelligible) and the visible realms—are equally important. One should take into account one's own capacities, emotions, advantages and disadvantages, as well as the possibilities of shaping one's own traits, both mental and physical. It has to be stressed that in the intelligible realm there exist no definite paradigms of human life which would contain specific aims to be reached by an individual in his 'external business'.[592] Virtues in themselves, belonging to the intelligible realm, are paradigms of 'what is within', 'what truly concerns him and his own'.[593] They provide paradigms for relations between parts of the soul. From the point of view of the aims pursued in 'doing externally', virtues are some kind of formal principles. The general goal is determined—it is obtaining

---

589 Plato, *Republic*, 501a–c.

590 Plato, *Republic*, 500e, trans. Grube.

591 Plato, *Republic*, 501b–c; Homer talks about a man as a divine image, for example, in the *Iliad* when Agamemnon speaks to Achilles: 'Do not thus, mighty though you are, godlike Achilles, seek to deceive me with your wit', Homer, *Iliad*, I, 130–132, trans. Murray; 'divine image' and 'godlike' are translations of the same word, 'θεοείκελος'.

592 Cf. Plato, *Republic*, 443c, trans. Bloom; Grube translates: 'someone's doing his own externally'.

593 Plato, *Republic*, 443c–d, trans. Bloom.

justice in the soul and acting justly—but there are no ready paradigms for how to achieve this goal; for instance, the beneficiary of just action is not determined. One should also remember that wisdom provides 'exact' knowledge about what should be avoided and not about what should be done in a given situation. Therefore, moral development (fulfilment and happiness) can be reached in different ways not only with regard to different individuals possessing different characteristics but also—as there is no reason to reject this possibility—with regard to the same, given individual.[594] There is place for self-determination, which is free in the sense that the shape of living justly and happily, the 'content' of life which is just and happy cannot be discovered solely by cognition of something objectively given. In other words—for a given individual there is usually more than one way of acting which is just (right, good). This is one of the lessons taught by Plato.

5.2.4.2 Long-term life planning

Views on freedom in shaping one's own life are also developed in the myth of Er, which concludes the *Republic*, and which concerns the choice of one's fate. The metaphor offered by Plato can be understood not only in the context of faith in metempsychosis (the transmigration of the soul), but also as a reflection upon taking decisions which radically change the shape of one's future life. Eric Voegelin remarks that

> In the language of the myth Plato has expressed the existential situation of every man at the dead point of decision between his past and his future, that is, the situation of his present in which mysteriously wells up the freedom of Arete.[595]

Plato clearly indicates that the myth not only can, but should be read as telling something about human life in the here and now. When summarising considerations about the criteria for right choices, Plato's Socrates notes that they should be applied to choices made 'whether in life or death',[596] 'both in this life and in all those beyond it'.[597]

According to the myth of Er, the message of Lachesis, the daughter of Necessity, to the souls which are to elect their fate in the afterworld, is the following:

---

594 This way of thinking about virtues and about the moral fulfilment of an individual (of a human person) was clearly expressed by Thomas Aquinas: 'virtutis moralis inclinatio convenit quodammodo cum inclinatione naturae, et quodammodo differt. Convenit in hoc, quia utraque inclinatio est in finem determinatum; differt autem in hoc quod in naturalibus sicut est finis determinatus, ita et ea quae sunt ad finem; sed in virtutibus moralibus est finis determinatus, non autem viae ad finem, quia potest medium inveniri in diversis diversimode', Thomas Aquinas, *Scriptum super Sententiis*, lib. 3, d. 33, q. 2, a. 3, ad 3.

595 Voegelin, *Plato and Aristotle*, pp. 111–112.

596 Plato, *Republic*, 618e, trans. Grube.

597 Plato, *Republic*, 619a, trans. Grube.

> Your daemon or guardian spirit will not be assigned to you by lot; you will choose him. The one who has the first lot will be the first to choose a life to which he will then be bound by necessity. Virtue knows no master; each will possess it to a greater or less degree, depending on whether he values or disdains it. The responsibility lies with the one who makes the choice; the god has none.[598]

The choice of a way of life is connected with the choice of a daimon (δαίμων)—the guardian spirit. He can be regarded as the same daimon whose voice was mentioned by Plato's Socrates in the *Apology*—'whenever it speaks it turns me away from something I am about to do, but it never encourages me to do anything'.[599] It can be observed, then, that this inner voice announces not only prohibitions which disclose general normative truths (general rules) applicable to all ways of life, but also prohibitions specific to a given way of life. In other words, it guards faithfulness to one's own choices and the way of life which results from them. Nevertheless, since it only turns one away from doing something and never encourages one to do anything, the space for short-term life planning or for making free choices is left open. One can say that in this element of the myth of Er, Plato repeats using a different metaphor his teaching on freedom as based on the conception of the voice of the conscience, understood as the voice of the daimon in the *Apology*.

Nobody is destined to be or not to be virtuous. Generally, there is no necessary connection between a chosen way of life and the moral quality achieved by the person who chose it. Moreover, the same chosen way of life can be—in principle—lived virtuously or not. At this point of the story, the conclusion can already be drawn that an individual can be virtuous in different ways of life. Knowing Plato's teaching on the Good, it can be observed that it would be against the nature of it to create a way of life that leads in itself (independently of who chooses it) and by necessity to something contrary to the good. Nevertheless, it seems that, depending on people's individual predispositions, there are certain ways of life which for certain individuals make it extremely difficult or even impossible to lead a virtuous life and to acquire justice.

The soul has to choose wisely. When it chooses more wisely, it can acquire justice more smoothly, although still not effortlessly:

> Then our messenger from the other world reported that the Speaker spoke as follows: 'There is a satisfactory life rather than a bad one [βίος ἀγαπητός, οὐ κακός]

---

598 Plato, *Republic*, 617d–e, trans. Grube; cf. idem, *Phaedrus*, 249a–b, trans. Nehamas, Woodruff: 'As for the rest, once their first life is over, they come to judgment; and, once judged, some are condemned to go to places of punishment beneath the earth and pay the full penalty for their injustice, while the others are lifted up by justice to a place in heaven where they live in the manner the life they led in human form has earned them. In the thousandth year both groups arrive at a choice and allotment of second lives, and each soul chooses the life it wants'.

599 Plato, *Apology*, 31c–d, trans. Grube.

> available even for the one who comes last, provided that he chooses it rationally [ἑλομένῳ] and lives it seriously [συντόνως]. Therefore, let not the first be careless in his choice nor the last discouraged.'[600]

The rational choice is denoted by Plato with the word 'ἑλομένῳ', a participle of 'αἱρέω'. The meaning of 'αἱρέω' combines grasping with the mind (understanding) with taking for oneself as something that is preferred. Therefore, one can also say that a choice is also wise when it takes into account the particular characteristics of the one who chooses. The wise choice is based on a consideration of the elements of the way of life which can be chosen as facilitating or impeding the acquisition of justice by a given individual:

> He should think over all the things we have mentioned and how they jointly and severally determine what the virtuous life is like. That way he will know what the good and bad effects of beauty are when it is mixed with wealth, poverty, and a particular state of the soul. He will know the effects of high or low birth, private life or ruling office, physical strength or weakness, ease or difficulty in learning, and all the things that are either naturally part of the soul or are acquired, and he will know what they achieve when mixed with one another.[601]

Having adequate knowledge, one 'will be able, by considering the nature of the soul, to reason out which life is better and which worse and to choose accordingly'.[602] It has to be pointed out—especially bearing in mind the accusations that Plato developed a totalitarian ideology—that the choice of a fate (of a future life) is made exclusively by an individual—'the responsibility lies with the one who makes the choice'.[603] Moreover, the decision is made exclusively on the basis of one's own knowledge and assessment, as well as one's admiration or disdain for virtue. Nobody can guide the choice of another, still less decide for someone else, whether acting as a friend or as one possessing authority.

Knowledge can help one avoid opting for a way of life in which justice is almost unachievable and the prospect of future punishment immense, as is the case when one chooses the fate of a tyrant.[604] Nevertheless, in the story about deciding on a future way of life, it is not stated that there is only one fate ascribed to a given individual, one which should be recognised and chosen by him. Knowledge itself—useful and even necessary in avoiding bad choices—seems to be insufficient to indicate the one and only one way of life which should be chosen. Much of the issue is depicted in the part of the story in which Odysseus decides on his future way of life. Here it should be recalled that Odysseus is someone of outstanding

600 Plato, *Republic*, 619b, trans. Grube.
601 Plato, *Republic*, 618c–d, trans. Grube.
602 Plato, *Republic*, 618c, trans. Grube.
603 Plato, *Republic*, 617e, trans. Grube.
604 Plato, *Republic*, 619c.

intelligence, and who is exceptionally talented in practical, especially political and military, matters. Plato writes:

> Odysseus got to make its choice last of all, and since memory of its former sufferings had relieved its love of honor, it went around for a long time, looking for the life of a private individual who did his own work, and with difficulty it found one lying off somewhere neglected by the others. He chose it gladly and said that he'd have made the same choice even if he'd been first.[605]

It is not said that the decision he made was the best possible in the sense that by choosing the life of a great warrior and prince he would be less just or less virtuous. The perspective of one's becoming more just (or not) is decisive in judging the rightness of the choice. The criteria of the goodness of life and—consequently—of the choice, are specified both generally (not only for Odysseus) and clearly. Someone who chooses wisely is 'calling a life worse if it leads the soul to become more unjust, better if it leads the soul to become more just, and ignoring everything else'.[606] The soul is led to become more just in such a life which is a mean between extremes: 'we must always know how to choose the mean in such lives and how to avoid either of the extremes, as far as possible, both in this life and in all those beyond it. This is the way that a human being becomes happiest'.[607]

Knowledge seems to suffice to indicate only one way of life which should be chosen if one were required to live the best life, as Berlin supposes (of course cognizable criteria of the best life and the uniqueness of such a life are also presupposed). Plato does not require one to opt for such a life, although some translations suggest it.[608] He writes about choosing a better life: 'so everywhere and always to choose the better from among those that are possible'.[609] Plato also provides explicitly an explanation of what 'a better life' means—a life is better 'if it leads the soul to become more just'.[610]

It should be noted that saying 'a best life' would be ambiguous. It could mean that it leads the soul to become as just as possible, or that it leads the soul along the best way to become more just, or that it leads the soul along the best way to become as just as possible. Moreover, it would also be unclear what 'the best way' means (does it mean 'the most certain', for example, or 'the easiest'?). It would also be necessary to take into account relationships between the degrees of goodness in

605 Plato, *Republic*, 620c–d, trans. Grube.
606 Plato, *Republic*, 618d–e, trans. Grube.
607 Plato, *Republic*, 619a–b, trans. Grube.
608 In an important introductory section to the considerations about criteria of choice (Plato, *Republic*, 618b–c), in Grube's translation one can read about making 'the best choice possible in every situation', and Shorey translates: 'always and everywhere to choose the best that the conditions allow'.
609 Plato, *Republic*, 618c, trans. Bloom.
610 Plato, *Republic*, 618e, trans. Grube.

leading to justice and the degrees of justice which is to be acquired. Plato does not write 'as just as possible' nor 'if it leads along the best way'. It suffices to answer the question—'does this way of life lead me to become more just?' This confirms, however, that Plato recognises the possibility that more than only one way of life may be lived as the good (just) one.

Odysseus chooses the life of a private individual 'since memory of its former sufferings had relieved its love of honor'.[611] A love of honour or lack of such love proves to be neutral from the point of view of acquiring justice, and therefore irrelevant to the rightness of the choice. Suppose that in spite of the memory of former sufferings Odysseus had retained his love of honour and decided on the life of a prince. Certainly this would have been a right choice. But would it be wrong to love honour and choose the life of a private person because of the memory of former sufferings? Answering this question seems to be not at all easy, and Plato invites his readers to consider this. Nevertheless, it is certain that this decision involves the whole human being, including emotions, passions, and desires which are not judged as good or bad in themselves.

Let us consider one more example, from the myth of Er. The soul of Atalanta, a mythical runner, 'saw great honours being given to a male athlete, she chose his life, unable to pass them by'.[612] Neither Plato's Socrates nor anybody else comments on her decision. Was it a choice of a better life or not? Perhaps it was a choice of a better life, but the way to becoming more just may lead through great suffering.

The myth can be read as describing the human condition in this world. There is no doubt that being bound by necessity to certain freely chosen projects of one's future life is also a part of the human condition in 'this world'. Although Odysseus was the last one to decide, he still had several possible ways of life to choose from. This can be interpreted as meaning that even though all around us have already taken on their social roles, although we might be the last to decide, our role is still not determined, and we still have several good options. It can also be interpreted in terms of growing older, which is associated with a diminishing range of possible ways of life. Therefore, the announcement of the Speaker in the afterworld that 'There is a satisfactory life rather than a bad one available even for the one who comes last, provided that he chooses it rationally and lives it seriously. Therefore, let not the first be careless in his choice nor the last discouraged'[613] could be read: 'There is a satisfactory life rather than a bad one available even for the one who *gets older*, provided that he chooses it rationally and lives it seriously. Therefore, let not *the young* be careless in his choice nor *the old* discouraged'.

---

611 Plato, *Republic*, 620c, trans. Grube.
612 Plato, *Republic*, 620b, trans. Grube.
613 Plato, *Republic*, 619b, trans. Grube.

5.2.5 Concluding remarks

Plato most probably believed in metempsychosis; nevertheless, he provides his reader with clear indications that the myth of Er should be read metaphorically. It is also a story about a human being who in the course of his life has to make choices which will change it deeply, and the consequences of which will be inseparable from his future fate.

In Plato's approach the shape of a good life (living justly) is not univocally determined by the knowledge which can be acquired by an individual. For a given individual there is usually more than one way of life which can be chosen as just (right, good), and there is usually more than one action which can be performed as just (right, good). This is not only a matter of knowledge or lack thereof. Both the social role which is to be played and the way one's own 'fate' is lived are determined by decisions made by the individual.

It is evident that an observer is not able to know the best life for someone else (the life which best leads the soul to become as just as possible). Moreover, an observer is not the right person to determine it. The one who decides on his fate is left alone—he cannot obtain advice from anyone wiser than he is. This issue is considered by Plato when his Socrates talks about the place of wives in the hypothetical state[614]—this matter is dealt with in Chapter 7. Last but not least, the one who chooses, and chooses rightly, is guided not only by his knowledge, but also by his emotions and desires.

5.3 Punitive justice

5.3.1 Preliminary remarks

The problem of punitive justice constitutes one of the principal threads in the dialogue *Gorgias*. Therefore, this dialogue will be the main point of reference for the present analysis. However, with regard to fundamental questions, it is difficult to find substantial differences in the articulation of the problem of punishment in this dialogue, especially in terms of its goals, from that in others, including the late dialogue *Laws*. Therefore, other dialogues will also be considered in the reconstruction of Plato's position, which is treated as remaining fundamentally consistent throughout the whole of his work.[615]

Plato's conception of punishment will be analysed here primarily from the perspective of the aims of punishment. On the one hand, this perspective will make it possible to situate Plato's concept within the context of the main rationales

614 Plato, *Republic*, 455d–456a.

615 See MacKenzie, *Plato on Punishment*, pp. 204–205; and, in more general terms, pp. 179–206.

articulated today for punishment—the concepts of retribution and prevention; on the other, it will make it possible to raise one of the fundamental questions concerning Plato's concepts of law and the state—the question of totalitarianism: does punishment, as decreed by law and executed by the state, have as its foremost aim the good of the state, or that of the individual? It transpires without any doubt that the justice of punishment is not intended as a means for realising the good of the state, of the legal order, or as something used to re-establish an abstractly understood justice 'separated' from individuals (such as cosmic justice). The justice of punishment, or simply just punishment, is first and foremost subordinated to the benefit of the punished. In rare cases when improvement of the punished is impossible, the primary beneficiaries become other individuals who are warned by the punishment; nevertheless, even in these extreme cases the good of the punished is also taken into account, and there is no crime which would be punished by the total destruction of the offender: although capital punishment is permitted as a medicine for a soul, there is no crime which would justify termination of the human soul itself. There is a principle—expounded in the Demiurge's speech in the *Timaeus*—that which is beautifully harmonised and in fine condition,[616] which possesses dignity, will never be destroyed, as it is willed by the Demiurge for its own sake and, accordingly, exists for its own sake.

An analysis of Plato's doctrine of fair punishment from an ontological perspective (which is generally underestimated in monographic studies), particularly in terms of the unwritten teachings concerning the Good and its relationship to unity as the basis for existence,[617] corroborates the importance of dignity for the understanding of punitive justice. The primary concern of punishment is shown to be the good of the offender—his own justice understood as internal unity, which is the basis of existence and, as such, is fundamental to the perfection of a human being as a whole.

5.3.2 Rhetoric as a counterfeit of punitive justice

In the *Gorgias*, the problem of punishment appears in the context of the question: is it appropriate (beneficial) to use rhetoric to avoid punishment, and—more broadly—is punishment something useful or not, does it contribute to happiness

---

616 Plato, *Timaeus*, 41b, trans. Zeyl.

617 The metaphysical context of Plato's doctrines on justice, according to which punishment returns the soul to health, is not considered by MacKenzie, *Plato on Punishment*. She regards the essential explanatory context to be his teaching on morality (in particular, ethical intellectualism) and the soul. However, she does not consider the metaphor of injustice as a sickness of the soul, as expressing problems about the strength of existence based on unity, and therefore on the justice or goodness of the soul. Nor is a metaphysical perspective taken into account by Saunders, *Plato's Penal Code*.

or does it limit it?[618] Plato is interested in just punishment, and in this dialogue he speaks of such punishment simply as justice. Punitive justice is, along with legislation (νομοθετική), an element of politics, characterised by Plato's Socrates as an art 'which concerns the soul'.[619] Both of these elements 'always bestow their care for the best advantage (...) of (...) the soul'.[620] This concept of politics is primarily concerned with the good of the individual, rather than that of the state. Punitive justice serves souls which are sick, and is aimed at returning their lost health; legislation serves healthy souls, sustaining and strengthening their health. These distinctions are based on a differentiation between the creation of laws and their implementation by the judicature.

Plato's Socrates points out an analogy between such a politics composed of two parts, as an art 'which concerns the soul', and another art, likewise composed of two parts, that concerns the body. He mentions that the latter does not have one name, though its parts are termed 'medicine' (the art of medicine) and 'gymnastic'. Medicine returns health to the sick body; gymnastic deals with healthy bodies and aims to strengthen and preserve their health.

Plato's Socrates characterises punitive justice through something that is, in a certain sense, its opposite, and which merely imitates it—the rhetoric taught and practised by the Sophists. The four arts correspond to four flatteries, which only pretend to be arts. Flattery 'is a disgrace [αἰσχρόν] (...) because it aims at the pleasant and ignores the best';[621] it 'cares nothing for what is the best, but dangles what is most pleasant for the moment as a bait for folly, and deceives it into thinking that she is of the highest value'.[622] Flattery is only 'a habitude or

618 A similar problem is introduced directly by Plato in the *Republic*, towards the end of Book IV, after having given basic answers to the question of what is individual justice: 'So it now remains, it seems, to inquire whether it is more profitable to act justly, live in a fine way, and be just, whether one is known to be so or not, or to act unjustly and be unjust, provided that one doesn't pay the penalty and become better as a result of punishment'. Plato, *Republic*, 444e–445a, trans. Grube. Plato's Glaucon, answering Socrates' proposal, considers that it is principally useless, when one knows what the justice of the soul is—'from this point on our inquiry becomes an absurdity—if (...) we are yet to be asked to suppose that, when the very nature and constitution of that whereby we live is disordered and corrupted, life is going to be worth living, if a man can only do as he pleases, and pleases to do anything save that which will rid him of evil and injustice and make him possessed of justice and virtue—now that the two have been shown to be as we have described them', ibid., 445a–b. Nonetheless Plato's Socrates stands by his proposition—'but nevertheless, now that we have won to this height, we must not grow weary in endeavoring to discover with the utmost possible clearness that these things are so', ibid., 445b.

619 Plato, *Gorgias*, 464b, trans. Lamb.

620 Plato, *Gorgias*, 464c, trans. Lamb.

621 Plato, *Gorgias*, 465a, trans. Lamb.

622 Plato, *Gorgias*, 464d, trans. Lamb.

knack',[623] for 'it has no account to give of the real nature of the things it applies, and so cannot tell the cause of any of them'.[624] Flattery is something irrational—an irrational, ill-considered work (ἄλογον πρᾶγμα)[625] and as such cannot be called an art.[626] A true art, through learning the nature of things and causes, searches for that which is best.[627] The rhetoric practised by the Sophists imitates punitive justice, which seeks to return health to the sick soul. It is called εἴδωλον—aptly translated by Benjamin Jowett as 'the ghost or counterfeit' element of politics.[628] Similarly, flattery is sophistry which imitates legislation that sustains and strengthens the health of the soul. Gymnastic, which sustains and strengthens the health and beauty of the body, is imitated by self-adornment (the 'art' of dressing up); medicine, which returns health to the sick body, is imitated by cookery.[629]

Making use of the language of mathematics and the study of proportions, Plato's Socrates notes that as self-adornment is to gymnastic, so is cookery to medicine:[630]

self-adornment: gymnastic = cookery : medicine

and further: 'as self-adornment is to gymnastic, so is sophistry to legislation':[631]

self-adornment: gymnastic = sophistry : legislation

and: 'as cookery is to medicine, so is rhetoric to justice':[632]

cookery : medicine = rhetoric : justice

Cookery, as the counterfeit of medicine, 'pretends to know what foods are best for the body; so that if a cook and a doctor had to contend before boys, or before men as foolish as boys, (...) the doctor would starve to death'.[633]

623 Plato, *Gorgias*, 463b, trans. Lamb.
624 Plato, *Gorgias*, 465a, trans. Lamb.
625 Plato, *Gorgias*, 465a.
626 Plato, *Gorgias*, 465a.
627 Plato, *Gorgias*, 465a.
628 Plato, *Gorgias*, 463d, trans. Jowett; Lamb translates 'εἴδωλόν' as 'a semblance'; Grube—'an image'.
629 Plato, *Gorgias*, 465b–c.
630 See Plato, *Gorgias*, 465b. In editions following those of Stallbaum or Deuschle-Cron: Plato, *Gorgias*, ed. Lodge; Plato, *Gorgias*, ed. Woolsey: 'ὅτι ὃ κομμωτικὴ πρὸς γυμναστικήν, τοῦτο ὀψοποιικὴ πρὸς ἰατρικήν· μᾶλλον δέ ὧδε, ὅτι ὃ κομμωτικὴ πρὸς γυμναστικήν, τοῦτο σοφιστικὴ πρὸς νομοθετικήν, καὶ ὅτι ὃ ὀψοποιικὴ πρὸς ἰατρικήν, τοῦτο ῥητορικὴ πρὸς δικαιοσύνην' (465b–c). In Burnet's edition, the first part of the quoted phrase 'ὅτι ὃ κομμωτικὴ πρὸς γυμναστικήν, τοῦτο ὀψοποιικὴ πρὸς ἰατρικήν· μᾶλλον δέ ὧδε' is missing; this part is also missing in Lamb's translation.
631 Plato, *Gorgias*, 465c, trans. Lamb.
632 Plato, *Gorgias*, 465c, trans. Lamb.
633 Plato, *Gorgias*, 464d–e, trans. Lamb.

In terms of self-adornment as the counterfeit of gymnastic, he writes that it is 'rascally, deceitful, ignoble, and illiberal',[634] and that 'it deceives men by forms and colors, polish and dress so as to make them, in the effort of assuming an extraneous beauty, neglect the native sort that comes through gymnastic'.[635]

Rhetoric is to the soul what cookery is to the body;[636] one can therefore characterise rhetoric as analogous to cookery, and punitive justice as the opposite of rhetoric. There is also an analogy between the properties of punitive justice and medicine. It follows that rhetoric as flattery—in line with the above—'cares nothing for what is the best, but dangles what is most pleasant for the moment as a bait for folly';[637] punitive justice, on the other hand, searches for what is best, without regard for whether it is pleasant or not. Rhetoric pretends to know what is best for the soul—those who lack reason consider it to be that which is the best, the most precious; in this way, the rhetorician in front of the court of 'boys, or before men as foolish as boys' will always win against those whose occupation is punitive justice. Rhetoric is experience and routine—it does not comprehend the nature of what it entails and with what it is occupied, nor does it know its causes; punitive justice is, on the other hand, a true art—in contrast to flattery, which is something irrational (ἄλογον πρᾶγμα):[638] it is well-considered work, it understands the nature of what it entails, and it can provide its causes. Whereas medicine entails the health of body, punitive justice entails the health of the soul; it is knowledgeable of it, and knows its causes.

5.3.3 The principal aims of punishment

The health of the soul turns out to be its justice, and the causes of justice are—like the causes of the health of the body—an inner organisation and order.[639] In the *Republic*, harmony[640] and the inner unity founded upon it comes to the fore, and the justice of the soul is closely connected to just action 'that preserves this inner harmony [of the soul] and helps achieve it'.[641] Punitive justice has as its aim the restoration of lost justice to the soul, and knowing its causes also comprises knowledge of how to achieve this aim. Rhetoric in the service of avoiding a penalty in court is only a semblance of care for 'afflicted souls'—for those who have committed wrongdoing.

The aim of punishment is not first and foremost the restoration of some abstract axiological order, or the rule of law and order in the state; the aim is rather the

634 Plato, *Gorgias*, 465b, trans. Lamb; illiberal (ἀνελεύθερος)—mean, rude.
635 Plato, *Gorgias*, 465b, trans. Lamb.
636 Plato, *Gorgias*, 465d.
637 Plato, *Gorgias*, 464d; see ibid., 465a: 'aims at the pleasant and ignores the best'.
638 Plato, *Gorgias*, 465a.
639 Plato, *Gorgias*, 504a–d.
640 Plato, *Republic*, 443d–444a.
641 Plato, *Republic*, 443e, trans. Grube.

good (internal regularity and order) of the punished, for whose soul the punishment is a kind of medicine.[642] Clearly visible is the instrumental role of the law and the state—they exist to serve individuals.

Punishment, though unpleasant, is nonetheless the best thing that can happen to those who have committed wrongdoing: 'paying the penalty is a relief from the greatest evil, wickedness' and 'the justice of the court reforms us [σωφρονίζει[643]] and makes us juster, and acts as a medicine for wickedness'.[644]

A wrongdoer should in his own self-interest bring himself before a judge, so that the latter may mete out punishment. A just punishment, though painful, constitutes medicine for the soul: it is useful, beautiful and good, as much for him who metes it out as for him who receives it;[645] it frees the soul from the greatest evil on earth, from that which is ugliest and brings the greatest harm; and it liberates one from injustice and the baseness of the soul.[646]

At the end of *Gorgias*, punishment is indicated as the second greatest good of man, after being just: 'when any one has been wrong in anything, he is to be chastised, and that the next best thing to a man being just is that he should become just, and be chastised and punished'.[647]

Punishment is thus directly connected with happiness:

> *Socrates*: Happiest therefore is he who has no vice in his soul, since we found this to be the greatest of evils.
> *Polus*: Clearly so.
> *Socrates*: Next after him, I take it, is he who is relieved of it.
> *Polus*: So it seems.
> *Socrates*: And that was the man who is reproved, reprimanded, and made to pay the penalty.[648]

Happiness is thereby an unquestioned good, and the possession of knowledge about happiness is 'most honourable [κάλλιστον]':

> the points which we have at issue are by no means of slight importance: rather, one might say, they are matters on which it is most honorable to have knowledge, and most disgraceful to lack it; for in sum they involve our knowing or not knowing who is happy and who is not.[649]

---

642 Plato, *Gorgias*, 478d–e, 480a.

643 'σωφρονίζω' means to call to order, to discipline; the accent falls on the return to order, which in the Greek world is always based on that which is rational.

644 Plato, *Gorgias*, 478d, trans. Lamb.

645 Plato, *Gorgias*, 476e–477a.

646 Plato, *Gorgias*, 477a–e; although the first place as the greatest evil is given to injustice, Plato's Socrates also speaks in this dialogue of other moral faults and generally about the baseness (πονηρία) of the soul.

647 Plato, *Gorgias*, 527b–c, trans. Jowett; see ibid., 472e.

648 Plato, *Gorgias*, 478e, trans. Lamb.

649 Plato, *Gorgias*, 472c, trans. Lamb.

At the fore here is the good of the punished, his improvement, which makes the one punished avoid unjust actions in the future. In the *Gorgias*, this question clearly dominates, and one of the reasons for this is the problem posed in that dialogue of whether punishment is worth avoiding.

Nonetheless, in Plato's reflections one can also find thinking based on prevention, on making it impossible for someone to act in a certain way. For example, Plato's Athenian in the *Laws* says of a guardian of the law who has harmed an orphan with his dishonesty: 'in addition to paying the sum assessed, he must be ejected from the office of Guardian of the Laws, and the government must supply the state and country with a fresh Guardian of the Laws to take his place'.[650]

5.3.4 The health of the soul as the foundation of justice

As the health of the soul, justice is grounded on internal regularity and order,[651] and therefore on that which is the basis of harmony and beauty. In a normal situation, where an individual does not commit an injustice, the soul becomes just through just actions.[652] The lack of justice, evil, is based on the lack of inner order, asymmetry and the ugliness of the soul.[653] Such a state is caused by unjust actions. A just punishment returns inner simplicity, and restores order, symmetry and harmony, which are the foundations of the justice of the soul.

This concerns, above all, the proper relation between the three principal elements of the soul – the rational, the spirited and the appetitive. In the *Republic*, Plato also writes about the consequences of punishment:

> in what way is it profitable to get away with doing injustice and not pay the penalty? Or doesn't the man who gets away with it become still worse; while, as for the man who doesn't get away with it and is punished, isn't the bestial part of him put to sleep and tamed, and the tame part freed, and doesn't his whole soul—brought to its best nature acquiring moderation and justice accompanied by prudence—gain a habit more worthy of honor than the one a body gains with strength and beauty accompanied by health, in proportion as soul is more honorable than body?[654]

---

650 Plato, *Laws*, 928d, trans. Saunders.

651 'ταῖς δέ γε τῆς ψυχῆς τάξεσι καὶ κοσμήσεσιν νόμιμόν τε καὶ νόμος, ὅθεν καὶ νόμιμοι γίγνονται καὶ κόσμιοι· ταῦτα δ' ἔστιν δικαιοσύνη τε καὶ σωφροσύνη'; 'And the regular and orderly states of the soul are called lawfulness and law, whereby men are similarly made law-abiding and orderly; and these states are justice and temperance [moderation]. Do you agree or not?' Plato, *Gorgias*, 504d, trans. Lamb; see Plato, *Republic*, 443c–e.

652 Plato, *Republic*, 443e.

653 'ἀσυμμετρίας τε καὶ αἰσχρότητος', Plato, *Gorgias*, 525a.

654 Plato, *Republic*, 591a–b, trans. Bloom.

Plato's teaching about punishment and justice in general must be seen in the light of his ontology—the connection between justice (the good based on internal unity) and the strength of existence, which is related to the degree of inner unity (and goodness). A just punishment, by returning order, renders a human being more just and contributes to his 'being more', even though by being punished he loses something of what he possesses and he 'has less'.

A human being who possesses the virtue of justice will act justly—his just actions originate from the justice of the subject (justice of the soul).[655] The return of the health of the soul, the re-establishment of justice in the soul, prevents unjust action. The linking of the justice of the subject to the justice of his actions has its foundations in Plato's metaphysics—in his teachings on the Good (the Form of the Good).[656] A man who becomes more just, and thus more unified, increasingly conforms to the Good, not merely becoming more so, but also—if he is indeed good—conducting himself in the manner in which good operates—*diffusivum sui bonum est* (good tends to spread)—out of the need to work for the existence of others. The just soul is actually unable to act unjustly: 'it is never just to harm anyone'.[657]

5.3.5 Equality of proportions as a basis for the determination of punishment

The determination of a just punishment is itself a type of just action. Such an action is based not on equality of an arithmetic type, but on proportional equality—geometric equality. This issue will be considered in more detail in the next chapter. Here it suffices to say that the proportional equality which underlies a just punishment 'consists in (...) the natural equality given on each occasion to things unequal'.[658] This equality:

> dispenses more to the greater and less to the smaller, giving due measure to each according to nature; and with regard to honors also, by granting the greater to those that are greater in goodness, and the less to those of the opposite character in respect of goodness and education, it assigns in proportion what is fitting to each.[659]

This equality 'produces all things good'[660] for man and the state.[661] The essence of just action, and of just punishment, which is a kind of just action, is doing that

655 Plato, *Republic*, 443e.

656 M. MacKenzie underestimates the metaphysical foundations of Plato's teaching on punishment, because she has some problems in his explanation of the links between justice as the well-being of the soul and the justice of actions; see MacKenzie, *Plato on Punishment*, p. 152.

657 Plato, *Republic*, 335e, trans. Grube.

658 Plato, *Laws*, 757d, trans. Bury.

659 Plato, *Laws*, 757c, trans. Bury.

660 Plato, *Laws*, 757c, trans. Bury.

661 Plato, *Laws*, 757b–c.

which is beneficial for others,[662] and the measure of being beneficial is whether the action 'builds' justice of the soul, consisting of inner regularity, order, and inner harmony, and—as a consequence—inner unity.[663]

Taking into account differences between subjects leads to considering the changes brought about by bad actions—the worse the action, the worse the damage to the soul, damage that should be repaired by punishment; so—the worse the action, the harsher the penalty. This results in proportions typical of Aristotle's concept of distributive justice based on the proportion of four elements as composed of at least two people and at least two assigned things,[664] for example, penalties, and, thus, at least two crimes and two corresponding penalties. Symbolically:[665]

action A (e.g. murder) : action B (e.g. theft)

=

punishment A (e.g. life imprisonment) : punishment B (e.g. a year's imprisonment)

One should note, however, that this type of proportion is secondary to equality understood as the primary suitability of the nature of a given individual, the nature which is to be repaired, to a punishment that should lead to such a repair. The punishment must be fitted to this nature. The basis of proportional equality is equality conceived as a mean between excess and scarcity, between too severe and too light punishment. At stake, then, is the equality described by Aristotle as the golden mean.[666] In the case of punishment, what is suitable is that which will return inner unity based on inner regularity, order and harmony, which will 'straighten out' that which has been 'twisted'.

In Plato's opinion, punishment is always a kind of affliction, something unpleasant. Plato's Socrates claims that the acquired injustice of the soul cannot be discarded otherwise than through pain and suffering:

> Those who are benefited by the punishment they get from gods and men are they who have committed remediable offences; but still it is through bitter throes of pain that they receive their benefit both here and in the nether world; for in no other way can there be riddance of iniquity.[667]

Determination of an adequate punishment requires, above all, a proper determination of the affliction. Although the basic measure is the state of the soul of the one punished, at times Plato identifies actions themselves and their external effects as the measure for determining a punishment. In the myth of Er that closes the *Republic*, for every unjust action a posthumous punishment is bestowed, meant to

662 See Section 4.2.
663 Plato, *Republic*, 443d–e.
664 Cf. Aristotle, *Nicomachean Ethics*, 1131a.
665 See Kaufmann, *Problemgeschichte*, p. 36.
666 Aristotle, *Nicomachean Ethics*, 1106a. See Plato, *Republic*, 619a–b.
667 Plato, *Gorgias*, 525b, trans. Lamb.

produce suffering ten times greater than that caused by the action. According to the tale of Er, people after death:

> For all the wrongs they had ever done to anyone and all whom they had severally wronged they had paid the penalty in turn tenfold for each (...); as for example that if anyone had been the cause of many deaths or had betrayed cities and armies and reduced them to slavery, or had been participant in any other iniquity, they might receive in requital pains tenfold for each of these wrongs.[668]

Trevor J. Saunders notes that pain and suffering are inherent to the healing of the soul in the early stages of restoring health, when it is necessary to stop behaviours consistent with the broken nature of the soul: 'All that is unnatural, we recall, is painful while all that occurs naturally is pleasant'.[669] Punishment is accompanied by pain and suffering, which as such are not a source of improvement; the soul can return to health by means of appropriate exercise, the acquisition of knowledge, and just actions, which, together with the recovery of health, becomes pleasant.[670]

The main measure of the severity of punishment remains the nature of the culprit, his interior state, and not the act itself, although, of course, it is the weight of the unjust act that causes lesser or greater harm in the subject. Plato likewise mentions circumstances, because these are what determine the level of harm caused to a subject through his behaviour, and whether the culprit's improvement requires a greater or lesser punishment; in the *Laws*, Plato writes:

> The penalty shall be lighter in the case of one who has done wrong owing to another's folly–the wrong-doer being over-persuaded because of his youth or for some such reason; and it shall be heavier when man has done wrong owing to his own folly, because of his incontinence in respect of pleasures and pains and the overpowering influence of craven fears or of incurable desires, envies and rages.[671]

There are also circumstances which make the punishment harsher due to qualities in those who were harmed. This is the case, for example, when those harmed are socially vulnerable people, such as orphans.[672]

5.3.6 Injustice which punishment cannot repair

In the *Gorgias*, Plato's Socrates also speaks of those who are so evil that no punishment can reform them. Making use of the ontological interpretation of justice sketched out earlier, this refers to those who are internally so 'twisted' and have

668 Plato, *Republic*, 615a–b, trans. Shorey.
669 Plato, *Timaeus*, 81e, trans. Zeyl.
670 See Saunders, *Plato's Penal Code*, pp. 174–178; cf. Plato, *Republic*, 443b–e, which refers to the deeds of the righteous as contributing to the justice of the soul.
671 Plato, *Laws*, 934a, trans. Bury.
672 Plato, *Laws*, 927d.

such internal disorder that no return to order is possible. It seems that in this case, the punishment inflicted does not serve the improvement of the criminal, but the improvement of others. In Plato's Socrates' narrative, the worst criminals, who can no longer be cured, receive eternal punishment—'undergoing for their transgressions the greatest, sharpest, and most fearful sufferings evermore'.[673]

The principle is that the punishment be beneficial for the punished, that it serve him and cure him of injustice. In the above scenario, concerning the most hardened criminals, there seems to be an exception to this rule. The punishment serves others, rather than the punished. The primary aim of this punishment is—to put it in contemporary terms—general prevention based on deterrence of potential culprits, and thus prevention of a negative type. Is not the punished treated here in a purely instrumental way—does his suffering not serve only others? However, in this case just punishment is also meant to be something that is suitable and tailored to the soul—that soul 'is to endure the sufferings that are fitting [τὰ προσήκοντα πάθη]',[674] an individual—the punished—himself provides a fundamental reason for the punishment and its severity. Nevertheless, the justification of punishment is at its core teleological—the punishment is justified by the good it causes in specific individual souls—either directly that of the punished, if it can be improved, or other souls. Plato's Socrates does not say that punishment returns some cosmic order, or is imposed with regard to the law itself, as would be typical of a justification based on retribution. The punishment is proportional to the crime—to the damage caused to the soul. The more damaged the soul, the heavier the punishment required so that it may be cured. The criterion of punitive justice is not simply proportion: a lighter sentence for a lesser fault, a harsher sentence for a more serious one. The fundamental criterion, the reason for the suitable measure of punishment, is its suitability to a given soul; the proportions between deserved punishments (a lesser crime—a lighter punishment, a more serious one—a harsher punishment) are secondary. Nevertheless, it seems that in the case of incurable injustice, one cannot say that punishment carries a certain weight for the reason that it is indispensable for the recovery of the soul of the punished. Is it possible to justify eternal punishment in terms of its consequences and not as retribution?

When posing the question of the purely instrumental treatment of the punished, it is necessary to pose yet another—why is there no reference in the narrative to the possibility of a punishment that could annihilate the soul of the most inveterate criminal—something of the order of the death of the soul? In the perspective of criminal justice, the simplest reply would be this: the deterrent factor, and thus, the benefit potential criminals could derive from it, is based on the severity of the penalty; the punishment would not be eternal, and thus, would not deter sufficiently and would not bring the desired benefit to others—what has to be feared most is not annihilation but eternal suffering. However, taking into account Plato's

673 Plato, *Gorgias*, 525c, trans.Lamb.
674 Plato, *Gorgias*, 525a.

argument for the immortality of the soul as presented in the Demiurge's speech in the *Timaeus*, it cannot be accepted that the needs of proper punishment are reasons for the immortality of the soul. Souls are immortal due to other reasons, due to their inherent excellence, which originates from the Demiurge. The reason for continuing existence is the inherent value of an individual that cannot be ignored or disrespected even by the Demiurge himself. He will never stop wanting the continuing existence of his direct creations because of their inherent goodness and not because they are useful for achieving the goodness of others. It is an important point that the Demiurge, while wanting existence, also wants the goodness even of the soul which is condemned to eternal punishment. Does such punishment then not inflict harm on the punished for the sake of the improvement of others? This cannot be accepted, since the basic principle which underlies Plato's conception of justice states that justice never harms and harms nobody.[675] Is it possible, then, to see any use of eternal punishment for the punished himself? In the framework of Plato's conception of justice, it is possible to argue that eternal punishment—having a deterrent value—contributes to the goodness of the punished. The essence of just action is not bringing harm to others and—as far as possible—acting for their benefit. Undergoing a punishment that has a deterrent value would liken the life of the punished, in some very modest— but nevertheless, as it seems, the only possible—way, to acting on behalf of the Form of the Good—of the Good itself. By receiving punishment, he contributes to the justice of others and, to the extent possible, comes to resemble the Good, and this contribution supports his inner unity and his existence, and makes him 'be more' than would be the case without punishment.[676]

Summing up the analysis concerning the main aims of punishment, it should be emphasised that Plato does not say that the good of the state is the main aim of punishment, nor does he speak of the return of some abstract order of justice—whatever has happened is accomplished and unchangeable. In the *Laws* there is a clear statement about the aims:

> he shall pay the penalty, not because of the wrongdoing,—for what is done can never be undone,—but in order that for the future both he himself and those who behold his punishment may either utterly loathe his sin or at least renounce to a great extent such lamentable conduct.[677]

Similarly in the *Gorgias*: 'everyone under punishment rightly inflicted on him by another should either be made better and profit thereby, or serve as an example

675 Plato, *Republic*, 335e.

676 M. MacKenzie does not take into account the metaphysical context of Plato's teaching on punishment, and does not perceive this kind of justification of punishment for 'incurable' injustice. See MacKenzie (1981), pp. 208–214.

677 Plato, *Laws*, 934a–b, trans. Bury.

to the rest, that others seeing the sufferings he endures may in fear amend themselves'.[678]

Thus, punishment serves a preventative aim, in particular—to put it in contemporary terms—within the domain of specific prevention (with respect to which the positive aspect—resocialisation, in modern parlance—is primary), although it is perceived by Plato also as general prevention based on deterrence. Seneca presents Plato's position in this domain with the famous formula: 'Nemo prudens punit, (...) quia peccatum est, sed ne peccetur'—'A sensible person does not punish a man because he has sinned, but in order to keep him from sin'.[679] Plato's approach does not exclude the death penalty, which destroys only the body. The effects of the punishment extend to the afterlife and to subsequent incarnations.

5.3.7 The inevitability of punishment by the gods and two aims of the law

Plato acknowledges the value that the inevitability of punishment has for the accomplishment of its aims. The gods watch over this inevitability, and in regard to punishment cannot be bought off through offerings: 'the next contention, that the gods can be won over by wrongdoers, on the receipt of bribes, is one that no one should admit, and we must try to refute it by every means in our power'.[680]

Plato's Athenian in the *Laws* speaks of a verdict imposed by the gods who ruled over Olympus, a verdict that was the first and most important, superior to all others. This was

> the decree that as thou becomest worse, thou goest to the company of the worse souls, and as thou becomest better, to the better souls; and that, alike in life and in every shape of death, thou both doest and sufferest what it is befitting that like should do towards like. From this decree of Heaven neither wilt thou nor any other luckless wight ever boast that he has escaped; for this decree is one which the gods who have enjoined it have enjoined above all others, and meet it is that it should be most strictly observed. For by it thou wilt not ever be neglected, neither if thou shouldest dive, in thy very littleness, into the depths of the earth below, nor if thou shouldest soar up to the height of Heaven above; but thou shalt pay to the gods thy due penalty, whether thou remainest here on earth, or hast passed away to Hades, or art transported to a region yet more fearsome.[681]

The gods' view on the impossibility of avoiding punishment is clearly expressed here; it is nonetheless worth mentioning yet another thought contained in the

678 Plato, *Gorgias*, 525b, trans. Lamb.
679 Seneca, *De ira—On Anger*, I, 19, 7, trans. Basore; somewhat further Seneca writes: 'Nec umquam ad praeteritum, sed ad futurum poena refertur', ibid., II, 31, 8.
680 Plato, *Laws*, 905d, trans. Bury.
681 Plato, *Laws*, 904e–905b.

quoted excerpt. The element of the gods' verdict that—as Plato's Athenian says—raises it above all others is not solely—and not especially—the inevitability of punishment. The verdict concerns both those who become worse and those who improve. In accordance with this verdict, everyone experiences from others and does unto others like himself—good unto good, evil unto evil. As stated above, the law, including criminal law, according to Plato, has the aim of making people more just, and thereby happier. Bearing in mind the verdict discussed here, which the gods have raised above all their other verdicts, the rise of the just leads not only to the emergence of happy individuals, but to the emergence of communities of the just who resemble one another in terms of their moral excellence, and who experience just actions towards themselves and themselves act in a just way towards others. A community thereby arises in which true friendship is realised. Plato refers to the truths contained in old maxims. In the *Gorgias* Plato's Socrates says: 'the closest possible friendship between man and man is that mentioned by the sages of old time as "like to like" [ὁ ὅμοιος τῷ ὁμοίῳ]'.[682] In the *Laws* we read: 'There is an old and true saying that "equality produces amity" [ἰσότης φιλότητα ἀπεργάζεται], which is right well and fitly spoken'.[683] Thus, the principal aim of the law designated by Plato is realised: 'to allow the citizens to live supremely happy lives in the greatest possible mutual friendship'.[684] In accordance with this statement, the aim of law is the emergence of a community of equals, of happy citizens. The opposite would be the emergence of a community of the unjust, who would inflict harm on each other, this being at the same time a punishment serving improvement.[685]

5.3.8 Civil law aspects of punishment

Plato's main reflection on punishment concerns the question of whether or not a penalty is something useful for the punished, and—as a consequence—whether punishment should be avoided. Thus, the perspective of the punished dominates. In the *Laws*, Plato also looks at punishment from the perspective of the judge and the lawgiver, and this perspective takes into account the victim of wrongdoing. Here the problem of punishment includes the question of the necessity of repairing inflicted harm, which is the concern of civil rather than criminal law. Plato places the compensation of the victim at the forefront:

682 Plato, *Gorgias*, 510b, trans. Lamb.
683 Plato, *Laws*, 757a, trans. Bury.
684 Plato, *Laws*, 743c, trans. Saunders.
685 Punishment consisting in living in a society of the unjust must be read in the light of the myth of Er, and the description of the choice of future fates; it must be acknowledged that one destined to live in a society of the unjust may choose a life in which he himself avoids acting unjustly and opens for himself the road to a better life; see Plato, *Republic*, 617e, 619b; cf. Plato, *Phaedrus*, 249b. See Section 5.2.4.

> In all cases where one man causes damage to another by acts of robbery or violence, if the damage be great, he shall pay a large sum as compensation to the damaged party, and a small sum if the damage be small; and as a general rule, every man shall in every case pay a sum equal to the damage done, until the loss is made good; and, in addition to this, every man shall pay the penalty which is attached to his crime by way of corrective.[686]

When the problem of punishment is expanded to include the dimension of compensating the victim, Plato does not discard the perspective of the individual, whose good constitutes the reason for inflicting a penalty.

Compensation can sometimes surpass the inflicted damage. This is so, for example, in the case of harm inflicted on orphans, who—finding themselves in an inferior situation to others in society—deserve exceptional care.[687] An orphan's caretaker who is accused of not caring for or harming the child, if found guilty, 'shall pay four times the damages assessed, and of this amount one half shall go to the child, the other half to the successful prosecutor'.[688]

The measure of compensation is determined, in part, by the particular situation of the victim and the resulting additional difficulties in his or her development, in the surmounting of which compensation may be of help; nonetheless the element of specific and general prevention is also present—higher compensation is an additional burden for the culprit, which may aid in his improvement, and also serves as a warning to others.

5.3.9 Concluding remarks

In Plato's conception of punishment one can discern elements of specific as well as general prevention. In the case of specific prevention, the positive element is foremost—punishment is a form of medicine which returns justice to the soul. The justice of actions is secondary to the state of the soul: a just individual will act justly. General prevention is also taken into consideration, especially with regard to the most serious offences, and is based on the deterrent function of punishment, especially eternal, everlasting punishment; the negative aspect of general prevention is thus the primary focus.

Nonetheless, the analysis here demonstrates that for Plato the principal aim of punishment is not the defence of values acknowledged by the legal system, whatever they might be, but the good of the individual—his personal development, which is, first of all, moral development, consisting of the attainment of the greatest excellence of the subject—situated on the level of existence—which is the virtue of justice, an inner unity based on inner regularity, order, harmony,

---

686 Plato, *Laws*, 933e–934a, trans. Bury; cf. ibid., 934b and E. B. England's notes on 'παντελῶς τῆς ἀξίας' (934b6), Plato, *Laws*, ed. England, p. 558.

687 Plato, *Laws*, 927e–928a.

688 Plato, *Laws*, 928b–c, trans. Bury.

and straightness. Attainment of the virtue of justice is likewise the attainment of happiness. In principle, punishment ought to be adapted and proportionate not to the act committed, but to the state of the subject, the state of his soul. It should be appropriate medicine, returning health to the soul, restoring inner order, harmony and straightness.

The elements of a retributive concept of punishment become salient, above all, in the case of the most hardened criminals, who are internally so spoiled that no amelioration is possible, no punishment can be a suitable, sufficient medicine. Yet, the punishment is deserved and possesses a deterrent value. Moreover, the suffering of the offender, since it is beneficial for others, contributes to his inner unity and his goodness.

The preceding analysis concerning Plato's conception of punishment clearly shows that the aim of punishment is not the good of the state, nor an abstractly conceived order of justice. The aims of punishment are not located beyond the individual (the individual soul). Therefore, in this conception of punishment there are no elements of thinking in the spirit of totalitarianism. The law and the state serve the good of the individual. This is an important argument in favour of a non-totalitarian interpretation of the *Republic* and Plato's other dialogues.

6 Equality

6.1 Initial remarks

The issue of equality underlies all of the principal dimensions of Plato's conception of justice. Plato recognises equal dignity and places proportional equality at the centre of his considerations about the content of just actions; this kind of equality is also fundamental for creating unity between the acting subject and the addressee of his action and for creating unity between elements, and therefore, for the construction of the universe as a whole. Last but not least, equality is a prerequisite for all friendship, and since it is one of the two principal aims of laws, they cannot fully reach their ends without advancing the equality of all members of the community.

6.2 Equality in dignity

Having sketched out Plato's conception of justice above, it is worth returning to the issue of dignity as encountered in the Demiurge's speech in the *Timaeus.* Plato's approach to dignity proves to be surprisingly modern in its recognition of the fundamental equality of all bearers of this perfection.

An inherent perfection is recognised both in the gods and in human souls, which provides the basis for postulating special treatment for beings endowed with such perfection. This perfection is the reason for the Demiurge's (and everyone's, inasmuch as one is good) willing of the continuing existence of such beings, independent of their way of acting, moral qualities, and other changeable traits. Such beings are wished by the Demiurge (and by everyone in as much as one is good) for their own sake. In respect to dignity as the basis for this special treatment, there is a fundamental equality—something either possesses this perfection, and should be treated accordingly as an aim in itself, or it does not. With respect to something's being an aim in itself, there is no spectrum of different 'stages'. Something is an aim in itself and its continuing existence is willed, or else it is not.

This dignity, this inherent perfection, is the perfection of existence based on being beautifully harmonised internally and on a unity established directly by the Demiurge himself. As has been shown, the question of unity is at the very centre of Plato's teaching on justice—the more someone is just, the more inner harmony and order is within him. The more he is internally united, the more strongly he exists. Striving for justice is striving for inner harmony (beauty), for increased unity and for stronger existence. Nevertheless, it is not the justice souls obtain that is the reason for wishing their continuing existence. The existence of even the most devious souls is wished by the Demiurge himself; therefore, even the worst criminals are recognised as worth lasting forever. What can be changed depending on the justice or the injustice obtained by the soul is its fate. In the

Phaedrus—according to the story about the soul as a tripartite chariot—souls incarnate into people performing different social roles, and they are bestowed with fates they deserve.[689] According to this story, they are not free to choose their fate—it depends on their moral perfection or imperfection, and takes place 'according to the law.'[690] In the *Laws* there is a famous depiction of God—the Supervisor of the Universe[691] as a draughts-player who assigns fates to souls according to their justice. This assignment is just in itself as it entails what is proper and appropriate in contributing to their goodness; the souls 'meet the fate they deserve [τῆς προσηκούσης μοίρας]',[692] which is to meet a fate which is appropriate for the given soul, a fate which fits it well. In assigning an appropriate (well-fitting) fate (τῆς προσηκούσης μοίρας) the divine draughts-player is—according to the description of just deeds in the *Gorgias* ('τὰ προσήκοντα πράττειν')[693]—exercising justice. He cares about each individual and acts to benefit him, creating opportunities for improvement, but eventually leaving this improvement to the free will of the individual. By moving a soul to an inferior situation the divine draughts-player assigns a kind of penalty (or reward) which creates an opportunity to improve, to make changes in the character of the soul. Nevertheless, 'he left it to the individual's acts of will to determine the direction of these changes'.[694] Therefore, there is no fundamental contradiction between the assignment of appropriate fates by the Supervisor of the Universe and the free choice of fate described in the myth of Er. There is an interplay between the two.

In considering the relationship between inherent dignity as a special unity and a special way of existence, and the justice of the soul, which is also a perfection of existence based on unity, it can be observed that the inner structure of an individual, which is decisive for the unity and for the strength of his existence, has two layers. The original one, which constitutes dignity, is unchangeable and is the reason why the Demiurge cares and will always care for the existence and for the well-being (happiness) of each individual endowed with dignity. The second dimension of the inner unity and the strength of existence can change and depends on the advancement of justice. This dimension shapes what is appropriate for the soul and underlies the diversity of the ways in which the postulate of caring is realised. This postulate itself applies, however, equally to all actions addressed towards those who are endowed with dignity. The Supervisor of the Universe described in the *Laws* as the draughts-player 'behaves' in relationship to human souls (to being endowed with dignity) as the Demiurge who cares for their continuing existence; both the Supervisor and the Demiurge act like the Good

689 Plato, *Phaedrus*, 248c–e.
690 Plato, *Phaedrus*, 248c, trans. Nehamas, Woodruff.
691 Plato, *Laws*, 904a.
692 Plato, *Laws*, 903d–e, trans. Saunders.
693 Plato, *Gorgias*, 507a–b.
694 Plato, *Laws*, 904b–c, trans. Saunders.

to which Plato refers in the *Republic*. Moreover, caring for continuous existence and being able to ensure it requires the Demiurge to have 'properties' which are ascribed to the Good—the Demiurge has to be the source of being, of existence. It should be stressed that in writing about the actions of the Demiurge as the Supervisor of the Universe, Plato unveils truths about the Good and about acting justly, about the actions of everyone in so far as one is good. In the reflection on justice, while considering the questions of how to be good and how to live a good life, the stories about the Supervisor of the Universe, the Demiurge and the Good seem to be designed to disclose knowledge about the foundations of being good and of good action. In that perspective there is no fundamental reason to conclude that three different 'entities' having divine character and performing analogous functions inhabit Plato's universe.[695]

It is worth noting that the equality of dignity is an equality based on a certain internal structure of a being—it relies on the special unity of certain elements and not on the equality of the 'content'. The elements involved can be very different—their harmony and order is what counts. Therefore, there is a fundamental equality of gods and human souls, of creatures that can be very different, in respect to their special ontological status and the postulates of special treatment (perpetual caring for their existence) related to it. It is not equality based on, for example, the possession (or exercising) of intellectual abilities (rationality), which can always be gradable. The fundamental equality in dignity, which is always preserved, is not only a foundation for the postulate of caring about everyone who possesses this perfection, but also—as will be argued below—for the formation of a community united by friendship.

6.3 Proportionate equality as a basis for shaping actions

6.3.1 Preliminary remarks

In the conclusion of his dialogue with himself in the *Gorgias*, Plato's Socrates explains to Callicles why their understandings of justice radically differ, redirecting his attention from human beings to the whole universe:

695 While analysing the myth of creation in the *Timaeus*, Kahn poses several fundamental questions about the ontological status of the Demiurge: 'Perhaps that is where the Demiurge is hiding: in the uncreated *nous* of an uncreated psyche? But then he appears again as an item in his own model for creation? Or is this simply one more inconcinnity in the cosmogonic narrative? I am afraid we must be resigned to leave these questions unresolved.' Kahn, *Plato and the Post-Socratic Dialogue*, p. 179. If I am right in focusing on justice (moral excellence) as the central problem of Plato's philosophy, and the myths and stories which are crucial in Plato's narrative should be read as means to resolve this problem, then the questions posed by Kahn are not the questions Plato wants us to ask and to seek answers to in his works.

> Yes, Callicles, wise men claim that partnership and friendship, orderliness, self-control, and justice hold together heaven and earth, and gods and men, and that is why they call this universe a world order, my friend, and not an undisciplined world-disorder.[696]

The diagnosis of why Callicles fails to understand or even notice the order of the whole universe is formulated by referring to proportionate—geometric—equality and geometry in general:

> I believe that you don't pay attention to these facts, even though you're a wise man in these matters. You've failed to notice that proportionate equality has great power among both gods and men, and you suppose that you ought to practice getting the greater share. That's because you neglect geometry.[697]

Neglecting geometry, overlooking the functions of the proportionate—that is, geometric—equality, turns out to be a fundamental flaw. An inquiry into why geometric equality is so important confirms the relevance of the issue of unity as ontic perfection for understanding justice. It also corroborates the conclusions reached above that just action is shaped by a certain congruence between an action and its addressee which is based on the relation of fitting (being appropriate for the concrete being) and not on a congruence between an action and general norms or abstract forms.

6.3.2 Arithmetic equality

In writing about the foundations of justice in the *Laws*, Plato distinguishes two types of equality: equality of 'measures, weights and numbers'[698] and a second type which 'needs the wisdom and judgment of Zeus'.[699] The former is also called arithmetic equality, the latter geometric equality. The equality which involves 'the judgment of Zeus' is geometric equality,[700] which in the *Gorgias* was required from Callicles by Plato's Socrates, and is 'the most genuine, and the best'[701] equality.

Arithmetic equality is easy to discern and to implement. It 'is within the competence of any state and any legislator: that is, one can simply distribute equal awards by lot'.[702] Exercising this kind of equality is sometimes 'necessary to avoid the anger of the man in the street by giving him an equal chance in the lot'.[703] Yet,

---

696 Plato, *Gorgias*, 507e–508a, trans. Zeyl.
697 Plato, *Gorgias*, 508a, trans. Zeyl.
698 Plato, *Laws*, 757b, trans. Saunders.
699 Plato, *Laws*, 757b, trans. Saunders.
700 Plato's teaching about geometric equality as a foundation of justice and of the universe in general is clearly influenced by Pythagorean philosophy; see Lengauer, *Pojęcie równości*, p. 80.
701 Plato, *Laws*, 757b, trans. Saunders.
702 Plato, *Laws*, 757b, trans. Saunders.
703 Plato, *Laws*, 757e, trans. Saunders.

it is contrary to true justice (παρὰ δίκην τὴν ὀρθήν).[704] When arithmetic equality is applied one should pray 'to the gods of good luck to make the lot give the right decision'.[705] The concept of justice based on an equality which does not take into account differences between people is developed later by Aristotle in his teaching on commutative justice;[706] however, he detaches it from the idea of deciding about the right share by lot.

6.3.3 Geometric equality as the foundation of true justice

Justice which needs the judgment of Zeus is based on geometric, proportionate equality. This is the most genuine and the best equality.[707] Exercising proportionate equality is exercising justice itself.[708] This kind of justice should be always strived for and is a paradigm which every legislator should concentrate on.[709] This equality takes account of inequalities between people and assigns to each what is fitting, according to his nature:

> The general method I mean is to grant much to the great and less to the less great, adjusting what you give to take account of the real nature of each—specifically, to confer high recognition on great virtue, but when you come to the poorly educated in this respect, to treat them as they deserve.[710]

This equality is based on a relation of commensurability, appropriateness, fittingness between something and someone. This something is an action or—rather—an intended effect of an action. The relation exists if an action (the intended effect of an action) fits the person who is the addressee of that action according to his nature. According to the nature of the addressee, something 'not too much' and 'not too little' is determined. 'Proportionate' means, first of all, well-fitted (appropriate commensurate, appropriate). Knowing Plato's considerations about justice, it can be added that the 'measure' of being well-fitted is being beneficial for the addressee of the action, and the criterion for being beneficial is the (direct or indirect) impact on the strength of existence, on the internal unity of the addressee.[711] However, there is something more about proportionate equality, since it is recognised to be the foundation of friendship, of a unity of a certain kind between people and gods. An action which is proportionate to its addressee is also in accord with the nature of the acting subject. On the one hand, it is a 'product' of a just soul, and

704 Plato, *Laws*, 757d–e.
705 Plato, *Laws*, 757e, trans. Saunders.
706 See Aristotle, *Nicomachean Ethics*, 1131b–1132a.
707 Plato, *Laws*, 757b.
708 Plato, *Laws*, 757d.
709 Plato, *Laws*, 757c–d.
710 Plato, *Laws*, 757c, trans. Saunders; cf. ibid., 744b–c.
711 See Chapter 4.

on the other, it fits the acting subject as contributing to his inner harmony and order as well as to his inner unity and justice, and therefore as strengthening his existence.[712]

Why is proportionate equality the foundation for the justice of the content of actions and, therefore, of the content of the law which shapes actions? This is because such equality is suited best to create a unity of elements. In the *Timaeus*, when the construction of the universe is discussed, the dialogue's title character explains:

> it isn't possible to combine two things well all by themselves, without a third; there has to be some bond between the two that unites them. Now the best bond is one that really and truly makes a unity of itself together with the things bonded by it, and this in the nature of things is best accomplished by proportion.[713]

Plato's Timaeus explains this kind of equality with an example involving numbers. Unification between two numbers is accomplished by a third, middle term:

> For whenever of three numbers which are either solids or squares the middle term between any two of them is such that
>
> [a] what the first term is to it, it is to the last,
> [b] and, conversely, what the last term is to the middle, it is to the first,
> [c] then, since the middle term turns out to be both first and last, and the last and the first likewise both turn out to be middle terms,
> [d] they will all of necessity turn out to have the same relationship to each other, and, given this, will all be unified.[714]

This kind of proportion takes place, for example, between

3—9—27.

This is a three-term relation in which 9 is the middle term. Then

$3 : 9 = 9 : 27$ — 'the first term is to it, it is to the last',

and, conversely,

$27 : 9 = 9 : 3$ — 'what the last term is to the middle, it is to the first'.

Thus

$9 : 27 = 3 : 9$ — 'the middle term turns out to be both first and last, and the last and the first likewise both turn out to be middle terms'.

712 Plato, *Republic*, 443d–e; see Section 3.7.
713 Plato, *Timaeus*, 31b–c, trans. Zeyl.
714 Plato, *Timaeus*, 31c–32a, trans. Zeyl.

Plato's Timaeus talks about proportionate—geometric—equality. Although the equations are composed of four elements, there are nevertheless only three different terms, and the three-element relation remains fundamental.

What are the main reasons for accepting geometric equality as a foundation of justice? In the foreground are ontological, not mathematical issues. Mathematical constructions are tools for directing one's attention (the learning power) to the problem of unity as being crucial for understanding justice, the human being, and being in general. In geometric equality, 'all elements will be unified'.[715] The middle term unifies the two other elements twofold. Firstly, from 'inside'—it is in between, in the middle, it is a kind of knot which ties external elements, like 9 in the proportion 3—9—27 (3 : 9 = 9 : 27).

Secondly, the middle term can become 'external', as in the equation 9 : 3 = 27 : 9. It then comprises the other elements, being a kind of border, a term—πέρας, something which surrounds and makes definite. This possibility of being regarded as both an internal and an external basis of unity is offered neither in harmonic nor arithmetic equality.

One of the commonly accepted ontological principles known in pre-Socratic philosophy states: 'to be'—'to exist as a given being' means 'to be definite',[716] 'to be determined', 'to be finite', 'to have a term (πέρας)', 'to be limited by boundaries which provide shape or form'.[717] There is a basic intuition that something which is not determined, which has no boundaries, simply falls apart. In opposition to contemporary thinking shaped by the Christian understanding of God as an infinite being, in ancient Greek thought only something that is finite can be perfect. An unfinished sculpture, which has not obtained its final shape, is of course not perfect. Only something finished can be something which is fulfilled.[718]

In the *Timaeus*, in the story about the universe coming into existence, two elements, two middle terms, bind all four elements together. The world is made up of four inter-related elements: 'the god set water and air between fire and earth, and made them as proportionate to one another as was possible, so that what fire is to air, air is to water, and what air is to water, water is to earth':[719]

$$\text{fire}\,(1) : \text{air}\,(3) = \text{air}\,(3) : \text{water}\,(9) = \text{water}\,(9) : \text{earth}\,(27).$$

715 Plato, *Timaeus*, 32a, trans. Zeyl.

716 Kahn, 'Being in Parmenides and Plato', p. 173 [244].

717 Kubok, *Problem apeiron*, p. 47.

718 This idea is present in the etymology of the word 'perfect', which derives from Latin '*per*'—'thorough', 'completely' and '*facere*'—'to make', Brown (ed.), *The New Shorter Oxford Dictionary*, p. 2154, 2158. According to Anaximander, the origin of all elements is ἄπειρον—that which is without boundary, limit, which is infinite, indefinite, or undetermined. The elements and beings come to be by determinations, by becoming definite, by boundaries.

719 Plato, *Timaeus*, 32b, trans. Zeyl.

However, considerations about the four elements of which the universe is built are based on three-fold proportions:

fire (1)—air (3)—water (9)

and

air (3)—water (9)—earth (27).

Applying simple mathematical rules, the first equation can be transformed in such a way that the middle terms—water and air—also become the first and the last term:

water (9) : air (3) = air (3) : fire (1) = earth (27) : water (9)

and

air (3) : fire (1) = earth (27) : water (9) = water (9) : air (3).

Plato's Timaeus stresses the issue of unity, which is based on proportional equality and which is also a foundation of friendship between elements.[720] The universe 'having come together into a unity with itself, (...) could not be undone by anyone but the one who had bound it together'.[721]

In human society, that which binds two subjects is acting justly. Schematically,

subject A (acting subject)—deed D—subject B (addressee).

Transforming this into a proportion with four terms, the middle term is repeated:

subject A (acting subject) : deed D = deed D : subject B (addressee).

Although mathematical formulae are used here as a means to express ontological and moral issues, and therefore metaphorically, it is nevertheless troublesome that the middle term belongs to an essentially different ontological category than the other two terms. In considerations about the elements in the universe, such incongruence is not present. Using Aristotle's terminology one can say that an action is, evidently, not a substance, like an acting subject and an addressee are, but belongs instead to the ontological category of properties (accidents). From the point of view of the acting subject, it is a property of doing; from the point of view of the addressee it is being-affected.[722] When only ontological categories are considered it is difficult to see any proportion (substance : property ≠ property : substance). However, the matter looks different if one considers that the problem of justice is apprehended by Plato as a problem on an existential level in which unity plays a crucial role. Constituting justice can be interpreted in terms of giving and receiving unity, which underlies any existence. The justice (the inner unity) of the

---

720 Plato, *Timaeus*, 32c.

721 Plato, *Timaeus*, 32c, trans. Zeyl.

722 The author wishes to thank Maurycy Zajęcki for his comments on this matter.

acting subject is then a precondition and a 'source' of just deed D.[723] On the other hand, deed D is something just for addressee B if it fits the addressee as being beneficial, as contributing to the inner unity, and therefore to the existence, of B. Deed D is then a 'source' of the unity of addressee B.

Introducing 'ontological units', these relations may be rendered in the following way:

acting subject A (source—a cause of unity) : deed D (effect—unity)
= deed D (source—a cause of unity) : addressee B (effect—unity).

According to basic mathematical rules, the middle term, which is deed D, can be substituted for with the other terms:

deed D (source—a cause of unity) : acting subject A (effect—unity)
= addressee B (source—a cause of unity) : deed D (effect—unity).

The deed which is just 'includes' both subjects; it forms a boundary (πέρας) and unifies the subjects. The aforementioned[724] etymology of 'δίκη' should be recalled here, which refers to the boundaries of a field. Justice creates a new entity, a community of subjects. Justice proves to be the foundation of friendship which, next to happiness, is one of the principal aims of the law.[725]

Plato's conception of proportionate equality can also be considered in relation to the concept of the 'golden mean.' For example, in Book X of the *Republic*, in considering the choice of a model for life, Plato's Socrates praises the mean, saying:

> we must always know how to choose the mean in such lives and how to avoid either of the extremes, as far as possible, both in this life and in all those beyond it. This is the way that a human being becomes happiest.[726]

In the *Laws*, while talking about marriage, Plato's Athenian evokes a general rule: 'in respect of excellence [πρὸς ἀρετήν] what is evenly balanced and symmetrical is infinitely superior to what is untampered.'[727]

6.3.4 Aristotle's continuation of Plato's teaching on geometric proportion

Plato's teaching on geometric equality or geometric proportion is referred to by Aristotle in his conception of distributive justice. However, he omits some important elements of Plato's conception; one may say that he loses something of its metaphysical depth.

---

723 Plato, *Republic*, 443b–e.
724 See Section 3.2.
725 Plato, *Law*, 743c, trans. Saunders.
726 Plato, *Republic*, 619a–b, trans. Grube.
727 'τὸ γὰρ ὁμαλὸν καὶ σύμμετρον ἀκράτου μυρίον διαφέρει πρὸς ἀρετήν', Plato, *Laws*, 773a, trans. Burnet.

Aristotle writes that distributive justice 'is found in the distribution of honours or wealth or anything else that can be divided among members of a community who share in a political system'.[728] In distribution, the particular differences between those who receive have to be taken into account: 'if the people involved are not equal, they will not receive equal shares'.[729] Aristotle observes that 'what is just requires four things at least; the people for whom it is just are two, and the [equal] things that are involved are two'.[730] This can be rendered by the formula:

person A : person B = thing received by A : thing received by B.

Following simple mathematical rules, this can also be given as:

person A : thing received by A = person B : thing received by B

or

thing received by A : person A = thing received by B : person B.

According to Aristotle, 'the other way of being just is the rectificatory, found in transactions both voluntary and involuntary'.[731] The justice of rectification—commutative justice—is characterised by numerical (arithmetic) proportion. From the formal point of view, however, justice in rectification can also be understood as a special instance of distributive justice which occurs when people are regarded as equal. Aristotle explains the justice of rectification in the domain of criminal law in the following way:

> the law looks only at differences in the harm [inflicted], and treats people involved as equals, when one does injustice while the other suffers it, and one has done the harm while the other has suffered it. Hence the judge tries to restore this unjust situation to equality, since it is unequal.[732]

The justice of rectification can be applied not only in the field of criminal law but also, for example, to contracts for buying and selling.[733] For a simple contract of this type, the following formula can be proposed:

value of what is assigned to A (value of thing bought) : person A(buyer)

=

value of what is assigned to B (value of paid money) : person B (seller).

Since:

person A = person B,

728 Aristotle, *Nicomachean Ethics*, 1130b, trans. Irwin.
729 Aristotle, *Nicomachean Ethics*, 1131a, trans. Irwin.
730 Aristotle, *Nicomachean Ethics*, 1131a, trans. Irwin; words in brackets added by Irwin.
731 Aristotle, *Nicomachean Ethics*, 1131b, trans. Irwin.
732 Aristotle, *Nicomachean Ethics*, 1132a, trans. Irwin.
733 Aristotle, *Nicomachean Ethics*, 1132a.

it follows that:

value of what is assigned to A = value of what is assigned to B.

Aristotle notes the difference between divided geometric equality, which always involves four elements, and continuous geometric equality with three terms. Nevertheless, he expresses no objections or reservations about replacing (as being equivalent) a tripartite proportion with a proportion composed of four elements: 'divided proportion clearly requires four terms. But so does continuous proportion, since here we use one term as two, and mention it twice'.[734] The tripartite proportion is, for Aristotle, an instance of a four-term proportion'.

In the *Timaeus*, however, the paradigm for understanding proportional equality is provided by a tripartite proportion in which one element binds the other two. In the example of the four elements in the universe, the structure of the proportions comprises not four but six elements:

fire (1): air (3) = air (3): water (9) = water (9): earth (27).

Of course, it is also the case that

fire (1): air (3) = water (9): earth (27).

Nevertheless, in such a simplification, the fundamental intuition linked with tripartite proportionate equality is lost. There is no longer one element which binds the other two together and is bound with them.

Aristotle's approach to distributive justice, based on a four-term proportion composed of four different elements, is characterised by Plato as 'the most genuine equality, and the best':[735] it grants 'much to the great and less to the less great'.[736] Nonetheless, treating Aristotle's approach to proportionate equality as fundamental, overlooks the one element which performs the binding function. For Plato, from an ontological point of view, the unifying function of proportionate equality is based on relations between three elements, where one of them—the middle one—binds the other two. In the Aristotelian approach the interpersonal character of just actions, and therefore an element which binds the members of a political community, is missing. In Plato's approach, just deeds link the giver and the beneficiary, and a new relational entity is created. In Aristotle's paradigmatic proportion with four different terms, the equality and the unity of the proportion (and therefore also its justice) are based in something 'external' to the elements; the basis for unification is 'somewhere' in the comparison of pairs of elements.

Without losing sight of the unifying functions of just actions, which is crucial in Plato's approach, the structure of distributive justice with four different elements (two subjects and two deeds) can be easily expressed applying basic mathematical

734 Aristotle, *Nicomachean Ethics*, 1131a, trans. Irwin.
735 Plato, *Laws*, 757b, trans. Saunders.
736 Plato, *Laws*, 757c, trans. Saunders; cf. ibid., 744b–c.

rules to Plato's formulae. From that point of view, Plato's approach proves to be more general than Aristotle's. If subject A is someone who is to distribute in a just way, and B and C are subjects who should receive the distributed goods and the addressees of A's actions D_1 and D_2, then

$$(\alpha)\ \text{subject A} : \text{deed } D_1 = \text{deed } D_1 : \text{subject B}$$

$$(\beta)\ \text{subject A} : \text{deed } D_2 = \text{deed } D_2 : \text{subject C}$$

Both D_1 and D_2 are proportional to A as their source:

$$(\gamma)\ \text{subject A} : \text{deed } D_1 = \text{subject A} : \text{deed } D_2$$

Therefore, it also holds that

$$\text{deed } D_1 : \text{subject A} = \text{deed } D_2 : \text{subject A}$$

The last formula can be interpreted as expressing the contribution which both the deed D_1 and the deed D_2 provide to the unity (to the justice) of the acting subject A.

Then applying (α) and (β) to (γ):

$$\text{deed } D_1 : \text{subject B} = \text{deed } D_2 : \text{subject C}$$

In this way, the Aristotelian formula with four different terms is reached.

6.3.5 Concluding remarks

The analyses of Plato's approach to equality confirm that unity as the foundation of existence is crucial for understanding justice. Just deeds bind acting subjects with the addressees of their actions. When a community is created, both the acting subject and the addressee benefit from a just deed—the acting subject benefits by building his own justice, his internal unity, by directly strengthening his existence; the addressee benefits by receiving that which fits him according to his nature. Respect for equality does not mean equal treatment. The disparities should, however, be justified by differences between the addressees of just actions. Nonetheless, all addressees should be equally respected as potential beneficiaries of such actions.

Geometric equality is a tool for exploration of the ontological foundations of justice as a binding force for community. A crucial role is played by just action, which is a middle term in the continuing proportion. Plato's teaching on geometric equality finds its continuation in the Aristotelian conception of distributive justice. There are, however, important differences. For Plato the three-term continuing proportion is the paradigm of geometric equality. Aristotle, however, prefers the four-term divided proportion as a starting point for understanding distributive justice, and the binding role played by just action itself is not as clearly expressed as in Plato's approach. In Plato's conception, increasing just actions leads not only to the growth of justice in souls, which increases happiness, but it also strengthens bonds between members of the community, and therefore life in the greatest possible mutual friendship is—alongside living supremely happy lives—the main aim of law. For Aristotle and the classical philosophical tradition regarding state and law, happiness remains the primary task of laws, whereas friendship loses its preeminent position.

6.4 Justice and friendship

6.4.1 Preliminary remarks

Friendship is evoked in different contexts in which justice is considered. There is friendship between parts of the soul and friendship with oneself. This turns out to be a basis for friendship with others and for building a community, just as justice in the soul is a basis for acting justly.

In Plato's approach to friendship, it is not only the proportionate equality involving just actions which is fundamental; the equality between an acting subject and the addressee of his actions also becomes an important issue. The equality of friends is a precondition for genuine friendship between people, and since friendship is one of the two primary aims of laws, equality of the members of the political community also becomes an objective of those laws and of political organisation.

6.4.2 Friendship with oneself

While talking about someone moderate (prudent), Plato's Socrates speaks about friendship between the parts of the human soul:

> And isn't he moderate because of the friendly and harmonious relations between these same parts, namely, when the ruler and the ruled believe in common that the rational part should rule and don't engage in civil war against it? Moderation is surely nothing other than that, both in the city and in the individual.[737]

To be one's own friend is the first dimension of being just. Plato's Socrates in the *Republic* identifies friendship with oneself, understood as caring about oneself, as the first dimension of the wisdom which is

> a kind of knowledge belonging to some of the citizens [to a part of the soul] that counsels not about the affairs connected with particular matters in the city [in a human being], but about how the city [a human being] as a whole would best deal with itself and the other cities [other people].[738]

---

737 Plato, *Republic*, 442c–d, trans. Grube; Bloom translates: 'Isn't he moderate because of the friendship and accord [φιλίᾳ καὶ συμφωνίᾳ] of these parts—when the ruling part and the two ruled parts are of the single opinion that the calculating part ought to rule and don't raise faction against it?'

738 Plato, *Republic*, 428c–d, trans. Bloom; see Section 3.6.2.

Friendship with oneself is mentioned in passages which can be regarded as highly important from a formal point of view. In the passage of the *Republic*, extensively commented on above, about what in truth justice is,[739] Plato's Socrates characterises a just man (one having justice in his soul) as someone who 'becomes his own friend [φίλον γενόμενον ἑαυτῷ]',[740] and 'then, and only then, he acts, if he does act in some way—either concerning the acquisition of money, or the care of the body, or something political, or concerning private contracts'.[741]

There is also a reference to being a friend to oneself in the final words of the *Republic*:

> if we are persuaded by me, we'll believe that the soul is immortal and able to endure every evil and every good, and we'll always hold to the upward path, practicing justice with reason in every way. That way *we'll be friends both to ourselves and to the gods* while we remain here on earth and afterwards—like victors in the games who go around collecting their prizes—we'll receive our rewards. Hence, both in this life and on the thousand-year journey we've described, *we'll do well and be happy* [*we shall fare well*—εὖ πράττωμεν].[742]

Friendship with oneself is—like justice in the soul—a prerequisite for acting in a just way, and therefore, also for happiness and friendship with other people.

6.4.3 Equality as the foundation of friendship

In the quotation above concerning moderation (prudence),[743] there is mention of friendship between parts of the soul—the ruling part and the ruled parts—which evidently are not equal. Nevertheless, in his considerations of friendship in interpersonal relations, Plato stresses equality as a precondition of genuine friendship. Equality is certainly a prerequisite for the 'the greatest possible mutual friendship [ὅτι μάλιστα ἀλλήλοις φίλοι]',[744] which is an aim of laws and therefore also an aim of the implementation of justice. As Plato's Socrates states in the *Gorgias*: 'the closest possible friendship between man and man is that mentioned by the sages of old time as "like to like"'.[745] This is not the only expression concerning friendship where Plato refers to the common wisdom present in Greek culture. In the *Laws* he writes: 'There is an old and true saying that "equality

---

739 Plato, *Republic*, 443c–444a; see Section 3.7.

740 Plato, *Republic*, 443d, trans. Bloom. Shorey omits to translate 'φίλον γενόμενον ἑαυτῷ' at all.

741 Plato, *Republic*, 443c–e, trans. Bloom.

742 Plato, *Republic*, 621c–d, trans. Grube, emphasis added.

743 Plato, *Republic*, 442c–d, trans. Grube.

744 Plato, *Law*, 743c, trans. Saunders.

745 'φίλος μοι δοκεῖ ἕκαστος ἑκάστῳ εἶναι ὡς οἷόν τε μάλιστα, ὅνπερ οἱ παλαιοί τε καὶ σοφοὶ λέγουσιν, ὁ ὅμοιος τῷ ὁμοίῳ', Plato, *Gorgias*, 510b, trans. Lamb.

produces amity" [ἰσότης φιλότητα ἀπεργάζεται], which is right well and fitly spoken'.[746] He univocally asserts that equality is an indispensable condition for establishing friendship:

> even if you proclaim that a master and his slave shall have equal status, friendship between them is inherently impossible. The same applies to the relations between an honest man and a scoundrel. Indiscriminate equality for all amounts to inequality, and both fill a state with quarrels between its citizens.[747]

This quotation indicates the type of equality Plato is most interested in. He starts with a comparison between a master and a slave—a grave social inequality well-known to his audience, but it is actually an illustration of an inequality of a moral kind: between an honest man and a scoundrel. Genuine friendship is friendship between people equal in being just or equally committed to justice.

Moral perfection, however, is not the only prerequisite of friendship that is an aim of laws. To determine the aspects of equality which underlie friendship, it is helpful to refer once again to the prayer of Plato's Socrates in the conclusion of the *Phaedrus.* Moral perfection proves to be not the only thing at stake. Socrates prays to the gods:

> grant that I may be beautiful inside. Let all my external possessions be in friendly harmony with what is within. May I consider the wise man rich. As for gold, let me have as much as a moderate man could bear and carry with him.[748]

And Phaedrus addresses Socrates saying: 'Make it a prayer for me as well. Friends have everything in common [κοινὰ τὰ τῶν φίλων].'[749] Because inner beauty is the foundation of inner harmony, unity and justice, and this is the first thing asked for in the prayer, it can therefore be concluded that inner harmony, unity and justice are also the first things which ought to be in common between friends. Justice is accompanied by wisdom. Nevertheless, account is also taken of that which is necessary for a good 'earthly' life of an embodied soul—symbolised by gold. What matters in equality is possessing a certain minimum; equality in overall wealth, however, is not required.

6.4.4 Friendship as an aim of laws

Next to happiness, friendship is one of the two primary aims of laws. Once more our leitmotif from the *Laws* should be recalled: 'The whole point of our legislation

746 Plato, *Laws,* 757a, trans. Bury.
747 Plato, *Laws,* 757a, trans. Saunders.
748 Plato, *Phaedrus,* 279b–c, trans. Nehamas, Woodruff.
749 Plato, *Phaedrus,* 279c, trans. Nehamas, Woodruff. The proverb about friendship Phaedrus refers to probably originates in the Pythagorean School; see Schofield, *The Stoic Idea of the City,* p. 97.

was to allow the citizens to live supremely happy lives in the greatest possible mutual friendship'.[750]

In the *Gorgias*, Plato's Socrates, after the dialogue with himself in which he explains what justice is, turns to considerations about the universe and remarks that 'wise men claim that partnership and friendship, orderliness, self-control, and justice hold together heaven and earth, and gods and men, and that is why they call this universe a world order, my friend, and not an undisciplined world-disorder'.[751]

Plato's Timaeus points to friendship, which is based on the proportions of the four elements, as the basis of the unity of the visible world—'the body of the Cosmos was harmonized by proportion and brought into existence. These conditions secured for it Amity [φιλίαν τε ἔσχεν ἐκ τούτων], so that being united in identity with itself it became indissoluble by any agent other than Him who had bound it together'.[752]

The analyses of equality reveal that proportionate (geometric) equality is used by Plato to explore the foundations of unity between people, and the bonds which rest on this equality can be called friendship. This unity is based on just action. Just deeds are a kind of expression of the justice of the acting subject and, at the same time, contribute to his own justice. On the other hand, just deeds are possible because of their addressees, and they are shaped to fit them, to benefit them.

If the best possible friendship is an aim of the laws, then these laws should also aim at equality, which is a prerequisite for genuine friendship. Bearing in mind the versatility of a just man,[753] there is no point in postulating equality only between rulers. If the action of the Demiurge is taken as an example of how to shape the deeds of human beings, it is of the highest importance to notice that human actions are regarded as secondary to the state of the soul. Changing deeds requires changing one's character. Justice of deeds requires justice of the soul.[754] There is no other way that just actions can be realised. This is fully consistent with Plato's approach to the factors which determine the shape of just actions—knowledge informs one, in principle, only about what should be avoided. Human beings, in acting justly, may refer—especially when ruling is concerned—to the example of the Demiurge himself, who does not impose the concrete shape of a just action, but strives only for a change in character, for the proper inner constitution of the soul.

It has to be pointed out here once again that wisdom is acquired not by receiving knowledge from someone, be it a ruler, a fellow man, a god or the Demiurge himself. It has to be acquired personally by looking in the right direction—education does not put knowledge into someone's mind, but consists in turning the power to learn towards proper objects. The need for education understood in such a way

750 Plato, *Laws*, 743c, trans. Saunders.
751 Plato, *Gorgias*, 508a, trans. Zeyl.
752 Plato, *Timaeus*, 32c, trans. Lamb.
753 See Section 3.7.6.
754 Plato, *Republic*, 443b–e.

reveals one more essential contribution of friendship and the community of equals to the acquisition of justice by individuals. Friendship creates conditions for developing 'the living, breathing discourse of the man who knows'.[755] Without this discourse, wisdom cannot be achieved.

At this point, the clash between the Platonic and the Sophists' approach to other people's actions is easily visible. Both Plato and the Sophists agree that to change someone's action the state of his soul has to be changed. The Sophists recommend influencing the appetitive part—the emotions, which are recognised as an overwhelming force driving their subject to a specific aim, the object of the induced desire. In Plato's approach such an influence is sought which enables the subject to follow his rational convictions, and what is more, no specific convictions are 'transmitted'; instead, the subject is enabled to acquire his own knowledge. This knowledge does not determine specific aims which are to be pursued, only specific aims which should be avoided.

Plato's perfect state—the one that should be strived for—is a state composed of individuals who are equal in virtues, because only a community of such subjects allows people 'to live supremely happy lives in the greatest possible mutual friendship.'[756] It is a community of citizens who, by participating in ruling, help each other to improve, to develop in a comprehensive way. This community is based on wisdom, which can only be acquired through dialogue and friendship.

Plato encourages reflection on freedom as an indispensable condition for the proper functioning of the state. In the *Laws* there are arguments that 'legislation providing for powerful or extreme authority is a mistake'.[757] Plato's Athenian remarks that 'a state ought to be free and wise and enjoy internal harmony',[758] and a lawgiver should always have an eye 'on three things: the freedom, unity and wisdom of the city for which he legislates'.[759]

Knowledge about the right laws and organisation, since it is formed in the 'the living and breathing discourse',[760] changes over time. It follows that there is no ready ideal model of the state and laws. Besides, Plato's Socrates expressly mentions that every form of political organisation is by its very nature only temporary, and necessarily changes to preserve its proper functions.[761]

This is a very important conclusion for reconstructing Plato's conception of justice. It confirms that the model of the hypothetical state should not be taken as a model of a perfect state. Plato aims to enable his pupils to discuss problems

755 Plato, *Phaedrus*, 276a, trans. Nehamas, Woodruff.
756 Plato, *Laws*, 743c, trans. Saunders.
757 Plato, *Laws*, 693b, trans. Saunders.
758 Plato, *Laws*, 693b, trans. Saunders.
759 Plato, *Laws*, 701d, trans. Saunders; similarly e.g. ibid., 694b.
760 Plato, *Phaedrus*, 276a, trans. Nehamas, Woodruff.
761 Plato, *Republic*, 546a–547d.

related to laws and to political organisation, and to implement solutions developed in the here and now.[762] The constants that are prerequisites for the successful organisation of any community are of formal character, and are the main subject of the *Republic*. The cardinal virtues are needed in any political organisation. Since Plato's teaching about dignity—understood as being an aim in oneself, an aim whose realisation has priority over the good of the state—underlies his approach to justice, it can be said that the recognition of dignity is one of a few constants which make Plato's thought surprisingly close to contemporary views on the axiological foundations of law.

Coming back to the problem of equality—following the symbolic stories presented by Plato, one can say that acquiring this ideal of equality is a task for generations and subsequent incarnations of human souls. In the words of Plato's Athenian in the *Laws*:

> 'This is the just decree of the gods who inhabit Olympus [Homer, *Odyssey*, XIX, 43]', O thou child and stripling who thinkest thou art neglected by the gods,—the decree that as thou becomest worse, thou goest to the company of the worse souls, and as thou becomest better, to the better souls; and that, alike in life and in every shape of death, thou both doest and sufferest what it is befitting that like should do towards like.[763]

Becoming more just leads to a life among equals practising friendship.

Before a perfect state is established, there are inequalities in the real state.[764] Nevertheless, an aim of laws and of political activity alike, is to support all members of the political community ('a visitor or townsman, a slave or free man'[765]) in striving for moral excellence—that is, for justice, which presupposes the development of other cardinal virtues and the attainment of the perfection of all parts of the soul. The commitment to care for moral development, which also means

762 D. Zygmuntowicz reaches similar conclusions, mostly on the basis of a careful analysis of the *Laws*; she writes: 'Since every form of political organisation, even the best one, is necessarily transitional, thus a philosopher/educator should focus not on the conditions of realising paradigmatic *polis* but on the comprehending of the dynamic character of political life and on enabling citizens and rulers to endure the necessary political changes and to introduce such changes if the situation requires it', Zygmuntowicz, *Praktyka polityczna*, p. 33, my translation.

763 Plato, *Laws*, 904d–905a, my translation.

764 Nevertheless, according to ancient sources, Plato sees the possibility of introducing some equality measures in the here and now: 'Pamphila in the twenty-fifth book of her Memorabilia says that the Arcadians and Thebans, when they were founding Megalopolis, invited Plato to be their legislator; but that, when he discovered that they were opposed to equality of possessions, he refused to go [ὁ δὲ μαθὼν ἴσον ἔχειν οὐ θέλοντας οὐκ ἐπορεύθη]', Diogenes Laertius, *Lives of Eminent Philosophers*, III, 23, trans. Hicks; the source text refers to equality in general, not equality of possessions specifically.

765 Plato, *Gorgias*, 515a, trans. Zeyl; see ibid., 515b–c, 517b–c.

'strict personal development', includes even slaves—a master should sow 'the seeds of virtue'.[766] Also in the case of a slave, his being, as an aim in himself (being related to personal development), should be equally taken into account; this is a postulate following the recognition of equal dignity. Ultimately, the Demiurge—the divine draughts-player who cares equally for the development of every soul (independently of an individual's social position, abilities, vices or virtues)[767]—is a role model for everyone living in the community, especially for those engaged in political activities.

6.4.5 Non-violence in implementing justice

Plato strongly opposes the use of violence in introducing the right political order. In the *Letter VII* he writes:[768]

> This is the principle which a wise man must follow in his relations towards his own city. Let him warn her, if he thinks her constitution is corrupt and there is a prospect that his words will be listened to and not put him in danger of his life; but let him not use violence upon his fatherland to bring about a change of constitution. If what he thinks is best can only be accomplished by the exile and slaughter of men, let him keep his peace and pray for the welfare of himself and his city.[769]

The primacy of an individual over the state is also seen in the content of the prayer: the man's own welfare is mentioned before that of his city. An attitude towards the state is shaped after the relations between people, especially in the family:

> a man who does not consult me at all, or makes it clear that he will not follow advice that is given him—to such a man I do not take it upon myself to offer counsel; nor would I use constraint upon him, not even if he were my own son. Upon a slave I might force my advice, compelling him to follow it against his will; but to use compulsion upon a father or mother is to me an impious act, unless their judgment has been impaired by disease.[770]

The principle of not using force in persuading others to act justly, or even in persuading them not to act unjustly, is applicable not only in the relationship with the political community, but also in relations with individuals. A reasonable man helps those who are willing to accept his help in acquiring goodness. Towards those who

766 Plato, *Laws*, 777d–e, trans. Saunders; cf. idem, *Gorgias*, 515a–b.
767 Plato, *Laws*, 903e.
768 See Voegelin, *The World of the Polis*, p. 71.
769 Plato, *Letter VII*, 331c–d, trans. Morrow.
770 Plato, *Letter VII*, 331b, trans. Morrow.

do not strive for goodness (justice) his attitude remains neutral, although he does not help them pursue their aims:

> If they are fixed in a way of life that pleases them, though it may not please me, I should not antagonize them by useless admonitions, nor yet by flattery and complaisance encourage them in the satisfaction of desires that I would die rather than embrace.[771]

It is worth noting that Plato opposes useless admonitions as antagonising. The relationships between people should as far as possible remain open to possible cooperation in striving for goodness, and therefore open to friendship based on pursuing genuine justice.

Plato's teaching that the will of others should not be violated even when they do not intend to act justly is not specific to *Letter VII*. In this respect, the relationship of the wise man towards other people and towards the political community is like the relationship of the Supervisor of the Universe—the Demiurge—to human souls. He provides conditions which encourage good changes of character, but 'he left it to the individual's acts of will to determine the direction of these changes'.[772]

Proceeding in a just way contributes to the justice of the soul, to happiness, and is the only path to fulfilment for a human being. The more just deeds are performed, the more strongly both the acting subject and the addressee of the deeds exist. Therefore, to have an opportunity to act justly is paramount.

One may argue that the best conditions for such actions exist between a rich and a poor man, or between an honest man and a scoundrel, since the rich man can give more to the poor man than to someone equal in wealth. However, equality in virtue and also in wealth may entail a higher quality in that which is given. What a superior can offer, such as a discussion on metaphysical issues, will not be interesting to those who are not advanced enough to follow the subject. The gift would be useless, and therefore it would be no gift at all, and sometimes even a burden.

6.4.6 Justice in giving and receiving

The analysis above of what is constitutive for the justice of the content of an action has shown that what is decisive is the relation of being fitting and being appropriate for the addressee of the action. If a deed D of subject A is just and it is addressed to B, then there are two relations of appropriateness. On the one hand, deed D is appropriate for B: it fits his nature as contributing to his perfections which strengthen his existence or his unity. On the other hand, deed D is appropriate for subject A, as his just action, as an action which is performed and formed by him, which stems from his inner unity and which is an 'expression' of all his

---

771 Plato, *Letter VII*, 331c, trans. Morrow.

772 Plato, *Laws*, 904b–c, trans. Saunders; see idem, *Republic*, 617e.

parts, and of him as a whole. This deed is appropriate for the acting subject in another sense too—it contributes to his inner unity, his existence and his justice.

It should be noted, however, that there are also two dimensions of appropriateness of the just action in relation to the subject B, its addressee. He is not purely receptive. Without an addressee, the acting subject A could not perform his just act; he needs an addressee to realise his virtue of justice, to act justly and to strengthen his own unity and existence. Addressee B has to be receptive ('open') to deed D of subject A. He or his part has to be at the disposal of the subject A. Therefore, one can say that addressee B of deed D also gives something to the acting subject A, who benefits from acting justly towards B. Thus addressee B, in accepting the deed D of the subject A, is acting justly towards A.

The postulate of the equality of the members of a community, including a political community, is fully understandable, since if there is greater equality, there is greater possibility of acting for the benefit of others (acting justly) and for happiness. Certainly the character of the goods which are given and received is of primary importance in 'measuring' the benefits and in 'measuring' to what degree the justice of the acting subject increases.

Plato's considerations of friendship and equality provide another argument against treating his hypothetical state presented in the *Republic* as a project for a perfect state. An exchange of goods between members of its different classes is hardly possible. The members of this community act first of all for the benefit of the state. The perfections specific to each particular class are 'attractive' only for representatives of the same class. The goods which develop philosophers are not appropriate for the development of soldiers or producers. Therefore, the members of different classes cannot be friends (and cannot benefit from giving and receiving) since as Plato's Phaedrus says: 'Friends have everything in common'.[773] Perhaps the philosophers would be the happiest or even the only happy people in the hypothetical state,[774] but they certainly would not 'live supremely happy lives

773 Plato, *Phaedrus*, 279c, trans. Nehamas, Woodruff.

774 Cf. Strauss, 'Plato', p. 47. Cf. Price, *Virtue and Reason in Plato and Aristotle*, p. 108. Price argues, interpreting Plato in reference to Aristotle's distinction of two modes of 'possessing' reason, that non-philosophers in Plato's hypothetical state can be happy since they have a share in wisdom because they 'possess' reason by 'listening to reason', though they do not 'possess' reason in the sense of being able to reason, cf. Aristotle, *Nicomachean Ethics*, 1098a. A different solution is provided by Vasiliou, *Aiming at Virtue in Plato*, pp. 259–267; he claims that there is habituated virtue which can be generated by a proper upbringing and 'non-philosophers are capable of realizing that they ought to be virtuous and thus do virtuous actions' (p. 266). According to Vasiliou, in the case of auxiliaries this 'realizing' is an effect of the education they receive (p. 262). Such an interpretation ignores, however, the teaching about education contained in the myth of the cave, which is of crucial importance, I believe, for the interpretation of the whole *Republic* (see Section 4.1.5.4); Vasiliou seems to have major problems with explaining this 'realizing' when it comes to the lowest class

in the greatest possible mutual friendship'[775] in comparison with comprehensively developed men and women who exercise true justice and who harmoniously cultivate all of the cardinal virtues.[776] The community of equal individuals striving for all virtues (not possessing wisdom[777] but striving for it) provides much better opportunities for exercising justice and being happy than the hypothetical state described in the *Republic*. Here is another dimension in which this state is seen to present only a phantom of justice, which is useful for understanding the justice of an individual. In the truly perfect state of equals there is no need to condemn whole large groups of individuals (the producers) to live a life which cannot be a happy one. It should be recalled here that being 'partners and helpers' was recognised in the *Republic* as a constitutive property of the real (earthly) state.[778] The hypothetical state is not one which actually possesses this property to a satisfactory extent.

It must be stressed that in Plato's approach the equality of citizens does not mean the equality of ways of life. Plato refers to equality in the existential aspect when he talks about justice as a virtue based on internal unity; and to the equality of certain structures (relations), not the equality of the elements involved in those structures, when he talks about other cardinal virtues. Wisdom is based on the relations of the learning power to its proper objects, which determine the content of knowledge; courage rests on relations between wisdom and action; moderation in the relations between the parts of the soul. All this contributes to the possibility of a diversity of ways of life which can fulfil human beings, and to the freedom to shape one's own life, which will be considered below.

---

which has not received an auxiliary's education (p. 262). Cf. Bobonich, *Plato's Utopia Recast*, pp. 7–8, 51–58 (all non-philosophers are unhappy and differ only in degrees of being unhappy). When Plato's hypothetical state is regarded as a model of the soul only, Price, Vasiliou, and Bobonich are trying to answer questions which Plato does not pose, as questions concerning a political project. R. Weiss argues that none of two paradigms for understanding who a philosopher is, which are present in the hypothetical state designed in the *Republic*, in fact represent an ideal of a true philosopher like Plato's Socrates; see Weiss, *Philosophers in the* Republic, esp. pp. 164–207. If only a true philosopher can be happy, even philosophers in the hypothetical state cannot be happy and should not be regarded as examples of how one could live a good (happy) life: 'Socrates fosters justice in others even at his own peril, and so is indeed in a class by himself. He thus represents a third paradigm—but one that lies outside the confines of the Republic: none of the philosophers described in the Republic can meet his standard'; ibid, p. 10.

775 Plato, *Laws*, 743c, trans. Saunders.

776 See Section 3.7.6.

777 Plato, *Phaedrus*, 278d.

778 'Many people gather in a single place to live together as partners and helpers. And such a settlement is called a city', Plato, *Republic*, 369b–c, trans. Grube.

6.4.7 Concluding remarks

It can be said that the issue of friendship crowns Plato's teaching about justice. Since friendship is a principal aim of laws, equality also becomes such an aim. The laws and the state that is based on them aim at happiness and the greatest possible friendship, a task that can be characterised as the greatest possible justice between members of a political community. The greatest possible justice of an individual is based on the highest possible degree of acting for the benefit of others. The possibility of giving presupposes the possibility of receiving that which is given. Especially, where goods of an intellectual and moral kind are concerned, the receiver has to be able and has to be willing to receive. Therefore, the recipient is also active: he opens himself to the action of the donor, and in some way, also gives; he cooperates with the donor in allowing him to be just. The greatest possible justice presupposes the greatest possible friendship, which in turn, requires the equality of donors and recipients. The more giving there is, the more justice there is, and the more happiness and friendship, the more equality between members of the community, is involved.

A political community which increases happiness and friendship is a community of equals who are able to fulfil different social roles. Such a community cannot be established forcibly, but only by using friendly means. Achieving this goal is a venture to be accomplished in generations and in numerous subsequent incarnations of human souls.

What are Plato's suggestions for us in the contemporary world? The law should create conditions for personal development, for a supremely happy life in the greatest possible mutual friendship. The benefits from living in the state are at least twofold. Firstly, people come together to get help from others, to obtain something they need, which is a primary aim of forming a community.[779] Secondly, people living together have an opportunity to do what is advantageous for others, to act justly and therefore to develop in the moral aspect, which is strictly personal. A long time before Christianity entered the stage of European culture, Plato saw that acting for others, including one's enemies, without expecting anything in return, is vital for the fulfilment of a human being, and that by acting in this way, human beings gain a share in that which transcends what is visible.[780]

---

779 Plato, *Republic*, 369b–c.

780 For a different approach see Hoelzl, 'Recognizing the Sacrificial', p. 55. Cf. *The Gospel according to St. Matthew*, 5, 43–48: 'Ye have heard that it hath been said, Thou shalt love thy neighbour, and hate thine enemy. But I say unto you, Love your enemies, bless them that curse you, do good to them that hate you, and pray for them which despitefully use you, and persecute you; That ye may be the children of your Father which is in heaven: for he maketh his sun to rise on the evil and on the good, and sendeth rain on the just and on the unjust. For if ye love them which love you, what reward have ye? do not even the publicans the same? And if ye salute your brethren

Acting justly is based on the unity and existence of the acting subject, and contributes to the existence of both the performer and the addressee of the just act, and therefore acting justly participates in the actions of the Good itself.

only, what do ye more than others? do not even the publicans so? Be ye therefore perfect, even as your Father which is in heaven is perfect', *Holy Bible*, King James Version.

7 Some key issues in Plato's conception of justice

7.1 What is more excellent—justice of the soul or justice of action?

Having outlined Plato's conception of justice, it is appropriate to now to focus on two specific issues that may give rise to certain objections from the point of view of commonly accepted interpretations of Plato's dialogues.[781] I am arguing that Plato places a priority on acting justly over the cognition or contemplation of truth, and that he believes that an individual, endowed with a body and being non-perfect, can be a proper object of love, understood as caring for someone. Before these issues are considered, it is important to pay attention to giving priority to the justice of actions over justice of the soul.

Plato makes a clear distinction between the justice of actions and the justice of an actor (justice of the soul).[782] As has been demonstrated, a just subject acts justly in virtue of being just; the doer's just actions contribute to his becoming just. To understand how one comes to excel in the virtue of justice, one has to accept that a kind of feedback loop exists between justice of the soul and just actions. Of course, everyone, given his existence, has some inner unity, and therefore, some justice as well. A person is able to produce just actions—which increase justice as a property in the acting subject—proportionally to his inner unity. Thus, as a consequence of acting justly an increased inner unity and justice of the soul are created, and thus the ability to act justly increases and the possibility for further development of justice of the soul is open.

To avoid a vicious circle in explaining the interrelationship between justice of the soul and just actions, one has to accept that just action 'bears' a certain 'power of justice' which is not simply a function of the justice of the soul, but comprises 'added' justice beyond that already present in the acting subject. It is difficult to identify the source of this 'added' justice. There seems to be four main possible explanations. The first is that the Demiurge himself rewards just action by directly giving its subject more unity. This explanation does not appear very plausible—the Demiurge, as the divine draughts-player, only moves souls to different places that are proper for them and provide conditions for development.[783]

781 As a representative statement of such interpretations I take Vlastos, 'The Individual as an Object of Love in Plato', first published in 1973.

782 E.g. Plato, *Republic*, 444b–c, 445a; idem, *Gorgias*, 507a–c.

783 Plato, *Laws*, 903d–e.

The second explanation focuses on the subject itself—acting justly is always based on establishing a unity between parts of the soul. A decision to act in a certain way could be regarded as the source of 'added' unity in the soul. This kind of explanation should not be excluded—Plato tends to understand the virtue of justice as 'something' inside a subject; however, his view on decision-making as an act that unifies different powers of the soul was never explicated by him in detail. In his consideration of actions, Plato is more interested in rational guidance than in decision-making itself. This guidance is found in wisdom as practical knowledge, in which the crucial point is the compatibility between an action and its addressee.

This leads to the third possible explanation of how justice of the soul develops—this 'surplus' of ('added') justice, of unity, rests on the relationship between an action and its addressee. As has been demonstrated, the justice of an action is based on its being 'fitted' to its addressee; this 'fittingness' is understood mostly as being beneficial, as contributing to the preservation or development of the addressee, and this is always a contribution to the existence (inner unity) of the addressee, and thus an acting subjects 'produces' a unity, a kind of power which is able to contribute to the unity of an acting subject itself, to 'add' justice. In acting justly, one resembles the Good itself, and in fact, cooperates in the creation of beings.

There is also a fourth explanation. Acting justly creates unity not only in the addressee of an action but also between its subject and its addressee. When acting justly is interpreted in terms of geometric proportion (proportionate equality), a just action unifies the acting subject and the beneficiary. Again, since unity is created, a good is also created, which by its nature provides unity, and a 'surplus' of unity for the soul itself can be added.

Independently of which of these explanations is chosen, the following question should be asked: what is more excellent for a subject—justice of his soul or justice of his actions? It is argued that acting justly takes precedence in excellence over justice as a state of the soul.

In the *Republic*, the first questions about justice are actually questions about a certain kind of acting, and the formulae analysed by Plato's Socrates at the beginning are formulae describing just actions: 'justice is speaking the truth and paying whatever debts one has incurred',[784] 'it is just to give to each what is owed to him',[785] 'to give to each what is appropriate to him'.[786] In the conclusion of Book I, when Plato's Socrates in a discussion with Thrasymachus names the problems to be considered, there is a clear statement that justice as a virtue of the soul makes it possible to perform well one's proper functions, such as taking care of things, ruling, deliberating, and—most of all—living.[787] To perform functions is to act, and

784 Plato, *Republic*, 331c, trans. Grube.
785 Plato, *Republic*, 331e, trans. Grube.
786 Plato, *Republic*, 332c, trans. Grube.
787 Plato, *Republic*, 353d.

questions about justice as a virtue of the soul are likewise questions about the conditions for acting justly:

> *Socrates*: (...) a bad soul rules and takes care of things badly and that a good soul does all these things well?
> *Thrasymachus*: It does.
> *Socrates*: Now, we agreed that justice is a soul's virtue, and injustice its vice?
> *Thrasymachus*: We did.
> *Socrates*: Then, it follows that a just soul and a just man will live well, and an unjust one badly.
> *Thrasymachus*: Apparently so, according to your argument.
> *Socrates*: And surely anyone who lives well is blessed and happy, and anyone who doesn't is the opposite.
> *Thrasymachus*: Of course.
> *Socrates*: Therefore, a just person is happy, and an unjust one wretched.[788]

Being happy is not based simply on a certain state of the soul; it is grounded in living and acting well.

The justice of the soul as a condition of just actions is highlighted in the *Republic*, in a crucial description of justice where Plato's Socrates says what justice is in truth (443c–e). The condition is a means to achieve an aim, which is acting justly.

The *Republic* closes with the words of Plato's Socrates:

> we'll always hold to the upward path, *practicing justice* with reason in every way. That way we'll be friends both to ourselves and to the gods while we remain here on earth and afterwards—like victors in the games who go around collecting their prizes—we'll receive our rewards. Hence, both in this life and on the thousand-year journey we've described, we'll *do well* and be happy.[789]

In the *Gorgias*, teaching about justice in the soul as a certain order in the soul (a certain internal state of the soul) is preparation for a consideration of acting justly. As demonstrated above, the structure of Socrates' dialogue with himself clearly indicates that deliberations about justice culminate in discussing the issue of just actions, and these deliberations are recognised by Plato's Socrates as the 'head'[790] of the overall argument about justice in his dialogue with himself. The justice of actions, living well, and the happiness bound to such a life are the aims and reasons for acquiring justice in the soul. At the end of the dialogue with himself, Plato's Socrates states that someone who obtains fundamental virtues (is self-controlled, brave, just and pious) 'is a completely good man, that the good man does well

788 Plato, *Republic*, 353e–354a, trans. Grube.
789 Plato, *Republic*, 621c–d, trans. Grube, emphasis added.
790 Plato, *Gorgias*, 505d.

and admirably whatever he does, and that the man who does well is blessed and happy'.[791]

In the *Phaedrus*, Socrates and Phaedrus pray for inner beauty and for the virtue of justice; the reason for this is their wish to become a true philosopher, who in this dialogue, is understood not as someone completely devoted to the contemplation of truth (of forms), but someone acting to benefit others by writing in their souls discourses 'concerning what is just, noble, and good'.[792]

An important argument for the priority of action can be drawn from the systemic context, especially from the teaching about the Good itself, which is the most perfect 'object' in Plato's universe. This highest form—the Form of the Good—is characterised in the *Republic* in terms of action—Plato's Socrates says what the Good does, rather than what it is. The observer thus draws conclusions about the highest rank of the Good from how it acts (for example, from the fact that it gives order, life, essence and existence to everything that is).[793]

The priority of action over the status of its subject is a fundamental assertion in the classical philosophical tradition. An action fulfils—makes real—possibilities which are in the subject. Aristotle expresses this view very clearly. For example, in the *Nicomachean Ethics* he writes: 'the human good turns out to be the soul's activity that expresses virtue. And if there are more virtues than one, the good will express the best and most complete virtue'.[794] This approach is also adopted by Thomas Aquinas: for example, in *Summa contra gentiles* he asserts that 'Each thing appears to exist for the sake of its operation; indeed, operation is the ultimate perfection of a thing'.[795]

It needs to be considered why Plato's Socrates, when talking about what justice in truth is, asserts that 'it isn't concerned with someone's doing his own externally, but with what is inside him, with what is truly himself and his own'.[796] This clearly indicates that just actions are a means to preserve and achieve justice in the soul.[797] This last view does not contradict the view that actions are an aim as the 'ultimate perfection' of a just man. In Plato's approach it would not be comprehensible to

791 Plato, *Gorgias*, 507c, trans. Zeyl.

792 Plato, *Phaedrus*, 278a, trans. Nehamas, Woodruff.

793 E.g. Plato, *Republic*, 517b–c.

794 Aristotle, *Nicomachean Ethics*, 1098a, trans. Irwin; cf. idem, *Metaphysics*, 1050a: 'the activity is the end, and the actuality is the activity; hence the term "actuality" is derived from "activity", and tends to have the meaning of "complete reality" ', trans. Tredennick; Aristotle, *Politics*, 1325a, trans. Rackham: 'to praise inaction more highly than action is an error, for happiness is an activity, and further the actions of the just and temperate have in them the realization of much that is noble. (...) the best thing is the most to be desired, and to do well is the best thing'.

795 'Omnis enim res propter suam operationem esse videtur: operatio enim est ultmia perfectio rei', Thomas Aquinas, *Summa contra gentiles*, lib. 3, cap. 113, trans. Bourke.

796 Plato, *Republic*, 443c–d, trans. Grube.

797 Plato, *Republic*, 443e.

say that a just man is the perfection of just deeds, and even less so the ultimate perfection. Justice of the soul is, of course, a necessary condition for just actions; nevertheless, it is not an object of them, not an aim directly intended by this kind of acting, it is not the final cause of just acts, it is neither reason for performing them nor for their shape.

It is impossible to characterise just actions, which contribute to the justice of the subject, purely in terms of the acting subject and without any reference to the addressee of the actions, who benefits from them. Without taking into account the relation between an action and its addressee, it is impossible to understand fully the justice of the soul, which is an effect of just actions. The addressee not only determines the shape of just action, but is also the reason for acting at all. Without an addressee there would not be any possibility of acting for the benefit of another. But there is more than a mere possibility at stake here. In some cases, an addressee 'provokes' an action, and thus does not allow one to stay uninvolved. The good of another, his existence, makes a just man act in a certain way. Just as the Demiurge will never 'consent to the undoing of what has been well fitted together [beautifully harmonised] and is in fine condition',[798] so every acting subject—in as much as he is good—will never consent to this and will act accordingly. Considering the acting subject itself, the principle of action is his striving for his existence and justice, his goodness based on inner unity. The addressee who 'has been well fitted together [beautifully harmonised]' causes a subject to act, and his benefit determines the shape of action—just is what 'fits', 'what's appropriate'.[799] The existence and content of laws which prescribe certain actions are secondary to the relations of an action to its addressee and to the acting subject; one first has to come to know these relations, then laws can be formulated.

In Plato's conception of justice, just deeds are linked both to an acting subject and to an addressee. Actions are also linked to the unique character of the subject and addressee as ends in themselves, and to their fulfilment. Moreover, just actions, which are based on giving and receiving, establish a kind of unity between a subject and an addressee. Therefore, just actions contribute to both fundamental aims of just laws—happiness and friendship. Separating a deed from its possible effects in the acting subject would make him a mere means for realising the law (the action would be performed for the sake of the law itself) or for realising the addressee of his action.

In considering the structure of a just deed, it should be borne in mind that Plato's conception is constructed to challenge the teaching of justice proposed by the Sophists. In the view of the latter, the foundations of justice rest on laws and on a relation of conformity between an action and laws. Following Antiphon the Sophist—'Justice, then, is a matter of not breaking the laws and customs (*nomina*) of the city in which one is a citizen'.[800] The content of laws has no objective

798 Plato, *Timaeus*, 41b, trans. Zeyl.
799 Plato, *Gorgias*, 507b, trans. Zeyl.
800 Antiphon, *On Truth*, Papyrus Oxyrhynchus XI, 1363; trans. Dillon, Gergel, p. 150.

foundations, as Protagoras of Abdera says, 'Whatever in any city is regarded as just and admirable is just and admirable, in that city and for so long as that convention maintains itself'.[801] The aim of a just action is to fulfil the laws; it is thus separated from the benefit of the addressee. Moreover, it is separated from the status of the acting subject—he acts for the sake of the laws themselves. In the Sophists' conception of justice, one has first to come to know the laws as a necessary condition for acting justly, because only laws allow one to determine which actions are just.

The recognition of just acting as an aim which is attained by being just accords with beliefs present in the culture of ancient Greece. In the well-known story *The Choice of Heracles* by Prodicus of Ceos—reported by Xenophon[802] and certainly known to Plato[803]—Heracles has to make a choice between personified Vice and Virtue, between two different kinds of life (a pleasant and easy life and a severe but glorious one). According to the story, virtue is acquired by good deeds and enables one to act well. Therefore, virtues have to be chosen. Someone who is virtuous becomes a doer of good [ἀγαθὸν ἐργάτην].[804] Personified Virtue says to Heracles: 'you will turn out a right good doer of high and noble deeds, and I shall be yet more highly honoured and more illustrious for the blessings I bestow'.[805] Virtue leads to deeds. Acquiring virtue is not an aim in itself.

All genuine rewards for a virtuous man are consequences of his actions; Virtue explains this to Heracles:

> For of all things good and fair, the gods give nothing to man without toil and effort. If you want the favour of the gods, you must worship the gods: if you desire the love of friends, you must do good to your friends: if you covet honour from a city, you must aid that city: if you are fain to win the admiration of all Hellas for virtue, you must strive to do good to Hellas: if you want land to yield you fruits in abundance, you must cultivate that land: if you are resolved to get wealth from flocks, you must care for those flocks: if you essay to grow great through war and want power to liberate your friends and subdue your foes, you must learn the arts of war from those who know them and must practise their right use: and if you want your body to be strong, you must accustom your body to be the servant of your mind, and train it with toil and sweat.[806]

It is because of their deeds that 'they are dear to the gods, lovely to friends, precious to their native land',[807] and after death 'they lie not forgotten and dishonoured, but

801 'ἐπεὶ οἷά γ' ἂν ἑκάστῃ πόλει δίκαια καὶ καλὰ δοκῇ, ταῦτα καὶ εἶναι αὐτῇ, ἕως ἂν αὐτὰ νομίζῃ', Plato, *Theaetetus*, 167c, trans. Levett.
802 Xenophon, *Memorabilia*, II, 1,21–34.
803 Plato, *Symposium*, 177b.
804 Pacewicz, 'The Concept of the Good', p. 22.
805 Xenophon, *Memorabilia*, II, 1, 27, trans. Marchant.
806 Xenophon, *Memorabilia*, II, 1, 28, trans. Marchant.
807 Xenophon, *Memorabilia*, II, 1, 33, trans. Marchant.

live on, sung and remembered for all time'.[808] Good actions themselves contribute even more directly to the well-being of virtuous men: 'with joy they recall their deeds past, and their present well-doing is joy to them';[809] and those who choose the path of vice obtain the opposite: 'their past deeds bring them shame, their present deeds distress'.[810]

7.2 Which activity is best and what is its best object?

7.2.1 Preliminary remarks

When asking about degrees in the excellence or perfection of something, one needs to specify the criteria of evaluation. Here the question is asked in respect to human fulfilment and happiness. The question 'what is more excellent?' can be substituted by the question 'what brings someone closer to their fulfilment?' Here, the fulfilment of a human being as a whole (a tripartite soul) must be considered. The fundamental dimension of such fulfilment is the 'strength' of the human being's existence. More excellent is that which makes the human soul's existence 'stronger'. The above analyses indicate that the highest virtue is justice, and the best activity that can be performed is practising justice. Wisdom is clearly subordinated to acting—it is a kind of knowledge about how a man as a whole would best deal with himself and other people.[811] There are, however, numerous passages which suggest that the contemplation of forms (ideas) is the best activity a human being (a human soul) can perform. Some of these have already been considered and shown to be consistent with regarding just actions as the best activity. Nevertheless, it is worthwhile to examine directly the question concerning the best type of activity. The answer to this question has far-reaching consequences for considerations about the objects of the best human activities. One may ask, after Gregory Vlastos: is an individual or an abstract form (idea) the proper object of love?[812]

It has been argued above that questions about justice are the most important ones.[813] One has to bear in mind the picture of souls choosing their fate, as depicted by Plato in the myth of Er, and the commentary that someone who has proper knowledge

> will be able, by considering the nature of the soul, to reason out which life is better and which worse and to choose accordingly, calling a life worse if it leads the soul

808 Xenophon, *Memorabilia*, II, 1, 33, trans. Marchant.
809 Xenophon, *Memorabilia*, II, 1, 33, trans. Marchant.
810 Xenophon, *Memorabilia*, II, 1, 31, trans. Marchant.
811 Cf. Plato, *Republic*, 428c–d; see Section 3.6.2.
812 Vlastos, 'The Individual as Object of Love in Plato', *passim*.
813 See Section 3.3.

> to become more unjust, better if it leads the soul to become more just, and ignoring everything else: We have seen that this is the best way to choose, whether in life or death.[814]

This statement is very clear. Nevertheless, there are also several remarks in the dialogues which suggest that contemplating truth and abstract forms (ideas) is the best thing a human being can do, and in the literature on Plato this view has prominent adherents, including Vlastos. It is therefore appropriate to have a closer look at some of the arguments in its favour.

7.2.2 What is a proper object of love? What is a proper object of just actions?

7.2.2.1 Abstract form or concrete individual—challenging Gregory Vlastos

The problem of establishing the ultimate aims of human lives, and questions concerning the priority of justice over wisdom, contemplation over acting justly, are strongly related to the problem of determining the best objects of human actions. This might be considered a problem concerning the proper (best, final) objects of love. The issue of objects of love is inseparable from the identification of a kind of action which fulfils a human being. Are these objects forms (ideas)—something perfect, immutable, abstract and general—or something incomplete, concrete and individual, like a human person is? In the first case there is, of course, no place for caring for the object of love—it is immutable and there is no possibility of contributing to its development or preservation. Love can be understood as striving 'to be with' or 'to join' the object of love. Only an intellect can obtain unity with its object by cognitive activity, and the other parts of the soul should help the intellect perform this activity. In the second case, if the proper subject of love is an individual, imperfect being, there is a place for caring for him, for acting for his benefit, for just action which engages the activity of all parts of the soul and knowledge about the invisible, general and abstract as well as the visible, concrete and individual.

Vlastos in his well-known essay *The Individual as Object of Love in Plato*[815] advocates the view that in Plato's approach to love 'the individual, in the uniqueness and integrity of his or her individuality, will never be the object of our love',[816] and he argues that—according to Plato—the fulfilment of love and the fulfilment of a human being are possible only in relation to abstract forms (ideas) as objects of true love. He makes his point clearly and unequivocally:

---

814 Plato, *Republic*, 618d–e, trans. Grube.
815 Vlastos, 'The Individual as an Object of Love in Plato', *passim.*
816 Vlastos, 'The Individual as an Object of Love in Plato', p. 31.

> As a theory of the love of persons, this is its crux: What we are to love in persons is the 'image' of the Idea in them. We are to love the persons so far, and only insofar, as they are good and beautiful. Now since all too few human beings are masterworks of excellence, and not even the best of those we have the chance to love are wholly free of streaks of the ugly, the mean, the commonplace, the ridiculous, if our love for them is to be only for their virtue and beauty, the individual, in the uniqueness and integrity of his or her individuality, will never be the object of our love. This seems to me the cardinal flaw in Plato's theory. It does not provide for love of whole persons, but only for love of that abstract version of persons which consists of the complex of their best qualities.[817]

Concluding his essay, he writes:

> In cosmology only the Forms represent completely lucid order; physical individuals, enmeshed in brute necessity, are only quasi-orderly, as they are only quasi-intelligible. In ontology there are grades of reality and only Forms have the highest grade. So too in the theory of love the respective roles of Form and temporal individual are sustained: the individual cannot be as lovable as the Idea; the Idea, and it alone, is to be loved for its own sake; the individual only so far as in him and by him ideal perfection is copied fugitively in the flux.[818]

Vlastos rightly links the problem of understanding objects of love, of their ontological structure, with the issue of someone's being loved for its own sake. If the love of something for its own sake is rational, justified by cognition of the object of love, then that object needs to have a certain characteristic—it should be an end in itself. But Vlastos misjudges Plato's views on what imperatives are to be accepted where our fellow men are considered. He writes that Plato

> has evidently failed to see that what love for our fellows requires of us is, above all, imaginative sympathy and concern for what they themselves think, feel, and want. He has, therefore, missed that dimension of love in which tolerance, trust, forgiveness, tenderness, respect have validity. Apart from these imperatives the notion of loving persons as 'ends in themselves' would make no sense.[819]

It should be noted that in this excerpt Vlastos understands love not as striving for unity with its object, as is the case in the *Symposium* when Eros is considered, but as caring for that which is loved. Vlastos merges two different kinds of love—love as aiming to acquire something, to unify with someone or something, and love as caring for someone or something. This second kind of love is actually equal to practising justice. He then concentrates on the first kind of love and regards the intellectual activities of contemplating forms (ideas) and striving for beauty

---

817 Vlastos, 'The Individual as an Object of Love in Plato', p. 31.
818 Vlastos, 'The Individual as an Object of Love in Plato', p. 34.
819 Vlastos, 'The Individual as an Object of Love in Plato', p. 32

as activities which fulfil a human being (the soul). In doing so, however, Vlastos concentrates only on the preliminary stages on the way to fulfilment and overlooks Plato's argumentation that this fulfilment can be completed only by the practising of justice by the whole human being (by the tripartite soul). True love, understood as caring for another, begins after acquiring knowledge and after attaining beauty, which is a kind of catalyst for acting for benefit of others. Eros himself, in causing a human being to gain beauty, strives for that which is necessary for love as active justice, as caring for fellow men. True love requires knowledge of something invisible, otherwise one is condemned to remain within the framework represented by the Sophists, where everybody competes with everybody in acquiring as many temporary, visible goods as possible. It also requires inner harmony, which rests on order and harmony and therefore also on beauty. Acting for the benefit of another requires justice in the soul, which is based on the special inner unity that makes a man a likeness of the Good itself. Practising love as caring for an individual is practising justice.

7.2.2.2 Engendering and birth as an aim of love

Plato's *Symposium*, which serves as the main source for Vlastos' argumentation, contains clear indications that striving for beauty in general and for pure beauty (the form of beauty) in particular, and for conjunction with beauty, which is the proper role of Eros, is not an aim in itself.

Diotima explains in her dialogue with Socrates:

> 'You see, Socrates', she said, 'what Love wants is not beauty, as you think it is.'
> 'Well, what is it, then?'
> 'Reproduction and birth in beauty.'[820]

The last statement, which in Greek reads 'τῆς γεννήσεως καὶ τοῦ τόκου ἐν τῷ καλῷ', can be also translated as 'engendering and parturition in beauty'. It is absolutely clear that an encounter with beauty is not the final stage of human activity related to beauty. It primes a subject to act creatively,[821] much like the Demiurge himself. It also perfectly fits into Plato's teaching on justice. Beauty provides harmony, harmony provides unity, unity provides justice in the soul. Justice in the soul is realised in just acting, and just acting also builds inner unity, and therefore, the true goodness of the soul.

---

820 Plato, *Symposium*, 206d–e, trans. Nehamas, Woodruff; cf. ibid., 206b: 'giving birth in beauty, whether in body or in soul'.

821 Cf. Kahn, *Plato and the Socratic Dialogue*, p. 269; at stake is immortality—on the biological level in reproduction; on the level of personal transcendence 'in noble deeds that secure undying fame, in great poetry and creative art, and (...) in legislation and the organization of virtuous cities', ibid. See Plato, *Symposium*, 208b.

7.2.2.3 *Loving imperfect creatures*

Diotima continues explaining why engendering is what love wants, and she says: 'A lover must desire immortality along with the good, if what we agreed earlier was right, that Love wants to possess the good forever. It follows from our argument that Love must desire immortality'.[822] The desire for immortality for someone who was created directly by the Demiurge follows from the very nature of the Good and of every good. This desire has its foundation in the ontological structure of such a creature: 'only one who is evil would consent to the undoing of what has been well fitted together [beautifully harmonised] and is in fine condition'.[823] This 'being well fitted together [beautifully harmonised] and being in fine condition', which rightly can be called 'dignity', is something that can never be lost, and therefore the desire of immortality for such a creature never stops. As the Demiurge states in the *Timaeus*—'you will not be undone nor will death be your portion, since you have received the guarantee of my will'.[824] This remains true whatever imperfections or vices are shared by a holder of dignity. And it remains true not only for the Demiurge himself, but also for any acting subject who is able to recognise this perfection, and to the extent that one—as an acting subject—is good, and thus is just. Who wants to act justly needs an addressee for his just deeds, needs someone who is able to receive, to 'absorb' such deeds, and therefore—at least in principle—someone who is not perfect, because it should be something beneficial for him. Of course, considering the quality rather than the quantity of that which is to be given, the better the addressee of an action, the greater 'gifts' he is able to absorb. Between virtuous people (or gods) greater friendship can emerge than between those who are not advanced in virtue, because greater goods can be given and received. Nevertheless, caring for imperfect creatures always expresses a striving for good, and does so in two dimensions—for the good of the acting subject and for the good of the addressee.

Because sustaining the existence of the addressee is a criterion for shaping just action, and because existence comprises the whole being, love as caring for one's fellow man means caring for a human being as a whole, contrary to what Vlastos claims.

7.2.2.4 *Loving an individual*

Vlastos also seems incorrect in concluding that 'the individual, in the uniqueness and integrity of his or her individuality, will never be the object of our love',[825] and therefore 'the notion of loving persons as "ends in themselves" would make no sense'.[826] Of course, if love as Eros is characterised, as striving for something

822 Plato, *Symposium*, 207a, trans. Nehamas, Woodruff.
823 Plato, *Timaeus*, 41b, trans. Zeyl.
824 Plato, *Timaeus*, 41b, trans. Zeyl.
825 Vlastos, 'The Individual as an Object of Love in Plato', p. 32.
826 Vlastos, 'The Individual as an Object of Love in Plato', p. 32.

common and invisible—for example, beauty as such—it does not have an individual as its proper object. This does not mean, however, that an individual cannot be a proper object of love understood as caring for an individual, which can be called active love, and which consists in acting justly. The story about love as Eros above all concerns striving for that which is necessary for acting justly, for active love. This story is strikingly analogous to the myth of the cave recounted in the *Republic*. It seems to be also about education as a means for turning the learning power in the right direction in order to acquire knowledge about something in the invisible realm, knowledge which is indispensable for understanding justice and for acting justly. In both stories it is pointed out that grasping for the invisible realm engages the whole soul—not only the intellectual part, but also the spirited and appetitive. Interpreting the speech of Diotima in the *Symposium*, it is clear that the described process of learning love starts in this visible world, that it is a part of living in flesh in the here and now. As was argued above, the myth of the cave should also be read as a story about education in the earthly life, and not (only) as a story about liberating the soul from the body in the cycle of incarnations.

Plato makes space not only for active love for imperfect creatures, but also for respecting their individuality. This is because wisdom provides knowledge which can directly instruct one only 'about what is to be feared and what isn't',[827] and therefore what specifically is to be done has to be determined by choosing between different options for realising that which is beneficial for the soul. Moreover, individuals themselves choose their own fate—this is their sole work,[828] and no one can do this for them. Plato also makes it clear that this choice cannot be made by the authorities of the state.

Moreover, education consists not of 'putting knowledge into souls'[829] but of turning a learner's power of knowledge in the right direction. Knowledge and wisdom are acquired only by the subject of an action himself. Teaching results in the writing of 'the living and breathing discourse'[830] in the mind of a learner by the learner himself. As Plato sees it, the content of this discourse can certainly be different in different minds, because he recognises that the knowledge of the teacher also changes in true teaching.

The individuality of the addressee of just action is beyond any question in the case of punitive justice, which is also a form of caring about someone who is to be punished. Punishment is a kind of medicine for the soul, something beneficial on the way to the fulfilment of the punished. It should also be noted that in the dialogue with himself in the *Gorgias*, where a general approach to the justice of actions is provided, Plato's Socrates characterises just action as something that is proper, that 'fits' a concrete human being (as something beneficial for a concrete

827 Plato, *Republic*, 442b–c, trans. Grube.
828 Plato, *Republic*, 617d–618b.
829 Plato, *Republic*, 518b–c, trans. Grube.
830 Plato, *Phaedrus*, 276a, trans. Nehamas, Woodruff.

being). The relation of true equality, which is a foundation of justice, as analysed above, is based on the congruence of an action (of something) with a given, specific, imperfect human being.

It can be observed that if just actions which fulfil their subject and make it happy are understood as active love, then to ask what should be the object of love—an individual or a perfect form (idea)—does not make much sense. Active justice presupposes that an addressee is vulnerable and the subject of just action should not harm it, or that an addressee needs something that an acting subject can provide. In the case of forms (ideas), neither of these presuppositions is fulfilled. Certainly, cognition of the truth can strengthen its subject, but fulfilment requires both giving and accepting that which is given; the more is given the more the subject of this action is just, the more he is good, and the more he exists. The justice of the object of just deeds is also at stake; his strength of existence, and therefore also his justice, is a primary criterion for that which is beneficial. Moreover, receiving—as was pointed out above[831]—requires, if it is intentional, an act of entrusting to the one who gives. The one who receives makes it possible for the giver to act justly. An act of accepting help is also an act of justice and contributes to the justice of the one who receives.

7.2.3 Just actions over contemplation

7.2.3.1 Back home from the top of the heavens—what are souls free of mortal deficiency doing?

It is not possible to accept the conclusion drawn by Vlastos that 'were we free of mortal deficiency we would have no reason to love anyone or anything except the Idea: seen face to face, it would absorb all our love'.[832] There is a fundamental reason in striving for existence based on unity, and therefore on the justice of the soul and just actions. Yet, it is hard to see how an intellect itself, even one contemplating the highest forms (ideas), could directly provide unity and existence for the whole soul.

Moreover, in the *Phaedrus*, Plato's Socrates tells a story about what the soul is like, likening the soul 'to the natural union of a team of winged horses and their charioteer'.[833] It should be noted that the soul which is free from the body is tripartite—the parts are symbolised by two horses and a charioteer. The same structure is to be found in the gods.[834] According to the metaphor proposed by Plato's Socrates, the crucial difference between gods and human souls is in the quality of the horses. Those with the gods both come from good stock and the driving of the chariot is

831 See Section 6.4.6.
832 Vlastos, 'The Individual as an Object of Love in Plato', pp. 32–33.
833 Plato, *Phaedrus*, 246a, trans. Nehamas, Woodruff.
834 Plato, *Phaedrus*, 246a.

easy.[835] With humans 'one of the horses is noble and of noble breed, but the other quite the opposite in breed and character. Therefore in our case the driving is necessarily difficult and troublesome'.[836] In their travel through the heavens, neither human souls nor the gods stop and rest in the place where true reality can be seen and where they nourish themselves. A god's soul 'rejoices in seeing reality for a space of time and by gazing upon truth is nourished and made happy until the revolution brings it again to the same place'.[837] The story about the gods, who certainly are 'free of mortal deficiency', is not complete at this stage. It closes with the following image:

> when the soul has seen all the things that are as they are and feasted on them, it sinks back inside heaven and goes home. On its arrival, the charioteer stables the horses by the manger, throws in ambrosia, and gives them nectar to drink besides.[838]

The story about the gods ends with resting at home, and this results from contemplation of true reality (ideas). What was the purpose of the journey to the top of the heavens to see what lies beyond? What is the purpose of nourishing the soul? Is it only to have enough strength to come to feast once again? To use a contemporary image, these questions resemble asking whether we refuel our cars merely for the purpose of driving to the petrol station again.

An answer can be found at the beginning of the story about the gods' travels. Resting at home precedes the next, busy day. Travel 'to the high tier at the rim of heaven'[839] is necessary 'when they go to feast at the banquet'.[840] But they do not feast all the time:

> Inside heaven are many wonderful places from which to look [μακάριαι θέαι] and many aisles which the blessed gods take up and back, each seeing to his own work, while anyone who is able and wishes to do so follows along, since jealousy has no place in the gods' chorus.[841]

The gods go to many different places and travel many different roads. Special attention should be given to the remark that while travelling through the heavens 'each [is] seeing to his own work [πράττων ἕκαστος αὐτῶν τὸ αὑτοῦ]'.[842] This description of acting justly is typical of Plato. The Greek 'θέαι' can mean not only 'places from which to look' but also 'places to look at', and 'going to a place to look at' it can be a prelude to looking after it, and thus to the work proper for a given deity.

835 Plato, *Phaedrus*, 246a.
836 Plato, *Phaedrus*, 246b, trans. Fowler.
837 Plato, *Phaedrus*, 247d, trans. Fowler.
838 Plato, *Phaedrus*, 247e, trans. Nehamas, Woodruff.
839 Plato, *Phaedrus*, 247b, trans. Nehamas, Woodruff.
840 Plato, *Phaedrus*, 247b, trans. Nehamas, Woodruff.
841 Plato, *Phaedrus*, 247a, trans. Nehamas, Woodruff.
842 Plato, *Phaedrus*, 247a, trans. Nehamas, Woodruff.

Also of primary importance is the phrase that directly follows recognition that the gods acts justly: 'anyone who is able and wishes to do so follows along'. Following the gods means acting in a just way. Plato's Socrates describes the difficulties which human souls encounter on the way to the top of heaven to nourish the soul. Nevertheless, a human soul—if it is able and wishes—can follow the gods actions (act justly) in their everyday business, and not only on their way to feast at a banquet.

Intelligence and pure knowledge are something which is appropriate (τὸ προσῆκον) for the intellectual part of the soul (both a god's and a human's), 'and so it is delighted at last to be seeing what is real and watching what is true, feeding on all this and feeling wonderful, until the circular motion brings it around to where it started'.[843] In describing human souls, Plato's Socrates observes:

> The reason there is so much eagerness to see the plain where truth stands is that this pasture has the grass that is the right food for the best part of the soul, and it is the nature of the wings that lift up the soul to be nourished by it.[844]

It should be noted that when knowledge and truth are considered, only the well-being of the intellectual part is directly concerned. Therefore, it can be concluded that contemplating truth (forms) is not an activity which fulfils the soul as a whole (a human being as a whole). It is, however, striking that—according to the story about the chariot—in the process of acquiring knowledge, the whole soul, with all its parts, is involved—just as in the description of the process of education in the myth of the cave.[845] The whole soul should be directed towards the Good. The myth about the winged chariot suggests that it is not enough to turn the appetitive part away from the visible realm. Both the desires of the appetitive part which push towards having more and more, and the striving for fame which is typical for the spirited part, can distract the soul from its path towards the Good even when the soul operates in the invisible realm.

The thesis concerning the priority of active justice over the contemplation of truth (forms) as an activity which fulfils the human soul is also supported by the description of the world of forms (ideas)—the world beyond heaven seen by the charioteer. Plato's Socrates begins describing the highest form (it can be assumed that it is the Good itself depicted in the *Republic* as the sun): 'What is in this place is without color and without shape and without solidity, a being that really is what it is [οὐσία ὄντως οὖσα], the subject of all true knowledge, visible only to intelligence, the soul's steersman'.[846] The forms (ideas) listed by name are strictly related to acting well: 'On the way around it has a view of Justice as it is; it has a view of Self-control; it has a view of Knowledge (...) it is the knowledge of what really is

---

843 Plato, *Phaedrus*, 247d, trans. Nehamas, Woodruff.
844 Plato, *Phaedrus*, 248b–c, trans. Nehamas, Woodruff.
845 Plato, *Republic*, 518c.
846 Plato, *Phaedrus*, 247c–d, trans. Nehamas, Woodruff.

what it is [ἀλλὰ τὴν ἐν τῷ ὅ ἐστιν ὂν ὄντως ἐπιστήμην οὖσαν]'.[847] If 'what really is what it is' is a description of the Good itself, also Knowledge here has a practical dimension and can be identified as the knowledge which is central to wisdom as a cardinal virtue. But even without such an identification the story about the soul as a winged chariot is not primarily about contemplation as an activity that fulfils a human soul. Contemplation of the forms (ideas) is a foundation for acting justly, a precondition of following the gods in their 'seeing to their own work'.

This interpretation fits well with the main conclusions of the *Phaedrus* regarding the aim of human life, especially the life of a philosopher, namely helping others and oneself to become just through active learning and teaching.[848] The prayer which concludes the dialogue is a prayer not for divine contemplation but for the prerequisites of acting justly: 'grant that I may be beautiful inside. Let all my external possessions be in friendly harmony with what is within. May I consider the wise man rich. As for gold, let me have as much as a moderate man could bear and carry with him'.[849] The fulfilment of a human being takes place by acting justly, mostly in relationship to imperfect human beings; moreover, their imperfection (lack of knowledge) seems to be one of the fundamental reasons for their being addressees of just actions.

7.2.3.2 Back to the cave from the light of the sun—what is the use of abstract forms?

At first glance, in the light of the myth of the cave, the contemplation of truth (forms) seems to be the best possible activity. Plato presents to readers of the *Republic* a very powerful image which appeals also to their emotions. The path upward, out of the cave, leads to genuine cognition—cognition in the proper sense of the word, and the intelligible realm is the object of this cognition. Plato's Socrates affirms that someone who has come out of the cave would 'feel, with Homer, that he'd much prefer to "work the earth as a serf to another, one without possessions," and go through any sufferings, rather than share their opinions and live as they [the prisoners in the cave] do'.[850] The one mentioned by Homer is the dead Achilles, who addressed Odysseus in Hades with the words: 'I should choose, so I might live on earth, to serve as the hireling of another, of some portionless man whose livelihood was but small, rather than to be lord over all the dead that have perished'.[851] Comparing the contemplation of the invisible realm to learning about visible things (something presented to sensual experience) is like comparing life to

847 Plato, *Phaedrus*, 247d–e, trans. Nehamas, Woodruff.
848 Plato, *Phaedrus*, 278a–b; see Section 3.6.3.
849 Plato, *Phaedrus*, 279b–c, trans. Nehamas, Woodruff.
850 Plato, *Republic*, 516d, trans. Grube.
851 Homer, *Odyssey*, XIX, 489, trans. Murray.

death. Plato's Socrates considers extensively how reluctant those who have come out of the cave are to go back into it.[852]

The myth of the cave, however, does not forejudge that for the fulfilment of a soul (of a human being) contemplation is better than practising justice. First of all, one has to remember that this myth, as was argued above,[853] is actually about education understood as turning the power to learn (intellect) towards that which is, and primarily towards the Good itself. The 'ascent from the cave' is made only by one part of the soul—the intellect.[854] Taking this part separately—which is feasible only theoretically—one can say that it tends to stay in contact with the intelligible realm. This illustrates the nature of philosophers in the hypothetical state. Plato's Glaucon explicitly asks if it were not an injustice to let them go back into the cave, because it would be 'making them live a worse life when they could live a better one'.[855] Plato's Socrates objects—compelling philosophers to guard and care for others in a manner that will not be an injustice to them, because 'the law produces such people in the city, not in order to allow them to turn in whatever direction they want, but to make use of them to bind the city together'.[856] Certainly they will not refuse to go down, 'for we'll be giving just orders to just people'.[857] In arguing for the justice of such orders, Plato's Socrates provides two reasons: firstly—philosophers should 'repay' the city for their education, and secondly—they are 'better and more completely educated than the others and are better able to share in both types of life'.[858] What can be learned from this image? It is clear that education, this turning around of the intellect, has as its aim 'to bind the city together', which means—to introduce justice (unity) in the soul. To care about justice in the soul is not 'a worse life' for the intellect. Indeed, asking whether a life is better or worse for one part of the soul does not make much sense. This is why Plato's Socrates considers this question in the context of the aims of the whole city, which means—of the whole soul. Shortly before considering whether it is just to compel philosophers to return to the cave—to compel the intellect to care about the unity of the soul—Plato's Socrates states that the best natures, the best part of the soul, should be compelled to undergo an education which leads to seeing the Good.[859] Such a process of education would involve the activity of the whole soul.

Plato's Socrates sees exceptions from the rule that philosophers should be compelled to care about the unity of the state, which means that there are exceptions

852 Plato, *Republic*, 519b–520e.
853 See Section 4.1.5.4.
854 Plato, *Republic*, 518b–c, 532b–d.
855 Plato, *Republic*, 519d, trans. Grube.
856 Plato, *Republic*, 519e–520a, trans. Grube.
857 Plato, *Republic*, 520e, trans. Grube.
858 Plato, *Republic*, 520b, trans. Grube.
859 Plato, *Republic*, 519c.

to the compulsion of the intellect to deal with earthly matters and to care about the unity of the soul. The founders of the state say to the philosophers:

> 'When people like you come to be in other cities, they're justified in not sharing in their city's labors, for they've grown there spontaneously, against the will of the constitution. And what grows of its own accord and owes no debt for its upbringing has justice on its side when it isn't keen to pay anyone for that upbringing.'[860]

'Other cities' designates, of course, other people, other souls. The translation of 'ἀκούσης τῆς ἐν ἑκάστῃ πολιτείας' as 'against the will of the constitution'[861] is too strong. The Greek 'ἀέκων' is closer to 'involuntary', 'unintentional' than 'against the will'; it stresses the lack of will and not active opposition to it. It is better here to follow Shorey's translation: 'from no volition of the government in the several states'. In trying to interpret this excerpt as pertaining to the situation of philosophers in other states, it is quite difficult to understand why Plato's Socrates introduces this remark here. Why only 'in other cities' and not also 'in our city'? In the individualistic interpretation, this is less mysterious. Plato's Socrates, knowing himself and—above all—his audience, realises that in the normal course of events people need education; they intentionally have to turn their power to learn away from visible things, things which are given in sensual experience, to the intelligible realm, to the Good itself. In an ordinary situation, the visible realm distracts the intellect from cognition of 'what truly is', from purely intellectual matters. But it is possible that all parts of the soul are well ordered spontaneously, and neither the appetitive nor the spirited part hinders the process of coming to know all that is necessary for acting justly. In that case, the intellectual part does not need to be concerned with ordering the soul as a whole and can study theoretical matters for their own sake.

There is also another interpretation which may explain Plato's Socrates' remarks about those who owe no debt for their education, and therefore should not be compelled to guard and care for others. As mentioned above,[862] in designing the shape of actions, the intellectual parts of souls, which are symbolised by philosophers in the model of the state, 'look away frequently in both directions, toward the just, fair, and moderate by nature and everything of the sort, and, again, toward what is in human beings'.[863] Coming out of the cave, viewed as turning the power of learning towards the intelligible realm, can be understood as an act of cognition or that which results from it. Therefore, those who are justified in not sharing in their city's labours, those who have grown spontaneously with an ability to cognise the invisible real, can be regarded as a metaphor for 'free thoughts', thinking which

---

860 Plato, *Republic*, 520a–b, trans. Grube, quotation in the source text.

861 Plato, *Republic*, 520b, trans. Grube; similarly Bloom: 'against the will of the regime in each'.

862 See Section 4.1.5.4.

863 Plato, *Republic*, 501b, trans. Bloom.

is not performed in order to shape actions, to oversee just actions, but for its own sake. And those who 'come to be in other cities'[864] can be viewed as representing other people's (other intellects') thoughts about the intelligible realm. Not 'automatically' applying other people's thoughts to shape one's own actions is fully compatible with Plato's teaching about education as a strictly personal process.

In any case, in the usual course of events, education is needed to come to know the Good and other beings in the intelligible realm, and this cognition is necessary for introducing justice into the soul and for shaping just actions.

Last but not least, the place of the myth of the cave must be accounted for within the overall structure of the *Republic*. It appears in Book VII and is clearly subordinated to the understanding of justice. The myth is not primarily intended to serve the interests of ontology or epistemology in general. It is about education and about the preconditions of being just and acting justly—above all, it is about knowing the Good as a precondition of being just and acting justly, a precondition for rejecting the Sophists' approach to justice.

In Book VI of the *Republic*, Plato clearly places the Good above knowledge, wisdom or truth:

> that what gives truth to the things known and the power to know to the knower is the form of the good. And though it is the cause of knowledge and truth, it is also an object of knowledge. Both knowledge and truth are beautiful things, but the good is other and more beautiful than they. In the visible realm, light and sight are rightly considered sunlike, but it is wrong to think that they are the sun, so here it is right to think of knowledge and truth as goodlike but wrong to think that either of them is the good—for the good is yet more prized.[865]

If justice—as was argued in the preceding paragraphs—is the goodness of the individual (the soul) as a whole and of his actions, then placing the good above knowledge, wisdom or truth is a powerful argument for regarding just actions as more excellent for a human being than the mere contemplation of truth (forms).

7.2.3.3 What does the Good—the Demiurge—do?

In seeking an answer to the question of what is the best thing for a human being to do, it is helpful to examine how in Plato's philosophy that which is best (or even relatively most perfect) is understood. This is also helpful in answering the question of what is the best quality, the highest perfection, of a human being (and any creature in general). It seems unnecessary here to resolve the question of whether the Good described in the *Republic* is the same as the Demiurge in the *Timaeus*. From both stories, the conclusion can be drawn that the highest perfection of a human being is his goodness based on internal unity. Where acting is concerned,

864 Plato, *Republic*, 520a, trans. Grube.
865 Plato, *Republic*, 508d–509a, trans. Grube.

the Good or the Demiurge is not devoted to purely intellectual activity, to cognition, like the first unmoved mover of Aristotle.[866] Both the Good and the Demiurge are busy with giving essence and existence, and especially with caring about the existence of the created world.[867] It is also clear that this kind of activity is proper for the Supervisor of the Universe in the *Laws*—he cares for concrete human souls and aims to strengthen their existence. When the governor of the world—'the divine draughts-player'[868]—and his relations to other beings are described, it is stated that he allocates the souls 'according to what best suits each of them, so that to each may be allotted its appropriate destiny'.[869] It can be said that the Good, the Demiurge or the Supervisor of the Universe exercises justice, or active love, in relation to the addressees of their activity. This is a type of activity which is proper to his nature, and in these activities an existential aspect is also visible.[870] 'Becoming as like God as possible'[871] means to exercise justice (active love) and not to contemplate truth.[872]

866 See Aristotle, *Metaphysics*, 1074b–1075a; cf. ibid., 1075a, trans. Tredennick: 'Therefore Mind thinks itself, if it is that which is best; and its thinking is a thinking of thinking [αὑτὸν ἄρα νοεῖ, εἴπερ ἐστὶ τὸ κράτιστον, καὶ ἔστιν ἡ νόησις νοήσεως νόησις]'.

867 See Plato, *Timaeus*, 68e; idem, *Republic*, 509b; ibid., 517b–c; see Section 4.1.5.3.

868 Plato, *Laws*, 903d, trans. Saunders.

869 'κατὰ τὸ πρέπον αὐτῶν ἕκαστον, ἵνα τῆς προσηκούσης μοίρας λαγχάνῃ', Plato, *Laws*, 903d–e, trans. Bury. Saunders translates 'τῆς προσηκούσης μοίρας' as 'the fate they deserve' which—bearing in mind the description of just actions in the *Gorgias*—is less accurate; see Section 3.7.1.4.

870 One of the finest examples of an analogous approach to love can be found in *On Love* by Jose Ortega y Gasset: 'Love (...) reaches out to the object in a visual expansion and is involved in an invisible but divine task, the most active kind that there is: it is involved in the affirmation of its object. Think of what it is to love art or your country: it consists of never doubting for an instant their right to exist; it is like recognizing and confirming at each moment that they are worthy of existence. (...) Falling in love even once is an insistence that the beloved exists; a refusal to accept (since everything depends on that one thing) the possibility of a universe without it. But notice that this reduces itself to the *same thing*, which is to continually and intentionally give life to *something which depends upon us*. Loving is perennial vivification, creation and *intentional* preservation of what is loved'. Ortega y Gasset, *On Love*, pp. 19–20, emphasis in the source text.

871 Plato, *Theaetetus*, 176b, trans. Levett.

872 See a direct statement in Plato, *Theaetetus*, 176b, trans. Levett: 'a man becomes like God when he becomes just and pious, with understanding'. See Price, 'Generating in Beauty', *passim*, esp. pp. 192–193. For a different approach cf. Sedley, 'The Ideal of Godlikeness', *passim*; D. Sedley argues for recognising a pure intellectual contemplation as the best activity which makes humans godlike; cf. Nussbaum, *The Fragility of Goodness*, pp. 136–164.

7.2.4 The *Timaeus* and Plato's teaching on justice

The journey through Plato's conception of justice starts with an analysis of the Demiurge's speech in the *Timaeus*, and eventually leads back to the same dialogue. The picture of justice sketched out above is enriched here with additional elements—additional perspectives for understanding justice which are related to questions about the best activity a human being can perform and about the object of just actions or the object of love as caring for others. In the *Timaeus*, Plato focuses the attention of his readers on the importance of the visible realm for the justice of an individual.

At first glance, the *Timaeus* gives strong evidence that the best activity which fulfils a human being (human soul) and gives him happiness is pure intellectual activity. Plato's Timaeus states:

> if a man has seriously devoted himself to the love of learning and to true wisdom, if he has exercised these aspects of himself above all, then there is absolutely no way that his thoughts can fail to be immortal and divine, should truth come within his grasp. And to the extent that human nature can partake of immortality, he can in no way fail to achieve this: constantly caring for his divine part as he does, keeping well-ordered the guiding spirit that lives within him, he must indeed be supremely happy.[873]

To care about the soul is 'to provide for it nourishment and the motions that are proper to it'.[874] This nourishment is truth, true wisdom. This point is analogous to the story about pasturing souls in the *Phaedrus*.[875] It may be additionally observed that for its well-being any part of the soul (any soul) needs the motions that are proper to it. The intellectual part obtains such motions by 'coming to learn the harmonies and revolutions of the universe'.[876] This learning brings 'into conformity with its objects our faculty of understanding'.[877] And finally, 'when this conformity is complete, we shall have achieved our goal: that most excellent life offered to humankind by the gods, both now and forevermore'.[878]

It would be inaccurate to conclude, however, that intellectual activity itself makes the human soul 'supremely happy', and that this activity is the 'most excellent life offered to humankind'. In contrast to the most excellent life, Plato does not place simply a life spent without learning the truth and without adjusting the revolutions in our heads to the harmonies and revolutions of the universe, but in opposition to the most excellent life he puts—clearly—the life of someone without justice in his soul who 'cultivates his mortality':

873 Plato, *Timaeus*, 90b–c, trans. Zeyl.
874 Plato, *Timaeus*, 90c, trans. Zeyl.
875 Plato, *Phaedrus*, 248b–c.
876 Plato, *Timaeus*, 90d, trans. Zeyl.
877 Plato, *Timaeus*, 90d, trans. Zeyl.
878 Plato, *Timaeus*, 90d, trans. Zeyl.

> if a man has become absorbed in his appetites or his ambitions and takes great pains to further them, all his thoughts are bound to become merely mortal. And so far as it is at all possible for a man to become thoroughly mortal, he cannot help but fully succeed in this, seeing that he has cultivated his mortality all along.[879]

The immediate context leaves no doubt that considerations about caring for the intellectual part of the soul and for learning are part of an answer to the more general question of 'how a man should both lead and be led by himself in order to have the best prospects for leading a rational life [κατὰ λόγον ζῴη]'.[880] And to secure a rational life we should do 'our utmost to make sure that the part that is to do the leading is as superbly and perfectly as possible fitted for that task'.[881] Learning truth and adjusting the movements of the intellect to the movements of the universe is not the ultimate aim of a human being, only a means to lead a rational life. The key to such a life is being guided by the intellectual part, which possesses knowledge about the intelligible realm. Although in the analysed passages of the *Timaeus* the word 'justice' itself does not appear, explicit consideration is given to how to lead a rational life, which is equivalent to acting justly.[882] It is worth noting that the adjustment of the intellectual part to the harmony of the universe not only contributes to harmony between the elements of the soul, but also makes 'stronger' the intellectual part itself, and prevents the learning power from being turned towards the sensual world when the foundations of justice are being searched for, and thus prevents one from regarding as a good life a life based on increasing one's possessions rather than strengthening one's being.

The aforementioned remark of Plato's Timaeus about the 'most excellent life offered to humankind by the gods' is in fact the last remark about a matter which is of great importance in the dialogue. Some supplementary considerations still remain, but in the text which follows, Plato explicitly belittles the new topic and the way it is examined: 'We should go on to mention briefly how the other living things came to be—a topic that won't require many words. By doing this we'll seem to be in better measure with ourselves so far as our words on these subjects are concerned'.[883] The new topic is introduced principally to close the composition and to complete the considerations about the history of the universe. This confirms the assumption made in the analysis of the Demiurge's speech in the *Timaeus*,

879 Plato, *Timaeus*, 90b, trans. Zeyl.
880 Plato, *Timaeus*, 89d, trans. Zeyl.
881 Plato, *Timaeus*, 89d, trans. Zeyl.
882 Problems adjusting the intellectual part of the soul to the harmony of the universe are also addressed in the *Republic*, where studying astronomy is considered an important part of the education of the perfect guardians (rulers). Studying astronomy has a moral dimension as it contributes to the inner harmony of the soul, and therefore to its justice. See Hutchison, 'Why Does Plato Urge Rulers to Study Astronomy?' *passim*.
883 Plato, *Timaeus*, 90e, trans. Zeyl.

that this dialogue should be read, first of all, as a continuation of the *Republic*, and therefore as a dialogue about justice in which the model of the soul is no longer a state (a city) but the universe.

The overall conclusion of the *Timaeus* is a splendid piece of literary art, worthy of being quoted in full:

> And so now we may say that our account of the universe has reached its conclusion. This world of ours has received and teems with living things, mortal and immortal. A visible living thing containing visible ones, perceptible god, image of the intelligible Living Thing, its grandness, goodness, beauty and perfection are unexcelled. Our one universe, indeed the only one of its kind, has come to be.[884]

If the *Timaeus* is read as a continuation of the *Republic*, and the (partially) visible universe is taken as a model of a human being, then it is striking that it is not a model of the human soul only, but of the human being as composed of both a soul and a body. It is certain that in talking about the human being, who is a part of the visible universe, Plato considers very seriously the visible, bodily dimension of a man. Creatures like human beings, composed of both an invisible element belonging to the intelligible realm and an element belonging to the visible realm, had to be formed, because otherwise the universe would be incomplete and therefore not the best one.[885] It is important to take into account the view expressed by Plato's Timaeus at the beginning of his story about how the universe came to being. 'The most preeminent reason for the origin of the world's coming to be'[886] was the goodness of the Demiurge: 'He was good, and one who is good can never become jealous of anything. And so, being free of jealousy, he wanted everything to become as much like himself as was possible'.[887] This also concerns human beings and their actions.

Plato evidently cherishes the visible universe. The reader's thoughts go straight to the universe and its splendour, but the quotation could and should be read as saying something important about every single human being. In cherishing the visible universe Plato also cherishes the visible, concrete human being, who is not only part of the universe, but also an image of it, and of the Demiurge himself. What Plato seems to want his reader to take into consideration—as a horizon for understanding who we are—is the magnificence of a human being as being composed of both soul and body: our one human being, 'indeed the only one of its kind, has come to be' who is an 'image of the intelligible Living Thing'.

What does the story contribute to an understanding of justice? Human beings are willed by the Demiurge as beings composed of soul and body. Justice, as inner harmony and inner unity, comprises not only the three parts of the soul but also

884 Plato, *Timaeus*, 92c, trans. Zeyl.
885 See Plato, *Timaeus*, 41b–c.
886 Plato, *Timaeus*, 30a, trans. Zeyl.
887 Plato, *Timaeus*, 29e, trans. Zeyl.

the bodily parts of the human being. Where just actions are concerned, their addressee is an entire human being, and they should be beneficial for that human being as a whole.

To make my point more apparent, it is useful to place the interpretation proposed here in the context of opposite views which seem to be generally accepted. A convenient point of reference is an argument presented by Martha Nussbaum in *The Fragility of Goodness.* She argues that Plato's considerations of justice, which are summed up in Book IV, end with a pure formal conception of just actions. She also argues that this formal conception should be supplemented with a claim—pertaining to the content of the just life—that this is a life devoted to learning and the contemplation of truth, a life organised around the activity of reasoning (and never a life devoted to rationally ordered activities aimed at satisfying persisting appetitive needs). Nussbaum claims that without this extension any well-ordered content should satisfy Plato's requirements;[888] and 'we risk turning the *Republic* into a comfortable expression of the liberal principle (mentioned in Book VIII) that it should be "open to each person to structure an arrangement for his own life, the one that pleases him" (557b)—rather than, what it is, a profound and unsettling attack on that principle as a basis for genuinely good living'.[889] She pays attention to Plato's Socrates' claim, in Book VI, that the earlier story was insufficient because it has not taken into account something which is more important than justice and the other virtues—the Form of the Good.[890]

According to her interpretation, on the way to the life devoted to learning and contemplation 'all of our appetites are lead weights'[891]; moreover, education—aiming at that which is in common—requires that the bodily dimension of a human being is rejected as something pertaining to his nature, since sensual feelings are genuinely and 'irreducibly one's own' (p. 160). She writes that 'the body is not only the biggest obstacle to stable life and to true evaluation; it is also the most dangerous source of conflict, and therefore the biggest obstacle to impartial and harmonious civic justice'.[892]

I agree with Nussbaum that the formal conception of justice presented in Book IV should be supplemented by elements which lead to determination of the content of just actions. But I do not agree with seeing this extension in a life entirely devoted to learning and contemplation of truth. From a recognition of the superiority of the Good over justice, it does not follow that acts of cognition of the Good are the best acts a human being could perform. Knowledge about the Good is necessary to make the considerations of justice complete.[893] I believe that the

888 Nussbaum, *The Fragility of Goodness*, p. 139.
889 Nussbaum, *The Fragility of Goodness*, pp. 140–141.
890 Nussbaum, *The Fragility of Goodness*, p. 139; see Plato, *Republic*, 504a–d.
891 Nussbaum, *The Fragility of Goodness*, p. 163.
892 Nussbaum, *The Fragility of Goodness*, p. 160.
893 See Plato, *Republic*, 504c.

necessary extension of the formal approach to justice is based on the teaching on the nature of the Good and on just actions as actions which fit their addressees, which do not harm and are beneficial for them. The criteria of just actions are based on their contribution to the existence of an addressee, which is something objective and—at least in principle—independent of that which simply pleases someone.

Getting 'out of the cave', turning the whole soul (including its appetitive part) from that which is sensual towards the invisible realm and towards the Good, is essential for the education which is necessary to lead a just and happy life. The description of the process of educating philosophers is interpreted here as pertaining to education as the process of turning 'learning power' in the right direction. Nussbaum is right that turning away from sensual feelings not only directs the soul towards an invisible realm but is also a process of leaving 'something irreducibly one's own' in favour of that which is in common. But I disagree that aiming at what is in common is a paradigm for social organisation. That which is 'in common' for all parts of the soul is necessary, since turning the learning power requires turning the whole soul.[894] Reversing from that which is one's own, be it sensual experience, property or family, is a step towards an understanding of the very nature of the Good and then of just actions, which—as much as they are just—are directed to the benefit of others.

Learning about the Good is necessary for becoming good, for becoming just and acting justly. Neither learning nor contemplating truth are activities performed by the Good which unveil its nature. Its nature is disclosed by giving, by giving essence, existence and perfections to everything in the universe. I think that this is a sufficient reason to reject interpretations of the *Republic* which conclude that the best life for a human being is a life devoted to learning and the contemplation of truth. To recognise the Good to be something more important than justice and the other virtues[895] does not mean that acts of cognition of the Good are the best acts a human being (as a whole) can perform.

The knowledge about the Good is necessary to understand that justice as the inner unity of the soul is its highest perfection since it pertains to the very existence of the soul—its 'to be', not 'to have', that this unity is a foundation of just actions and that just actions are those which are beneficial for others, which contribute to the existence of their addressees. And this takes place after returning to the cave, in the visible world, where even private property is nothing shameful, even in the case of the paradigmatic philosopher—Plato's Socrates, who in the conclusion of the *Theaetetus* prays for gold.[896] The principal measure of perfection is acting for the benefit of others, and that is far from being devoted to that which pleases them. Acts of learning and contemplating truth are not godlike. Acts of learning and contemplating truth themselves are not acts of justice and they do

894 Plato, *Republic*, 518c.
895 Plato, *Republic*, 504d.
896 Plato, *Phaedrus*, 279c.

not contribute to the unity of the soul and its existence, as long as they are not a part of helping others, for example by educating them. A life devoted to satisfying one's own appetitive needs is certainly not a just and happy life. But what about rationally organised activities which focus on satisfying appetitive needs of other people which are rationally organised? What about actions which—by satisfying appetitive needs—help to act for the benefit of others and which do not encourage other people to focus on their own needs?

7.2.5 The elderly Cephalus on justice: foreword as epilogue

The priority of the individual over the state in terms of the 'place' for realising justice was already visible at the very beginning of the discussion on justice in the *Republic*, in the introductory conversation between Socrates and the elderly Cephalus—the father of Polemarchus, whose house hosted all of those who would discuss the issue of justice. Plato's Socrates' first observation was that Cephalus 'looked quite old',[897] and second—'he had been offering a sacrifice in the courtyard'.[898] Socrates then addresses him directly: 'I enjoy talking with the very old, for we should ask them, as we might ask those who have travelled a road that we too will probably have to follow, what kind of road it is, whether rough and difficult or smooth and easy'.[899] The crucial part of Cephalus' answer points to the way people live as being a decisive factor in determining whether old age is bitter or not: 'If they are moderate and contented [κόσμιοι καὶ εὔκολοι], old age, too, is only moderately onerous; if they aren't, both old age and youth are hard to bear'.[900] Plato's Socrates is evidently delighted by this statement.[901] Cephalus then says that concrete deeds, whether just and pious or not, are decisive for the quality of life. Moreover, what matters is their benefit or harm for a specific man or what is owed to a specific god, not that which would be beneficial for the state or legal order as such, nor the fulfilment of general precepts. Cephalus remarks that an older man

> is filled with foreboding and fear, and he examines himself to see whether he has been unjust to anyone. If he finds many injustices in his life, he awakes from sleep in terror, as children do, and lives in anticipation of bad things to come. But someone who knows that he hasn't been unjust has sweet good hope as his constant companion—a nurse to his old age.[902]

Similarly, it is an individual man or an individual god that is concerned when Cephalus considers the question of compensation for harming somebody or for

---

897 Plato, *Republic*, 328b, trans. Grube.
898 Plato, *Republic*, 328c, trans. Grube.
899 Plato, *Republic*, 328d–e, trans. Grube.
900 Plato, *Republic*, 229d, trans. Grube.
901 Plato, *Republic*, 229d.
902 Plato, *Republic*, 330e–331a, trans. Grube.

neglecting sacrifices. According to Cephalus, wealth is most valuable because it makes such compensation possible.[903] Nevertheless, wealth is most valuable 'not for every man but for a decent and orderly one'.[904] Justice in the soul is regarded as a precondition of just actions—they are the deeds of someone who is decent and orderly.[905] He does not simply 'buy' inner peace and a better afterlife by buying a better condition of the soul. Cephalus supposes that he is already decent and orderly. What he considers and thinks about is not his inner peace itself, but the harm he has done to others, for which compensation should be given. Peace appears as a side effect of just actions.

The priority of deeds over the state of the soul is also suggested by the fact that considerations about the consequences of human actions in the afterlife are an important component of Plato's reflections on justice in both the *Republic* and the *Gorgias*.

With regard to wealth, Cephalus is described by Plato's Socrates as a man of moderation—someone who is quite rich and who has increased his inherited wealth, but nevertheless does not 'seem to love money too much',[906] he does not devote his life to making money, nor does he bother about money at the end of his life—at 'the threshold of old age'.[907] He is far from treating wealth as an absolute good, although he believes that for a decent person it is a good which can be used as a means for accomplishing justice.[908]

Plato's Socrates neither objects to Cephalus' views nor tries to convince him of something else; on the contrary, he is content with what Cephalus says.[909] Socrates endeavours to draw him into a discussion, but Cephalus does not intend to take part in the debate and shows no interest as to whether there are arguments which would confirm or undermine his views. Instead he prefers to perform his sacrifice. Cephalus gives priority to pious actions (acting justly towards the gods) over intellectual inquiries about justice itself. He already knows what is important in human life. Action addressed to a concrete addressee takes priority over theoretical inquiry about justice as such.

The picture of Cephalus given by Plato at the very beginning of the *Republic*, considered from the perspective of a comprehensive analysis of the conception of justice, turns out to announce several elements of thinking about justice which Plato advocates as essential, namely the higher excellence of just deeds over the justice of the soul, and the priority of the individual over the state or legal order as

903 Plato, *Republic*, 330e–331b.
904 Plato, *Republic*, 331a, trans. Grube.
905 Plato, *Republic*, 331a.
906 Plato, *Republic*, 330b, trans. Grube.
907 Plato, *Republic*, 328e, trans. Grube.
908 Plato, *Republic*, 331b.
909 'I admired him for saying that', Plato, *Republic*, 329d; 'A fine statement, Cephalus', ibid., 331b, trans. Grube.

such. The voice of Cephalus is not, however, the voice of someone who expresses knowledge in the full sense, but someone who speaks from his own experience,[910] an experience that confirms the findings of philosophical enquiry.

7.2.6 Closing remarks

The above analysis confirms that according to Plato, it is not justice in the soul alone that provides happiness to its subject. Acting justly is a key to fulfilment and happiness, although justice in the soul is a necessary condition for such acting. Cognition of the truth and contemplation of the forms (ideas) are only means to achieve justice in the soul and to act justly. An individual, endowed with an imperfect body, can be a proper object of loving care, of actions which are beneficial for their addressee and—at the same time—fulfil an acting subject and make him happy. Moreover, active justice presupposes a kind of imperfection on the side of the addressee of actions, and therefore cannot be practised in relation to perfect forms (ideas). In acting towards perfect forms (ideas), it is impossible for a human being to act like the Good or the Demiurge, and so it is impossible to act accordingly to being an image of God.

7.3 The sharing of wives: testing the interpretation on a 'hard case'

7.3.1 Preliminary remarks

The parts of the *Republic* treating the question of women in the state present a 'hard case' for testing the correctness of the proposed interpretation of Plato's conception of justice. Plato's Socrates' approach to women seems to favour a totalitarian interpretation of the whole of Plato's conception of justice. However, there are grounds for taking a dignitarian perspective if one examines more closely Plato's Socrates' attitude to his own assertions, which indicates that the passages about the sharing of wives should not be read as a direct project for organising society, but rather as an intellectual exercise, an exercise in wisdom, based on jesting and

910 Cf. Aristotle, *Nicomachean Ethics*, 1143b, trans. Irwin: 'while no one seems to have natural wisdom, people seem to have natural consideration, comprehension and judgment. A sign [of their apparent natural character] is our thinking that they also correspond to someone's age, and the fact that understanding and consideration belong to a certain age, at though nature were the cause. We must attend, then, to the undemonstrated remarks and beliefs of experienced and older people or of intelligent people, no less than to demonstrations. For these people see correctly because experience has given them their eye'.

irony.[911] Moreover, it turns out to be also an exercise in the courage and moderation of the reader.

Plato's Socrates discusses the position of women in the state extensively from the beginning of Book V up to the end of Book VII. Even though they are not the only subject of these books, they are included in considerations of the earlier developed model of the state, and are therefore important for the interpretation of Plato's overall project to present the hypothetical state. On the other hand, as a part of the project to design a model of a hypothetical state, the considerations about women in the state should be read taking due account of the heuristic functions of this model and of Plato's explicit reservations against treating this model as an ideal for an actual state, expressed clearly in the remark that justice in this model is only a phantom [εἴδωλον] of justice.[912]

The topic of wives is already briefly mentioned in Book IV, as a matter which is not difficult to deal with. Plato's Socrates points out that in some matters the proper education of the guardians suffices, and they have no need for numerous orders:

> if by being well educated they become reasonable men, they will easily see these things for themselves, as well as all the other things we are omitting, for example, that marriage, the having of wives, and the procreation of children must be governed as far as possible by the old proverb: Friends possess everything in common.[913]

However, this passage seems to be only a kind of provocation, and the matter proves to be far more complex and not easy at all, as Plato's Socrates admits himself in Book V.

When Plato finally tackles the issue, he clearly marks both the beginning and the end of the elaboration of the problem. The beginning is marked by a discussion among the members of the audience, who request to return to the question of wives;[914] the end is indicated by the statement: 'And as for your question, I think that we have reached the end of this topic',[915] as well as by a short conclusion formulated at the beginning of Book VIII.[916] The main point established in the discussion is as follows:

> If a city is to achieve the height of good government, wives must be in common, children and their education should be in common, their way of life, whether in peace or

911 Plato's views on the sharing of wives expressed in the *Republic* are notoriously taken seriously and directly as a social project; see e.g. Vlastos, 'The Individual as Object of Love in Plato', pp. 17–18; S. Rosen, *Plato's Republic*, pp. 171–197; Annas, 'Plato's *Republic* and Feminism', *passim.*

912 Plato, *Republic*, 443c, trans. Bloom; see Section 3.7.

913 Plato, *Republic*, 423e–424a, trans. Grube.

914 Plato, *Republic*, 449a–b.

915 Plato, *Republic*, 542b, trans. Grube.

916 Plato, *Republic*, 543a–c.

war, must be in common, and their kings must be those among them who have proved to be best, both in philosophy and in warfare.[917]

The issue of wives in the state is also clearly sectioned off by a kind of a frame provided by the considerations of different kinds of constitutions of states and—related to them—the different kinds of characters of individuals. Immediately before the issue of wives is taken up, the discussion of kinds of constitutions and characters is suddenly interrupted;[918] Plato's Socrates returns to this discussion immediately after closing the issue of wives.[919]

7.3.2 The dolphin of Arion—an introduction by Plato's Socrates

The main passage related to the issue of women in the state opens with an exceptionally long introductory part (from 449a to 453d) in which Plato's Socrates expresses his reluctance to develop the topic because he does not feel entirely secure and confident in talking about it, and indicates that he does not know the truth about these matters and still searches for it.[920] This remark is clearly incongruent with his earlier statement in Book IV that the issue is among the matters which reasonable men 'will easily see'.[921]

One must not underestimate the remark, placed right at the end of this introductory part, about being rescued by a dolphin. Plato's Socrates compares tackling the law concerning the possession and upbringing of women to swimming in the middle of the largest ocean of argument: 'Then we must swim too, and try to save ourselves from the sea of argument hoping that a dolphin will pick us up or that we'll be rescued by some other desperate means'.[922]

Plato's Socrates evidently refers to the story of Arion, which can be found in Herodotus' *Histories*.[923] Arion was a great half-mythical Dionysiac poet from the seventh century BC, the best lyre-player and singer of his time. Born on Lesbos, he spent most of his life at the court of Periander, the tyrant of Corinth. Herodotus says that he was considered to be the inventor of the dithyramb.[924] According to the story told by Herodotus, the crew of the ship which was to carry Arion from

917 Plato, *Republic*, 543a, trans. Grube.
918 Plato, *Republic*, 449a.
919 Plato, *Republic*, 543c.
920 Plato, *Republic*, 450d–451a, trans. Grube: 'Your encouragement would be fine, if I could be sure I was speaking with knowledge, for one can feel both secure and confident when one knows the truth about the dearest and most important things and speaks about them among those who are themselves wise and dear friends. But to speak, as I'm doing, at a time when one is unsure of oneself and searching for the truth, is a frightening and insecure thing to do'.
921 Plato, *Republic*, 423e, trans. Grube.
922 Plato, *Republic*, 453d, trans. Grube.
923 Herodotus, *Histories*, 1, 23–24.
924 Herodotus, *Histories*, 1, 23.

Tarentum to Italy decided to rob him and cast him overboard. When beseeched to spare his life, the sailors left him a choice: 'either to kill himself and so receive burial on land or else to jump into the sea at once'.[925] Arion pretended to choose killing himself, and his last wish was to sing one more time. The crew agreed. After singing a dithyramb in honour of Apollo, Arion threw himself into the sea only to be rescued by a dolphin, which carried him to a shore close to Corinth.

When approaching difficult and important problems, Plato's Socrates commonly resorts to the help of gods and prayer;[926] here he rests his hopes in a dolphin. One can conclude that Plato's Socrates intends to perform like a poet who, in spite of not possessing knowledge, is sometimes able to say something true, and for whom entertainment is an important function of the performance. At one point in his considerations, Plato's Socrates reflects upon his way of speaking: 'I forgot that we were only playing [jesting], and so I spoke too vehemently'.[927] This remark seems to be very general. The fact that the story about women was referred to as being like poetry, having been told in jest, is confirmed by Plato's Socrates' characterisation of poetry as something which is based on imitation. He mentions 'that an imitator has no worthwhile knowledge of the things he imitates, that imitation is a kind of game and not something to be taken seriously'.[928]

7.3.3 Non-geometrical but erotic necessities

Another clear indication that Plato's Socrates performs as if on stage is a remark made by Glaucon about Socrates' statement on the necessities in sexual relations. Glaucon observes that 'the necessities aren't geometrical but erotic'.[929] Departure from the geometrical necessities is equivalent to departure from true philosophy.[930]

In the context of playing with the audience and jesting, it is useful to examine the first argument that Plato's Socrates provides to support the view that the guardians should have their wives in common. This argument is formulated immediately after the description of the regulation of the sexual life of the guardians and is based on 'erotic necessities'.

A careful reader is certainly surprised how easily, almost directly, Plato's Socrates links the good with the pleasant, given that he usually strictly separates these two things, and sometimes vigorously defends their separation.[931] There is an argument here which takes for granted a positive connection of the good with the pleasant. It runs as follows:

---

925 Herodotus, *Histories*, 1, 24, trans. Godley.
926 Plato, *Republic*, 432c, 443b, 536c.
927 Plato, *Republic*, 536c, trans. Grube.
928 Plato, *Republic*, 602b, trans. Grube.
929 Plato, *Republic*, 458d, trans. Grube.
930 Cf. Plato, *Gorgias*, 507e–508a.
931 See e.g. *Gorgias*, 506c; see Section 4.1.3.

Socrates: Is there any greater evil we can mention for a city than that which tears it apart and makes it many instead of one? Or any greater good than that which binds it together and makes it one?

Glaucon: There isn't.

Socrates: And when, as far as possible, all the citizens rejoice and are pained by the same successes and failures, doesn't this sharing of pleasures and pains bind the city together?

Glaucon: It most certainly does.

Socrates: But when some suffer greatly, while others rejoice greatly, at the same things happening to the city or its people, doesn't this privatization of pleasures and pains dissolve the city?

Glaucon: Of course.

Socrates: And isn't that what happens whenever such words as 'mine' and 'not mine' aren't used in unison? And similarly with 'someone else's'?

Glaucon: Precisely.

Socrates: Then, is the best-governed city the one in which most people say 'mine' and 'not mine' about the same things in the same way?

Glaucon: It is indeed.[932]

It can be observed that this argument needs to be understood as an element of the construction of the model of the hypothetical state because it is assumed that the unity of the state is an indisputable, supreme aim of the organisation of the state. This premise is not applicable to a real state, where the development of each member of the political community is recognised as taking precedence over the existence and unity of the state.[933]

If the above quoted text is read with an open mind and without the prejudice that everything written by Plato must be entirely serious, the reader would then naturally react: 'Plato, you're joking, aren't you?' And Plato would most certainly answer: 'Yes, of course, I am!' There is, for example, the question concerning the one, most beautiful woman in the city who is able to give her lover supreme pleasure. If every man in the city could call her 'mine', would it contribute to the unity of the state based on the unity of experiencing pleasures? Would a lottery solve the matter? What about the tacit premise that everybody would experience similar emotions and, therefore, pleasures or pains in relation to the things which are common to all? Many pleasures and pains are tied to emotions, which are irregular, variable, and not ordered by themselves, as is clearly recognised by Plato when he criticises the Sophists and proposes Typhon as an image of a man governed by emotions.[934] Here the argument seems to presuppose that there is a

932 Plato, *Republic*, 462a–c, trans. Grube.

933 Plato, *Laws*, 770e; see Chapter 5.

934 Plato, *Phaedrus*, 230a; see Section 3.6.1.

constant regularity based on 'erotic necessities', which—if unrestricted by cultural conventions—leads straight to the unity of a state. Plato's Socrates seems to speak in unison with Callicles in saying that calling something 'mine' is based on 'these contracts of men that go against nature, they're worthless nonsense!'[935] 'Erotic necessities', which are obviously not 'geometrical' and therefore not philosophical, not rational, underlie the entire argument. If the solutions posed are to be opposite to those of the Sophists, the argument should be based on the ordering of 'erotic necessities' by reason. The whole story about the sharing of wives is constructed as a kind of test of the courage and moderation of Plato's Socrates' male audience. Courage is understood here in the specific Platonic sense, as a power to preserve rational convictions not only in the face of danger, fear and pain, but also in relation to pleasures and desires.[936] What about the prospect of having an erotic relationship with the most beautiful woman in the city? The *Republic* proves to be not only a challenge for the intellect of its readers, but also a trial of their courage and a test of their moderation. Will rational convictions stand this test? In spite of the clear reservations expressed by Plato's Socrates that he talks about matters he has no knowledge about, his audience eagerly admits that the sharing of wives is 'by far the best'[937] arrangement in the state. The audience of Plato's Socrates do not pass this test of courage.

One can ask why Plato's Socrates, when in Book X he advises banning poetry from the state, does not take into account the pleasure-giving functions of poetry as something that could contribute to the unity of the state. What could be more common than Homer's poetry and the pleasures and pains experienced while listening to it? Yet Plato's Socrates aims to discredit Homer as a poet and advocates the view that 'if you admit the pleasure-giving Muse, whether in lyric or epic poetry, pleasure and pain will be kings in your city instead of law or the thing that everyone has always believed to be best, namely, reason'.[938] One may argue that a state could survive without poets but not without women; but why trust that sexual intercourse, unlike poetry, would not likewise lead to the reign of pleasure and pain in the city?

In the context of 'erotic necessities' and the clearly poetic narrative about relations between men and women in the state, Plato's Socrates observes that 'it looks as though our rulers will have to make considerable use of falsehood and deception for the benefit of those they rule. And we said that all such falsehoods are useful as a form of drug'.[939] In the hypothetical state only the rulers should be free from

935 Plato, *Gorgias*, 492c, trans. Zeyl.
936 Plato, *Republic*, 429b–d; see Section 3.6.3.
937 Plato, *Republic*, 461e, trans. Grube.
938 Plato, *Republic*, 607a, trans. Grube; cf. ibid. 607c, see Pacewicz, *Hēdonē*, pp. 206–207; Plato's Socrates seems to be ready to accept the pleasure which is given by poetry if poetry proves to be beneficial; nevertheless, the unifying function of pleasure is not mentioned.
939 Plato, *Republic*, 459c–d, trans. Grube.

falsehood.[940] All the others are destined to be permanently deceived and to live their lives being led by the lies they are told. They are destined to be ignorant about vital matters all their lives. Already in Book II Plato's Socrates distinguished true (pure) falsehood, which is 'ignorance in the soul of someone who has been told a falsehood',[941] from falsehood in words.[942] The former, 'the thing that is really a falsehood is hated not only by the gods but by human beings as well'.[943] The latter can be permitted as useful against one's enemies and as a useful drug preventing evil if someone attempts, through madness or ignorance, to do something bad.[944] Using falsehood in words certainly causes 'ignorance in the soul'. Such an ignorance, as being contrary to the reason which is present in every human soul, could be accepted—in principle—only temporarily. Considerable and permanent use of falsehood in words as a drug could be permitted if all citizens, except the rulers themselves, were everlasting enemies of the rulers or were permanently insane. Both premises seem to be unacceptable. Not ill will but friendship between all citizens is the foundation of both the real and the hypothetical state. Similarly, a state in which the vast majority of inhbitants are perpetually insane could not be a paradigm for any reasonable political project.

Plato's Socrates could rightly expect his audience to object to his proposal to make considerable use of falsehood and deception; this proposal went clearly against some fundamental reasonable convictions. Of course he provided some arguments. The main justification for lying was that it was necessary to regulate sexual intercourse in the state and that such a regulation is required as the best means to strengthen the unity of the state. This argument presupposes a doubtful premise that the benefit of the state takes priority over the soundness of the souls of its citizens. The thesis that the sharing of wives best secures this unity seems also be underargued. In the course of the argumentation Plato's Socrates clearly pointed out that the extensive use of deception makes it possible that the best males, the rulers, can have sex with potentially every attractive woman in the state. Such a prospect is evidently something desirable for Plato's Socrates' audience—young men who see themselves as rulers in the hypothetical state.

Talking about making considerable use of falsehood is understandable if it is interpreted not in terms of a political project but in terms of the inner relations of an individual. If those who are ruled represent the emotions—'the many-headed beast'[945]—then, indeed, there is no point in caring whether truth or falsehood is presented to rule over them or to exercise them. Emotions, as they are understood

940 Plato, *Republic*, 459d–e, trans. Grube.
941 Plato, *Republic*, 382b, trans. Grube.
942 Plato, *Republic*, 382c–d, trans. Grube.
943 Plato, *Republic*, 382c, trans. Grube; see a broader consideration of falsehood, ibid., 382a–c, 485c.
944 Plato, *Republic*, 382c–d, trans. Grube.
945 Plato, *Republic*, 589b, trans. Grube.

by Plato, are not able to learn anything about reality, they are simply not a cognitive power (one can, of course, learn something about reality interpreting emotional reactions but this is a work of the intellect).

One more observation should be made. When the problem of poets in the state is formulated in Book X, Plato's Socrates mentions that in the case of poets as imitators, their works 'are easily produced [ῥᾴδια ποιεῖν] without knowledge of the truth'.[946] This remark should be taken into account in the interpretation of the issue of women in the state, formulated in Book IV. According to this formulation, the guardians 'will easily see [ῥᾳδίως διόψονται] (…) for themselves'[947] how to deal with this matter. When this problem returns in Book V, and Plato's Socrates is asked to develop an argument, he declares that he has no knowledge and is reluctant to speak. He knows that he does not know, and this is why it is not easy for him to speak on the subject. Finally, when he conceals his face under a mask of poetry, everything related to women starts to be easily seen. The announcement formulated in Book IV, when the model of hypothetical state was under construction, that guardians 'will easily see' is realised, again—in the framework of the model of the state. Is this not because they are only a theoretical construct, part of an intellectual game, which as such is without knowledge of the truth? Is this not a clear warning not to take the story about the hypothetical state directly as a project for the organisation of a real state?

And one further remark. Plato's Socrates' presentation of the question of women, accompanied by his declaration of not knowing the truth and performed in the mask of a poet, would never be allowed in the hypothetical state in the light of the conclusions drawn in Book X, where the problem of poets and poetry in the imaginary state is extensively developed. In the hypothetical state, imitative poetry 'should be altogether excluded. (…) all such poetry is likely to distort the thought of anyone who hears it, unless he has the knowledge of what it is really like, a drug to counteract it'.[948] In his exposition of the issue of women in the state, Plato's Socrates—not having knowledge about the truth in these maters—can offer only an imitation of a state and does not have a proper drug to counteract the distortion of thought it may cause. Again, the story about the sharing of wives turns out to be a test of the courage and moderation of Plato's Socrates' listeners (and of the readers of the *Republic*) who are confronted with their desires.

7.3.4 Some instructions on how to read Plato

How might these incongruities be resolved? The answer seems not to be very difficult if Plato's dialogue is read with an intellectual distance, without the assumption that Plato always speaks very seriously. Plato plays with the reader, trying

946 Plato, *Republic*, 599a, trans. Grube.
947 Plato, *Republic*, 423e, trans. Grube.
948 Plato, *Republic*, 595a–b, trans. Grube.

to force him to think independently. He expects his reader to write himself, in his own mind 'the living, breathing discourse of the man who knows'.[949] Therefore, the interpretation of Plato's texts always remains an open undertaking.

Nevertheless, Plato expects from his reader an ability to distinguish irony and jest from earnest statements; to distinguish a model, an icon and—most of all—a phantom from reality. This is certainly not always an easy task, although when it comes to vital questions, Plato provides his reader with clear guidance. This is the case when in the *Republic* Plato's Socrates starts his crucial statement about justice with the words—'And in truth [τὸ δέ γε ἀληθές] justice is',[950] and at the same time, justice in the state based on strict division of occupations is called 'a phantom' ['εἴδωλον'] of justice,[951] and—to leave no doubts—the description of a just man which follows is not the description of a perfect guardian or a pure philosopher, but a man who integrates features of all the basic types of citizen in the hypothetical state and performs different types of activities in the real state.[952] In the *Gorgias* the discussion of the most important questions about justice ends with an earnest and straightforward statement: 'So this is how I set down the matter, and I say that this is true [ἀληθῆ εἶναι]'.[953] Generally, Plato is very careful when he writes what 'in truth' is or what 'is true'. Quite contrary instructions are given to the reader when it comes to the question of women. There is no prayer; no gods are expected to come with help, but a dolphin; and there is a clear suggestion that what is said is more like a song performed by a poet, a jest, than a philosophical dispute. What is more, Plato's Socrates plainly states that he has no knowledge about the issue at hand. Of course, Plato is sometimes less unequivocal in his instructions. And no wonder—learning to think independently involves exercises in discerning models (shadows, icons, phantoms) from reality. In any case, where is joy to be found in reading instruction manuals?

Last but not least, the story about the sharing of wives is to be read as an exercise not only in searching for wisdom, but also in courage and moderation.

7.3.5 What can be gained from the discussion about women?

7.3.5.1 Fundamental equality of the sexes

The story about the sharing of wives in Books VI and VII is clearly a part of the model of the hypothetical state, and although it presents only a phantom of reality, it should prove useful. Although poets above all serve Dionysus, who symbolises

949 Plato, *Phaedrus*, 276a, trans. Nehamas, Woodruff.
950 Plato, *Republic*, 443c, trans. Grube.
951 Plato, *Republic*, 443c.
952 Plato, *Republic*, 443e.
953 Plato, *Gorgias*, 507c, trans. Zeyl.

vitality, appetites and desires, the song of Arion is sung to Apollo, who symbolises arts and reason. Plato's Socrates' remark about jesting certainly refers to the discussion of questions about women, but Plato's Socrates speaks earnestly about education and about the Good in Book VII, and in Book VI the accusation of ignorance against the Sophists is also serious and direct.[954] However, the question remains as to why Plato devoted so much attention, so much space in the *Republic*, to women in the hypothetical state. In seeking an answer, one should adopt an interpretative key based on a dignitarian approach; therefore the issue should be considered, first of all, from the perspective of individuals—their justice and happiness.

The question that arises is whether people of both sexes are equally able to pursue justice and happiness. Plato's answer is 'yes'—there are no fundamental differences in this respect. In assigning different types of activity, the nature of anybody and of anything should be viewed from the perspective of the tasks proper for a given activity. Plato's Socrates argues:

> *Socrates*: isn't one woman philosophical or a lover of wisdom, while another hates wisdom? And isn't one spirited and another spiritless?
> *Glaucon*: That too.
> *Socrates*: So one woman may have a guardian nature and another not, for wasn't it qualities of this sort that we looked for in the natures of the men we selected as guardians?
> *Glaucon*: Certainly.
> *Socrates*: Therefore, men and women are by nature the same with respect to guarding the city, except to the extent that one is weaker and the other stronger.
> *Glaucon*: Apparently.
> *Socrates*: Then women of this sort must be chosen along with men of the same sort to live with them and share their guardianship, seeing that they are adequate for the task and akin to the men in nature.
> *Glaucon*: Certainly.
> *Socrates*: And mustn't we assign the same way of life to the same natures?
> *Glaucon*: We must.[955]

From an individualistic perspective there is an assertion that in every woman, just like in every man, the same fundamental (for acquiring justice) types of inner activity and parts of the soul can be found: 'isn't one woman philosophical or a lover of wisdom, while another hates wisdom? And isn't one spirited and another spiritless?'[956] Moreover, 'men and women are by nature the same with respect to

954 Plato, *Republic*, 493b, trans. Grube: 'In truth, he knows nothing about which of these convictions is fine or shameful, good or bad, just or unjust'.
955 Plato, *Republic*, 456a–b, trans. Grube.
956 Plato, *Republic*, 456a, trans. Grube.

guarding the city'.[957] There is no reason to assign different tasks to these parts—'mustn't we assign the same way of life to the same natures?'[958]

7.3.5.2 No justification for subordinating weaker minds to stronger ones

In analysing the quoted excerpt, attention should be paid to the reservation made by Plato's Socrates: 'men and women are by nature the same with respect to guarding the city, *except to the extent that one is weaker and the other stronger*'.[959] This is a repetition of the view that 'women share by nature in every way of life just as men do, but in all of them women are weaker than men',[960] which was expressed by Plato's Socrates shortly before. This cannot be regarded as a marginal remark that could be explained by the social context of the story. It is intriguing also because there are quite obviously women who, in respect to guarding the state, are stronger than many men.[961] Therefore, there are good grounds to pay special attention to this general remark about women's being weaker in respect to guarding the city. Translating this remark into an individualistic perspective, a view of primary importance for organising a real state is disclosed: the fact that someone's reason is weaker does not justify denial of its role in guiding that individual, nor does it justify a general subordination to the dictate of a more brilliant mind or minds. Such subordination is justified only 'when the best part is naturally weak in someone, it can't rule the beasts within him but can only serve them and learn to flatter them',[962] or when someone is not educated, as in the case of

---

957 Plato, *Republic*, 456a, trans. Grube; cf. ibid., 455d–e: 'there is no way of life concerned with the management of the city that belongs to a woman because she's a woman or to a man because he's a man, but the various natures are distributed in the same way in both creatures. Women share by nature in every way of life just as men do, but in all of them women are weaker than men'.

958 Plato, *Republic*, 456b, trans. Grube. On how Plato's Socrates' argumentation in favour of equality of the sexes is revolutionary in the context of ancient Greek culture, see Freudiger (1995), *passim*. S. B. Pomeroy notes that 'The utopian literature of the Classical period recommended a return to what were thought to be some primitive features of Athenian society. In terms of women's lives, these would include the elimination of monogamous marriage and known paternity of children, and the opportunity to play a role in public affairs and enjoy sexual freedom'. According to a myth, marriage was instituted by the legendary first king of Athens, Cecrops, and marriage accompanied by the loss of women's political equality was meant as a punishment for women, since they voted for Athena as a patroness of their city, against men who preferred Poseidon; Pomeroy, *Goddesses, Whores, Wives, and Slaves*, p. 115. Cf. description of Phaeacia in Homer, *Odyssey*, VI–VIII.

959 Plato, *Republic*, 456a, trans. Grube, emphasis added.

960 Plato, *Republic*, 455d–e, trans. Grube.

961 Plato's Socrates recognises the general superiority of women in several domains; see Plato, *Republic*, 455c.

962 Plato, *Republic*, 590c, trans. Grube.

children.[963] In the first case, when someone cannot rule 'the beast within him'—not reason but the spirited part—it is a question of will. Nevertheless, even individuals with weaker reason or with weaker spirited parts are fully entitled to a proper education: 'We've come round, then, to what we said before and have agreed that it isn't against nature to assign an education in music, poetry, and physical training to the wives of the guardians'.[964] This statement closes a longer deliberation on the place of women in the city, and this provides additional justification for paying attention to the hidden meaning of Socrates' remark about the weaker nature of women.

7.3.5.3 The highest standards of friendship

Particular attention should be given to the formulation of the issue of women in Book IV (423e–424a), reiterated in Book V (449c). In both formulations, Plato's Socrates points to the old proverb that 'friends possess everything in common' as establishing the principle which should govern considerations about women in the state. The original formula 'πάντα ὅτι μάλιστα κοινὰ τὰ φίλων' could also be translated: 'everything should be in common between friends as far as possible'. What is of primary concern here is not the common possession of things in a literal sense, but rather sharing a common fate and forming a community of friends. Plato's Socrates considers the second main aim of laws, after the happiness of all citizens, to be 'the greatest possible mutual friendship'.[965] One has to remember that a basic condition for friendship—commonly recognised in the Greek world—was equality.[966] Equating relations between citizens and between parts of the soul with relations between members of a good family—as Plato's Socrates does in his deliberations about women—sets the highest possible standards for friendship; it is like saying—'always think whether higher friendship is possible'.

Advocacy of a general equality between men and women in respect to cardinal virtues has, as has been shown above, deeply rooted justifications in Plato's philosophy: justice is 'produced', above all, by acting for the benefit of others—this is the way a man or a woman can best resemble the Good itself, to be godlike. But such acting is limited by the ability of an addressee to take, to 'absorb' the gift; for example, it is impossible to share deep philosophical ideas with someone who is far from being equal in his philosophical education. Equality in virtues facilitates further development of the justice of souls and of action, and lack of equality limits the quality of such development.

963 Plato, *Republic*, 590e.
964 Plato, *Republic*, 456b, trans. Grube; cf. ibid., 589a–b.
965 Plato, *Laws*, 743c, trans. Saunders.
966 Plato, *Gorgias*, 510b; *Laws*, 757a; see Section 6.4.3.

7.3.5.4 How to establish friendship in the soul

The discussion concerning women may also be read in the context of the fundamental problem of how to establish friendship in the soul, which is something proper for justice. When explaining what in truth justice is, Plato's Socrates describes a just man as someone who 'puts himself in order, is his own friend, and harmonises the three parts of himself'.[967] This friendship should be as great as possible. But how to gain such friendship with oneself? The difficulty of this question resembles the difficulty of how to deal with relations between men, women and children in the state. At first glance, it does not seem to be a complicated issue, but later on it turns out to be very challenging. How to establish friendship between the three parts of the soul when each deals with different matters, has different tasks to fulfil, and—taken separately—has different aims? The first thing that has to be accepted is the community (unity) not only of all three parts of the soul, but also of all of the elements which can be identified in each part. Recognising these elements as 'mine' is a precondition for cultivating relations between the elements and for forming the unity of the soul. In Book IX, a soul is compared to a compound consisting of a human being (the rational part), a lion (the spirited part), and a many-headed beast (the appetitive part). Plato's Socrates observes:

> all our words and deeds should insure that the human being within this human being has the most control; second, that he should take care of the many-headed beast as a farmer does his animals, feeding and domesticating the gentle heads and preventing the savage ones from growing; and, third, that he should make the lion's nature his ally, care for the community of all his parts, and bring them up in such a way that they will be friends with each other and with himself.[968]

Again, there is no direct answer to the question of how to 'care for the community of all his parts, and bring them up in such a way that they will be friends with each other'. It should be done—but how? Plato's Socrates, as he admitted in Book V, does not know. He suggests considering whether the community of the pleasant and the painful might help.

7.3.6 Closing remarks

The dignitarian interpretation of Plato's conception of justice has been shown to withstand a confrontation with a 'hard case'. It remains fruitful and allows the writing of 'the living and breathing discourse'[969] in the reader's mind. Moreover, the analysis of the 'hard case' confirms that Plato's teaching on justice is intended to give an understanding of individual justice, that the model of the hypothetical

---

967 Plato, *Republic*, 443d, trans. Grube.
968 Plato, *Republic*, 589a–b, trans. Grube.
969 Plato, *Phaedrus*, 276a, Nehamas, Woodruff.

state and justice based on a strict division of occupations are only a means for understanding an individual and must not be regarded as Plato's proposals for the organisation of a real state. They are a kind of phantom which is useful for understanding certain aspects of reality. The story about the sharing of wives provides reasons for recognising the general equality of the sexes in respect to gaining moral development and happiness. It also provides reasons for recognising personal responsibility in directing one's own life rationally, and for rejecting the governance of people with weaker minds (once they reach a certain level of maturity) by the more brilliant, which is evidently contrary to the solutions depicted in the model of the hypothetical state.

The sections devoted to the sharing of wives in the state turn out to challenge not only the intellect of the reader, but also his spirited and appetitive parts, and to test both his moderation and his courage, understood as the power to preserve rational convictions in the face of desires and pleasures.

8 Conclusions

8.1 Dignity

The question of whether what is nowadays called 'dignity' was recognised by Plato has been answered in the affirmative, and this certainly speaks in favour of the thesis of the universality of human dignity, which underlies the modern-day protection of human rights in international law and in many constitutional orders. Plato reflects upon 'something' which has properties that are nowadays recognised in legal instruments as fundamental for dignity. This reflection cannot be held to be a marginal part of his thought; rather it should be regarded as fundamental to the whole of Plato's theory of justice, and indeed to the whole of his philosophy. His considerations relating to dignity appear in the context of enquires about justice; the fundamental statements relevant to dignity are to be found in the speech of the Demiurge. This speech can be regarded as one of the most important parts of the *Timaeus*, a dialogue written as a continuation of the *Republic*, which has the justice of an individual as its primary object.

Unlike modern legal approaches to dignity, Plato offers an answer to the question of what is dignity, which is placed on the level of existence: it is a special, exceptionally perfect way of existence based on an inner unity which is constituted by a special, exceptionally perfect harmony and order. As the Plato's Demiurge describes this special inner constitution of creatures composed directly by him, they are 'beautifully harmonised and in fine condition',[970] and 'only one who is evil would consent to the undoing'[971] of such creatures. And the Demiurge, who provides this inner unity, is not evil, and therefore can never want them to be undone; to the contrary—he will always want their existence. The will of the Demiurge not to consent to the undoing has objective foundations in the inner constitution (dignity) of the addressee of his actions and in his being good. Therefore everyone, in as much as he is good, cannot consent to the undoing of what has been beautifully harmonised and are in fine condition.

This inner unity is the foundation of existence. Since dignity rests on existence, it is not a trait in an ordinary sense, it is not simply possessed—it is of the order of being, rather than having. In Plato's theory of justice, as in modern approaches, this special way of existence can be characterised in terms of one's being an aim in oneself. The 'possessors' of dignity are willed by the Demiurge for themselves and not as mere means, and their way of existence is congruent with the way something is willed by the 'provider' of existence.

970 Plato, *Timaeus*, 41b, trans. Zeyl.
971 Plato, *Timaeus*, 41a–b, trans. Zeyl.

In Plato's conception of justice, like in contemporary reflections on the foundations of law, the recognition of dignity leads to recognition of the postulate that someone endowed with dignity should always be treated as an end in himself, never merely as a means. To treat someone as an end means to care about their flourishing and the accomplishment of their aims. From the perspective of the Demiurge, who is the pure Good and, at the same time, the source of existence, to care means, above all, to provide existence. The Demiurge cares not only for the existence but also for the flourishing of someone endowed with dignity (someone created directly by him). He is like a draughts-player who moves pieces on the board of the universe, creating opportunities for people to improve. He does not compel anybody to improve, as Plato makes very clear, he only creates opportunities. Treating a person as an end (in oneself) does not exclude the recognition that he is a part of a certain whole which is also an end in itself; in Plato's philosophy this is the universe. Treating someone as a means does not contradict his dignity. The point is that a person is not treated *only* as a means, and in all actions addressed to him, even if he is treated as a means, he is regarded *at the same time* as an end in himself. Plato fully recognises this. The postulate that a bearer of dignity is to be treated as an end in himself is a universal principle which is to be realised by everybody in as much as they are good—as far as they are just and strive for justice.

In Plato's approach, dignity—being a special way of existence—is universal in a radical sense: it has always been and will always be present where there is a human being. It is inherent and inalienable. Without it no human being can exist. Losing dignity would mean the loss of existence and dismemberment of the parts, which would necessarily involve destruction of the special harmony and order and of the principle of the life of a human being. Dignity neither increases nor decreases based on any particular trait; it cannot be lost either by any action of its bearer or by any action of other people; it is independent of the circumstances of one's life and, moreover, of one's moral stances. Being independent of any particular trait, it is equally 'possessed' by men and women, slaves and free men. Therefore, the development of every human being (the acquiring of moral perfections) is equally important and should be taken into account by everyone.

Since dignity 'belongs' directly to the soul, which is a principle of the living, existing and acting of the whole human being, it is suited to be a foundation for postulates concerning caring for a human being as a whole. This is congruent with the contemporary recognition of dignity as a source of all human rights and of their integrity.

When Plato is read from this perspective, the importance of the *Timaeus* for the understanding of justice and of a human being significantly increases. And, since this dialogue deals with the creation of the visible universe, this leads to an appreciation of the bodily dimension of human existence. Although only a part of the human soul is created by the Demiurge directly, human souls are nevertheless created as principles of life of creatures composed also of flesh. Such creatures are wished by the Demiurge as an element which is necessary for the universe to be perfect. But there is much more in the *Timaeus* that speaks for an appreciation of existence in the soul and flesh. If the *Timaeus* is read as a continuation of the *Republic*, and therefore as a dialogue about the justice of an individual, then the final delight in the universe as a perceptible god whose 'grandness, goodness, beauty, and perfection are unexcelled'[972] is—*mutatis mutandis*—also a delight in the human being, who is an image of the universe and also of the god. Since human beings are wished by the Demiurge in soul and flesh, then existing 'in flesh' is not against the nature of the human soul. Acknowledging this affects an understanding of the other dialogues.

The myth of the cave in Book VII of the *Republic* provides a good example. The way out of the cave cannot be interpreted as a way out of the body to the afterworld, but—in accordance with Plato's remarks on how to read it—as a metaphorical story about education understood as turning the power of learning towards its proper objects situated in the invisible realm in order to acquire the knowledge necessary for acting justly and becoming just. In principle, one comes out of the cave to return back and live a good (better) life, and that means that cognition of the invisible, which involves the active cooperation of all parts of the soul, provides knowledge which is necessary to order and harmonise all parts of the soul and to act justly.

Since an inherent dignity is constituted by a special unity between elements and not by the particular 'content' of those elements, it can be ascribed not only to human souls but also to other entities. Plato ascribes dignity to the gods and also to the universe as a whole, but he does not ascribe it to any state or city.

8.2 Justice of the soul

Dignity, understood as a special way of existence which can be characterised as a special inner unity based on an original harmony and order created by the Demiurge himself, cannot be lost. It is the reason for the immortality of the soul. Nevertheless, a human being can develop himself in the existential aspect, in his unity. This takes place through advancement in the moral aspect, by becoming just and by acting justly. This can be said to be the development of dignity. Therefore, it is appropriate to distinguish between an inherent and inalienable dignity and dignity as a moral stance, a moral quality of an individual. Overall moral perfection as a characteristic of a person equals justice understood as an existential excellence: the more one is just, the more—the more strongly—one exists. Justice of the soul is based on increasing the unity (harmony, order, integrity) of its three parts—the rational, spirited and appetitive. This unity is built up by an acting subject; it is an addition and enhancement to the original unity (the original strength of existence based on inherent dignity). The thought that an inner unity of reason (reasonable convictions) and the way one acts are crucial for the moral quality

972 Plato, *Timaeus*, 92c, trans. Zeyl.

of an individual is present also in the intuitions contained in contemporary natural language—in English 'integrity' means 'honesty', 'goodness', 'rightness', and 'virtuousness'.

Justice as an inner unity—as a virtue—is expressed by external action; nevertheless, what is constitutive for justice in the soul is the very decision to act in accordance with reason, and therefore unforeseeable obstructions to the external fulfilment of an action do not jeopardise the positive contribution of such uncompleted deeds to the justice of the acting subject.

Justice in the acting subject is characterised directly by a certain structure—by relations between certain elements and not by the 'content' of those elements. This opens up the possibility of being just in a variety of ways. Nevertheless, this variety is not unlimited. Obtaining justice presupposes the mastery of three other cardinal virtues—wisdom, courage and moderation.

Wisdom is a kind of knowledge which oversees just actions. This is practical knowledge concerning how to deal best with oneself and other people. It is essential for wisdom to consider this 'best' from the point of view of the acting subject as a whole, and also from the point of view of the addressees of one's actions. Since the way of existence comprises the whole being, this holistic perspective favours the existential aspect (and the perfection of this aspect, namely acquiring justice) and provides a general perspective for understanding wisdom.

Courage as a virtue is understood by Plato in a way that differs from its common understanding as a virtue typical of soldiers and concerned with acting in the face of mortal threat. Plato emphasises that courage consists in preserving one's own, rationally acquired convictions concerning what should be avoided. Courage proves itself in the face of strong emotions—not only fear and pain (as on the battlefield), but also—and equally—desires and pleasures. Plato stresses that the knowledge to which an acting subject should be faithful indicates only specific actions which should not be performed, not specific actions which should be done. If one accepts that this knowledge is expressed by the conscience, then according to Plato—'whenever it speaks it turns me away from something I am about to do, but it never encourages me to do anything'.[973] This knowledge—represented by the 'personal' daimon—is not the same for all, but it is crafted for one's chosen way of life. Plato's approach to courage clearly goes beyond the intuitions relating this virtue to a military context. Plato's examination of courage in the *Republic*, which can hardly be taken as specifically applicable to the military class in the state, favours the thesis that the model of the hypothetical state is essentially subordinated to considerations about an individual.

Moderation is a virtue which spreads throughout the whole soul; it is not a perfection solely of the appetitive part, as was accepted in the later ancient tradition. Plato does not advocate suppressing desires or emotions. His goal is to appoint them to play their role in relation to the other parts and to the whole

973 Plato, *Apology*, 31d, trans. Grube.

of the human being. On the one hand, they should not set the aims, although they are helpful in reaching the aims determined by reason. On the other hand, reason should not ignore the spirited or appetitive part. Since specific tasks are not determined solely by knowledge, there is space to take into account one's own desires and emotions. Moderation is a kind of concord, a kind of harmony of the parts of the soul concerning which part is to rule, determining the objectives of actions, and which parts are to execute actions. Since reason is the part which ought to rule, moderation is more closely related to prudence than to temperance. Like justice, moderation extends throughout all parts of the soul. Above all, however, it is characterised by the role accepted by each part—that it agrees, executes, rules or is ruled. Therefore, like both wisdom and courage, it directly concerns the content of the being. It belongs, along with wisdom and courage, to the essential rather than the existential aspect of the soul—unlike justice, which concerns the existential one.

8.3 Justice of actions

Happiness derives not from justice of the soul, from inner unity in itself, but from acting justly. Bearing in mind Plato's account of the Good, such acting flows from the very nature of being just, that is, of being good. In determining the shape of just actions, justice means the benefit of others—this thought, which will lie at the very foundation of reflections on justice in the centuries to come, finds theoretical justification in Plato's approach. Those deeds are just which are in accordance with the nature of the addressee of the action—those which are appropriate and fitting to the addressee. This appropriateness of actions is measured by their contribution to the strength of existence—that is, the justice—of the addressee. Just deeds are characterised negatively by a version of the harm principle—'it is never just to harm anyone'.[974] Plato is radical in that he includes even enemies among those who should be treated justly. In the positive characterisation of just actions, it is stated that they should be aimed at the advantage of their addressees.

Just actions, on the one hand, 'flow' from the justice of the acting subject, and on the other, contribute to his justice. They contribute also to the justice of their addressees. Moreover, just actions are a means of creating friendship, a certain unity between people which is the basis of a community. Just actions enhance also the unity of the universe as a whole (its goodness and beauty). Nevertheless, existence for the benefit of the universe does not compromise the dignity of an individual (being an end in himself) as long as he is not treated purely instrumentally and his individual aim (development) is recognised and respected.

By placing moral excellence on the level of existence, Plato succeeds in explaining the phenomenon that, although acting justly involves the loss of something which belongs to the acting subject (possessions, time, health and sometimes

974 Plato, *Republic*, 335e, trans. Bloom.

even one's own life), nonetheless, someone who acts justly gains a kind of advantage. One has less but is more. Justice as moral perfection is a matter of being, of the strength of existence, and not of having and increasing one's possessions.

What should be cared about—in other words, what should be loved—is not abstract perfections in our fellow creatures, but is each being as an existing whole which by its nature is directed towards fulfilment—happiness. The Demiurge cares for concrete beings which have received from him (directly or indirectly) their existence. He cares especially for those beings which were created directly by him, and although they are not immortal in themselves, they will always exist, since—due to their special inner harmony and order (unity, beauty, dignity)—he cannot stop wishing their continuing existence: 'only one who is evil would consent to the undoing of what has been well fitted together [beautifully harmonised] and is in fine condition'.[975] Human beings, in so far as they are good, participate in the Demiurge's caring about other creatures, and out of their very goodness, caring about others is congruent with their nature.

Entities which belong to the invisible realm of forms (entities which do not act like human beings, souls or gods) are perceived by Plato evidently not as addressees of just actions, which are the highest expressions and the highest perfections of an individual as a whole. They are clearly understood as 'nourishment' indispensable for acting justly[976] or as a kind of a catalyst, like beauty, which is necessary for engendering and parturition.[977] Contemplation is not a final end of the efforts of a human being to become good; it is only a necessary step on his journey to fulfilment by acting justly.

Knowledge about the Good itself is necessary to understand justice and moral development as a whole. Knowledge about that which is invisible makes it possible to overcome the Sophists' approach to justice, and to comprehend why justice is about the benefit of another, why justice never harms anybody, and why practising justice is the best thing of all that a human being can do. Without knowledge about that which is invisible, principally about the Good, it is impossible to understand that existence based on harmony, order and unity is the most fundamental perfection of every being. This knowledge enables one to understand how it is possible to lose one's possessions and still benefit. Without knowledge about the invisible, it is impossible to understand that the knowledge that counts most is knowledge about what should be avoided, that courage is faithfulness to one's moral knowledge, that emotions should not determine the aims of actions, but should help in achieving those aims. Last but not least, knowledge about the invisible is necessary to comprehend that there are certain special creatures that 'have been well fitted together and are in fine condition', who independently of their virtues or vices

975 Plato, *Timaeus*, 41b, trans. Zeyl.
976 Plato, *Phaedrus*, 247d.
977 Plato, *Symposium*, 206d–e.

deserve continuing care about their existence and well-being as far as it is possible; they are ends in themselves—they have dignity.

The conclusions about the priority of acting justly over contemplating truth are confirmed by Plato's teaching about the Demiurge. Unlike Aristotle's god, Plato's is not focused on getting to know himself, but by his very nature, creates and cares for that which has been created. A human being striving for goodness participates in this undertaking.

Because without acting justly the full development and happiness of the acting subject is not possible, and accepting that one has rights to the necessary conditions for development and happiness, acting justly is not only an obligation towards other people but the acting subject also has a right to act justly—a right which is based on the very constitution of the human being, on his inherent property. Of course, acting justly itself cannot be a direct object of rights, but the conditions for such acting can. Therefore, human rights also include the right to social conditions which foster acting for the benefit of others.[978]

8.4 Justice of laws and the state

Given Plato's remarks concerning the methodology underpinning the construction of the hypothetical state in the *Republic*, and the way in which the argument is developed, the importance of the model of the state for understanding justice of the state proves to be quite limited. What seem to be crucial conclusions with regard to the model state—for instance, that the members of two classes should be completely subordinated to wise rulers, that the good of the state is the supreme aim, that everyone should perform only one job—Plato places in clear opposition to that which is said after the phrase 'what in truth justice is'. Moreover, the argument which leads from the construction of the hypothetical state to conclusions about justice in it has fundamental flaws related to its simple presuppositions, explicitly formulated by Plato's Socrates, namely, that in the state there are exactly four basic virtues, those examined in the argument. Plato provides no thoughtful reason to accept these presuppositions, and, moreover, in his writings he often does not adhere to them himself.

Social life organised by laws, in the form of a state as well, clearly has a moral dimension. Laws should contribute to the development of cardinal virtues. Since acquiring justice presupposes the presence of wisdom, courage and moderation, it can be said—in short—that the social order should aim at justice. The acquisition of cardinal virtues does not predetermine what model of life should be lived or which particular deeds should be performed.

Laws and the state, and their justice, should be judged according to their contribution to the goodness—justice—of individuals and their just deeds, which are the foundation of their happiness. The second criterion is the intensity of friendship

978 Cf. Art. 28 of the *Universal Declaration of Human Rights* (1948).

between them, which both presupposes the justice of the members of the community, and contributes to acting justly and to the justice of individuals.

Plato, recognising individuals as ends in themselves and subordinating law and the state to the happiness and friendship of citizens, evidently supplies no foundations for totalitarianism, as a view according to which the state would be the supreme good and individuals would exist for its sake. Moreover, Plato's approach is not totalitarian in terms of rulers controlling and shaping the lives of individuals. Plato's conception of justice gives acknowledgment to the specific traits of individuals, their own knowledge about what is right and wrong. Because wisdom only discourages people from performing unjust actions, and never encourages them to perform a specific action, there is space for individual choices. Moreover, knowledge does not point unambiguously at any particular model of life. Adherence to one occupation throughout one's whole life Plato himself calls a phantom of justice. A just man or woman would more likely exercise the virtue of magnanimity, which presupposes versatility and requires involvement in different kinds of activity in the state.

When Plato talks about penal justice, it is always for the benefit of someone, and not the benefit of any state or the re-establishment of a legal or moral order, that is said to be the reason for just punishment, which is understood chiefly as a kind of medication for the soul; in rare cases, when no improvement is possible, a punishment is beneficial as a deterrent. Punishment does not cause the improvement by itself, but only provides an opportunity for it.

It needs to be pointed out that Plato does not ascribe dignity to any state, even to the best one. There is no mention that any state was directly created by the Demiurge; to the contrary, there are many statements implying that laws and the state have an instrumental value, and can be treated only as means. If a state fails to fulfil its tasks and makes its people worse, it is better that the state fall apart or the citizens go into exile. The state is only a relational entity which comes to be because people have many needs which they cannot satisfy by themselves, and thus come together to help each other. Since helping each other is the basic reason for forming a state, the principle of subsidiarity is anticipated—the state should create the conditions for people's helping one another and not act as a substitute for the members of the community helping each other, otherwise the very foundations of friendship would be undermined.

Unlike in the Sophists' approach, members of the community are not competitors in possessing more and more. If they compete in something, it is in moral excellence—justice in the soul and acting justly. Since justice is an advantage for others, contributing to the moral development of an individual is potentially advantageous for each member of the community. These are the very foundations of the classical tradition of reflection on the common good, which at its core, in its subjective aspect, is the happiness of the members of the community, derived from their acting justly. Acting justly and individual happiness, which are the subjective aspect of the common good, can be accomplished directly only by particular members of the society and not by the state or laws. Nevertheless, social arrangements can contribute to achieving these gals. Social arrangements come to be the objective aspect of the common good if they contribute to the development of the justice of all members of the community. Creating such arrangements is fully compatible with recognising the dignity of individuals, and their being ends in themselves. Moral development can be achieved only by an individual himself, though the conditions of life can ease or obstruct it. Because an increase in justice inevitably increases mutual friendship, social arrangements aimed at moral development are aimed at building the community as well; moral development cannot be achieved by coercion. An example is set by Plato's Demiurge, who places individuals where they may have an opportunity to improve, but never tries to cause this improvement directly.

Maximisation of happiness and friendship—which is the primary aim of laws (and of the state)—presupposes maximisation of the equality of members of the community. Therefore, equality also becomes an aim of laws. This aim is certainly not to be attained at once. Its realisation is, for Plato, a matter not of years but of successive incarnations; nevertheless, it is an aim which should shape legislation and action in general—it should shape the content of both laws and deeds which are just in the here and now.

Mutual help concerns, first of all, acquiring practical knowledge which belongs to wisdom and is necessary to act justly. This knowledge—and not any coercion—is the key to shaping one's actions. It has to be stressed that—where possible—this should be knowledge acquired by an individual himself, not taught by someone, not simply transferred into one's mind by someone who knows. Education consists in turning the learning power in the right direction. Acquiring wisdom is a venture of a social kind. Others are needed to write 'the living and breathing discourse'[979] in one's soul, and this concerns both the learner and the teacher. Since the wisdom contained in this discourse is knowledge which enables just action, it is indispensable for organising social life. Consequently, laws should be based on this knowledge. It follows, then, that laws can be carved only for a given community by its members, and should change according to changes in the living discourse written in their minds.

Nevertheless, knowledge and virtues themselves are not the only aspect of creating a community. The equality which is gained is not only equality in terms of moral stance nor only equality in an existential aspect. Just actions also require something that one can give and another can receive. The common prayer of friends also includes 'bodily' aspects of living—in the words of Plato's Socrates in the *Phaedrus*: 'as for gold, let me have as much as a moderate man could bear and carry with him'.[980]

At first glance, Plato does not seem to expound the importance of individuality and autonomy as crucial elements for the fulfilment of an individual. While

979 Plato, *Phaedrus*, 276a, trans. Nehamas, Woodruff.
980 Plato, *Phaedrus*, 279b–c, trans. Nehamas, Woodruff.

in the Middle Ages, in the thought of Thomas Aquinas, special individuality and particularity are constitutive of dignity, understood as an especially perfect way of existence,[981] in Plato the importance of individuality and particularity seem to be overshadowed by the reality of abstract forms. Nonetheless, on closer inspection, Plato refers to all of the important pieces that are essential for an appreciation of individuality as a fundamental perfection of a human being. The first perfections of a human being—dignity and justice—are based on unity and belong to the existential dimension, which comprises the whole being. Taking into account the intuitions contained in language, which are developed in the mediaeval theory of universals, individuality is actually the flip side of unity, since it is based on being internally undivided. Inner unity is built from human actions, which are always something particular and not abstract. Moreover, acting justly is based on the congruence between deeds and knowledge; and as Plato stresses, this knowledge can be acquired only by an acting individual himself, and its content is always specific for a given person. Moreover, both particular actions and the project of one's whole life—though coordinated and overseen by reason—are shaped not only by cognitive elements, but also by volitional and emotional ones.

The primacy of individuality is reinforced when Plato points to the inner relations (structures), and not the content of the terms of these relations, as the foundation of dignity and justice, and therefore of the goodness of a person as a whole. The unity of elements, based, for instance, on a conformity of actions with the rational convictions of an acting subject, does not predetermine the content of just actions. Similarly, dignity as unity based on a special harmony and order does not determine univocally what the content of the elements that are harmonised and ordered is.

Plato teaches his readers to deliberate in a community with others on the issues of political organisation and laws in the here and now. The results of these deliberations should be put into practice. Social arrangements which contribute to a happy life for the members of the political community vary in time and space. Nevertheless, he argues that there are prerequisites for any political system and any laws which claim to be just. These prerequisites are moral in character and include a striving for cardinal virtues. Since recognising dignity underlies Plato's teaching about justice, the recognition of dignity, understood as one's being an end in oneself, is one of a few basic conditions of just political order and just laws. Plato's thought turns out to be strikingly contemporary.

981 See Thomas Aquinas, *Summa theologiae*, I, q. 29, a. 1, co.; Piechowiak, 'Thomas Aquinas—Human Dignity and Conscience as a Basis for Restricting Legal Obligations', pp. 71–79; idem, 'Tomasza z Akwinu egzystencjalna koncepcja osoby', *passim*.

Bibliography

I Works of Plato

a Collections

Platonis Opera (in Greek). Ed. John Burnet. Oxford: E. Typographeo Clarendoniano, 1903 ff. (*The Perseus Project*. Ed. G. R. Crane. http://www.perseus.tufts.edu (2016)).

Plato. Complete Works. Ed. John M. Cooper. Indianapolis—Cambridge: Hackett, 1997.

b Dialogues

Alcibiades. Trans. D. S. Hutchinson. In: *Plato. Complete Works*. Ed. John M. Cooper, pp. 557–595.

Apology. Trans. G. M. A. Grube. In: *Plato. Complete Works*. Ed. John M. Cooper, pp. 17–36.

Charmides. Trans. Rosamond Kent Sprague. In: *Plato. Complete Works*. Ed. John M. Cooper, pp. 639–663.

Crito. Trans. G. M. A. Grube. In: *Plato. Complete Works*. Ed. John M. Cooper, pp. 37–48.

Euthydemus. Trans. Rosamond Kent Sprague. In: *Plato. Complete Works*. Ed. John M. Cooper, pp. 708–745.

Gorgias. Trans. Walter Hamilton, Chris Emlyn-Jones. London: Penguin, 2004.

——. Trans. Benjamin Jowett. In: *The Dialogues of Plato*. Vol. 2, New York—London: Oxford University Press, 1892, pp. 267–431.

——. Trans. Walter Rangeley Maitland Lamb. In: *Plato in Twelve Volumes*. Vol. 3, Cambridge: Harvard University Press—London: William Heinemann, 1967 (*The Perseus Project*).

——. Ed. Gonzalez Lodge, edited on the basis of the Julius Deuschle and Christian Cron edition. London—Boston: Ginn & Co, 1896.

——. Ed. Theodore Dwight Woolsey, *Chiefly According to Gottfried Stallbaum's Text*. Boston—Cambridge: J. Munroe & Company, 1856.

——. Trans. Donald J. Zeyl. In: *Plato. Complete Works*. Ed. John M. Cooper, pp. 791–869.

——. *Gorgiasz*. Trans. Władysław Witwicki. In: Platon. *Dialogi*. Kęty: Wydawnictwo ANTYK, 1999, pp. 333–452.

Laches. Trans. Rosamond Kent Sprague. In: *Plato. Complete Works*. Ed. John M. Cooper, pp. 664–686.

Laws. Ed. E. B. England. *The Laws of Plato*. Vol. 1–2, Manchester: The University Press—London: Longmans, Green & Co, 1921.

——. Ed. G. Burges. In: *The Works of Plato: A New and Literal Version*. Vol. 5, London: H. G. Bohn, 1852.

——. Trans. R. G. Bury. Vol. 1, Cambridge: Harvard University Press—London: William Heinemann, 1961; Vol. 2, London: William Heinemann—New York: G. P. Putnam's Sons, 1926 [The Greek text based on the Baiter—Orelli—Winckelmann (Zurich 1839) edition].

——. Trans. Trevor J. Saunders. In: *Plato. Complete Works*. Ed. John M. Cooper, pp. 1318–1616.

Letter VII. Trans. R. G. Bury. In: *Plato in Twelve Volumes*. Vol. 7, Cambridge: Harvard University Press—London: William Heinemann, 1966 (*The Perseus Project*).

——. Trans. Glenn R. Morrow. In: *Plato. Complete Works*. Ed. John M. Cooper, pp. 1646–1667.

Phaedo. Trans. G. M. A. Grube. In: *Plato. Complete Works*. Ed. John M. Cooper, pp. 49–100.

Phaedrus. Trans. H. N. Fowler. In: *Plato in Twelve Volumes*. Vol. 9, Cambridge: Harvard University Press—London: William Heinemann, 1925 (*The Perseus Project*).

——. Trans. Alexander Nehamas, Paul Woodruff. In: *Plato. Complete Works*. Ed. John M. Cooper, pp. 506–556.

Protagoras. Trans. Stanley Lomardo, Karen Bell. In: *Plato. Complete Works*. Ed. John M. Cooper, pp. 746–790.

Republic. Trans. Allan Bloom. *The Republic of Plato*. New York: Basic Books, 1968.

——. Trans. Paul Shorey. In: *Plato in Twelve Volumes*. Vols. 5 & 6, Cambridge: Harvard University Press—London: William Heinemann, 1969 (*The Perseus Project*).

——. Trans. G. M. A. Grube. In: *Plato. Complete Works*. Ed. John M. Cooper, pp. 971–1223.

——. *Państwo*. Trans. Władysław Witwicki. In: Platon. *Państwo, Prawa*. Kęty: Wydawnictwo ANTYK, 2003, pp. 11–338.

Statesman. Trans. Christopher Rowe. *Complete Works*. Ed. John M. Cooper, pp. 294–358.

Theaetetus. Trans. Harold N. Fowler. In: *Plato in Twelve Volumes*. Vol. 12, Cambridge: Harvard University Press—London: William Heinemann, 1921 (*The Perseus Project*).

——. Trans. M. J. Levett, rev. Myles Burnyeat. In: *Plato. Complete Works*. Ed. John M. Cooper, pp. 157–234.

Timaeus. Trans. W. R. M. Lamb. In: *Plato in Twelve Volumes.* Vol. 9, Cambridge: Harvard University Press–London: William Heinemann, 1925 (*The Perseus Project*).

——. Trans. Donald J. Zeyl. In: *Plato Complete Works.* Ed. John M. Cooper, pp. 1224–1291.

II References

Aeschylus. *Seven Against Thebes.* Trans. Herbert Weir Smyth. Cambridge: Harvard University Press–London: William Heinemann, 1926.

Annas, Julia. *Platonic Ethics, Old and New.* Ithaca–London: Cornell University Press, 1998.

Antiphon. *On truth.* Trans. John Dillon, Tania Gergel. In: *The Greek Sophists.* London: Penguin Books, 2003, pp.146–158.

Aristotle. *Eudemian Ethics.* Trans. Harris Rackham. Cambridge: Harvard University Press–London: William Heinemann, 1981 (*The Perseus Project*).

——. *Metaphysics.* Trans. Hugh Tredennick. Cambridge: Harvard University Press–London: William Heinemann, 1989 (*The Perseus Project*).

——. *Nicomachean Ethics.* Trans. Terence Irwin. Indianapolis–Cambridge: Hackett, 1985.

——. Trans. Harris Rackham. Cambridge: Harvard University Press–London: William Heinemann, 1934 (*The Perseus Project*).

——. *Politics.* Trans. Harris Rackham. Cambridge: Harvard University Press–London: William Heinemann, 1944 (*The Perseus Project*).

Aristoxenus. *Elementa Harmonica. The Harmonics by Aristoxenus.* Ed. Henry Stewart Macran. Oxford: Clarendon Press, 1902.

Bacon, Francis. *Novum organum.* Ed. Joseph Devey. New York: Callier, 1902.

Balot, Ryan K. *Courage in the Democratic Polis: Ideology and Critique in Classical Athens.* Oxford: Oxford University Press, 2014.

Barney, Rachel, Tad Brennan, Charles Britain, eds. *Plato and the Divided Self.* Cambridge: Cambridge University Press, 2012.

Basic Law for the Federal Republic of Germany (1949) [*Grundgesetz für die Bundesrepublik Deutschland*]. Adopted 23 May 1949. Trans. Christian Tomuschat, David P. Currie. http://www.gesetze-im-internet.de/englisch_gg (2017).

Basilicorum libri LX. Ed. Karl Wilhelm Ernst Heimbach.Lipsiae: Barth, 1933.

Berlin, Isaiah. 'Two Concepts of Liberty', (1958). In: idem. *Four Essays on Liberty.* Oxford: Oxford University Press, 1969, pp. 118–172.

Blackburn, Simon. *Plato's Republic: A Biography.* New York: Grove Press, 2007.

Blandzi, Seweryn. *Henologia–Meontologia–Dialektyka. Platońskie poszukiwanie ontologii idei w Parmenidesie* [*Henology–Meontology–Dialectics: Plato's Search for Ontology of Forms in the Parmenides*]. Warszawa: Instytut Filozofii i Socjologii PAN, 1992.

——. *Platoński projekt filozofii pierwszej* [*Plato's Project of the First Philosophy*]. Warszawa: Instytut Filozofii i Socjologii PAN, 2002.

Bobonich, Christopher. *Plato's Utopia Recast: His Later Ethics and Politics*. Oxford: Clarendon Press, 2008.

——, ed. *Plato's Laws: A Critical Guide*. Cambridge: Cambridge University Press, 2010.

Brown, Lesley, ed. *The New Shorter Oxford English Dictionary*. Oxford: Clarendon Press, 1993.

Bundy, Elroy L. *Studia Pindarica*. Berkeley: University of California–Department of Classics, Digital Version 2006. http://escholarship.org/uc/item/2g79p68g (2017). Originally: *Studies in Classical Philology* 1962, Vol. 18, No. 1 (February 27) and No. 2 (April 13).

Burnyeat, Myles, Michael Frede. *The Pseudo-Platonic Seventh Letter*. Ed. Dominik Scott. Oxford: Oxford University Press, 2015.

Charter of Fundamental Rights of the European Union. 2000. *Proclaimed* 7 Dec. 2000, *Official Journal of the European Communities* 18.12.2000, C 364/01.

Carone, Gabriela Roxana. *Plato's Cosmology and Its Ethical Dimension*. Cambridge: Cambridge University Press, 2011.

The Constitution of the Republic of Poland (1997) *[Konstytucja Rzeczypospolitej Polskiej], adopted* 2 April 1997. *Dziennik Ustaw* (*Journal of Laws*) Vol. 78, item 483. Trans. Albert Pol, Andrew Caldwell. In: *Polish Constitutional Law: The Constitution and Selected Statutory Materials*. Eds. Ewelina Gierach, Piotr Chybalski. Warsaw: Chancellery of the Sejm, 2009, pp. 19–68.

Convention on the Rights of Persons with Disabilities (2006), *adopted* 13 Dec 2006, G.A. Res. 61/106, Annex II, U.N. GAOR, 61st Sess., Supp. No. 49, at 80, U.N. Doc. A/61/49.

Cooper, John Madison. *Reason and Emotion: Essays on Ancient Moral Psychology and Ethical Theory*. Princeton: Princeton University Press, 1999.

——. 'Socrates and Plato in Gorgias'. In: idem. *Reason and Emotion*, pp. 29–75.

Corey, David D. *The Sophists in Plato's Dialogues*. Albany: SUNY Press, 2015.

Cornford, Francis MacDonald. *Plato's Cosmology: The* Timaeus *of Plato*. London: Routledge, 1935. Reprinted: Indianapolis: Hackett, 1997.

Dembiński, Bogdan. *Późny Platon i Stara Akademia* [*Late Plato and the Old Academy*]. Kęty: Wydawnictwo Marek Derewiecki, 2010.

Dahl, Norman O. 'Plato's Defence of Justice'. In: Fine, ed. *Plato 2*, pp. 207–234.

Diogenes, Laertius. *Lives of Eminent Philosophers.* Trans. Robert Drew Hicks. London: Heinemann–New York: Putnam's, 1925.

Dover, Kenneth James. *Greek Popular Morality in the Time of Plato and Aristotle.* Indianapolis–Cambridge: Hackett, 1994.

Euripides. *Children of Heracles. Hippolytus. Andromache. Hecuba.* Trans. David Kovacs. Cambridge: Harvard University Press, 1995.

Ferber, Rafael. *Warum hat Platon die „ungeschriebene Lehre" nicht geschrieben?* 2nd edition. München: Beck, 2007.

——. *Platos Idee des Guten.* 3rd edition. Sankt Augusitn: Academia Verlag, 2015.

Ferrari, Giovanni R. F. *City and Soul in Plato's Republic.* Chicago: The University of Chicago Press, 2003.

——, ed. *The Cambridge Companion to Plato's Republic.* Cambridge: Cambridge University Press, 2007.

Fine, Gail, ed. *Plato 1: Metaphysics and Epistemology.* Oxford: Oxford University Press, 1999.

——, ed. *Plato 2: Ethics, Politics, Religion and the Soul.* Oxford: Oxford University Press, 1999.

Freudiger, Jürg. 'Platon und die Sache der Frau'. *Kriterion.* 1995. Vol. 10, pp. 14–27.

Gadamer, Hans-Georg. *Wahrheit und Methode.* Tübingen: Mohr, 1975.

Gagarin, Michael. *Writing Greek Law.* Cambridge: Cambridge University Press, 2008.

Gaiser, Konrad. *Platons ungeschriebene Lehre. Studien zur systematischen und geschichtlichen Begründung der Wissenschaften in der Platonischen Schule.* 3rd edition. Stuttgart: Klett-Cotta, 1998.

——. *Testimonia platonica. Le antiche testimonianze sulle dottrine non scritte di Platone.* Milano: Vita e Pensiero, 1998.

Gajda, Janina. *Platońska droga do idei* [*The Platonic Road to Forms*]. Wrocław: Wydawnictwo Uniwersytetu Wrocławskiego, 1993.

Galewicz, Włodzimierz. 'Leontios i trupy. O Platońskiej etyce godności' [Leontios and Corpses: On Plato's Ethics of Dignity]. *Kwartalnik Filozoficzny* 1998, Vol. 26, No. 2, pp. 47–69.

Gerson, Lloyd P. *Knowing Persons: A Study in Plato.* Oxford: Oxford University Press, 2006.

Grimal, Pierre. *Concise Dictionary of Classical Mythology.* Ed. Stephen Kershaw from the translation by A. R. Maxwell-Hyslop. Oxford: Blackwell, 1990.

Guthrie, William Keith Chambers. *The Greek Philosophers: From Thales to Aristotle.* London–New York: Routledge, 2013.

Havelock, Eric A. *The Greek Concept of Justice: From its Shadow in Homer to its Substance in Plato.* Cambridge: Harvard University Press, 1978.

Heidegger, Martin. *The End of Philosophy and the Task of Thinking*. In: idem. *Basic Writings*. Ed. David Farrell Krell. London: Routledge & Kegan Paul, 1978, pp. 369–392.

Herodotus. *The Histories*. Trans. Alfred Denis Godley. Cambridge: Harvard University Press, 1920 (The Perseus Project).

Hesiod. *Theogony. The Homeric Hymns and Homerica*. Trans. Hugh G. Evelyn-White. Cambridge: Harvard University Press—London: William Heinemann, 1914 (*The Perseus Project*).

Hippocrates. '*De capitis vulneribus*'. In: *The Genuine Works of Hippocrates*. Ed. Francis Adams. New York: W. Wood & Co.,1886 (*The Perseus Project*).

Hoelzl, Michael. 'Recognizing the Sacrificial Victim: The Problem of Solidarity for Critical Social Theory'. *Journal for Cultural and Religious Theory* 2004, Vol. 6, No. 1 (Winter), pp. 45–64.

Homer. *Odyssey*. Trans. Augustus Taber Murray. Cambridge: Harvard University Press—London: William Heinemann, 1919 (*The Perseus Project*).

Holy Bible. King James Version. Glasgow: Collins, 1991.

Hutchison, Keith. 1996. 'Why Does Plato Urge Rulers to Study Astronomy?' *Perspectives on Science* 1996, Vol. 41, pp. 24–58.

Incampo, Antonio. *Sul fondamento della validità deontica. Identità non-contradictione*. Bari: Giuseppe LaterzaEditore, 1996.

International Covenant on Economic, Social and Cultural Rights. 1966. Adopted 16 Dec. 1966, G.A. Res. 2200 A (XXI), U.N. GAOR, 21st Sess., U.N. Doc. A/6316, 993 U.N.T.S. 3.

International Covenant on Civil and Political Rights. 1966. Adopted 16 Dec. 1966, G.A. Res. 2200 A (XXI), U.N. GAOR, 21st Sess., U.N. Doc. A/6316, 999 U.N.T.S. 171.

Irwin, Terence. *Plato's Ethics*. Oxford: Oxford University Press, 1995.

——. 'Questions about Justice'. In: Fine, ed. *Plato 2*, pp. 164–185.

Jaeger, Werner. *Paideia: The Ideals of Greek Culture*. Trans. Gilbert Highet. Vol. 1: *Archaic Greece—The Mind of Athens*. Oxford: Blackwell, 1946.

——. *Paideia: The Ideals of Greek Culture*. Trans. Gilbert Highet. Vol. 2: *In Search of the Divine Centre*. Oxford: Blackwell, 1947.

Janik, Joanna. *Terms of the Semantic Sphere of* δίκη *and* θέμις *in the Early Greek Epic*. Kraków: Polska Akademia Umiejętności, 2003.

Jarra, Eugeniusz. *Idea państwa u Platona i jej dzieje* [Plato's Concept of State and Its History]. Warszawa: Gebethner & Wolff, 1918.

Kahn, Charles H. 'Being in Parmenides and Plato (1988)'. In: idem. *Essays on Being*, pp.167–191.

——. *Plato and the Socratic Dialogue: The Philosophical Use of a Literary Form.* Cambridge: Cambridge University Press, 1996.

——. 'Why Existence Does Not Emerge as a Distinct Concept in Greek Philosophy (1976)'. In: idem. *Essays on Being*, pp. 62–74.

——. *The Verb 'Be' in Ancient Greek.* Indianapolis—Cambridge: Hackett, 2003.

——. *Essays on Being.* Oxford: Oxford University Press, 2009.

——. *Plato and the Post-Socratic Dialogue: The Return to the Philosophy of Nature.* Cambridge: Cambridge University Press, 2013.

——. 'Review: Myles Burnyeat and Michael Frede, *The Pseudo-Platonic Seventh Letter*, Ed. Dominic Scott, Oxford University Press, 2015'. *Notre Dame Philosophical Reviews*, 2015.11.06. http://ndpr.nd.edu/news/the-pseudo-platonic-seventh-letter/ (2017).

Kant, Immanuel. *Critique of Practical Reason.* Trans. Werner S. Pluhar. Indianapolis—Cambridge: Hackett, 2002.

——. *Fundamental Principles of the Metaphysic of Morals* [*Grundlegung zur Metaphysik der Sitten*]. Trans. Thomas Kingsmill Abbott. New York: Cosimo, 2008.

——. *Prolegomena to any Future Metaphysics that can Present itself as a Science.* Trans. Peter G. Lucas. Manchester: Manchester University Press, 1962.

Kateb, George. *Human Dignity.* Cambridge: Harvard University Press, 2011.

Kaufmann, Arthur. '*Problemgeschichte der Rechtsphilosophie*'. In: *Einführung in Rechtsphilosophie und Rechtstheorie der Gegenwart.* Eds. Arthur Kaufmann, Winfried Hassemer. 5th edition, Heidelberg: Müller, 1989, pp. 25–142.

Koszkało, Martyna. 'Rozwój pojęcia woli w pogańskiej filozofii starożytnej – Sokrates, Platon, Arystoteles' [The Development of the Notion of Will in the Ancient Pagan Philosophy—Socrates, Plato, Aristotle]. *Roczniki Filozoficzne* 2015, Vol. 63, No. 2, pp. 157–186.

Kraut, Richard, ed. *The Cambridge Companion to Plato.* Cambridge: Cambridge University Press, 1999.

Krämer, Hans Joachim. '*Epekeina tēs ousias*: On Plato, Republic 509B'. In: Nikulin, ed. *The Other Plato*, pp. 39–64.

Kubiak, Zygmunt. *Mitologia Greków i Rzymian* [*The Mythology of the Greeks and Romans*]. Warszawa: Świat Książki, 1998.

——. *Literatura Greków i Rzymian* [*The Literature of the Greeks and Romans*]. Warszawa: Świat Książki, 1999.

Kubok, Dariusz. *Problem apeiron i peras w filozofii przedsokratejskiej* [*On Apeiron and Peras in Presocratic Philosophy*]. Katowice: Wydawnictwo Uniwersytetu Śląskiego, 1998.

——. *Prawda i mniemania. Studium filozofii Parmenidesa z Elei* [*Truth and Belief: A Study in Parmenides*]. Katowice: Wydawnictwo Uniwersytetu Śląskiego, 2004.

Legutko, Ryszard. *Sokrates. Filozofia męża sprawiedliwego* [*Socrates: Philosophy of the Man of Justice*]. Poznań: Zysk i S-ka, 2013.

Lengauer, Włodzimierz. *Pojęcie równości w greckich koncepcjach politycznych. Od Homera do końca V w.* [*The Notion of Equality in Greek Political Concepts: From Homer to the End of the Fifth c.*]. Warszawa: Wydawnictwo Uniwersytetu Wrocławskiego, 1988.

Leo XIII. *Rerum novarum: Encyclical on Capital and Labor* (1891). http://w2.vatican.va/ (2017).

Leuprecht, Peter. *Reason, Justice and Dignity: A Journey to Some Unexplored Sources of Human Rights.* Leiden— Boston: Martinus Nijhoff Publishers, 2012.

Levinson, Ronald Bartlett. *In Defense of Plato.* Cambridge: Harvard University Press, 1953.

Lewis, Charlton T., Charles Short. *A Latin Dictionary.* New York—Cincinnati—Chicago: American Book Company, 1879.

Liddell, Henry G., Robert Scott, Henry S. Jones. *A Greek-English Lexicon.* With a revised supplement. Oxford: Oxford University Press, 1996.

MacKenzie, Mary Margaret. *Plato on Punishment.* Berkeley—Los Angeles—London: University of California Press, 1981.

McPherran, Mark L., ed. *Plato's Republic: A Critical Guide.* Cambridge: Cambridge University Press, 2010.

The Merriam-Webster Dictionary. Springfield: Merriam-Webster. www.merriam-webster.com (2017).

Mróz, Tomasz. 'Rola dialogu Gorgias w Karla R. Poppera interpretacji Platona i w pierwszych głosach krytycznych' [The Role of the Dialogue Gorgias in Karl Popper's Interpretation of Plato and the First Critical Voices]. In: *Kolokwia Platońskie – ΓΟΡΓΙΑΣ.* Ed. Artur Pacewicz. Wrocław: Instytut Filozofii Uniwersytetu Wrocławskiego, 2009, pp. 189–203.

Nails, Debra. *The People of Plato: A Prosopography of Plato and other Socratics.* Indianapolis—Cambridge: Hackett, 2002.

Nikulin, Dmitri, ed. *The Other Plato: The Tübingen Interpretation of Plato's Inner-Academic Teachings.* Albany: SUNY Press, 2012.

Nussbaum, Martha C. *The Fragility of Goodness: Luck and Ethics in Greek Tragedy and Philosophy.* Revised edition. Cambridge: Cambridge University Press, 2013.

O'Grady, Patricia, ed. *The Sophists: An Introduction.* London: Duckworth, 2008.

Olejarczyk, Anna. *Dialogi Platona. Dzieło otwarte* [*Plato's Dialogues: An Open Work*]. Wrocław: Wydawnictwo Uniwersytetu Wrocławskiego, 2001.

Olson, Halsten. 'Socrates Talks to Himself in Plato's Hippias Major'. *Ancient Philosophy* 2000, Vol. 20, pp. 265–287.

Ortega y Gasset, Jose. *On Love: Aspects of a Single Theme* (1957). Trans. Toby Talbot. Eastford: Martino Fine Books, 2012.

Ovidius, Publius Naso. *Metamorphoses*. Trans. Brookes More. Boston: Cornhill Publishing Co., 1922.

Owen, Gwilym Ellis Lane. 'The Place of the "Timaeus" in Plato's Dialogues'. *Classical Quarterly*, N.S. 1953 Vol. 3, No. 1–2, pp. 79–95.

Pacewicz, Artur. *Między Dobrem a Jednością. Związek Dobra i Jedna w filozofii Platona, Starej Akademii i Arystotelesa* [*Between Good and Unity: The Relationship between Good and One in the Philosophy of Plato, the Old Academy and Aristotle*]. Wrocław: Wydawnictwo Uniwersytetu Wrocławskiego, 2004.

——. 'O ewolucyjnym charakterze filozofii Platona' [On the Evolutionary Character of Plato's Philosophy]. In: *Philosophiae itinera. Studia i rozprawy ofiarowane Janinie Gajdzie-Krynickiej*. Eds. Artur Pacewicz, Anna Olejarczyk, Janusz Jaskóła. Wrocław: Instytut Filozofii Uniwersytetu Wrocławskiego, 2009, pp. 373–390.

——. 'The Concept of the Good (tagathon) in Philosophy before Plato'. *Studia Philosophica Wratislaviensia*, Supplementary Volume, English edition, 2012, pp. 11–25.

——. *Hēdonē. Koncepcja przyjemności w filozofii Platona* [*Hēdonē: A Conception of Pleasure in Plato's Philosophy*]. Wrocław: Oficyna Nukowa PFF, 2016.

Paczkowski, Przemysław. '*Timajos* Platona: Kosmologia w służbie Paidei' [Plato's *Timaeus*: The Cosmology in the Ministry of *Paidea*]. In: *KolokwiaPlatońskie. ΤΙΜΑΙΟΣ*. Eds. Anna Olejarczyk, Maciej Manikowski. Wrocław: Wydawnictwo Uniwersytetu Wrocławskiego, 2004, pp. 227–233.

——. 'Klasyczna filozofia grecka wobec problemu wolności i wolnej woli' [Classical Greek Philosophy and the Question of Liberty and Free Will]. *Studia Philosophica Wratislaviensia* 2009, Vol. 4, No. 4, pp. 71–83.

Pawłowski, Kazimierz. 'Zasada „niekrzywdzenia" w kontekście mitu eschatologicznego w Platońskim "Gorgiaszu"' [The 'Harm Principle' in the Eschatological Myth in Plato's *Gorgias*]. In: *Kolokwia Platońskie. ΓΟΡΓΙΑΣ*. Ed. Artur Pacewicz. Wrocław: Instytut Filozofii Uniwersytetu Wrocławskiego, 2009, pp. 53–70.

Pico della Mirandola, Giovanni. *Oration on the Dignity of Man*. Trans. Robert Caponigri. Chicago: Henry Regnery Co., 1956.

Piechowiak, Marek. 'Negative Freedom or Objective Good: A Recurring Dilemma in the Foundations of Politics'. In: *Dokąd zmierza Europa—przywództwo—idee—wartości. Where Europe Is Going—Leadership—Ideas—Values*. Eds. Halina Taborska, Jan S. Wojciechowski. Pułtusk: Akademia Humanistyczna im. Aleksandra Gieysztora, 2007, pp. 537–544.

——. 'Sokrates sam ze sobą rozmawia o sprawiedliwości' [Socrates in a Dialogue with Himself on Justice]. In: *Kolokwia Platońskie. ΓΟΡΓΙΑΣ*. Ed. Artur Pacewicz. Wrocław: Instytut Filozofii Uniwersytetu Wrocławskiego, 2009, pp. 71–92.

——. 'Auf der Suche nach einer philosophischen Begründung der Würde des Menschen bei Thomas von Aquin und Immanuel Kant' [In Search of a Philosophical Justification of Human Dignity according to Thomas Aquinas and Immanuel Kant]. In: *Würde—dignité—godność—dignity. Die Menschenwürde im internationalen Vergleich*. Eds. Christine Baumbach, Peter Kunzmann. München: Herbert Utz Verlag, 2010, pp. 289–319.

——. 'Tomasza z Akwinu egzystencjalna koncepcja osoby i jej godności. Komentarz do *Summy teologii*, część I, kwestia 29, artykuł 1' [Thomas Aquinas's Existential Conception of Person and His Dignity: A Commentary to the *Summa Theologiae*, I, q. 29, a. 1]. In: *Szkice o godności człowieka*. Eds. Marek Piechowiak, Tomasz Turowski. Zielona Góra: Oficyna Wydawnicza Uniwersytetu Zielonogórskiego, 2012, pp. 35–47.

——. 'Przemowa Demiurga w Platońskim „Timajosie" a współczesne pojęcie godności' [Demiurge's Speech in Plato's *Timaeus* and the Contemporary Notion of Dignity]. In: *Abiit, non obiit. Księga poświęcona pamięci Księdza Profesora Antoniego Kościa SVD*. Eds. Antoni Dębiński et al. Lublin: Wydawnictwo KUL, 2013, pp. 655–665.

——. 'Kallikles i geometria. Przyczynek do Platońs kiejkoncepcji sprawiedliwości' [Callicles and Geometry: On Plato's Conception of Justice]. In: *Księga życia i twórczości. Księga pamiątkowa dedykowana Profesorowi Romanowi A. Tokarczykowi*. Ed. Zbigniew Władek. Lublin: Wydawnictwo Polihymnia, 2013, Vol. 5: *Prawo*, pp. 281–291.

——. 'Platońskie widziadło sprawiedliwości' [Plato's Semblance of Justice]. *Themis Polska Nova* 2013, Vol. 1, No. 4, pp. 5–18.

——. 'Tomasza z Akwinu koncepcja prawa naturalnego. Czy Akwinata jest myślicielem liberalnym?' [Thomas Aquinas' Conception of Natural Law: Is Aquinas a Liberal Thinker?]. *Przegląd Tomistyczny* 2013, Vol. 19, pp. 301–337.

——. 'Plato and the Universality of Dignity'. *Themis Polska Nova* 2015, Vol. 9, No. 2, pp. 5–25.

——. 'Plato's Conception of Punitive Justice'. In: *Universality of Punishment*. Eds. Antonio Incampo, Wojciech Żełaniec. Bari: Cacucci, 2015, pp. 73–96

——. 'Thomas Aquinas—Human Dignity and Conscience as a Basis for Restricting Legal Obligations'. *Diametros* 2016 (March), Vol. 47, pp. 64–83.

Pinckaers, Servais T. *The Sources of Christian Ethics*. Trans. M. T. Noble. Washington, D. C.: CUA Press. 1995.

Pindar. *Odes*. Trans. Diane A. Svarlien. 1990 (*The Perseus Project*).

Pius XI. *Quadragesimo anno: Encyclical on Reconstruction of the Social Order* (1931). http://w2.vatican.va/ (2017).

Pomeroy, Sarah B. *Goddesses, Whores, Wives, and Slaves: Women in Classical Antiquity.* London: The Bodlay Head, 2015.

Popper, Karl R. *The Open Society and Its Enemies,* Vol. 1: *The Spell of Plato.* 5th edition. Princeton: Princeton University Press, 1971 (1st edition. London: Routledge, 1945).

Price, Anthony W. 'Generating in Beauty for the Sake of Immortality: Personal Love and the Goal of the Lover'. In: *Plato's Symposium: A Critical Guide.* Eds. Pierre Destrée, Zina Giannopoulou. Cambridge: Cambridge University Press, 2017, pp. 176–193.

——. *Love and Friendship in Plato and Aristotle.* Oxford: Oxford University Press, 2004.

——. *Virtue and Love in Plato and Aristotle.* Oxford: Clarendon Press, 2011.

Proclamation of Teheran (1968). Final Act of the International Conference on Human Rights, Teheran, 22 April to 13 May 1968, U.N. Doc. A/CONF. 32/41 at 3.

Reale, Giovanni. *History of Ancient Philosophy,* Vol. 2: *Plato and Aristotle.* Trans. John R. Catan. Albany, NY: State University of New York Press, 1990.

——. *Autotestimonianze e rimandi dei dialoghi di Platone alle "dottrine non scritte".* Milano: Bompiani, 2008.

Rosen, Michael. *Dignity: Its History and Meaning.* Cambridge–London: Harvard University Press, 2012.

Rosen, Stanley. *Plato's Republic: A Study.* New Haven–London: Yale University Press, 2005.

Roskal, Zenon. *Astronomia matematyczna w nauce greckiej. Metodologiczne stadium historyczno-przyrodnicze* [*A Mathematical Astronomy in Greek Science. Natural Science – History Methods*]. Lublin: Redakcja Wydawnictw KUL, 2002.

Santas, Gerasimos. 'The Form of the Good in Plato's Republic'. In: Fine, ed. *Plato 1,* pp. 247–274.

——. *Goodness and Justice: Plato, Aristotle and the Moderns.* Malden: Blackwell Publishers, 2001.

——. *Understanding Plato's Republic.* Malden: Wiley-Blackwell, 2010.

Saunders, Trevor J. *Plato's Penal Code: Tradition, Controversy, and Reform in Greek Penology.* Oxford: Clarendon Press, 1991.

Schofield, Malcolm. *The Stoic Idea of the City.* Chicago–London: The University of Chicago Press, 1999.

——. *Plato: Political Philosophy.* Oxford: Oxford University Press, 2011.

Sedley, David. 'The Ideal of Godlikeness'. In: Fine, ed. *Plato 2,* pp. 309–328.

Seneca, Lucius Annaeus. *De ira—On Anger.* Trans. John W. Basore. In: Lucius Annaeus Seneca. *Moral Essays.* London: William Heinemann, 1928, Vol. I, pp.106–355.

Shorey, Paul. 'The Unity of Plato's Thought'. In: *Decennial Publications of the University of Chicago.* First Series, Vol. 6 (*Investigations Representing the Departments: Greek Latin Comparative Philology, Classical Archaeology*), Chicago: The University of Chicago Press, 1904, pp. 129–214.

Sieroń, Józef. *Status jednostki i państwa w greckiej πόλις w świetle filozofii Sokratesa, Platona i Arystotelesa* [The Status of the Individual and the State in the Greek πόλις: The Philosophy of Socrates, Plato and Aristotle]. Katowice: Wydawnictwo Uniwersytetu Śląskiego, 2003.

Smith, Nicholas D. *Images, Education and Paradox in Plato's Republic.* In: *Recognition, Remembrance & Reality.* Ed. Mark L. McPherran. Kelowna: Academic Printing and Publishing, 2000, pp. 125–141.

——. 'Return to the Cave'. In: *Plato's Republic: A Critical Guide.* Ed. Mark L. McPherran. Cambridge: Cambridge University Press, 2010, pp. 83–102.

Stauffer, Devin. *Plato's Introduction to the Question of Justice.* Albany: State University of New York Press, 2001.

——. *The Unity of Plato's 'Gorgias': Rhetoric, Justice, and the Philosophic Life.* Cambridge: Cambridge University Press, 2009.

Strauss, 'Plato'. In: *History of Political Philosophy.* Eds. Leo Strauss, Joseph Cropsey. Chicago: The University of Chicago Press, 1987, pp. 33–89.

Szlezák, Thomas A. *Reading Plato.* Trans. G. Zanker, London: Routledge, 1999.

——. 'The Idea of the Good as *Arkhē* in Plato's *Republic*'. In: Nikulin, ed. *The Other Plato,* pp. 83–142.

Taylor, Christopher Charles Whiston. 'Plato's Totalitarianism'. In: Fine, ed. *Plato 2,* pp. 280–296.

Tell, Håkan. *Plato's Counterfeit Sophists.* Cambridge: Harvard University Center for Hellenic Studies, 2011.

Thomas Aquinas. *De potentia.* Trans. English Dominican Fathers. Westminster: The Newman Press, 1952. Reprint of 1932 edition.

——. *Scriptum super Sententiis,* www.corpusthomisticum.org (2017).

——. *Summa contra gentiles.* Trans. Anton C. Pegis (lib. 1), James F. Anderson (lib. 2), Vernon J. Bourke (lib. 3), Charles J. O'Neil (lib. 4). New York: Hanover House, 1955–1957.

——. *Summa Theologica* [*Summa theologiae*]. Trans. Fathers of the English Dominican Province, e-artnow, 2013. Reprint Benziger edition: New York: Benziger, 1947–1948.

Universal Declaration of Human Rights. 1948. Adopted 10 Dec. 1948, G.A. Res. 217 A (III), U.N. GAOR, 3rd Sess., U.N. Doc. A/RES/3/217A.

Vasiliou, Iakovos. *Aiming at Virtue in Plato.* Cambridge: Cambridge University Press, 2008.

Vienna Declaration and Programme of Action (1993) *adopted* 25 June 1993 by the World Conference on Human Rights, U.N. Doc. A/CONF. 157/23.

Vlastos, Gregory. 'The Individual as Object of Love in Plato'. In: idem. *Platonic Studies.* 2nd print., with corrections. Princeton: Princeton University Press, 1981, pp. 3–34. Reprinted in *Plato 2.* Ed. G. Fine, pp. 137–163.

——. 'Socratic Piety'. In: Fine, ed. *Plato 2,* pp. 56–77.

Voegelin, Eric. *The World of the Polis* (*Order and History.* Vol. 2). Ed. Athanasios Moulakis. Columbia–London: University of Missouri Press, 2000.

——. *Plato and Aristotle* (*Order and History.* Vol. 3). Ed. Dante Germino. Columbia–London: University of Missouri Press, 2000.

Vries, Gerrit Jacob de. *Antisthenes Redivivus. Popper's Attack on Plato.* Amsterdam: North-Holland Publishing Co., 1952.

Waldron, Jeremy. *Dignity, Rank, and Rights.* Oxford: Oxford University Press, 2012.

Walgrave, Jan Hendric. 'Reason and Will in Natural Law'. In: *Lex et Libertas: Freedom and Law according to St. Thomas Aquinas.* Eds. L. J. Elders, H. Hedwig. Città del Vaticano: Libreria Editrice Vaticana, 1987, pp. 67–81.

Weiss, Roslyn. *Philosophers in the Republic: Plato's Two Paradigms.* Ithaca: Cornell University Press, 2012.

Wesoły, Marian. 'Platońska koncepcja harmonii w świetle dialogów i nauk niespisanych' [Plato's Conception of Harmony in the Light of his Dialogues and Unwritten Teachings]. In: *Platon: nowa interpretacja.* Eds. Agnieszka Kijewska, Edward Iwo Zieliński. Lublin: Redakcja Wydawnictw KUL, 1993, pp. 107–132.

Whitehead, Alfred North. *Process and Reality* (1929). Corrected edition. Eds. D. R. Griffin, D. W. Sherburne. New York: Free Press, 1978.

Wild, John Daniel. *Plato's Modern Enemies and the Theory of Natural Law.* Chicago: The University of Chicago Press, 1953.

Xenophon. *Memorabilia. Oeconomicus. Symposium. Apology.* Trans. Edgar Cardew Marchant, O. J. Todd. Cambridge: Harvard University Press–London: William Heinemann, 1923 (*The Perseus Project*).

Zygmuntowicz, Dorota. *Praktyka polityczna. Od Państwa do Praw Platona* [Political Praxis: Plato–From the Republic to the Laws]. Toruń: Wydawnictwo UMK, 2011.

Indexes

Index Locorum

Plato

A

Alcibiades
- *Alcibiades*, 128e–129a 70

Apology
- *Apology*, 21a 123
- *Apology*, 23a–b 123
- *Apology*, 30d 147
- *Apology*, 31c–d 87, 166, 169
- *Apology*, 31d 258
- *Apology*, 40b–c 87

C

Charmides
- *Charmides*, 161b 92

Crito
- *Crito*, 49c 145

E

Euthydemus
- *Euthydemus*, 281d–e 76

G

Gorgias
- *Gorgias*, 447c 58
- *Gorgias*, 448c 58
- *Gorgias*, 449b 124
- *Gorgias*, 454b 59
- *Gorgias*, 454b–c 125
- *Gorgias*, 458a–b 59
- *Gorgias*, 460a 59
- *Gorgias*, 460b 130
- *Gorgias*, 461d 124
- *Gorgias*, 461e–462a 124
- *Gorgias*, 463b 103, 176
- *Gorgias*, 463c–d 103
- *Gorgias*, 463d 103, 176
- *Gorgias*, 464a 109
- *Gorgias*, 464b 155, 175
- *Gorgias*, 464c 155, 175
- *Gorgias*, 464d 175, 177
- *Gorgias*, 464d–e 176
- *Gorgias*, 465a 58, 103, 175–177
- *Gorgias*, 465b 176–177
- *Gorgias*, 465b–c 103, 176
- *Gorgias*, 465c 176
- *Gorgias*, 465d 177
- *Gorgias*, 465d–466a 125
- *Gorgias*, 466a 125
- *Gorgias*, 469b 60
- *Gorgias*, 470b–c 60
- *Gorgias*, 470e 61
- *Gorgias*, 472c 61, 178
- *Gorgias*, 472e 61, 178
- *Gorgias*, 473a 60
- *Gorgias*, 474b 60
- *Gorgias*, 474d 62
- *Gorgias*, 474e 62
- *Gorgias*, 475a 62
- *Gorgias*, 475a–b 62
- *Gorgias*, 476e–477a 62, 178
- *Gorgias*, 477a–e 178
- *Gorgias*, 477c 62–63
- *Gorgias*, 477d–e 63
- *Gorgias*, 478c 62
- *Gorgias*, 478d 178
- *Gorgias*, 478d–e 61, 178
- *Gorgias*, 478e 178
- *Gorgias*, 479c–d 60
- *Gorgias*, 479e 60
- *Gorgias*, 480a 178
- *Gorgias*, 480d 60
- *Gorgias*, 482a–b 60
- *Gorgias*, 483d 73–74, 135
- *Gorgias*, 483e–484b 73
- *Gorgias*, 491e–492a 72
- *Gorgias*, 491e–492c 135
- *Gorgias*, 492a–b 73
- *Gorgias*, 492b–c 73

- *Gorgias*, 492c 74, 245
- *Gorgias*, 503e–504a 110
- *Gorgias*, 504a–d 177
- *Gorgias*, 504b 109
- *Gorgias*, 504d 179
- *Gorgias*, 505b 123
- *Gorgias*, 505c 124
- *Gorgias*, 505c–d 123, 126
- *Gorgias*, 505d 124, 126, 131, 215
- *Gorgias*, 505e 126
- *Gorgias*, 506a 123
- *Gorgias*, 506c 243
- *Gorgias*, 506c–507c 89, 122, 129, 159
- *Gorgias*, 507a 131–132, 134
- *Gorgias*, 507a–b 132, 190
- *Gorgias*, 507a–c 213
- *Gorgias*, 507b 66, 94, 148, 151, 217
- *Gorgias*, 507c 61, 132–133, 143–144, 216, 248
- *Gorgias*, 507c–d 144
- *Gorgias*, 507d 156
- *Gorgias*, 507d–e 144
- *Gorgias*, 507e 144
- *Gorgias*, 507e–508a 192, 243
- *Gorgias*, 508a 192, 204
- *Gorgias*, 508b 61, 145
- *Gorgias*, 508c 145
- *Gorgias*, 508e 147
- *Gorgias*, 510b 186, 202, 251
- *Gorgias*, 513e–514a 155
- *Gorgias*, 515a 206
- *Gorgias*, 515a–b 207
- *Gorgias*, 515b–c 155, 206
- *Gorgias*, 517b–c 206
- *Gorgias*, 525a 179, 183
- *Gorgias*, 525b 49, 181, 185
- *Gorgias*, 525c 183
- *Gorgias*, 527a 40
- *Gorgias*, 527b 147
- *Gorgias*, 527b–c 178
- *Gorgias*, 527e 156

H

Hippias Major (*Greater Hippias*)
- *Hippias Major* (*Greater Hippias*), 286c ff. 123

L

Laches
- *Laches*, 193e 85
- *Laches*, 198b 86, 160

Laws
- *Laws*, 626b–628e 65
- *Laws*, 630c 84
- *Laws*, 631b–c 25
- *Laws*, 633c–d 84
- *Laws*, 634a–c 84
- *Laws*, 689d 139
- *Laws*, 693b 26, 205
- *Laws*, 693c 26
- *Laws*, 694b 205
- *Laws*, 697a–b 25
- *Laws*, 701d 205
- *Laws*, 707c 26
- *Laws*, 728e–729a 108
- *Laws*, 743c 13, 25–26, 30, 74, 82, 97, 113–114, 144, 153, 156, 186, 197, 202, 204–205, 210, 251
- *Laws*, 744b–c 193, 199
- *Laws*, 757a 186, 203, 251
- *Laws*, 757b 192–193, 199
- *Laws*, 757b–c 180
- *Laws*, 757c 180, 193, 199
- *Laws*, 757c–d 193
- *Laws*, 757d 180, 193
- *Laws*, 757d–e 193
- *Laws*, 757e 192–193
- *Laws*, 770c–e 26, 154
- *Laws*, 770e 148, 244
- *Laws*, 770e–771a 154
- *Laws*, 773a 197
- *Laws*, 777d–e 67, 146, 207
- *Laws*, 777e 146
- *Laws*, 887b 37
- *Laws*, 889c 37
- *Laws*, 889d–e 37
- *Laws*, 903b–c 50
- *Laws*, 903b–e 45, 47

- *Laws*, 903d 232
- *Laws*, 903d–e 190, 213, 232
- *Laws*, 903e 207
- *Laws*, 904a 190
- *Laws*, 904b–c 190, 208
- *Laws*, 904d–905a 206
- *Laws*, 904e–905b 185
- *Laws*, 905d 185
- *Laws*, 926c–928d 146
- *Laws*, 927d 146, 182
- *Laws*, 927e–928a 187
- *Laws*, 928b–c 187
- *Laws*, 928d 179
- *Laws*, 933e–934a 187
- *Laws*, 934a 182
- *Laws*, 934a–b 184
- *Laws*, 934b 187

Letter VII
- Letter VII, 331b 207
- Letter VII, 331c 208
- Letter VII, 331c–d 207
- Letter VII, 342a 101
- Letter VII, 343d 101
- Letter VII, 344b 101

P

Parmenides
- *Parmenides*, 132c 100

Phaedo
- *Phaedo*, 105c 40
- *Phaedo*, 78b–80b 40
- *Phaedo*, 95c–d 41
- *Phaedo*, 99b–c 38
- *Phaedo*, 99c 136

Phaedrus
- *Phaedrus*, 229a–230b 69
- *Phaedrus*, 230a 71, 74, 244
- *Phaedrus*, 235c–d 123
- *Phaedrus*, 245c 40
- *Phaedrus*, 246a 47, 91, 225–226
- *Phaedrus*, 246a–d 47
- *Phaedrus*, 246a–257b 50
- *Phaedrus*, 246b 226
- *Phaedrus*, 246d–248e 47, 50, 102, 139
- *Phaedrus*, 247a 47, 226
- *Phaedrus*, 247b 226
- *Phaedrus*, 247c–d 136, 227
- *Phaedrus*, 247d 226–227, 260
- *Phaedrus*, 247d–e 228
- *Phaedrus*, 247e 226
- *Phaedrus*, 248b–c 227, 233
- *Phaedrus*, 248c 190
- *Phaedrus*, 248c–e 190
- *Phaedrus*, 249a–b 169
- *Phaedrus*, 249b 186
- *Phaedrus*, 275c–d 105
- *Phaedrus*, 276a 105, 107, 159–160, 205, 224, 248, 252, 263
- *Phaedrus*, 276c 104, 107
- *Phaedrus*, 276e 104
- *Phaedrus*, 276e–277a 105, 107
- *Phaedrus*, 277d–e 104
- *Phaedrus*, 277e 105
- *Phaedrus*, 278a 216
- *Phaedrus*, 278a–b 105, 228
- *Phaedrus*, 278d 88, 160, 210
- *Phaedrus*, 279b–c 107–108, 115, 203, 228, 263
- *Phaedrus*, 279c 107, 203, 209, 237

Protagoras
- *Protagoras*, 330b 94

R

Republic
- *Republic*, 229d 238
- *Republic*, 328b 238
- *Republic*, 328c 238
- *Republic*, 328d–e 238
- *Republic*, 328e 239
- *Republic*, 329d 239
- *Republic*, 330b 239
- *Republic*, 330b–c 114
- *Republic*, 330c 114
- *Republic*, 330e–331a 146, 238
- *Republic*, 330e–331b 239
- *Republic*, 331a 239
- *Republic*, 331b 147, 239
- *Republic*, 331c 64, 131, 214

- *Republic*, 331e 64, 129, 214
- *Republic*, 331e ff. 63
- *Republic*, 332a–b 65
- *Republic*, 332c 65, 67, 214
- *Republic*, 334b 65
- *Republic*, 334e 65
- *Republic*, 335a–e 143
- *Republic*, 335d 145
- *Republic*, 335e 65–66, 142, 145, 180, 184, 259
- *Republic*, 336a 66
- *Republic*, 336c–d 30, 149
- *Republic*, 337d 149
- *Republic*, 338c 135
- *Republic*, 339b–342e 67
- *Republic*, 339b–347e 148
- *Republic*, 342e 149
- *Republic*, 343c 150
- *Republic*, 343c–d 67
- *Republic*, 343d–344c 109
- *Republic*, 344d 124
- *Republic*, 344e 63
- *Republic*, 345c–d 150
- *Republic*, 345e 150
- *Republic*, 346e 150
- *Republic*, 352d 63
- *Republic*, 353d 47, 110, 142, 214
- *Republic*, 353e 110
- *Republic*, 353e–354a 215
- *Republic*, 358e–359b 135
- *Republic*, 362b 66
- *Republic*, 366e 59, 64
- *Republic*, 368b 68
- *Republic*, 368c–d 68
- *Republic*, 369a–b 68
- *Republic*, 369b 156
- *Republic*, 369b–c 115, 156, 210–211
- *Republic*, 369c 77
- *Republic*, 370a 115
- *Republic*, 382a–c 246
- *Republic*, 382b 246
- *Republic*, 382c 246
- *Republic*, 382c–d 246
- *Republic*, 420b–421c 20
- *Republic*, 421b–c 96
- *Republic*, 423d 20, 96, 118, 126
- *Republic*, 423d–e 83
- *Republic*, 423e 242, 247
- *Republic*, 423e–424a 241, 251
- *Republic*, 427e–428a 80
- *Republic*, 428b 80
- *Republic*, 428c–d 80, 107, 121, 130, 161, 201, 219
- *Republic*, 429b 159–160
- *Republic*, 429b–c 139, 166
- *Republic*, 429b–d 84, 86, 245
- *Republic*, 429c 161
- *Republic*, 430a–b 86
- *Republic*, 430e 89
- *Republic*, 430e–431a 90
- *Republic*, 431c–d 90
- *Republic*, 431d–e 90
- *Republic*, 431e 89, 129
- *Republic*, 431e–432a 89, 91
- *Republic*, 432a 90–91, 129
- *Republic*, 432b 29, 91, 106
- *Republic*, 432b–d 91
- *Republic*, 432c 91–92, 243
- *Republic*, 432d–e 93
- *Republic*, 433a 32, 92, 94
- *Republic*, 433a–b 92, 94, 126
- *Republic*, 433b 92
- *Republic*, 433b–c 94–95, 151
- *Republic*, 433c 30, 80, 84, 86, 91
- *Republic*, 433c–d 79
- *Republic*, 433d 92, 95
- *Republic*, 433e 92
- *Republic*, 433e–434a 92
- *Republic*, 433e–434c 111
- *Republic*, 434a–b 79
- *Republic*, 434b 30, 112
- *Republic*, 434c 30, 79
- *Republic*, 435b–c 93
- *Republic*, 435c 93
- *Republic*, 435d 93
- *Republic*, 437a–441c 77
- *Republic*, 439a–b 78
- *Republic*, 439b 78

- *Republic*, 439c 78
- *Republic*, 439d 78
- *Republic*, 439e–440a 78
- *Republic*, 440a 78
- *Republic*, 440a–b 78
- *Republic*, 440b 78
- *Republic*, 440d 79
- *Republic*, 441a 79
- *Republic*, 441a–b 79
- *Republic*, 441c 77
- *Republic*, 441e 81
- *Republic*, 442b 81
- *Republic*, 442b–c 84–86, 166, 224
- *Republic*, 442c 82
- *Republic*, 442c–d 201–202
- *Republic*, 442d 97
- *Republic*, 443b 98, 243
- *Republic*, 443b–c 98
- *Republic*, 443b–e 182, 196, 204
- *Republic*, 443b–444a 110
- *Republic*, 443c 25, 30, 68, 99–100, 110–112, 121, 126, 158, 167, 241, 248
- *Republic*, 443c–d 167, 216
- *Republic*, 443c–e 24, 32, 99, 101, 108, 116–117, 132, 158, 179, 202, 215
- *Republic*, 443c–444a 68–69, 126, 161, 202
- *Republic*, 443d 202, 252
- *Republic*, 443d–444a 177
- *Republic*, 443d–e 121, 181, 194
- *Republic*, 443e 107, 113, 117, 130, 161, 177, 179–180, 216, 248
- *Republic*, 444a 99
- *Republic*, 444b–c 213
- *Republic*, 444d 109
- *Republic*, 444e–445a 175
- *Republic*, 445a 213
- *Republic*, 445a–b 109, 175
- *Republic*, 445b 175
- *Republic*, 449a 242
- *Republic*, 449a–b 241
- *Republic*, 449c 251
- *Republic*, 450d–451a 242
- *Republic*, 453d 31, 242
- *Republic*, 455c 250
- *Republic*, 455d–456a 173
- *Republic*, 455d–e 250
- *Republic*, 456a 249–250
- *Republic*, 456a–b 249
- *Republic*, 456b 250–251
- *Republic*, 457b 151
- *Republic*, 458d 243
- *Republic*, 459c–d 245
- *Republic*, 459d–e 246
- *Republic*, 461e 245
- *Republic*, 462a–b 20
- *Republic*, 462a–c 244
- *Republic*, 485c 246
- *Republic*, 493b 249
- *Republic*, 500e 167
- *Republic*, 501a–c 167
- *Republic*, 501b 142, 230
- *Republic*, 501b–c 167
- *Republic*, 504c 236
- *Republic*, 504d 237
- *Republic*, 504e–505a 136
- *Republic*, 508d–509a 231
- *Republic*, 509a 130
- *Republic*, 509b 23, 42, 136–137, 232
- *Republic*, 514a 133–134
- *Republic*, 515a 140
- *Republic*, 515d 136
- *Republic*, 516a 101
- *Republic*, 516b–c 136
- *Republic*, 516d 228
- *Republic*, 517a 140
- *Republic*, 517b 140
- *Republic*, 517b–c 137, 216, 232
- *Republic*, 517c 136, 141
- *Republic*, 517d 134, 141
- *Republic*, 518b–c 82, 125, 138, 159, 224, 229
- *Republic*, 518c 82, 138–139, 227, 237
- *Republic*, 518c–d 82, 136, 138
- *Republic*, 519b–520e 229
- *Republic*, 519c 141, 229
- *Republic*, 519d 229
- *Republic*, 519e–520a 20, 96, 229

- *Republic*, 520a 231
- *Republic*, 520a–b 230
- *Republic*, 520b 229–230
- *Republic*, 520c 102
- *Republic*, 520e 229
- *Republic*, 525b 112
- *Republic*, 528a–d 140
- *Republic*, 532b 140
- *Republic*, 532b–d 141, 229
- *Republic*, 533d–e 149
- *Republic*, 536c 31, 243
- *Republic*, 542b 241
- *Republic*, 543a 242
- *Republic*, 543a–c 241
- *Republic*, 543c 242
- *Republic*, 546a 40
- *Republic*, 546a–547d 205
- *Republic*, 580a 147
- *Republic*, 580b 59
- *Republic*, 580b–c 60
- *Republic*, 589a–b 251–252
- *Republic*, 589b 246
- *Republic*, 590b 70
- *Republic*, 590c 250
- *Republic*, 590c–d 146
- *Republic*, 590e 251
- *Republic*, 591a–b 179
- *Republic*, 591b 94, 111
- *Republic*, 591c 111–112
- *Republic*, 591d 112
- *Republic*, 592a 68
- *Republic*, 592b 68–69
- *Republic*, 595a–b 247
- *Republic*, 599a 247
- *Republic*, 600e 95, 102
- *Republic*, 601b–c 103
- *Republic*, 602b 243
- *Republic*, 607a 245
- *Republic*, 607c 245
- *Republic*, 609a–611b 41
- *Republic*, 615a–b 182
- *Republic*, 615e 49
- *Republic*, 617d–618b 224
- *Republic*, 617d–e 48, 87, 169
- *Republic*, 617e 170, 186, 208
- *Republic*, 618b–c 171
- *Republic*, 618c 170–171
- *Republic*, 618c–d 170
- *Republic*, 618d–e 171, 220
- *Republic*, 618e 168, 171
- *Republic*, 619a 168
- *Republic*, 619a–b 171, 181, 197
- *Republic*, 619b 170, 172, 186
- *Republic*, 619c 170
- *Republic*, 620b 172
- *Republic*, 620c 119, 172
- *Republic*, 620c–d 171
- *Republic*, 621c–d 202, 215

S

Sophist
- *Sophist*, 234c 104
- *Sophist*, 234c–e 104

Statesman
- *Statesman*, 261e 30
- *Statesman*, 267e 57
- *Statesman*, 275e 57
- *Statesman*, 276d 57
- *Statesman*, 286a 100–101

Symposium
- *Symposium*, 177b 218
- *Symposium*, 206b 222
- *Symposium*, 206d–e 222, 260
- *Symposium*, 207a 223
- *Symposium*, 208b 222
- *Symposium*, 219d–221c 115

T

Theaetetus
- *Theaetetus*, 148e–151d 123
- *Theaetetus*, 150a–c 104
- *Theaetetus*, 150c–d 105, 160
- *Theaetetus*, 150e 104
- *Theaetetus*, 167a–b 63, 72, 135
- *Theaetetus*, 167c 218
- *Theaetetus*, 176b 232

Timaeus
- *Timaeus*, 19b 102

- *Timaeus*, 19b–c 36
- *Timaeus*, 20a 36–37, 116
- *Timaeus*, 20d–26c 37
- *Timaeus*, 26c 102
- *Timaeus*, 29a 44
- *Timaeus*, 29b 39
- *Timaeus*, 29b–c 39
- *Timaeus*, 29c 39
- *Timaeus*, 29e 235
- *Timaeus*, 30a 235
- *Timaeus*, 31b–c 194
- *Timaeus*, 31c–32a 194
- *Timaeus*, 32a 195
- *Timaeus*, 32b 195
- *Timaeus*, 32c 196, 204
- *Timaeus*, 37a 44
- *Timaeus*, 41a–b 39, 44, 255
- *Timaeus*, 41b 41, 46, 174, 217, 223, 255, 260
- *Timaeus*, 41b–c 45, 47–48, 235
- *Timaeus*, 41c 45
- *Timaeus*, 41c–d 46
- *Timaeus*, 59c–d 38
- *Timaeus*, 68e 136–137, 232
- *Timaeus*, 69a–81e 48
- *Timaeus*, 71a 104
- *Timaeus*, 77a 49
- *Timaeus*, 77c 49
- *Timaeus*, 81d–e 48
- *Timaeus*, 81e 49, 182
- *Timaeus*, 87c 112
- *Timaeus*, 87d 113
- *Timaeus*, 88c–d 113
- *Timaeus*, 89d 234
- *Timaeus*, 89d–90d 36
- *Timaeus*, 90a 46–48
- *Timaeus*, 90b 234
- *Timaeus*, 90b–c 233
- *Timaeus*, 90c 48, 233
- *Timaeus*, 90d 233
- *Timaeus*, 90d–e 36
- *Timaeus*, 90d–92c 49
- *Timaeus*, 90e 234
- *Timaeus*, 92c 48, 235, 257

Aeschylus
Seven Against Thebes, 610 94

Antiphon
On Truth, Papyrus Oxyrhynchus XI, 1363 217

Aristotle
Eudemian Ethics, 1218a 42
Metaphysics
- *Metaphysics*, 987b–988a 42
- *Metaphysics*, 1022a 71
- *Metaphysics*, 1032b 71
- *Metaphysics*, 1050a 216
- *Metaphysics*, 1074b–1075a 232
- *Metaphysics*, 1075a 232
- *Metaphysics*, 1091b 42

Nicomachean Ethics
- *Nicomachean Ethics*, 1095a–b 42
- *Nicomachean Ethics*, 1098a 209, 216
- *Nicomachean Ethics*, 1106a 181
- *Nicomachean Ethics*, 1106a–b 132
- *Nicomachean Ethics*, 1107b 89
- *Nicomachean Ethics*, 1115a 83
- *Nicomachean Ethics*, 1123a–1125a 115
- *Nicomachean Ethics*, 1129b 117
- *Nicomachean Ethics*, 1130a 116, 150
- *Nicomachean Ethics*, 1130b 198
- *Nicomachean Ethics*, 1131a 181, 198–199
- *Nicomachean Ethics*, 1131b 198
- *Nicomachean Ethics*, 1131b–1132a 193
- *Nicomachean Ethics*, 1132a 198
- *Nicomachean Ethics*, 1134b 150
- *Nicomachean Ethics*, 1137b 132
- *Nicomachean Ethics*, 1143b 240
- *Nicomachean Ethics*, 1156a–b 28

Politics
- *Politics*, 1252b 26
- *Politics*, 1325a 216

Aristoxenus
Elementa harmonica, II, 39.8–40.4 42

Diogenes Laertius
Lives of Eminent Philosophers
- *Lives of Eminent Philosophers*, I, 94–100 66
- *Lives of Eminent Philosophers*, III, 23 206

Euripides
Hippolytus, 380–381 76

Herodotus
Histories
- *Histories*, 1, 23 242
- *Histories*, 1, 23–24 242
- *Histories*, 1, 24 243

Hesiod
Theogony, 306–307 71

Hippocrates
De capitis vulneribus, 3 55

Holy Bible
The First Epistle General of John 2, 16 66
The Gospel according to St. Matthew 5, 43–48 211

Homer
Iliad, I, 130–132 167
Odyssey
- *Odyssey*, IV, 689 ff. 55
- *Odyssey*, VI–VII 250
- *Odyssey*, XIV, 58 ff. 55
- *Odyssey*, XIX, 489 228

Kant Immanuel
Critique of Practical Reason, 161 131
Fundamental Principles of the Metaphysic of Morals
- *Fundamental Principles of the Metaphysic of Morals*, 64–65 (428) 45–46
- *Fundamental Principles of the Metaphysic of Morals*, 66–67 (429) 46
- *Prolegomena to any Future Metaphysics*, 367 13

Ovidius
Metamorphoses, 7.20–21 76

Seneca
De ira
- *De ira*, I, 19, 7 185
- *De ira*, II, 31, 8 185

Thomas Aquinas
De potential, q. 7, a. 2, ad 9 43
Scriptum super Sententiis
- *Scriptum super Sententiis*, lib. 3, d. 33, q. 2, a. 3, ad 3 168
- *Scriptum super Sententiis*, lib. 3, d. 35, q. 1, a. 4, qc. 1, co. 45
Summa contra gentiles, lib. 3, cap. 113 216
Summa theologiae, I, q. 29, a. 1, co. 264
Summa theologiae, II-II, q. 47, a. 15, co. 163

Xenophon
Memorabilia
- *Memorabilia*, II, 1, 28 218
- *Memorabilia*, II, 1, 31 219
- *Memorabilia*, II, 1, 33 218–219
- *Memorabilia*, II, 1, 21–34 218
- *Memorabilia*, II, 1, 27 218
- *Memorabilia*, III, 9, 4 76
- *Memorabilia*, III, 9, 5 76
- *Memorabilia*, IV, 2, 33 61, 76

General Index

A
Aeschylus 55, 79, 94
anamnesis / recollection 41, 54
Anessi T. 15
anger 57, 78, 185, 192
Annas J. 31, 241
Antiphon 217
Apollo 54, 243, 249
appetitive part 78, 85, 89–90, 104, 205, 227, 237, 252, 258
Arion 31, 242–243, 249
Aristotle 28, 45, 83, 89, 116–117, 132, 181, 193, 196–200, 216, 232, 261
Aristoxenus 42
arithmetic equality 192–193, 195
astronomy 140, 234
auxiliaries / auxiliary class 79, 85–87, 90, 96, 112, 117–118, 139, 159, 209
Averroes 19
Avicenna 19

B
Bacon F. 100
Balot R. 85
Barney R. 76
Bartolomé de las Casas 19
'be' (εἶναι) 23
beauty 35, 38, 41, 45, 61–62, 106–108, 130, 142, 151, 167, 170, 176–177, 179, 189, 203, 216, 221–222, 224, 232, 235, 257, 259–260
beneficial 30, 34, 56, 81, 103, 110, 122, 136, 141, 146, 148–151, 160, 174, 181, 183, 188, 193, 197, 214, 223–224, 236–238, 240, 245, 262
Berlin I. 15, 162–166, 171
Bias of Prien 66
birth in beauty / parturition in beauty 222
Blackburn S. 27, 64
Blandzi S. 41, 43
Bobonich C. 25–26, 210
body 39–40, 47–49, 81, 99, 103, 108–113, 116–117, 121, 127, 132, 138, 141, 157, 175–177, 179, 185, 202, 204, 213, 218, 222, 224–225, 235–236, 240, 257
border (πέρας) 41
Bourke V. J. 216
Brennan T. 76
Britain C. 76
Brown L. 157, 195
Bundy E. L. 70
Burges G. 154
Burnyeat M. 101, 218
Bury R. G. 64, 154

C
capital punishment 174
Carone G. R. 35
Catlow J. 15
cave 23, 33, 44, 50, 71, 82, 85, 95, 101–102, 122, 133–143, 159, 209, 224, 227–231, 237, 257
Cephalus 64, 113, 146–147, 238–239
chariot 50, 102, 139, 190, 225, 227–228
child / children 34, 66, 70, 79, 87, 105, 114, 126, 146, 158, 187, 206, 238, 240–243, 247–249, 251–252
Cleanthes Stoicus 75
common good 26, 157, 262
community of wives, *see* sharing of wives
compel / compulsion 20, 96, 141, 207, 229–230, 256
Confucius 19
conscience 87, 166, 169, 258
contemplation 34, 80, 100, 107, 133, 141, 213, 216, 219–220,

225–229, 231–232, 236–237, 240, 260
Cooper J. M. 20
Corey D. D. 71
Cornford F. 37
counsel 80–81, 201, 207
counsellors 79
courage 24, 26, 33–34, 72–73, 77, 79, 81–87, 89, 93–95, 113, 115–118, 133, 139, 143, 159, 161, 167, 210, 241, 245, 247–248, 253, 258–261
craftsmen / money-makers / producers 79, 85, 90, 96, 110, 116–117, 209–210
Cron C. 176
Czarnowski J. 15

D
Dahl N. O. 27
daimon 48, 57, 87, 159, 169, 258
Dembiński B. 24, 158
Demiurge 15, 31–32, 35, 39–41, 43–49, 74–75, 81, 137, 146, 148, 153, 174, 184, 189–191, 204, 207–208, 213, 217, 222–223, 231–235, 240, 255–257, 260–263
desire 45, 72–74, 78, 83–86, 89–90, 105, 108, 153, 172–173, 182–183, 205, 208, 216, 218, 223, 227, 245, 249, 253, 258
Deuschle J. 176
dignity 15, 17–23, 27–31, 33, 35, 41–45, 48, 50, 122, 136, 139, 159, 174, 189–191, 206–207, 223, 255–257, 259–264
Dike 54–55
Diogenes Laertius 66, 206
Diotima 222–224
dolphin (of Arion) 31, 242
Dover K. J. 145
draughts-player 190, 207, 213, 232, 256
drug 245–247

E
education 33, 36, 38, 50, 73–74, 82–85, 106, 112, 118, 121, 133–134, 138–142, 159, 180, 204, 209, 224, 227, 229–231, 234, 236–237, 241, 249, 251, 257, 263
Emlyn-Jones C. 103
England E. B. 154, 187
equality 32, 34, 57, 74, 131, 153, 180–181, 186, 189, 191–204, 206, 208–211, 214, 225, 248, 250–251, 253, 263
Er, *see* myth of Er
Erinyes 57
erotic necessities 34, 243, 245
essence 42, 54, 67, 70, 83, 98, 135, 138, 161, 180, 184, 216, 232, 237
Euripides 76
exile 33, 148, 154, 207, 262
existence 19–21, 23, 26, 29, 33, 37, 42–45, 48–49, 51, 56–57, 64, 74, 81, 89, 91, 96, 108, 110, 116, 136–137, 141–143, 147–148, 150–151, 153, 174, 180, 184, 187, 189–191, 193–196, 200, 204, 208–209, 212–214, 216–217, 219, 223, 225, 232, 237–238, 244, 255–260, 264
external acting 112

F
falsehood 245–246
fear 55, 57, 83–84, 86, 146, 160, 182, 185, 238, 245, 258
Ferber R. 42–43
Ferrari G. R. F. 25
Ficino M. 154
final cause (*causa finalis*) 25, 217
fine condition (ἔχον εὖ) 42
flattery 70, 103, 176–177, 208
formal 30, 33–34, 39–40, 121, 123, 160–161, 167, 198, 202, 206, 236–237
Fowler H. N. 72, 104, 147
Frede M. 101

freedom 18, 33, 74, 82, 86, 88, 124, 157–158, 160, 162–163, 165, 167–169, 205, 210, 250
Freudiger J. 250
friend 65–66, 97, 99, 107, 121, 128, 131, 139, 141, 145, 170, 192, 201–204, 209, 215, 218, 242, 251–252, 263
friendship 13, 25–26, 30, 32, 34, 65, 74, 82, 97, 113–114, 144, 153, 156, 186, 189, 191, 193, 196–197, 200–206, 208–211, 217, 223, 251–252, 259, 261–263

G

Gadamer H.-G. 27
Gagarin M. 57
Gaia 54
Gaiser K. 43
Gajda J. 23
Galewicz W. 81
generation 42, 206, 211
geometric equality 180, 192–193, 195, 197, 199–200
geometric proportion 34, 197, 214
geometrical necessities 34, 243
Gerson L. P. 41, 104
god, 31, 35, 37, 39–41, 43–44, 46–51, 54, 57, 75, 88, 94, 97–98, 101, 107, 123, 131–134, 144, 147–148, 151, 153, 160, 167, 169, 181, 185–186, 189–193, 195, 202–204, 206, 215, 218, 223, 225–226, 228, 232–235, 238–240, 243, 246, 248, 257, 260–261
Godley A. D. 243
godlike 64, 110, 167, 232, 237, 251
gold 107–108, 115, 203, 228, 237, 263
golden mean 181, 197
Good / good 20–21, 23, 25–26, 28–29, 31, 33, 36–38, 41–51, 55, 57–59, 61–63, 65, 67, 69–70, 73–76, 79–80, 82, 84–85, 94–97, 99, 102, 104–112, 114–117, 119, 121, 123, 127–131, 133–138, 140–148, 150–151, 153–155, 157–170, 172–175, 178, 180, 183–184, 186–190, 193, 202–203, 206–208, 210–212, 214–219, 221–223, 225, 227, 229–232, 234–241, 243, 249–251, 255–257, 259–262
Grimal P. 57
Grube G. M. A. 80, 90, 95-96, 98, 100, 111, 161, 167, 171, 176
guardians / rulers 30, 33, 57, 66, 79–80, 82–83, 85–86, 88, 90, 92, 96, 106, 111, 113, 116–118, 137, 139, 150, 153, 167, 204, 206, 234, 241, 243, 245, 247, 249, 251, 261–262
Guthrie W. K. C. 54–56, 98
gymnastics 103, 113

H

Hades 54, 185, 228
Hamilton W. 103
happiness / happy 13, 20, 25–26, 30, 34–35, 49, 57–62, 67, 74, 82, 88, 96–97, 105, 107, 113–114, 118, 128, 133, 139, 143–144, 153–154, 156, 159–160, 162–164, 168, 174, 178, 186, 188, 190, 197, 200, 202–205, 208–211, 215–217, 219, 225–226, 233, 237–238, 240, 249, 251, 253, 259–264
harm principle 145, 148, 159, 259
harmony 20, 26, 33, 41, 43–45, 89–90, 93, 107–108, 111–112, 118, 121, 129–130, 137, 142, 150, 153, 177, 179, 181, 187, 189, 191, 194, 203, 205, 222, 228, 234–235, 255–257, 259–260, 264
Havelock E. A. 24, 55
health 60, 63, 78, 99, 103, 108–110, 112, 143, 150, 155, 174–177, 179–180, 182, 188, 259
Heidegger M. 17
Herodotus 242–243
Hesiod 54–55, 71
Hippocrates 55
Hoelzl M. 211

Homer 55, 93–94, 98, 102, 167, 206, 228, 245, 250
hunt / hunting (bloodless) 91–92, 95–96, 106
Hutchison K. 234

I

Ibn Khaldun 19
ignorance 68, 76, 104–105, 121, 123, 246, 249
image 38, 71, 100–101, 103–105, 140, 142, 167, 176, 221, 226, 228–229, 235, 240, 244, 257
immortality / immortal 23, 29, 38–42, 46–48, 50, 75, 105, 184, 202, 223, 233, 235, 257, 260
inalienable 17, 28, 256–257
Incampo A. 43
inherent 18–19, 22, 28–29, 44, 122, 153, 182, 184, 189–190, 256–257, 261
injustice 41, 59–61, 64, 66, 68, 92, 97, 109, 135, 146–147, 157, 169, 174–175, 178–179, 181, 183–184, 189, 198, 215, 229
intellect 40, 78, 81, 85, 141–143, 160, 165–166, 220, 225, 229–230, 234, 245, 247, 253
intelligible realm 121–122, 136, 140–141, 167, 228–231, 234–235
Irwin T. 25, 83, 116–117, 198–199, 216, 240
Ismenias of Corinth 66

J

Jaeger W. 58, 79, 109
Janik J. 54
Jarra E. 27
Jowett B. 176
justice 17–18, 21–27, 30–38, 42–43, 46–47, 49, 53–69, 71, 73, 75, 77, 79, 81, 89, 91–104, 106–114, 116–118, 121–123, 126, 129–135, 137–139, 141–151, 153, 155–163, 166–170, 172–184, 187–211, 213–217, 219–222, 224–225, 227, 229–241, 248–249, 251–252, 255–262, 264
- in truth 32, 102, 111, 248
- phantom of 15, 33, 81, 100, 106, 112, 158, 210, 248, 262
- just acting / acting justly 26, 33–34, 42, 47, 53, 62, 64, 74, 82, 87, 126, 139, 142, 144, 150, 161–162, 168, 191, 196, 201, 204, 209, 212–215, 218, 220, 222, 224, 226, 228, 230–231, 234, 237, 239, 257, 259–262, 264
- as a virtue 26, 93, 116
- of law 25, 32–33, 261
- of the state 31–32, 53, 59, 153, 158, 261

K

Kahn C. H. 23, 31, 56, 101, 191, 195, 222
Kant I. 13, 19, 45–46, 63, 131
Kateb G. 29
Kaufmann A. 181
king 54, 66, 212, 250
knowledge 18–19, 23, 32–34, 38, 41, 48, 54, 61, 72, 74, 80–83, 85–88, 90, 94, 100–101, 103–107, 109–110, 118, 121, 123, 125–126, 130, 133, 135–136, 138–139, 142–143, 159–164, 166–168, 170, 173, 177–178, 182, 191, 201, 204–205, 210, 214, 219–220, 222, 224, 227–228, 231, 234, 237, 240, 242–243, 245, 247–248, 257–260, 262–264
Koszkało M. 130
Krämer H. J. 23, 42–43
Kraut R. 25
Kubiak Z. 57, 66
Kubok D. 56, 195
Kurp P. 70

L

Lamb W. R. M. 20, 37, 42, 66, 103, 131–132, 176

learning power / power of learning 33, 83, 125, 159–160, 195, 210, 224, 230, 234, 237, 257, 263
legislation 13, 25–26, 37, 82–83, 97, 103, 144, 153, 155, 175–176, 203, 205, 222, 263
Legutko R. 65, 130
Lengauer W. 192
Leo XIII 137
Leontius 78
Lethe 54
Leuprecht P. 19
Levett M. J. 72
Levinson R. B. 158
Lewis Ch. 77
Liddell H. G. 57, 65, 75, 101, 161
Lodge G. 176
love / loving / lover 28, 34, 88, 107, 114, 155, 160, 167, 171–172, 211, 213, 218–225, 232–233, 239–241, 244, 249
– active love / love as caring 221–225, 232–233
– lover of wisdom 88, 107, 160, 249
Lucas P. G. 13

M

MacKenzie M. M. 173–174, 180, 184
magnanimity 115, 262
Marchant E. C. 76, 218–219
marriage 66, 197, 241, 250
McPherran M. L. 25
medicine 62, 81, 103, 109, 155, 174–178, 187–188, 224
madness 135, 246
Mencius 19
midwife / midwives / midwifery 103–105, 123, 126
Mnemosyne 54
moderation 79, 83, 89–91, 93–95, 108, 110–111, 113, 116–117, 129–131, 143–144, 151, 167, 179, 202, 210, 239, 241, 245, 247–248, 253, 258–259, 261
Moirai 57
money 66, 70, 79, 85, 90, 93, 99, 108, 111–114, 116–117, 132, 146–147, 155–156, 198, 202, 239
money-makers, *see* craftsmen
Morrow G. R. 101
mortality / mortal 39–40, 46–48, 225–226, 233–235, 258
Moszyk M. 15
Mróz T. 158
music 41, 140, 251
myth of Er 48, 87, 119, 145, 168–169, 172–173, 181, 186, 190, 219

N

Nails D. 78
Nemesis 57
Nikulin D. 31
non-violence 207
Nussbaum M. 232, 236–237
Nyx 57

O

O'Grady P. 71
Olejarczyk A. 31
Olson H. 123
one's own work 32, 53, 92–95, 98–99, 104, 113, 126
order 20–21, 33–34, 38, 43, 48, 50, 53, 56–59, 69, 71–72, 80, 89–90, 96, 99, 107, 109–110, 112, 121, 127–130, 135, 137, 141–142, 157, 162–165, 174, 177–181, 183–185, 187–189, 191–192, 194, 204, 207, 215–216, 221–222, 224, 229, 231, 234, 238–239, 252, 255–257, 260–262, 264
Ortega y Gasset J. 232
Ovidius 76
Owen G. E. L. 37

P

Pacewicz A. 31, 43, 218, 245
Paczkowski P. 35, 37–38, 115
Pawłowski K. 147
Perdiccas 66

Periander 66, 242
phantom 15, 33, 38, 66, 68, 81, 99–106, 110, 112, 126, 153, 155, 158, 210, 241, 248, 253, 262
philosopher 35, 37, 75, 88, 107–108, 112, 115–118, 139, 160, 206, 210, 216, 228, 237, 248
Pico della Mirandola 19
Piechowiak C. 15
Piechowiak M. 18–19, 162, 264
piety / pious 79, 94, 128, 132, 143, 148, 151, 215, 238–239
Pinckaers S. T. 165
Pindar 70
pious, *see* piety
Pittakos of Mytilene 66
Pius XI 157
pleasure 38, 62, 76, 84, 127, 244–245
political 21–22, 24–27, 31–32, 34, 36, 63, 66, 99, 102, 111, 113, 117, 132, 148, 154, 162–166, 171, 198–199, 201–202, 205–211, 244, 250, 264
– activity 206
– community 21–22, 26, 32, 34, 165, 199, 201, 206–209, 211, 244, 264
Pomeroy S. B. 250
Popper K. R. 20–21, 27, 98, 157–158
possessions 53, 62, 64, 107, 143, 147, 150, 160, 203, 206, 228, 234, 259–260
power of learning, *see* learning power
prayer 93, 107–108, 115, 203, 207, 228, 243, 248, 263
Price A. W. 28, 209–210, 232
producers, *see* craftsmen
prudence 72, 74, 89–90, 130–131, 143–144, 179, 202, 259
Przylepa E. 15
punishment 33, 49, 60, 103, 123, 169–170, 173–175, 177–188, 250, 262

R

Rackham H. 26, 150, 216
rational part 47–48, 78–79, 85, 139–140, 201, 252
Reale G. 41, 43–44
recollection, *see* anamnesis
rhetoric 58–59, 103, 123, 127, 129, 174–177
Rosen M. 26, 29
Rosen S. 241
Roskal Z. 35
rulers, *see* guardians

S

Santas G. 25–26, 42
Saunders T. J. 154, 174, 182, 232
Schofield M. 25–26, 203
Sedley D. 232
self-control 26, 61, 73, 85, 89–90, 144, 156, 192, 204
Seneca 185
senses 63, 72, 74, 138
sensible 38, 132, 137, 146, 185
sensual 25, 64, 72, 101, 106, 109, 135, 141–143, 228, 230, 234, 236–237
shame / shameful 61–62, 73, 103, 145, 147, 219, 237, 249
sharing of wives / community of wives 34, 158, 240–241, 245–248, 253
Shorey P. 31, 42, 66, 100, 149, 161, 171, 202, 230
Short Ch. 77
Sieroń J. 155
Simonides of Ceos 64
slaves 67, 146, 207, 256
Sobczak J. 15
Smith N. D. 106, 141
sophistry 103, 176
Sophists 59, 63, 71–72, 74, 135, 176, 205, 218, 231, 260, 262
spirited part 70, 78–79, 88, 161, 227, 230, 251–252
Stallbaum G. 176

Stauffer D. 58, 63, 131
Strauss L. 24, 209
subsidiarity 34, 157, 262
Supervisor of the Universe 44, 50, 190, 208, 232
Szlezák T. 43, 136

T
Taylor C. C. W. 21–22
Tell H. 71
temperance 77, 89, 94, 118, 130, 179, 259
Themis 54
Thomas Aquinas 15, 19, 43, 45, 163, 165, 168, 216, 264
totalitarian / totalitarianism 17, 19–22, 33–34, 51, 81–82, 88, 154–155, 157–159, 162–165, 170, 174, 188, 240, 262
tripartite proportion 199
truth 24–25, 30, 32, 40, 54, 64, 68–69, 73–74, 93, 97–104, 107–108, 110–112, 116–117, 121, 123, 126, 130, 132–133, 137, 141, 158, 161, 202, 213–216, 220, 225–228, 231–234, 236–237, 240, 242, 247–249, 252, 261
– speaking the truth 64, 214
– *see* justice in truth
tyrant / tyrannical 29, 60, 73, 147, 170, 242

U
unanimity 90–91, 129
unity 23, 29, 33–34, 38, 40–45, 64, 75, 89, 91, 96, 99, 107–108, 110, 118, 137, 139, 142, 147, 150–151, 153, 160, 174, 177, 180–181, 184, 187–197, 199–200, 203–205, 208–210, 212–214, 217, 220–222, 225, 229, 231, 235, 237, 244–245, 252, 255, 257–260, 264
universal 18, 20, 22, 29, 45, 76, 145, 164, 256
universe 35–36, 39, 44, 46–51, 72, 95, 113, 137, 189, 191–192, 194–196, 199, 204, 216, 232–235, 237, 256–257, 259
unwritten teachings / doctrins 31, 42–43, 125, 137, 174
Uranus 54

V
Vasiliou I. 25–26, 209–210
versatility 99–100, 108, 112, 115, 118, 137, 204, 262
violence 55, 187, 207
virtue 25, 32–33, 53, 56–57, 59, 62, 71–72, 75, 83, 89, 93–94, 102, 108–110, 113, 115–117, 129, 131, 138, 146, 151, 154, 170, 175, 180, 187, 193, 207–210, 213–216, 218–219, 221, 223, 228, 258, 262
– as a kind of order 129
– cardinal virtues 33, 69, 77, 91, 100, 113, 117–118, 121, 129, 160–162, 206, 210, 251, 258, 261, 264
visible realm 102, 106, 111, 114, 136, 138–139, 141, 160, 227, 230–231, 233, 235
Vlastos G. 94, 151, 213, 219–223, 225, 241
Voegelin E. 69, 168, 207
Vries J. de 158

W
Waldron J. 29
Walgrave J. 165
Weiss R. 110, 151, 210
Wesoły M. 42
Whitehead A. N. 17
Wild J. D. 158
wisdom 30, 33–34, 75–77, 79–83, 85–90, 93–95, 107, 113, 116–118, 121, 123, 126, 130, 133, 157–161, 168, 192, 201–205, 209–210, 214, 220, 224, 228, 231, 233, 240, 248–249, 258–259, 261–263

wise 26, 32, 37, 64, 66, 75–76, 80, 82, 88–89, 105, 107, 123, 140, 160, 162, 170, 192, 203–205, 207–208, 228, 242, 261
wives 34, 40, 158, 173, 240–243, 245, 247–248, 251, 253
women 210, 240–243, 245, 247–252, 256
Woolsey T. D. 176
Wroczyński K. 15

X
Xenophon 61, 75–76, 218–219
Xerxes 66

Z
Zajęcki M. 196
Zeyl D. J. 37, 103, 126, 131
Żełaniec W. 15
Zygmuntowicz D. 15, 39, 154, 158, 206

Philosophy and Cultural Studies Revisited / Historisch genetische Studien zur Philosophie und Kulturgeschichte

Editd by/herausgegeben von Seweryn Blandzi

Band 1 Dorota Muszytowska / Janusz Kręcidło / Anna Szczepan-Wojnarska (eds.): Jerusalem as the Text of Culture. 2018.

Band 2 Dorota Probucka (ed.): Contemporary Moral Dilemmas. 2018.

Band 3 Ján Zozuľak: Inquiries into Byzantine Philosophy. 2018.

Band 4 Marek Piechowiak: Plato's Conception of Justice and the Question of Human Dignity. 2019.

www.peterlang.com

www.ingramcontent.com/pod-product-compliance
Ingram Content Group UK Ltd.
Pitfield, Milton Keynes, MK11 3LW, UK
UKHW041826100926
8556IPUK00002B/40

9 783631 659700